A HUNDRED YEARS
OF ANTHROPOLOGY

DUCKWORTH'S 100 YEARS SERIES

A HUNDRED YEARS OF PSYCHOLOGY (*New Edition* 1964)
   By J. C. Flugel, B.A., D.Sc.

A HUNDRED YEARS OF MUSIC (*New Edition* 1964)
   By Gerald Abraham

A HUNDRED YEARS OF CHEMISTRY (*New Edition* 1964)
   By Alexander Findlay, C.B.E., D.Sc., LL.D.

A HUNDRED YEARS OF ECONOMIC DEVELOPMENT
      IN GREAT BRITAIN
   By G. P. Jones, M.A., Litt.D., and A. G. Pool, B.Sc., Ph.D.

A HUNDRED YEARS OF PHYSICS
   By William Wilson, D.Sc., F.R.S.

A HUNDRED YEARS OF ARCHAEOLOGY
   By Glyn E. Daniel, M.A., Ph.D.

A HUNDRED YEARS OF ENGLISH LITERATURE
   By W. Sherard Vines, M.A.

A HUNDRED YEARS OF BIOLOGY
   By Ben Dawes, D.Sc.

A HUNDRED YEARS OF EDUCATION (*New Edition* 1960)
   By A. D. C. Peterson, O.B.E., M.A.

A HUNDRED YEARS OF WAR (*New Edition* 1961)
   By Cyril Falls

A HUNDRED YEARS OF GEOGRAPHY
   By T. W. Freeman, M.A.

A HUNDRED YEARS OF PHILOSOPHY
   By John Passmore

A HUNDRED YEARS OF METALLURGY
   By W. H. Dennis, B.Sc., M.I.M.M.

A HUNDRED YEARS

OF

ANTHROPOLOGY

by

T. K. PENNIMAN

*Curator of the Pitt Rivers Museum, Head of the Department
of Ethnology and Prehistory and Diploma Secretary for
Anthropology in the University of Oxford 1939—1963*

With contributions by

BEATRICE BLACKWOOD, B.Sc., M.A., F.S.A.

and

J. S. WEINER, M.Sc., M.A., Ph.D., M.R.C.S.

GERALD DUCKWORTH & CO. LTD.

3 Henrietta Street, London, W.C.2.

First Published in 1935
Second Edition, Revised, 1952
Third Edition, Revised, 1965

© 1965 by T. K. PENNIMAN, BEATRICE BLACKWOOD
AND J. S. WEINER

PRINTED IN GREAT BRITAIN BY
COX & WYMAN LTD., LONDON, FAKENHAM AND READING

To My Friends
in the Village of Llangennith in Gower
and Especially to
Miriam Taylor of Delvid Farm
and to
George Ernest Rees of The King's Head Farm
and The College Farm

CONTENTS

PREFACE TO THE FIRST EDITION

ANTHROPOLOGY is the science of man, a master-science, embracing first, such biological studies as help to explain what man is and was, and his place in the realm of animated nature. These shade into a second group, that of psychological studies, as is clearly shown by physiologists who have studied behaviour experimentally. And since beliefs underlie institutions, psychological studies shade into yet a third group, that which studies cultures, material and spiritual, past and present. All of these must be studied in connexion with the organic and inorganic environment, the medium in which man and his cultures develop.

Ethnology is the application of any or all of the methods of anthropology to the comparative study of races or peoples, a race like the Nordic or Alpine being distinguished by physical characters, and a people like the English or the Jews by cultural characters. Ethnography is the study of a particular race, people, or area by any or all of the methods of anthropology.

The history of the subject displays in a remarkable way its nature in being and in becoming. First, there is a long formulary period, when the elements of the science are scattered throughout all the others. Secondly, there is a convergent period, when efforts are made to relate the various sciences that bear on man, ending with the admission of the high antiquity of palaeolithic man and the publication of *The Origin of Species* in 1859. These events brought order out of chaos in the biological world and furnished principles which allowed the integration of biological and cultural studies. The constructive period up to 1900 shows a steady and confident development for the most part on evolutionary lines. The rediscovery of Mendel's work in 1900 introduced a more austere and critical mood, and the present century has seen at the same time more intensive and specialized work and a great enlargement of the field of work in each of the branches of anthropology, now appearing more clearly as distinct entities, yet shading into each other and being closely connected. The earlier history is dominated by the interaction between the discoveries of voyagers and travellers and social theory;[1] in the later, the interaction

[1] For this reason, fairly full lists of ethnographical works are given in early chapters. In the later chapters such lists would overweight the narrative, and choice would be invidious. But some outstanding ones are included in the text.

9

between social studies and the increase in biological knowledge is perhaps more prominent.

While no one man can be expert at the whole subject, it is advisable that any anthropological training which covers the period required for a university degree should require a general acquaintance with what each of the branches is trying to do before specialization begins. A man is all the better for knowing where he and his work belong in the world, and less apt to run a theory too hard in one direction if he is aware of other ways of looking at his subject.

If I had had the services of a team of workers during the past year, skilled in various branches of the subject, this book might have been differently balanced, and I should not lay myself open to the reproach levelled at a famous series of volumes by a specialist, who declared that their author had done a wonderful piece of work as far as the rest of the book went, but was very ignorant about the specialist's own subject.

But any book of this kind is bound to be an interpretation, and there may be something to be said for the interpretation of a single mind, rather than a series of separate monographs on various aspects of the subject. A single author's attitude to a vast subject, and to its place in life as a whole, gives a unity which the public may approve or condemn, while a series of valuable expositions of its various parts might appeal only to the specialists who have no need to read discussions of their own subject.

As the specialist in one subject is very often a layman in another, perhaps the author is justified in writing the whole book for the layman, hoping at the least to make would-be anthropologists aware of the greatness of their territory, and praying those who have become eminent in some part or other of it to remember that one man cannot know all parts of it equally well. A general map is all that is intended.

Those whose work has been especially useful to me have been mentioned wherever I have used their material or ideas. But I am especially indebted for historical details to Dr R. R. Marett, Professor J. L. Myres, Sir Grafton Elliot Smith, Professor A. C. Haddon, Marcellin Boule, Professor Pitrim Sorokin, Professor Thomas Achelis, Dr Paul Topinard, Salomon Reinach, Father W. Schmidt, Professor J. C. Flugel, Professor J. D. Cunningham, Dr Dudley Buxton, Henry Balfour, and Thomas Bendyshe esq., all of whose works are noted in the text as being historical, or as giving some historical information.

I am very grateful to T. T. Ford, and especially to R. J. Bates, of the

Radcliffe Science Library at Oxford, for looking out a considerable number of references for me.

Finally, the debt I owe to Miss Taylor, of Delvid, and to Mr and Mrs G. E. Rees, of King's Head and College, Llangennith, is more than I can express. I can only record it.

T. K. PENNIMAN

Written between June, 1934, and June, 1935, at Acland House, 40 Broad Street, Oxford, and at Delvid Farm and the King's Head Farm, Llangennith, Gower.

PREFACE TO THE SECOND EDITION

AFTER the greater part of the first edition was destroyed by enemy action during the late war, requests for this book began to accumulate, and now the publishers have asked me to prepare a new edition. Up to page 344, the book has been reproduced photographically, with minor emendations.

After page 344, a chapter on anthropology since 1935 has been substituted for the former chapter on the future, and in writing this, I have fortunately had the help of my colleagues Professor Evans-Pritchard on social anthropology, B. M. Blackwood on Americanist Studies, and Dr J. S. Weiner on palaeontology and physical anthropology. I am also indebted to Miss Blackwood and to R. C. Gurden for help with the Bibliography. For the section on prehistory and technology, I alone am responsible, as I have been for the rest of the book apart from this new chapter.

In this final chapter I have sometimes referred to events before 1935, partly because I ought to have mentioned them in the first edition, and partly because some events since 1935 are the outcome of what happened earlier.

The Bibliography has been photographically reproduced, and a Supplement added at the end. Appendixes I and II to the first edition have been omitted, partly to gain space, and partly because it seems invidious for an author to bring a list of men and events up to date with his colleagues looking on, and the list of museums and societies would need to become an encyclopaedia to be really useful. Again, at the moment, such works of reference as the *Index Generalis*, *Minerva*, the

World List of Scientific Periodicals, and the Museums Association's lists of museums in the British Isles and Empire have brought out no new editions since 1939.

T.K.P.

April, 1951

PREFACE TO THE THIRD EDITION

WHEN I knew that the first edition would appear in 1935, I found that the title *A Hundred Years of Anthropology* was very apt, as 1835 was the year when Darwin visited the Galapagos Islands (page 56) and discovered the key to his future researches which were to culminate in *The Origin of Species* in 1859. In the second edition of 1952, I added a section on later developments, with the help of Beatrice Blackwood and J. S. Weiner, as my position kept me fully occupied in one branch of the subject, and I was no longer capable of keeping up with fast-moving developments which presented a different picture from that in which I could estimate past events in the light of the verdict of history. In the present edition, I stilll have the help of these colleagues, to whom I am grateful. In the first five sections, I have indicated a Formulary, a Convergent, a Constructive, and a Critical Period, and in the sixth, the account of what came after the original hundred years (with a long look backward to begin), I have ventured to use the title 'Convergence and Consolidation' with a short chapter entitled 'Trends towards a New Constructive Period' included. The postscript especially indicates my change of view about the method of integrating the branches of anthropology as things appear to me now, though of course I make no prediction how things will appear in the long run to me, or more likely, to my successors.

When the time came for publication, it was apparent that additions to history had made one book so long that if I included the extensive bibliography, the price would be more than most students would pay. I therefore asked my colleagues to extend their shortened references, and have added a short list of abbreviations and their full forms for periodicals and books which might otherwise be difficult to find.

I am happy to thank members of my Staff, Miss Blackwood, Dr A. J. Butt, Dr K. O. L. Burridge, Dennis Britton, and D. F. W. Baden-

Powell, as well as other colleagues, such as Professor E. E. Evans-Pritchard, the Reverend A. G. Mathew, Professor Robert Braidwood, W. C. Brice, Seton Lloyd, James Mellaart, and G. E. S. Turner, whom Miss Blackwood especially wishes to thank for reading her section on Americanist Studies and making useful suggestions.

This time I terribly miss the help of R. C. Gurden, Administrative Secretary and Librarian of the Pitt Rivers Museum, my friend and colleague for thirty years, who died of lung cancer on July 8, 1961. His ability in finding material and in ordering it well was beyond anything I have ever known, or am likely to know again.

T.K.P.

Pitt Rivers Museum,
Oxford.
June, 1962—1964

1

THE SCOPE OF ANTHROPOLOGY

ANTHROPOLOGY is the science of man. In one aspect it is a branch of natural history, and embraces the study of his origin and position in the realm of animated nature. In so far as it is a comparative study of the anatomical and physiological characters which determine man's zoological position, it forms a part of the general study of zoology. The search for man's ancestors, involving geological evidence to tell the conditions of the world when he appeared, zoological evidence to discover his companions, and anatomical to demonstrate his likenesses to and differences from modern man, is known by the name of palaeontology. The study of the physical characters which distinguish the principal races of mankind from each other, of the classification and geographical distribution of races and sub-races, and of the influence of environment upon physique, together form a branch of ethnology. This whole group of studies may be linked together under the name of PHYSICAL ANTHROPOLOGY. Each of the sciences from which it draws its material is an independent science, and even these sciences have independent disciplines which serve them, and each other, and also serve the study of physical anthropology, such as geography, botany, forestry, agriculture (soil sciences), genetics, biochemistry, psychology, and statistics. Yet the study is no mere collection of subjects which could be dealt with entirely under other sciences, for none of these several sciences can attempt to deal with the whole study of man as an animal, alone, and in relation to his fellows, and to his environment.

In another aspect, anthropology is the science of history, in that it explains how 'man, in his collective capacity, must needs act in order to furnish the material of that regular sequence of events which may be recorded or not, but which when it is recorded, goes by the name of history'.[1]

This side of the subject may be called CULTURAL ANTHROPOLOGY, and falls naturally into two parts, that dealing with material cultures, or the arts and industries of man, and that dealing with social phenomena,

[1] T. Bendyshe, 'The History of Anthropology,' *M.A.S.L.*, I, 1865, p. 335.

or man's mental and spiritual adjustment to the universe, and to his fellow men. Neither of these parts can be wholly independent of a study of the natural history of man, nor of each other, for man's physique and temperament and environment are all intimately bound up with his methods of gaining a living and adorning himself and his surroundings, and with his attitude to the problems of a life which must be lived among his fellow men, in a world which is ever furnishing experiences demanding a skill and power which seem to be above that which is required for the everyday work of life.

That branch of the study of material cultures which deals with the antiquity of man as ascertained by the earliest remains of his handiwork is called ARCHAEOLOGY. This subject embraces the characteristics of the prehistoric periods, the methods employed in determining their sequence and duration, and the persistence of early conditions of material culture in later times. In some periods, excavation furnishes our only evidence; in others, it supplements the evidence of written documents. It is a necessary part of the study of material cultures, for without it, there is no perspective of the development of modern arts and crafts. The comparative study of the origin, historical development, and geographical distribution of the principal arts and industries with their appliances, is called TECHNOLOGY. The study of the geographical distribution, affinities, and contacts, of the material cultures of ancient and modern peoples, and of man's response to and control of environment, including his fellow men, show TECHNOLOGY and ARCHAEOLOGY in their ethnological aspect.

That part of cultural anthropology which treats of social phenomena is called SOCIAL ANTHROPOLOGY. Under the title 'sociology' we may include the comparative study of social phenomena, their geographical distribution and historical development. Such phenomena embrace social organizations including marriage customs, economics, government and law, moral ideas and codes, folklore, and magical and religious beliefs and practices. The subject also includes a study of psychology and linguistics, including the relation of language to thought. Like the other divisions of anthropology, this has an ethnological aspect in the comparative study and classification of peoples based on conditions of language, and religious and social institutions and ideas. The reciprocal influence of environment and of social and moral development is an important part of this subject.

Cultural Anthropology, like physical, embraces a number of disciplines, some of which are independent. But the anthropologist, even though his main interest and labour may lie in one of them, must be aware of all the forces at his command, for no one of them alone can explain man and his cultural activities. The science of man implies a synthesis of all the disciplines that throw light on him and his creations, and to this synthetic study we give the name anthropology.

Some writers, particularly on the Continent, prefer to keep the word 'anthropology' for physical anthropology and to call cultural anthropology 'ethnology', but in this book we shall use the word 'anthropology' to mean the whole science of man, and consider it as having the threefold division which has been described—the division which has always been observed in the University of Oxford, and has been followed by the schools of Cambridge and London. ETHNOLOGY is that part of anthropology which deals with the comparative study of the physical characters and material and social cultures of the races of mankind, based on the methods, and under the headings, described for anthropology. In other words, it is a study of the formation and distribution of ethnic types or peoples, with their varying physical and cultural conditions. For example, Buxton's *Peoples of Asia* is an ethnological work, in which he employs the methods of physical anthropology for distinguishing the races of Asia. ETHNOGRAPHY is the intensive study and description of a group of people or of an area by the methods and under the headings which have been described for anthropology. It furnishes the data required by anthropology, and employs the methods based on such data.

Such studies can be pursued solely to find out what is true, to discover what happens, how it happens, and why it happens. Indeed, if we are to be competent workers, we must in the first stage of inquiry keep strictly to the facts of observation, and use common sense to interpret them. We are engaged with a 'pure science' in our attempt to find out the truth, and must maintain a rigidly impartial attitude, even when the facts lead us where we would hesitate to go. But many will ask of what use our discoveries may be, or in other words, whether anthropology may be an 'applied science', of value to the community. Apart from the value of well-disciplined minds to society, it may be said that the researches on which they are engaged are essential in determining the composition of all living populations and their cultures, and such questions as their reactions to diseases, urban conditions, the nervous stresses incident upon a clash of cultures, or upon our own social and industrial life, acclimatization, and maintenance. Any exact knowledge of what man is and does, how he happens to be thus or so and comes to act in particular ways, and why he so is and so acts, must be of value in dealing with the multitude of problems that arise in any community. Even

17

palaeontology, at first sight incapable of application to the problems of everyday life, might one day discover the secret of man's origin, and put us in the way of knowing whether his nature or his nurture is responsible for the major evils of civilization.[1]

It is unfortunate that the science of man should be so generally taken to be a study of primitive peoples only. This is due to several reasons. First, there is the belief that various of the specialized departments of learning deal with all the questions which affect civilized man and his institutions. This is only partially true, for when we are dealing with man, we need a master-science which will collect the harvest of these special sciences, and apply them to the study of man, racially, culturally, and in relation to his environment. None of the departmental sciences alone can tell the whole tale. Anthropology must act as the liaison of all of them.

Secondly, when anthropology became conscious of itself as a science, many of these specialized disciplines were already in being, engaged in the study of peoples akin to ourselves, and in periods of history for which there was literary record. Thus anthropologists found themselves working with peoples remote from us in culture, whose activities had not hitherto been considered as affecting us deeply.

Thirdly, it is easier and safer to study a primitive people; easier, because there is not as a rule so vast an amount to study, and novelty makes the outlines clearer and more interesting, and safer, because the majority of men do not so much care what we say about savages who live at a distance, so long as they can keep a good conceit of themselves and not upset any respectable and well-established prejudices.

Fourthly, the spread of European and American power over so much of the earth has brought us into close contact with a great number of races and customs alien to our own, and the necessity for dealing with this enormous amount of new material has preoccupied the attention of anthropologists faced with the practical problems raised when peoples of very different cultures must live in the same territory.

There have been anthropologists ever since man began to reason, but for the most part the earlier ones were like M. Jourdain, who talked prose before he was conscious of the fact. It is only yesterday that anthropology became conscious of itself as a science, and many of its pioneers are still with us.[2] This is not surprising.

For one thing, many of the sciences which throw light on man's

---

[1] Cf. Karl Pearson, *R.B.A.*, Cardiff, 1920; J. L. Myres, *J.R.A.I.*, LIX, 1929.

[2] They were in 1935, when I wrote. But the ranks of the old guard are now very thin.

origin and nature are creatures of the last hundred years, and a science which attempts to deal with man as a whole can hardly advance its forces on so wide a front until they are properly equipped.

Again, it is only now that we have become dimly conscious that there must be bridges between many of the sciences, or that we can explore the territory where chemistry ends and life begins, or the no-man's-land between physiology and psychology, to mention only two examples. To search for man in no-man's-land requires courage, money, brains, and leisure, a rare, but fortunately not impossible combination.

The reason for the slow growth and late development of anthropology will become evident in the study of its history, which displays in a remarkable way its nature in being and in becoming. The earlier part will necessarily read like a history of human progress, with the main emphasis on the interaction between voyages, travels, and discoveries on the one hand, and social philosophy and natural science on the other. Following chapters will show these same interactions, and in addition, the interaction between biological discoveries and the development of social studies. It is only in the chapter on the present that we can attempt to show clear-cut divisions of the subject, with each of these divisions, however, overlapping, or shading into each other at their margins.

This history falls naturally into four periods, the Formulary, the Convergent, the Constructive, and the Critical. We are still in a Critical Period.

The main part of the history of anthropology occupies the last hundred years, and properly begins with what we have called the Convergent Period, between 1835 and 1859, the year of the publication of *The Origin of Species*, and of the recognition of the high antiquity of palaeolithic man. During these years, the social scientists, the archaeologists and students of material cultures, and the ethnologists and biologists were all coming into relation with each other, and breaking down the compartments in which their sciences were imprisoned from each other. Further, all were trying to find principles of origin and development. Darwin provided the evolutionist view of nature which furnished such principles and so integrated all these studies, and thus made possible the science of man as a unified subject. In the same year, the geologists admitted that epochs, rather than a few millenia, were involved in man's development.

To explain the slow growth of conditions which ultimately made this convergence possible, the chapter on the Convergent Period is preceded by one showing the debt of anthropology to the Greek freedom of speculation to which we owe philosophy and science, to the Renaissance, with its widening of the mental horizon, and to the Revolutionary period which began towards the end of the eighteenth century, and prepared the way for a wide and general interest in the problems of society. As Chapter 2 will show, questions were asked, and general principles were formulated in separate departments of learning, but there was little attempt to co-ordinate all the facts that bear on the understanding of man, nor was any co-ordinating principle discovered. This long period in our history is somewhat analogous to the period in Roman legal history when laws were formulated to meet particular cases, and the idea of the law as a codified whole had not arisen. The title 'Formulary Period' has been borrowed from writers on Roman legal history to fit a similar period in the history of anthropology.[1]

With Darwin, the history of anthropology as a single, though many-sided, science begins. 'The origin of species by means of natural selection, or the preservation of favoured races in the struggle for life' offered the first hypothesis respecting the origin and development of organic forms which did not assume the operation of any causes except those which could be proved to be actually at work. In language that everyone could understand, Darwin put before the world his evidence of spontaneous variations under domestication and in natural conditions, gathered from experiment at home and from his voyage on the *Beagle*. His readers themselves could see that these variations were facts, and that some of them were transmissible. He showed both artificial and natural selection at work in the perpetuation or extinction of varieties. The struggle for existence and the progress or survival of certain elements in the community were patent and ever-present facts in the industrialized society of his day.

His theory then, not only brought order out of chaos in the biological sciences, but also furnished a rational method of studying the origin and development of human institutions and beliefs. It was now possible to bring under one scheme all the variations and developments which would otherwise have remained as unrelated inventories, and to study society as an organism, whose development results from natural and social selection operating in the struggle for existence of the materials of which society is composed. For the next forty years, the great pioneers in the study of anthropology in all its branches followed Darwinian principles, and constructed a science of man out of what had hitherto been little better than an inventory of all kinds of men. This period,

[1] Flight-Lieutenant A. G. C. Somerhough, a pupil of mine, suggested this parallel.

following Marett's account of 'The Growth and Tendency of Anthropological and Ethnological Studies' read at the First International Congress of Anthropological and Ethnological Sciences held in London in 1934, has been called the Constructive Period.

Marett takes the year 1900, when Mendel's earlier discoveries first became generally recognized, and a critical mood began to succeed the previous one of enthusiastic construction, as the beginning of a new stage in the history of anthropology, and calls it the Critical Period. A more exact study of the causes of variation and examination of the laws of heredity have made both the biologists and social scientists proceed more slowly, and re-examine much that had been taken for granted. The period is a critical one for anthropology in another sense, because of a tendency to split up into many independent disciplines. These, however, group themselves into three main branches. *There are the biological sciences which work to understand what man is and was, and these link up through psychological studies with studies of man's cultures, now, and in the past.*[1] In addition, there are the studies of environment, the medium in which man and his cultures develop. In the biological and psychological parts of the subject, there have been great advances and even greater hopes in the study of genetics and biometry, and as the functions of the endocrine glands come to be better understood, and the soil sciences develop, efforts will be made to study more subtly than was before possible the interplay of environment and of race and individual. While the study of osteology will always be valuable, as in the past century, there is a growing emphasis on other parts of the body. In cultural anthropology, the notion of unilinear evolution held by uncritical Darwinians, though never by Darwin or by those who understood him, is dead. Beside the old comparative and evolutionary school, there has grown up another, the historical, which distrusts the earlier use of world-wide analogies with its assumption that men are fundamentally the same the world over, and pays attention to differences rather than similarities, refusing to consider parallels unless it can be proved that they are due to actual borrowing. The new German school does not allow one great epic of humanity, but postulates a number of smaller tales, of cultures arising in many areas, spreading and overlaying others. The evolutionary school has benefited by this insistence on differences and diffusion, though the more critical have never admitted the possibility of independent origin of ideas and institutions until the possibilities of

[1] This may yet prove to be right. It ought to be right. But at the end of the book, I have given what seems now to be a better working hypothesis, that the branches of anthropology find their link in ethnology.

diffusion have been exhausted. The natural tendency of the historians has been to concentrate on particular areas or peoples. There has also been a growing insistence on a functional method of study, which takes into account all the inter-play of factors that constitute a particular society. Here again, the more critical of the evolutionists have benefited from this more exact examination of the functions of such traits as they may be considering in particular societies, and of the inter-relations of these traits with all the rest. In one respect at least, the oldest of the three schools will never be superseded. Its approach was psychological, and all of the older evolutionists assumed the psychic unity of mankind. Without saying absurdly that one people is exactly like another, we may say that unless there is a common denominator, it would be impossible for diffusion to occur. The truth is that the work of the three schools is complementary, and a good anthropologist will need to comprehend all three methods if he is to study man, and not merely develop his own notions.

While admitting and acknowledging throughout the book the tremendous importance of those who collected the evidence on which a succession of social philosophies and natural sciences was based, the main emphasis will be placed on the use made of the evidence. In the first place, it is impossible to do more than mention the nature of evidence from the field without compiling an encyclopaedia. In the second place, it is the man who examines the evidence who lays down the principles by which science advances, and thereby plays a greater part in its history.

Emphasis will be placed on the main lines of development, but variations which have been forgotten will be included, partly because a re-examination of them might possibly be fruitful, and partly because some of them furnish a warning that the experiment has been tried, and has failed.

2

THE FORMULARY PERIOD
BEFORE 1835

THE first, and by far the longest period in the history of anthropology, extends from the time of the Greek historians, philosophers, and naturalists, until the thirties of the last century. During all this time, its rudiments were scattered throughout the writings of natural historians, physicians, travellers, and social philosophers. Pertinent questions were asked, and laws were formulated in separate departments of learning, but there was no co-ordination of all the facts that bear on man. There was no fundamental principle by which various physical and cultural data and laws could be integrated as a science of man. This period is in some ways analogous to what students of Roman law have called the formulary period, the time in which laws were formulated to meet particular cases, before the law was codified, and considered as a whole.

This period then begins in Greece, the country where freedom of thought was first born, whose philosophy and science are the foundation of modern civilization. Great periods in history have often had their inception in voyages and travels which have brought Europeans into contact with many peoples of alien cultures, promoting a spirit of free inquiry, and causing philosophers and scientists to question their own institutions. Seeing what man is, they try to discover what he ought to be. Why the splendid Egyptian and Sumerian civilizations did not promote a similar spirit of inquiry is a mystery. It may be that as pioneers in discovering the elements of civilization, developing in a uniform environment, they became specialized for development in one direction. 'The beginning of civilization is marked by an intense legality; that legality is the very condition of its existence, the bond which ties it together; but that legality—that tendency to impose a settled customary yoke upon all men and all actions—if it goes on, kills out the variability implanted by nature, and makes different men and different ages facsimiles of other men and other ages, as we see them so often. Progress is only possible in those happy cases where the force of legality has gone far enough to bind the nation together, but not far enough to kill out all varieties and destroy nature's perpetual tendency to change.'[1] The background of both these pioneers in civilization was the conflict between the desert and the sown, and it remained a constant fact in all their progress from small cities to great empires. Even when the marauders of the desert conquered in part, they were in turn conquered by the law devised to maintain the sown. The very struggle to establish and maintain necessary institutions in countries where the fundamental problems did not vary specialized them for unilear development, and prevented the consideration of variants.

The Greeks were the heirs of some of their painfully acquired knowledge, and lived in a more churlish land, which forced the more adventurous to go abroad and accommodate themselves to a variety of places, men, and customs. Much information was collected by these earlier voyagers, but it was not until their small nation had repulsed the advance of the great Persian Empire that Herodotus was inspired 'to procure that human acts should not be obliterated by time, and that great deeds, wrought some by the Greeks, some by men of other speech, should not come to lose their fame', and first 'to discover, besides, the reason why they fought with one another'.

Herodotus (c. 484–425 B.C.) may be regarded as the first anthropologist. His compilation of the travels of the seventh and sixth centuries before Christ, and his own travels and researches, brought him face to face with races and customs entirely foreign to his own, and forced him to ask questions. Can climate alter character or physique? Can the mode of life and diet affect them? Is the father the natural head of the family, or the mother? Can customs spring up independently of each other, or must we look for a historical connexion? How long a time must be allowed for the development and diffusion of human varieties? These and many other questions exercised the Greeks of the fifth century before Christ. We do not know enough about contemporary or earlier authors to say how much Herodotus is indebted to ideas current in his time, and how much is due to his original way of collecting and evaluating evidence and in drawing conclusions from it and raising questions. But he appears to be the earliest author to collect so vast an amount of facts about peoples varying from the highest civilization to the lowest savagery, and to be the first to apply the comparative method to a study of the protean multiformity of customs and beliefs throughout the known world. It was his delight to place the most glaring contrasts in antithesis, and to attempt to answer the questions arising from it. To his view of a nation defined as of one blood and one speech, with

[1] Walter Bagehot, *Physics and Politics*, London, 1872, II, ii.

dwelling-places of gods in common, and with similar customs, we can add little. His honesty in collecting and sifting evidence, and his ability as an exact observer, have sometimes come in question, but modern investigations have more often confirmed than refuted his statements. And he is one of the most entertaining writers of all time.[1]

His contemporary, Hippocrates (c. 460–377 B.C.), was the first fully to separate the profession of the physician from that of the witch-doctor, and to seek for natural causes for the effects observed in the bodies of men. His accounts of the Scythians and of the people about the Phasis River show that he considered both physical and mental traits as plastic, and subject to climate and environment, though his remark that the Scythians were naturally inclined to be beardless implies that he took account of racial factors as well. Apparently he believed in the inheritance of acquired characters, as well as of natural, for his account of artificial deformations of the head includes: 'At the beginning the practice itself had the result that their mode of growth was of this kind. But as time went on, it came to be inbred so that their law was no longer compulsory': ἐν φύσει ἐγένετο, ὥστε τὸν νόμον μηκέτι ἀναγκάζειν.[2]

The great systematizers of the third century before Christ were more interested in the problems of the ideal state in which the good man can live the good life, and paid less attention to the multiplicity of data furnished by barbaric or savage societies.

Plato (c. 428–347 B.C.) built his theory of the State on his conception of the nature of the soul, and it is therefore necessary to explain briefly his general system of philosophy on which his conception of an ideal society rests. For him, there were three primary principles, God, Matter, and Ideas. All things, animate and inanimate, are fashioned by God from Matter, which may be regarded as the Mother of Forms, since it is capable of receiving any impress. Intellect is co-existent with Matter, and both precede Forms. Of the existence of God, he writes: 'All in the world is for the sake of the rest, and the places of the single parts are so ordered as to subserve to the preservation and excellency of the whole; hence all things are derived from the operation of a Divine intellectual cause'. The reason of God contemplates and comprehends the original models of all natural Forms, and these Ideas or patterns are the only true reality. They are the Universals, of which particular objects are only material embodiments. For example, all horses are things of a kind, although they may differ widely in appearance. But

---

[1] Cf. J. L. Myres, in *Anthropology and the Classics* (ed. Marett), Oxford, 1908.

[2] Hippocrates, περὶ Ἀέρων (ed. Kuhn), p. 550. Quoted by J. L. Myres in *Anthropology and the Classics* (ed. Marett), Oxford, 1908.

they are fashioned according to a common model, and this model is the Universal or Idea of 'Horse'. Our knowledge of Ideas cannot come from the senses, but must come from reflexion.

Behind the world of appearances, then, given by the senses, there is the world of Ideas, the true world, and we are like prisoners chained in a cave, our faces from the light, seeing only the shadows of reality cast upon the wall before us. Ideas seem to be implanted in the human mind, and as they are not communicated by the senses, they must be due to recollection of what the soul formerly knew, either in the world of pure Ideas, or in former states of existence, and this sentiment of pre-existence proves that the soul existed before the body. Each soul is an Idea, and of Ideas generally, the lower are held together by the higher, and all by the Supreme, for God is the sum of all Ideas. Everyone has two parts, a body and a soul, and of the soul the immortal part is Reason, and of the mortal, Appetite. Uniting these parts is the daemonic part, or Spirit. Each part has its appropriate virtue, that of the Reason being Wisdom, that of the Spirit, Courage, and that of the Appetite, Temperance. Justice is the virtue regulating the relations of the three.

His triple constitution for a good state follows his division of the soul. The guardians represent Reason, his military class, Spirit, and his labourers, Appetite, and Justice is ensured when all are interacting harmoniously for the good of the state as a whole. The citizens of his state are to possess property in common, even women and children. Plato had observed that any ordinary city, however small, was really two cities, one of the poor, and one of the rich, and that they were at war with each other. Poverty is the parent of meanness and viciousness, and wealth of luxury and indolence. The guardians especially then must not have private property to distract their attention from their duties to the state, and their common property must not be sufficient to encourage luxury, but enough to prevent them from preying on the citizens. Marriage was to be regulated by the state, and undesirable infants exposed, the children belonging to the state and not to the parents. To eugenic selection at marriage and at birth was to be added selection by education, also a state duty. Individuals were not to be considered as such, but only as elements of the perfect state, and the higher a citizen's position, the greater his duty to repress his individual appetites. The improvement of the state is to be brought about by selection and training, which will gradually modify the social environment. Man outside of social control is but an animal. When the reasoning and ruling part is asleep, the beast in our nature starts up naked, ready for any crime. It is really the society that makes the individual, and allows his development for the best. 'If the Constitution of States are five, the dispositions of individual minds will also be five.'[1]

Like Plato, Aristotle (384–322 B.C.) based his view of the State and Man on his whole philosophy of life. It was his fortune, after a long period with his teacher Plato, to be appointed as tutor to Alexander, and his friendship with the conqueror was a fact of great importance in the intellectual development of Europe, for it was to Alexander and his captains that he owed the vast collection of facts which enabled him to write his *Historia animalium* and other biological works. While Plato had started with Universals, and from these had deduced particulars, Aristotle took the fact as the starting point, and by inductive reasoning arrived at Universals.

How far does he differ from the modern biologist? Dr Draper[2] admirably summarizes his view that 'there is an unbroken chain from the simple element through the plant and animal up to Man, the different groups merging by insensible shades into one another: thus zoophytes partake partly of the vegetable and partly of the animal, and serve as an intermedium between them'. Certainly Aristotle understood clearly the difference between analogies and homologies, that is, between functional and developmental or structural resemblances, for he classified the bats with the mammals and not with birds, and the whales with the mammals and not with the fishes. He may justly be called the first zoologist, the first and only scientist before Linnaeus who knew that man must be classified with the other animals.

It is probable that Aristotle's whole system of philosophy would have prevented his ever arriving at any theory of the origin of species by natural selection, because of his belief in the fixity of forms. The moving cause, ἀρχὴ τῆς κινήσεως, by which any particular member of a natural kind is brought into being, is a previous member of the species, which when mature transmits the specific characteristics to its offspring. Man generates man. The end, or final cause, τέλος, is the preservation of the species. Aristotle's view of immanent form received from a previous member of the species then implies the same archetypes of creation as Plato's Ideas, and both are opposed to the theory of natural selection. And it was Aristotle's belief in the fixity of forms, rather than his scientific method of observation, associated with the traditions of the Old Testament, that set authority against inquiry until in the reign of King Charles II, the Royal Society was founded on the

---

[1] Cf. Plato, *Republic, Laws*; John William Draper, *A History of the Intellectual Development of Europe*, 2 vols., New York, 1861, London (revised), 1875, s.v. *Plato*.

[2] Draper, *Op. cit.*, 1875, I, 180.

principle of Horace, *Nullius addictus jurare in verba magistri*, and experimental science was born.

Like Plato, Aristotle believed that the state determined the behaviour of men. 'Without law and justice, man would be the worst of all animals.' Both believed in the innate inequality of men, and of races. Aristotle especially stressed the point that there were men by nature slaves and by nature masters. Both, like other great sociologists, made their theory of society a part of a scheme which embraced all the sciences, and thus were true anthropologists. Pitrim Sorokin in his book on *Contemporary Sociological Theories*, published in 1928, writes: 'Whether we take the *Republic* of Plato, or the *Politics* of Aristotle, *La Scienza Nuova* by Vico, *Discourse on Livy* by Machiavelli, Montesquieu's *The Spirit of Law*, Malthus' *Essay on Population*, or the works of Adam Smith, Saint-Simon, I. Kant, Auguste Comte, H. Spencer, and so on—all these great works are composed from, and on the basis of, the data of various sciences, to such an extent that we cannot say exactly to what "department" of science . . . they really belong.'

Aristotle's view of man as a social animal was based on his biological studies, and those formed a part of a scheme which embraced physics and metaphysics, a theory binding all in the universe together, and logic, a theory of the method of scientific research. In the *Nicomachean Ethics* and the *Politics*, he raises the question, 'What is man's chiefest good?' in the *Ethics* considering it as the well-being of the individual, and in the *Politics*, since man as a social animal cannot realize himself except as a citizen, as the well-being of the state. Man's well-being consists in the performance of such functions as are distinctively human, and to find these, Aristotle rejects nutrition and growth as shared alike with plants, and sensation, as shared with animals, and concludes that man's distinctive functions are reason, and the rational control of appetites and passions. The virtues[1] of these functions are of two sorts; moral, shown when the soul's appetitive part obeys its rational part; and intellectual, shown by the rational part. Among the moral virtues are courage, temperance, generosity, self-respect, and justice. The intellectual virtues are prudence or practical wisdom, and speculative wisdom, which is the virtue of the purely intellectual part or reason. Since the exercise of pure reason is the most distinctively human function, the life of the student is the best of all and brings the greatest well-being.

Such a student must, however, realize and do his duty to his family and state, for it is only as a citizen that he can realize such well-being.

The *Politics* is based on a study of a multitude of constitutions

[1] The word ἀρετή is translated as 'virtue'.

collected by the author. With the evidence before him, he asks which are suitable for particular sorts of peoples, how to establish and maintain them under particular conditions, what circumstances tend to maintain or change them, and which is the best for the generality of states. To Aristotle, as to Plato, the state means the city, a theory which controlled the world until the death of Caesar, when the boundaries of the city were extended so far as to create an almost universal state. Moreover, the well-being of the city meant the well-being of free men only, and this rested on the drudgery of slaves. The later Athenian Empire, and the Roman Republic, rested on the idea of the well-being of the dominant city, and the subjection of the rest. The answer to the question, 'Who is my neighbour?' had a very limited answer. Aristotle regards the city as an organism, developed from the village, which in turn has developed from the patriarchal family. He considers right polities, where the sovereign, one, few, or many, rules for the good of the society, and per-versions, where the sovereign uses power for personal advantage. The right polities are aristocracy, monarchy, and true polity. The per-versions are democracy, oligarchy, and tyranny. While Plato hoped by eugenic and social selection and education to develop a perfect state, Aristotle was less optimistic. He considered monarchy and aristocracy as perfect polities to be unattainable, because of the impossibility of finding suitably gifted rulers. In the true polity, all free men are admitted to a share in government, and all in turn rule and are ruled, under a constitution to which all occasional laws must conform. Of the perversions which are likely to happen, tyranny is the worst, and democracy, with the least power for evil, the least bad.[1]

Aristotle's approach to biological and sociological problems differed from that of Plato, in that Plato was more the speculative philosopher, and Aristotle more the scientist, as we now understand science. Aris-totle's collection of 158 constitutions, and his vast collection of bio-logical, astronomical, and other facts, as a basis for induction, brings him into line with the moderns. It was fortunate for the progress of European intellectual development that he was the friend of Alexander, and that Alexander, like so many other great soldiers and sailors, was interested in gaining new and exact knowledge. 'Perhaps it may be inferred that the practical habit of thought and accommodation of theory to the actual purposes of life pre-eminently required by their profession, leads them spontaneously to decline speculative uncertainties, and to be satisfied only with things that are real and exact.'[2]

[1] Cf. Henry Jackson, s.v. Aristotle in Hastings E.R.E.

[2] Draper, op. cit., 1875, I, 192.

Aristotle, as Draper justly observes, is the link between philosophy and science in the history of European intellectual progress. It was due to his teaching, and the conquests of Alexander, that the Alexandrian school, a superb organization of all the branches of human knowledge, grew up under the Ptolemies. The library had over 700,000 volumes, and the museum contained a botanical garden, a menagerie, an anatomical school for the dissection of the human body and the practice of surgery, and schools for the study of geography, astronomy, mathematics, and other sciences. Among the great names associated with the school are Euclid, Archimedes, and Apollonius Pergaeus, in the physical and mathematical sciences; Ptolemy, Hipparchus, and Eratosthenes, in geography and astronomy; and Galen, the anatomist and physician, whose work was based on the tradition of the school as developed from Hippocrates. The work of Galen (A.D. *c.* 130–200) was founded solidly on anatomy, the dissection of apes and possibly men. He was the founder of experimental physiology, and considered that theology should be based on the teleological doctrine of physiology.

The influence of Athens gave way to that of Alexandria, and in its turn, Alexandria yielded to Rome. The only great Roman philosopher who really contributed to the progress of the science of man was Lucretius (*c.* 98–55 B.C.) in his poem *De Rerum Natura*. In his work we find a final summary of the naturalistic view of the universe as held by the ancients. The world and all in it were formed by natural causes through the chance concourse of some part of an infinity of atoms in some part of infinite space. The belief in gods arose from visions seen by the mind in sleep and in waking hours. On the whole, religion has worked for evil and enslaved mankind. He shows civilized society as the product of a long course of development. In the beginning, men were hardier and more like the brutes than now. They could not till the soil, and knew nothing of fire, but lived on raw acorns and berries, went naked, lived in caves, and had no laws, government, or marriage. Their common foes were the beasts. Then began the use of huts and skin garments, and family life. Next came contracts with neighbours for friendship and alliance, and then speech, a natural impulse roused by necessity, and not invented by any single person. Fire was discovered from the effects of lightning or from the chance rubbing of tree-branches together. The first arms were nails and teeth and stones and wood and fire. Then copper was discovered, and used to till the soil and fight. Then by slow steps the iron sword gained ground, and the copper sickle fell out of use. With iron men ploughed the soil, and war became more general. The ores were first discovered when wood fires caused the ores to run from the stone (v. 922–1457). This general scheme of the development of civilization was placed on a sound scientific basis in the nineteenth century by the work of Councillor Thomsen at Copenhagen.[1] Needless to say, it is the precise opposite of the views of Hesiod and Moses, in which man began in a golden age or Garden of Eden, and degenerated from a former high estate.

From the outset, the Roman military class regarded religion as little more than a useful tool of government, and as they gradually conquered the world round the Mediterranean, both they and the conquered, from seeing so vast a multitude of gods in juxtaposition, came to think the lot of little account. To this attitude was added the disappointment of the conquered, whose gods had failed them. The general result throughout the civilized world was either a contempt for religion on the part of the abler or better-placed people, or a constant preoccupation with religious matters among the less fortunate, whose main hope of alleviation was to look for a better world after death. Among these, the early Christian missionaries spread their doctrines.

It is not within the scope of this history to examine the various modifications of early Christianity. Suffice it to say that it is but natural that the teaching of our Lord, so infinitely better than the world had ever known, and so little understood even now, should be corrupted and altered by peoples according to their own background and circumstances. But one thing all the sects had in common, although they quarrelled bitterly with each other, and this was intolerance of other religions. Thus an empire grew up within an empire. The Christians, certain of their own faith, refused homage to the deity of the Emperor. The ease of communications throughout the civilized world allowed their doctrines to spread, and caused great alarm at Rome. Persecution only served to bind the various Christian communities more closely together.

To the astute Emperor Constantine occurred the idea of alliance with the Christian power in the state. Thereby he would gain throughout the empire and in every legion men and women who had shown that they were ready to endure fire and rack and sword and wild beasts, even to the death. Moreover, imperial unity demanded religious unity, and the Christians were the most unified body within the state. Again, it served his purpose to foster the importance of the Church, in order that the ambitious might rise to power and dignity within it, and thus be removed from political life dangerous to his supremacy. His policy in allowing the Church to receive bequests endowed it with temporal

[1] See Chap. 3, p. 55.

power, and at the same time linked it with the civil power. Henceforward, Church and State were bound together, and the Church became the vassal of the State. And while polytheism allowed a multitude of views, monotheism linked with temporal power could not admit dissension, for the struggle of religious sects was also the struggle of political sects, and their striving for power shook the civil government. Thus Constantine summoned the Council of Nicaea in A.D. 325 to define the position of the Son in the Trinity, and enforced the decision of the Council.

The union of Church and State made heresy and civil dissension the same. Freedom of thought was dead. The ecclesiastical organization had little use for any of the sciences or institutions of the pagans who had persecuted it. In A.D. 415 the ignorant and fanatical Archbishop of Alexandria, Cyril, jealous of the growing power of Hypatia, whose lectures on philosophy and mathematics were drawing the populace away from his unintelligible sermons, caused her to be murdered with every shame and indignity possible, and thus struck the death-blow to scientific inquiry.[1]

During the next thirteen years, St Augustine was writing *De Civitate Dei*, a work which had a powerful effect in stamping orthodox scientific views on the world for centuries to come. He supported uncompromisingly the orthodox Mosaic or monogenist view of the descent of all mankind from Adam and Eve, in opposition to the polygenist view of multiple origin. Antipodal man and the globular earth were dismissed as absurd. Any history which pretended to cover many thousands of years was absurd, since according to Scripture, there are not yet six thousand years since the creation of man.

Bendyshe in his *History of Anthropology*[2] is unduly severe in saying: 'It is not, perhaps, too much to say of this work, that it has done more to destroy all love for the investigation of truth, and to retard human progress, than any other composition whatever.' It is true that there was very little progress in the natural sciences, and in anthropology in particular, during the Middle Ages, though there were great travellers, like Marco Polo[3] in Cathay, and Ibn Batuta[4] in Asia and Africa. But this is not entirely due to the activities of the Church or her teachers. The struggle to maintain Western civilization against Islam, and the struggle to maintain its unity against disruptive forces within its own borders, preoccupied men's minds. The Roman Empire had for a time given the

---

[1] Cf. Draper, *op. cit.*, 1875, I, 322, 324; Kingsley, *Hypatia*.
[2] *M.A.S.L.*, 1865, I, 347.
[3] 1254–1323.
[4] 1304–77.

idea of a great and peaceful universal state to the world, and the Church, allied to temporal power, was its heir. This ideal had to be maintained at all costs against the Mohammedan threat and the tendency of feudal times to split up into smaller units. Rebellion from accepted authority in any sphere was dangerous to an ideal which had been achieved with difficulty, and must be maintained with difficulty. Ideas from pagan or Mohammedan sources were a part of a system which the Church regarded as evil. Here and there, of course, there were Christian students who attended the courses at Cordoba, and quietly influenced the universities of Paris, North Italy, and Oxford, so that there were ultimately students able to take advantage of the discoveries and spirit of the Renaissance. Among Arabian philosophers of the Middle Ages may be named Ibn-Rushd, better known as Averroës (1126-98), who based his work on Aristotle, but sharply divided religious from scientific truth. His is a great name in the history of the liberation of science from theology. Then there was Mohammed ibn Mûsâ, who invented the zero, and first used decimal notation and gave the digits the value of position. Ibn-Sina, or Avicenna of Bokhara (980-1037) could with some justice be called the founder of modern medicine. Had the Mohammedan powers shown the ability to evolve any other form of government than that of unstable despotism, they would have played a far larger part in the history of European civilization.

Such influences from without prepared the world for progress. The great influence from within was the teaching of the Church that every individual was unique, and of equal value in the eyes of God, a teaching so absolutely contrary to that of ancient society, which rested on slavery, that it was a long time in taking root. But by the end of the sixteenth century, slavery was abolished almost everywhere in Europe. Whether they were conscious of it or not, later reformers were able to build because of this foundational idea of the equality of men before God.

We have seen that one great period in the history of civilization was quickened to life by travel and discovery which brought Europeans into contact with different peoples and with ideas and facts which aroused their curiosity, promoting a spirit of free inquiry, and causing philosophers and scientists to examine and question their own institutions. So it was also at the Renaissance.

Three great events in the fifteenth century were powerful agents to change the course of Western civilization. The first was the discovery of printing, about the year 1446, and the introduction of paper making from the Arabs, who had taken their knowledge from the Chinese. A widespread knowledge and general interest are the soil in which great ideas can grow. The second was the fall of Constantinople in 1453, and the migration of its scholars westward, bringing with them the Aristotelian spirit of scientific inquiry. The third was the voyage of Columbus in 1492–93, and his discovery of America, at first supposed to be Asia. All classes of men were deeply affected. The desire for profit and the love of adventure sent the whole European world on voyages of exploration for the next three centuries. In 1497, Cabot claimed a part of North America for Henry VII. In May, 1498, Vasco da Gama reached India by sailing round Africa.

These voyages completely changed the outlook of Europe. The old mercantile supremacy of Italy with her routes via Egypt came to an end. Henceforward, the western nations looked towards the sea and maritime development. Spain, Portugal, and England, and shortly afterwards France and Holland, were the leaders in commercial enterprise, and since such enterprise brings with it a concentration of people and wealth, and a lively intellectual condition, it is to the nations facing the Atlantic that we must look in our study of the Renaissance. The east and centre of Europe were still occupied with holding their own against the Mongol and Turk. Germany was under the dominion of Spain.

Of all the early voyages, the most heroic was that of Magellan, whose expedition was the first to encircle the globe. He lost his life in the attempt, but his lieutenant, Juan Sebastian d'Elcano, completed the voyage, and arrived at Seville in the *San Vittoria* in 1522. If the discoveries of Columbus and Vasco da Gama had cast doubts on the patristic geography, the expedition of Magellan destroyed its very foundations. Whether the idea was impious or not, the globular earth and the existence of antipodes were facts, and authority set against them could only destroy itself. 'But, though the Church hath evermore from Holy Writ affirmed that the earth should be a widespread plain bordered by the waters, yet he comforted himself when he considered that in the eclipses of the moon the shadow cast of the earth is round; and as is the shadow, such, in like manner, is the substance.' It is good to know that a traveller with such a heart learned before his death that his faith was justified.[1]

The first of the sciences to take advantage of revolt against authority was that of medicine, whose empirical nature must always have been fretted by dictation, for facts are stubborn witnesses for or against authority. During a millenium, the only anatomy taught was that of Galen. But in 1543 appeared *De humani corporis fabrica* by Andreas Vesalius (1514–64), a young Belgian twenty-eight years old. He

[1] Draper, *op. cit.*, 1875, I, 170 ff.

demonstrated that the anatomy of Galen was not the anatomy of man, but in large measure the anatomy of an ape, and placed the study of human anatomy on the foundation of direct observation. Besides comparing man and ape, he noted certain racial differences in head form, which he considered to be due originally to artificial deformation.[1] As might be expected, he was prosecuted by the Inquisition on the trumped-up charge that he dissected men alive. The death sentence was commuted to a pilgrimage to the Holy Sepulchre, from which journey he never returned.

The discovery of America soon raised the question of the origin and descent of the races of mankind. Patristic ethnology had divided the old world between the descendants of Shem, Ham, and Japhet, and thus made all men descendants of Adam, and participators in his sin and fall. The first view of the Spaniards, as soon as they knew that the Americans were a new race, was that they were outside the grace of God, and therefore their natural prey. In spite of the papal declaration of 1512 that the Amerindians were descended from Adam and Eve, the fact that the Pope had divided the world between Spain and Portugal, and the desire for gold, gave a sort of crude justification to the appalling cruelty of Cortez (1519) in Mexico, and of Pizzarro (1533) in Peru. Various authors of the sixteenth century contradicted the monogenistic view of the Church. For example, Paracelsus in 1520 was of the opinion that people in out-of-the-way islands were the children of another Adam, and not allied to us in flesh and blood. These various and diverse peoples must have sprung not from one parent, but from many. Moses wrote purely as a theologian, and not as a scientist, 'according to the faith for the weaker brethren'. And Giordano Bruno in 1591 declared that 'no sound thinking person will refer the Ethiopians to the same protoplast as the Jewish one'.[2] The discovery of America then raised anew the old controversy between monogeny and polygeny which St Augustine had so effectually buried.

That there was an eager curiosity to learn about the different races of mankind during the sixteenth century is shown by the great collections of travels and voyages printed. Among the many may be mentioned: Olaus Magnus, *Historia de Gentibus Septentrionalibus*, in 1555, an account containing much about Scandinavian folk-lore and customs; *Da Asia* de João de Barros, begun in 1552, with an Italian version in two volumes printed at Venice in 1561–62; A. Thévet's *Cosmographie du Levant*, 1575; Richard Hakluyt's *Divers Voyages touching the Discovery*

[1] J. D. Cunningham, 'Presidential Address,' *J.R.A.I.*, XXXVIII, 1908.

[2] T. Bendyshe, 'The History of Anthropology,' *M.A.S.L.*, I, 1865, pp. 353–55.

of America, London, 1582, and *The Principal Navigations, Voyages, Traffiques, and Discoveries of the English Nation*, London, 1598–1600; José d'Acosta's *De Natura Novi Orbis*, two volumes, Salamanca, 1588–89, and *Historia natural y moral de las Indias*, Seville, 1590; and F. Pigafetta, *Relatione del Reami di Congo* (from the accounts of Lopez), published at Rome in 1591.[1]

These sixteenth-century accounts found their echo in the popular literature and general ideas of the day. Caliban appears in *The Tempest* as the natural man, guarding his island property against invaders, gathering roots, berries, and honey for his food, haunted by the spirit Ariel, in fear of the magician Prospero, abasing himself before drunken sailors and putting offerings before them as though they were gods.

It cannot be said that this knowledge of the natural man played any direct part in the political thinking of the century. The pioneers of trade and expansion and missionary effort were inclined to 'Observe ye Beastly Devices of ye Heathen',[2] and to crush or Christianize them. But European nations came into conflict with each other in the New World, and the idea of nations and of national expansion began to take the place of the idea of universal empire. The sixteenth and seventeenth centuries saw once more the rise of nations, and in the Reformation, beginning with Luther's theses at Wittenberg in 1517, the end of the general view that uniformity of religious belief was essential.

Jean Bodin (1530–96) attempted to reconcile the ideas of unity and tolerance, and found the solution in the state with an absolute centralized sovereignty, not bound by past laws or the consent of subjects, but obliged to obey the law of God and nature. He went so far as to show the falsity of the assumption that there must be an all-embracing political and religious imperium, and showed great courage in opposing the efforts of the nobility and clergy to enforce conformity. But it was left to other centuries to ask the question, 'Whom should the subject obey if the sovereign breaks the law of God and nature?' Another question arose out of the great expansion of the mercantile class, and the protection of its gains in each of the several countries. The provision of strong governments and of armies and navies would give a certain amount of protection to their peoples, but still there was an increase of poverty and a general rise of prices, in spite of the fact that the amount of money in circulation continued to increase. Bodin was the first to point out that the amount of money in circulation did not constitute the wealth of the

[1] See *J.R.A.I.*, LVIII, p. 231.

[2] Quoted by Andrew Lang in *Anthropology and the Classics* (ed. Marett), Oxford, 1908.

community, and to grapple with the problem of the relation of currency to the market value of commodities and labour. He advocated energetic state interference in fixing the relation, and high taxes on foreign manufactures, and low taxes on raw materials and food. He believed that taxes must be impersonal rather than personal, so as to prevent the poorer and more numerous classes from paying more than their share.

One of the most valuable of his contributions is his attempt to explain religious, moral, and intellectual differences as an interaction of human and environmental factors. True, his geography is Ptolemaic, and his world ends at the Sahara. His environments run from the cold North to the hot South, and his cultures from civilized East to savage West. He was at one with the ancients in believing that intellectual and moral characteristics respond to climatic differences, but considered that man can, by virtue of his reason, overcome some of the injurious effects of nature and climate. Environment was the medium in which culture developed, but was by no means the only determining factor. Man himself was no less important.[1]

In the sixteenth century the establishment of the independent state and its maintenance against others was the central problem. In the seventeenth and eighteenth centuries the main interest was the basis of authority within the state. Widespread trading and adventure had developed a large mercantile or middle class of people, and their growing power and desire to protect their interests, together with the general diffusion of knowledge about many polities other than their own, led them to inquire why customs and governments differ so much in different places, and how the various societies or polities revealed by a multitude of voyagers came into being. Such questions force philosophers to investigate the nature of their own society, and these speculations invariably lead to a study of origins. Aristotle had taken it for granted that man is a social animal by nature. The Greeks generally had been forced to unite against an almost overwhelming enemy, and thus to realize that apart from the state there was no safety or freedom for the individual.

After the Renaissance, the world saw the struggle of nation against nation, and then the struggle of class against class, and of individuals with authority. It was not so much man's social nature, as 'man's

---

[1] Alfred C. Haddon, History of Anthropology, London, 1934, p. 106; Jean Bodin, Six Livres de la République, Paris, 1576 (Six Books of a Commonweale . . . tr. R. Knolles, London, 1606); Jean Bodin, Discours sur les causes de l' extrème cherté qui est aujourd'huy en France, 1574; Jean Bodin, Responsio ad Paradoxa Malestretti (Malestroit was Comptroller of the Mint), 1588.

inhumanity to man', abroad and at home, that impressed the social philosophers of the seventeenth and eighteenth centuries. His unnatural behaviour towards his fellows in society made it difficult for the greater number of political writers to assume that society had always existed, and forced them to the belief that it was a compromise, or contract made to avoid a worse condition. Men had voluntarily given up their pre-social state, or state of nature, and submitted to the evils of society for their mutual advantage, in order to escape the worse evils of a life that was 'solitary, poor, nasty, brutish, and short'. Hobbes's state of nature, Locke's Indian in the backwoods of America, Defoe's Man Friday, Montesquieu's Iroquois and Huron, Captain Cook's Boy Omai, and Rousseau's Carib on the banks of the Orinoco[1] are all commonplaces of our literature, and have played a great part in the moulding of people's minds towards a revolution in outlook and government. Inevitably the question arises, 'If we individuals made a contract for our mutual advantage, why should we not review the contract when occasion arises, so that it will serve our purpose even better?'

The material for comparison was at hand for such social philosophers as Hobbes and Locke, Montesquieu, Rousseau, and Voltaire, and they made use of it. By far the most imposing collections of ethnological data are the seventy-three volumes of the Jesuit *Relations*, between the years 1610 and 1791. Various other accounts of peoples, and certain of the *Relations* may be mentioned to give a small idea of the vast amount of material at the disposal of sociologists. Garcilasso de la Vega published *Comentarios reales que tratan del origen de los Yncas* at Lisbon in 1609, and his *Historia general del Peru*, the second part, was published in the year after his death in 1617, also at Lisbon. His work is very well informed, as he was the son of a Spanish father and Peruvian mother and lived in Peru. It was translated into English by Sir Paul Rycraft in 1688. *Purchas his Pilgrimage, or Relations of the World and the Religions observed in all Ages* (by Samuel Purchas), was published in 1613 in London. Gabriel Sagard's *Le grand Voyage du Pays des Hurons* appeared in 1632, and C. de Rochefort's *Histoire naturelle et morale des Iles Antilles de l'Amérique* (Rotterdam), in 1665. A most remarkable book is Olfert Dapper's *Description de l'Afrique*, Amsterdam, 1686. The late Emil Torday praises him very highly for giving ample details of every-day life rather than publishing merely curious or quaint customs. His method has much of the precision of Spencer's *Descriptive Sociology*, and his understanding of the position of the various customs in their several societies entitles him to rank as the first of the functional anthro-

[1] J. L. Myres, 'Presidential Address', *J.R.A.I.*, LIX, 1929.

pologists.[1] J. F. Lafitau's *Moeurs des sauvages américains comparées aux moeurs des premiers temps*, Paris, 1724, interprets ancient peoples in the light of modern savages. He considers them as witnesses of stages in the history of civilization. Another early comparative ethnologist was Charles de Brosses, whose *Du culte des dieux fétiches, ou parallèle de l'ancienne religion de l'Egypte avec la religion actuelle de la Nigritie* was published in Paris in 1760. The pioneer of the animistic school was N. S. Bergier, whose idea that fetishism and astrolatry grew out of a childish state of mind which supposed everything to be full of genies or spirits is stated in his book *L'origine des dieux du Paganisme*, Paris, 1767.[2] P. F. X. de Charlevoix showed a wide range in his *Histoire de la nouvelle France*, 1744, and *Voyage dans l'Amérique septentrionale*, its continuation, *Histoire de Paraguay*, 1756, and *Histoire et description générale du Japon*, 1736, all published in Paris. D. Crantz's *History of Greenland* was published in London in 1767. Captain James Cook's great voyages, with their wealth of material, especially about the South Seas, were between 1768 and 1780. Various early editions of the *Voyages* were published in 1773, 1777, 1784, and 1788. L. A. de Bougainville printed his *Voyage autour du monde* at Paris in 1771. One of the Melanesian islands bears his name, and also the plant and genus Bougainvillaea. P. S. Pallas, a German naturalist, published his *Reise durch verschiedene Provinzen des russischen Reichs* at St Petersburg in 1771–76, M. Dobrizhoffer his *Historia de Abiponibus* at Vienna in 1784, and D. Collins his *An Account of the English Colony in New South Wales* at London in 1798.

So much for first-hand travels. Among the compilers and systematizers may be mentioned William Camden, whose second edition of the *Britannia* in 1607 placed early English history on a sound foundation. *The Estates, Empires, and Principalities of the World*, translated out of the French by Edward Grimstone in 1615, omits America as having no constitutions; all of those collected, with the exception of a few European republics, are monarchies. Peter Heylin in his *Microcosmus* published at Oxford in 1636 concentrates on despotisms, and arrives at Hobbes's idea that peoples more or less voluntarily submitted to rule to escape a worse condition.[3] Christoph Meiners may be said to have laid the foundation of modern comparative ethnology in his

[1] E. Torday, 'African Races, compiled and abstracted upon the plan organized by Herbert Spencer', *Descriptive Sociology*, 4, London, 1930.

[2] W. Schmidt, *The Origin and Growth of Religion*, London, 1931 (tr. Rose), p. 31.

[3] For all of the political thinkers of the seventeenth and eighteenth centuries see J. L. Myres, 'Anthropology and Political Science,' *R.B.A.*, Winnipeg, 1909.

Grundriss der Geschichte der Menschheit (Lemgo), 1785, and Herder's *Ideen zur Philosophie der Geschichte der Menschheit*, published at Riga and Leipzig in 1789-90, disregarded speculation and followed experience, attempting to show what man was on the earth in general and in every region in particular. He and Voltaire were almost alone in the seventeenth and eighteenth centuries in the Aristotelian view of man's social nature. It was the idea of the pre-social state and the revokable contract that shaped political history. The wild parts of the earth rather than the civilized had captured the minds of the social philosophers.

Thomas Hobbes first published *Leviathan* in 1651, two years after the execution of King Charles I. Hobbes wrote in the midst of rebellion, and to him the first need of society was order and absolute authority to enforce it. Conditions in England showed clearly how prone men were to resent authority, and it seemed as though the natural condition of men was one of war of all against all. When he looked abroad for an explanation, the American Indian appeared to show best the original condition of mankind. 'For the savage people in many places of America, except the government of small families, the concord whereof dependeth on natural lust, have no government at all, and live at this day in that brutal manner' (*Leviathan*, xiii). Society then was begun as a purely rational act for the sake of self-preservation, and could only be held together by the sanction of absolute authority. This authority rested in the sovereign, and his only title to hold it was his power to enforce it. Once he failed, the contract was dissolved, and the subjects owed no further obedience. The sovereign might be a monarch—and Hobbes preferred such a solution as the most efficient—or an aristocracy, or a democracy. Justice was as artificial as society itself; it could exist only in society as the law imposed by the sovereign. In short, the state was a leviathan, tolerable only because without it, man's life would be uncertain, and like that of the American Indians, 'solitary, poor, nasty, brutish, and short.'

John Locke's *Two Treatises on Civil Government* were published in 1690 under very different conditions, his thesis of constitutional government as the defender of rights in person and property being a theoretical version of the results of the Revolution in 1688. The social compact is one 'of agreeing together mutually to enter into one community and make one body politic', and rests on the consent of those who made it. Hobbes did not distinguish between society and government. With him, the compact was the setting up of the government. In Locke's view, the people always remain sovereign, and can recall or abolish the government, or limit it. He recognizes society as natural to men, and, while he points out from a comparison of African, American, and other examples that the rule of virtue in one place is not the same as in another, believes that certain of the principles necessary to hold society together are innate, or at least universal. He takes the Indian in the backwoods of America as the natural man, and America as 'a pattern of the first ages in Asia and Europe'. From American examples he shows that every man has a property in his own person, and in the products of his labour. These principles, and 'truth and the keeping of faith, belong to men as men, and not as members of society', and can exist in a state of nature so long as the people are too few for their country, and there is no temptation to enlarge boundaries because of the accumulation of wealth or overcrowding. It is then necessary to make a compact, and to delegate to a government the duty of upholding these natural rights. If this government is false to its trust, the people may abolish it.

Locke's theories and examples are based on very wide reading, as may be seen in the *Two Treatises*, the *Essay on the Conduct of the Human Understanding*, and the *Thoughts concerning the Reading and Study for a Gentleman*. Among them are Sir Thomas Roe's Journal of his voyage to the East Indies, F. T. de Choisy's *Journal du Voyage de Siam*, Fernandez Navarette's *Tratados . . . de la Monarchia de China*, and the works of Garcilasso de la Vega and of José d'Acosta on America. He quotes widely from the Jesuit *Relations* generally, and is supposed to have written the preface to A. and J. Churchill's *Collection of Voyages and Travels*.[1]

Locke's works were widely read on the Continent, especially in France, where they deeply impressed Montesquieu, who adapted from him the threefold classification of powers as legislative, executive, and judicial, and insisted that unless these powers were exercised by different authorities, there was no civil or political liberty within the state. The Constitution of the United States of America was written on this principle, expressed in *L'Esprit des Lois* (1748), and that country is still governed by the political doctrines of the eighteenth-century French philosopher. Like Aristotle, Montesquieu based his theories on the analysis and comparison of a vast number of constitutions, ancient and modern. Like his contemporaries, he made great use of travels and voyages. He appears to have been deeply impressed by Lafitau, and regularly uses the Iroquois or Huron as an example of natural man. He quotes Dampier on the South Seas, Hyde's *Persia*, Pyrard on Turkey, Perry's *Russia*, Kaempfer on Japan, and a great number of others. Man

[1] J. L. Myres, *R.B.A.*, Winnipeg, 1909.

was made for a life in society, but before all, the laws which govern him now are the laws of nature, so called because they are derived solely from the constitution of our being. To understand these laws, we must consider what man was before society was formed, for under such conditions these laws would be obeyed. It appeared to him that the natural man would be timid, and would tend to run away from everything. Mutual fear, and the pleasure that animals take in the society of their kind, would draw men together. The four laws of nature are the sense of weakness, the sense of hunger and the desire to satisfy it, the sense of mutual support, and the natural need for society in the sense of mere acquaintance. The first three are concerned with the maintenance of animal life, the fourth is an appeal to the experience of human societies. The first condition of primitive man is one of peace. Then in association, they feel strength, and war begins. Thence arises the law of nations. 'All peoples have a law of nations. Even the Iroquois, who eat their prisoners, have one. They send and accept embassies, they recognize laws of war and laws of peace.'[1]

Rousseau was the first to introduce the noble savage to the world's literature. After his time the publication of Cook's *Voyages*, and of novels and tales about the American Indian, confirmed people in their sentimental notions about the innocence and happiness of primitive man, and this popular fallacy is still with us. Was not Adam thus, before his fall from grace? The *Contrat Social* was published in 1762. It begins with the well-known words, 'Man is born free, and everywhere he is in chains'. The state of nature is the natural state of man, in which he is free and fearless. He takes the Carib of Venezuela as his type of natural man, and uses such data as he can collect to illustrate his thesis. He argues that the family is the most ancient of societies, and the most natural. But the tendency is for even the family to break up. Children leave their parents and become independent. This desire for liberty is in human nature. He agreed with Hobbes that sovereignty is indivisble and arises when the social contract is made, and with Locke that the sovereignty is in the whole people. But he wished to make his sovereign people active in government, rather than passive, not delegating authority to a government, but exercising it themselves as a whole. Such a theory of course denies that any society larger than the small city state can rest on any legitimate principle. But the idea that the people as a whole should rule caught the imagination of the world, and was responsible for the French Revolution, and its ideas appear at length in the American Declaration of Independence.

[1] See J. L. Myres, *R.B.A.*, Winnipeg, 1909.

Almost the only dissentient from the general idea of a pre-social state of affairs was Voltaire (1694–1778). He was more impressed by the civilization of China as shown by the Jesuit missions. In his time any civilization that went back two or three thousand years must be near the beginning of the world. He agreed with Aristotle that man is a social creature. He always shows affection for himself, the companions of his labour, and his children. As these affections form the basis of society, society has always been in existence. But *chinoiserie* was for the court. The wild man held the popular imagination.

We have attempted to show the growth of free inquiry in the social sciences during the seventeenth and eighteenth centuries. The same spirit of experiment was abroad among the natural historians, and discoveries were made which accelerated their progress. For example, William Harvey demonstrated the circulation of the blood in 1628, and Leeuwenhoek (1632–1723) discovered the microscope, and opened a new world for study. When he brought his microscope to London in the late seventeenth century, he was able to convince Fellows of the Royal Society of the existence of unicellular animals, or Protozoa, those present signing a declaration that they had really seen these animalculae. Not only the study of diseases due to micro-organisms, but the whole possibility of analysing the elements of which the higher animals are composed, begins with this epoch-making invention.

The Royal Society received its charter from Charles II in 1662. In the previous century, Vesalius had been punished by the Inquisition when he dared to compare man with ape and to dissect the human body, but in 1669 the Royal Society sponsored Tyson's demonstration that a 'pygmy' was a missing link between man and monkey. True, the pygmy was a chimpanzee, but that did not alter the fact that Tyson was free to make the comparison.[1] In 1655, Isaac de la Peyrère in his book *Prae-Adamitae* raised again the idea of polygenesis. The first creation of man occurred many thousands of years before Adam. Thus we may account for the Gentiles. The peoples of the New World could not be the descendants of Adam, but must have sprung from the pre-Adamites. The book was publicly burnt at Paris, which gave it more importance than it deserved. Bendyshe in his 'History of Anthropology'[2] discusses this book at some length, as well as the collection of answers to these arguments 'perverted from Scripture' made by Fabricius in 1721. Bendyshe also notes that the word 'anthropology' first appeared in

---

[1] Edward Tyson, *Orang-Outang, sive Homo Sylvestris: or, The Anatomy of a Pygmie compared with that of a Monkey, an Ape, and a Man*, 1699.

[2] *M.A.S.L.*, I, 1865, s.v.

English in the title of an anonymous book treating of the subject as the history of human nature in two parts, psychology, 'the nature of the rational soul discoursed', and anatomy, 'the structure of the body of man revealed in dissection'. The same history mentions Hundt's *Anthropologeion*, a work on anatomy, printed at Leipzig in 1501, and Capella's *L'Anthropologia*, published by Aldus in 1533, a fanciful discourse on personal singularities. According to Bendyshe, these are the earliest uses of the word 'anthropology' in the modern world. Aristotle of course used the word in the *Ethics*, but in a far from complimentary sense. The great-minded man is οὐκ ἀνθρωπόλογος, not a gossip, nor talker about himself.

In 1737, Linnaeus published the first edition of his *Systema Naturae*. Bendyshe,[1] who gives a very full account of the twelve editions between that year and 1760, says: 'It is difficult at the present day to form an idea of the courage that must have been necessary to put forth these few folio pages, at the end of which man, for the first time, was classed as one with the rest of the animal creation'. Certainly no one since Aristotle had so classified man with the other animals. In the first edition, man appears in the class Quadrupedia, and the order Anthropomorpha, along with the apes and the sloth, man being distinguished by the motto 'Nosce te ipsum', a pretty piece of wit which cast the onus of distinction on the reader. In 1740 the ant-eater is added to the order, and in the tenth edition, the Primates include man, the apes, the lemurs, and the bats, man being divided into Homo sapiens, Homo ferus, americanus, europaeus, asiaticus, afer, and monstrosus; Homo ferus embracing various 'wild men' observed in Europe, and Homo monstrosus, dwarfs and giants, and various artificially deformed peoples. The bats and wild men and monsters have since been thrown out of their place, but in other respects, man remains where Linnaeus placed him.

Linnaeus is a very dull writer in comparison with the brilliant and dashing Buffon, who had a great dislike for the painstaking detail which was so important to the Swedish naturalist. Fortunately, Buffon had a most accurate anatomist, Daubenton, as his colleague. Daubenton's careful descriptions of the structure of animals form a most valuable part of Buffon's works. The reader will be able to test his quality in such a work as *La Situation du trou Occipital dans l'Homme et les Animaux*, published in 1764. Buffon and Daubenton knew much more about the structure of apes than Linnaeus, as their descriptions show. Buffon believed in the unity of the origin of man, and in the two volumes of the *Variétés Humaines*, discussed such features as hair, colour, stature, and

[1] *M.A.S.L.*, I, 1865, s.v. *Linnaeus*.

44

features, explaining how individual variations are due to climate, food, and habits, and how such influences produce races when acting over large areas and groups of people.[1]

Johann Friedrich Blumenbach (1752–1840) was the true founder of craniology. The importance of his contribution to anthropological study was realized by the Anthropological Society of London, one of whose earliest publications was *The Anthropological Treatises of Johann Friedrich Blumenbach*, with memoirs by Marx and Flourens, 'and an account of his anthropological museum by Professor R. Wagner', published in London in 1865. This book contains Blumenbach's *De Generis Humani Varietate Nativa*, Göttingen, 1775, and *Beyträge zur Naturgeschichte*, Göttingen, 1795, translated by Thomas Bendyshe.

According to Marx's memoir, Blumenbach's interest in the study of man began with Büttner's collection at Göttingen. His efforts to reduce this collection to order resulted in the thesis 'On the Natural Variety of Mankind'. The book shows a wonderful range of knowledge, and very remarkable critical power. He appears to have read a vast number of voyages and travels, and to show great judgement in sifting true from false evidence, as well as considerable ability in direct observation. He classifies mankind into five varieties under one species, to wit, the Caucasian, the Mongolian, the Ethiopian, the American, and the Malay, using hair, colour, bodily structure, and especially the form of the skull as criteria. The Caucasian is the highest and most primitive form, and the others have degenerated from it. Skull-form is of especial importance, the norma verticalis, the shape of the skull as seen from above, being used to distinguish three types, the Mongols having a square shape, the Negroes a long and laterally compressed form, and the Caucasians an intermediate. His classification and collection became world famous, and it was for a long time the fashion to visit his museum to view the various cranial types. Broca, Flower, Turner, and many today have followed in his path, and developed the study of craniology. It is perhaps not surprising that the subject has come to occupy more attention than it should have in the general study of man as an animal. Blumenbach displayed a clear and well-defined department within a chaotic science, and the majority of people prefer to work within limits, rather than explore with the hope of finding something useful to do.

Blumenbach deserves the greatest credit for his careful investigation of Homo ferus. Linnaeus had collected accounts of a number of wild

[1] D. J. Cunningham, *J.R.A.I.*, XXXVIII, 1908; Paul Topinard, *L'Anthropologie*, Paris, 1876.

men that had been noted in various parts of Europe, and there was a general belief that such men were a distinct variety. Wild Peter was discovered as a naked brown boy near a village in Hanover in the year 1724. He showed very poor intelligence, had dirty and savage habits, and could not speak. The philosophers and naturalists considered this foolish, dumb boy to be of great importance, as showing the original type of natural man. Blumenbach investigated carefully, and pointed out that when Peter was first seen, he had the torn fragments of a shirt about his neck, and that the whiteness of his thighs as compared with the brownness of the rest of his body showed that he had worn breeches. He finally proved that Peter was the dumb child of a widower, put out of his home by a stepmother.[1]

Other writers of the century who deserve mention are Peter Camper, especially his *Sur les Différences que présente le Visage dans les Races Humaines*, published after his death in 1791; Charles White, who wrote in 1799 *An Account of the Regular Gradation in Man, and in different Animals and Vegetables from the Former to the Latter*; and Henry Home Lord Kames, who published his *Sketches on the History of Man* at Edinburgh in 1774. Camper is chiefly remembered for his attempt to measure the facial angle, and for realizing the importance of facial form, White for his comparative anthropometric work on the upper limbs of the chimpanzee, Negro, and European, and Lord Kames as one of the earliest of the polygenists in England.

Just as Alexander's collections gave an impetus to Aristotle and the Alexandrian school to classify and systematize, and to attempt to discover general principles, so did the collections made by voyagers and travellers from the Renaissance onward stimulate the natural scientists of western Europe. The very inrush of new material enlarges the horizon, and gives a sense of freedom, and one discovery leads to another. When there is a general interest in any problem, authority has little chance to prevent its discussion. As we have seen, this new freedom had most effect in the social sciences. The search for the origin of society had led to the theory of the revocable contract, and the theory was popular.

Thus the end of the eighteenth and the beginning of the nineteenth centuries saw a period of revolution towards popular government. Locke's Indian in the backwoods of America had impressed Montesquieu and Rousseau. The Declaration of Independence and the Constitution of the United States were the direct outcome of the views of Rousseau and Montesquieu, and the French Revolution was the child of

[1] Cunningham, *J.R.A.I.*, XXXVIII, 1908.

Rousseau. The practical result of the teaching of English social philosophers and French Encyclopaedists terrified the world. The young and threatened Republic of France was forced to accept the dictatorship of Napoleon. In England the fulminations of Edmund Burke roused the governing class to repress every form of Radical activity. In Germany, Hegel glorified the authority of the State, a sort of mystical entity in which the individual must realize himself through his contribution to its life.

But the teaching that man was naturally free, and that he could break the chains of his own making, or in other words, that social progress was possible, did not end, though these views simmered rather than boiled over during the early years of the nineteenth century. The ideas which had the most effect in the steady progress of human development were those of Lamarck. It is true that both Prichard and Lawrence held evolutionary views, as shown in Prichard's second edition of *Researches into the Physical History of Man* in 1826 and Lawrence's *Lectures on Comparative Anatomy, Physiology, Zoology, and the Natural History of Man*, delivered between 1816 and 1818. But Prichard suppressed his views in later editions, and while Lawrence's were widely read, they made no apparent headway for a long time against the violent attack of the reactionaries. Their work will then be considered in the next chapter.

According to Topinard, the contest between Lamarck and Cuvier had a good deal to do with the events that culminated in the French Revolution of 1830. In 1809 J. B. A. Lamarck's *Philosophie zoologique* departed from the old idea of the fixity of species, and bound all animated nature together by the evolutionary doctrine of transformism. External circumstances modify the way of living and create new habits and necessities which bring about a change in the structure of organs. In this way, species pass from one to the other by a multitude of transitions, and man himself is no exception to this law of development. Moreover, there is an inward urge of the organism to realize its inmost wants, and to express this urge in change of habits and structure. Lamarck's doctrine was violently opposed by Cuvier (1769–1832), who believed that a series of catastrophes had occurred, with a change of plants and animals after each, miraculously supplied by the Divine Will.

Geoffroy de Saint-Hilaire supported Lamarck in France, and Goethe in Germany. Goethe perhaps expressed most clearly the innate tendency of living creatures to full self-realization. Indeed, Faust shows the principle of Lamarck applied to the moral sphere, the ideal of *reine*

Menschlichkeit achieved by progressive development. The idea of 'la carrière ouverte aux talents' and of every soldier carrying a field-marshal's baton in his knapsack were Lamarckian ideas which ultimately triumphed over autocracy.[1]

[1] Paul Topinard, *L'Anthropologie*, Paris, 1876, pp. 547–49; Geddes and Thomson, *Evolution*, London, 1934 (12th imp.), Chap. 7.

3

THE CONVERGENT PERIOD
c. 1835–1859

THE history of a hundred years of anthropology properly begins with
this chapter. The previous chapter showed its rudiments scattered
throughout the writings of social philosophers, naturalists, and voyagers,
and how the collection of ethnological material affected the thought of
Europe during various periods. The rate of progress in the several
departments of learning differed enormously, and there was no anticipation of an integrated science of man. The troops were in the field,
but widely scattered, and in various stages of advance and equipment,
fit to advance as an undisciplined mob, but hardly as a disciplined
army.

With the early thirties of the last century began a series of movements and investigations which prepared the civilized world to recognize an integrated science of man in evolution. This period from the
thirties until 1859 may be called the Convergent Period, for its events all
tended to prepare the world for such an integrated view.

In the political sphere, the peoples of Europe made a determined
stand against reactionary autocracy. The July revolution of 1830 in
France forced Charles X to abdicate in favour of Louis Philippe of
Orleans as a constitutional King, prepared to grant measures of reform.
France remained in a fairly peaceable condition until 1848, when
another revolution caused Louis to abdicate in favour of a republic.
The July revolution in France brought matters to a head in Belgium,
which rose in revolt against Holland. France and England intervened,
and made Belgium independent, under Prince Leopold of Saxe-Coburg
as Ring. So far were the rights of the people beginning to take a hold on
the affairs of state. The Poles rose against their masters in 1831, but
were no match for the armies of Nicholas of Russia, who put down the
revolt, and brought them under a more autocratic rule than they had
endured before. In the same year, Bologna and other of the Papal
States rose against the temporal power of the Pope, and in 1846 the first
measures of reform were granted by Pius IX. The German states,

influenced by the July revolution in France, agitated for general reforms, which were offensive to Metternich and his party of reaction. By 1848, however, all Germany, including German Austria, was for a brief time united under the Frankfort Parliament. The Greeks secured their independence from Turkey in 1833, and the long struggle of Hungary for independence under the patriot Louis Kossuth brought her a brief autonomy in 1849. Agitation in England, and the final passing of the Reform Bill in 1832, showed that England also was affected by these revolutionary movements, and that the party of reform was a power in the country.

In the first place, these movements had their origin in the diffusion of the ideas of the Encyclopaedists and of the English social philosophers of the previous centuries, and their ideas of the natural man and the social contract and the possibility of its revision had grown out of European contact with primitive peoples.

During the reaction that followed revolution, and in the later period of reaction against authority, with which we are now dealing, these ideas of the relation between individuals and the state took different turns in England and on the Continent.

In England, Jeremy Bentham (1748–1832) and J. S. Mill (1806–73) agreed with Locke in desiring to restrict state action, and give as much freedom as possible to private initiative. Their question about any institution was, 'How far does it minister to human happiness?' Their test of political right was expediency, or utility, and the promotion of the greatest happiness or good of the greatest number. The question as to what is expedient or useful or the greatest happiness of the greatest number is one which would allow a variety of answers and a good deal of violent disagreement. In the statement that 'push-pin is as good as poetry' we have the gist of the assumption of the Utilitarian school, namely, that one man's happiness is as good as another, and that what matters is the happiness of individuals, and not any well-being of society as distinguished from the individuals who compose it. The theory fitted very well with the industrial and economic changes resulting from the invention of machinery. The best course was for the state to leave matters alone as much as possible, and allow the interests of individuals to adjust themselves to each other. This *laissez-faire* attitude coloured Herbert Spencer's later attempt to take an organic view of society, and Darwin's 'struggle for existence' and 'survival of the fittest' were seized upon by a whole school of so-called evolutionists who later considered society to be the scene of an everlasting struggle in which the fittest would survive, if nature were allowed to take her course. These ideas reached their popular apotheosis in some of the works of Kipling in England and Nietzsche in Germany, whose notions about the fittest in societies and in individuals bring us back to the ethics of the jungle.

On the Continent, G. W. F. Hegel (1770–1831) and Karl Marx (1818–83) were respectively developing theories which, carried to their logical conclusion, would set state against state, and on the other hand, class against class throughout the world. Both these theories would very well fit in with the idea of the struggle for existence and the survival of the fittest. Hegel believed that the individual could realize himself only through his contribution to the state, the highest form of human achievement. It is plain that in the course of its self-realization, war and the consequent spread of its beneficent power may be desirable and necessary, and as all cannot contribute alike to the well-being of the state, individuals are going to be sorted out and take their places according to their several capacities. Progress within the state is a matter of the dominant idea conflicting with its opposite, and a fusion of old and new bringing about a higher idea which is dominant until a new conflict arises.

Hegel saw the evolution of the state as the evolution of the dominant ideas which gave it its material form. Marx looked rather at the evolution of the means of production. His and F. Engels's (1820–95) *Communist Manifesto* was published in London in 1848, and Marx's *Zur Kritik der Politischen Oekonomie* in 1859. Both, and especially the latter, brought the idea of development into the economic organization of society. In social production, men enter into definite relations which are necessary and independent of their will. These relations of production correspond with a definite stage of development in their power of production, and the sum total of these relations of production constitute the economic structure of society. On this foundation rise legal and political superstructures. The mode of production determines the general character of their social and political and religious thinking. At various stages of history, the material forces of production conflict with the relations of production, and there is social revolution. Marx distinguishes the Asiatic, ancient, feudal, and bourgeois epochs. In feudal days, for example, society was constructed in accordance with the needs of the great landlords. Then came the industrial revolution, with power in the hands of the capitalists, and the proletariat collected into factories to serve their needs. This makes the final struggle clear. It is now between the capitalists and the proletariat, and when the proletariat have the power there will be no subject class to be exploited, and the whole community will govern its means of production in the interests of all.[1]

The ideas of Hegel dominated Germany until its failure to spread the *Kultur* of a dominant state in 1918. But under Hitler in Germany, and Mussolini in Italy, a kind of Hegelianism was in force. For Germans and Italians, the true reality was the dominant national idea, and the duty of individuals was to make the nation great. This idea, if carried to its logical extreme, results in the struggle of idea against idea, and of state against state. The ideas of Marx appeared in the founding of the International Working Men's Association in 1864, and the growth of the Labour parties. In our own day, since the Russian revolution of 1917, we have seen an intermediate stage of 'dictatorship of the proletariat', a struggle of class against class, a stage in the evolution of the hoped-for classless society in which struggle will come to an end.

A great deal of the revolutionary movements of the period were due to the changes brought about by the invention of machines, as Marx saw. These inventions were the outcome of the accumulating knowledge and confidence of the few scientists who had carried on their labours with very little encouragement from governments, and without creating very general interest. Machinery forced a revolution in outlook. Previously, society depended on the slave or the illiterate drudge. But stupid drudges cannot run complicated machines. By the thirties and forties of the last century, religious and other teachers who had been making spasmodic efforts to educate the people, found the more energetic manufacturers eager to help them to educate their workers, or at least to train them to a higher level of efficiency.

The mechanical revolution pressed education on the whole community, preparing it to understand and support those who attempted to reform a society which was developing into two classes, the employers and the employed, on a scale so vast that its terrible consequences could not be hidden. It was during this period of industrial ferment that modern socialism was born. The word itself was first used in connexion with the work of Robert Owen, about 1835.[2] Distressed by the conditions among his own cotton-spinners, he established a model settlement at New Lanark, of a type foreshadowing the Ford business in America, and Lord Leverhulme's in England, and advocated a resettlement of all the industrial populations of the world on similar lines. At the same time the trade union movement with its idea of collective bargaining

[1] Cf. Pitrim Sorokin, *Contemporary Sociological Theories*, 1928; G. D. H. Cole, 'Theories and Forms of Political Organization' in *An Outline of Modern Knowledge* (ed. Dr William Rose), 1931.
[2] H. G. Wells, *The Outline of History*, 1932 (7th rev.), p. 964.

with employers was rising. Karl Marx brought the two movements into relation. While Owen had looked to every class in the community to help in the reorganization of society according to his plan, Marx depended on the union of labour against capital throughout the world, with the ultimate idea of replacing private-owner capitalism by state capitalism.

On August 1, 1834, slavery came to an end throughout the British Empire. Ministers of religion, like Wilberforce, Wesley, and Paley, had attacked the institution for many years previously, but it was not possible for them to succeed against heavily vested interests. For one thing, the public knowledge of what was occurring abroad was insufficient. For another, public sympathy was hardly strong enough before the time when people engaged with ameliorating their own lot could realize the sufferings of alien and distant people in a worse condition.

In 1837, Dr Thomas Hodgkin, who had been involved in the movement which culminated in abolition, was a prime mover in the establishment of 'The Aborigines Protection Society'. In the following year, M. Edwards founded the 'Société Ethnologique de Paris'. In 1839, Dr James Cowles Prichard read a paper on 'The Extinction of Native Races' before the British Association at Birmingham, which excited so much attention that a grant was made to a committee for the purpose of drawing up a questionnaire to serve as a guide for all who came into contact with native races. Hodgkin, Prichard, and Owen were members of the committee, and finished their work in 1843, the year which saw the foundation of 'The Ethnological Society' to be a 'centre and depository for the collection and systematization of all observations made on human races'. The presidential address declared that the ethnological harvest was ripe, and must be gathered now, if at all. The questionnaire was the first edition of the present *Notes and Queries on Anthropology*, formerly published by the British Association and now published by Routledge & Kegan Paul.

While the thirties saw a general tendency towards liberalism in social studies, archaeological discoveries had to wait longer for recognition. Both in 1838 and in 1846,[1] Boucher de Perthes' discoveries of flint implements at Abbeville, and his deductions concerning their immense antiquity, were received with derision by those who followed the Mosaic chronology as set out by Archbishop Ussher. A great deal of archaeological work had been done since 1800 and continued throughout the period of which we are writing. Its significance was largely obscured by the great authority of William Buckland. In 1816 he visited the caves

---

[1] *De l'industrie primitive ou des arts à leur origine*, Vol. I of Boucher de Perthes' *Antiquités celtiques et antédiluviennes*.

in Franconia, long famous as the source of a panacea for human ills, the horn of the unicorn. By this time, the true nature of these bones had been discovered. Systematic investigations at Gailenreuth had shown that man existed at the same time as various mammals now extinct in Europe. Buckland's *Reliquiae Diluvianae*, published in 1823, accepted the current geological theory of a universal deluge, and thus retained the Mosaic chronology as a framework for archaeology. In the same year he presented the famous 'Red Lady of Paviland' which he had discovered in a cave in Gower, to the University Museum at Oxford, where it lay for a long time forgotten. In 1825 he was confronted with the evidence of the Rev. J. MacEnery, who had found the tooth of a rhinoceros with a flint weapon in Kent's Cavern at Torquay. He explained this by the theory that the ancient Britons had scooped out ovens in the stalagmite floor, and had thus allowed the flint implements to fall into the cave earth with the bones of extinct animals. In 1833 he kept the same uncompromising attitude in the face of the evidence presented by Dr Schmerling from Liège, who had discovered a human cranium at Engis in an osseous breccia with the bones of now extinct mammals.[1] The only people to support the view that man was of immense antiquity and that he was coexistent with extinct mammals which had lived ages before the Biblical narrative began, were W. Pengelly, who investigated Mac-Enery's claims for the Torquay Natural History Society in 1846, and Dr Rigollet, who discovered flint axes in gravel at Saint-Acheul in 1854. Pengelly agreed with MacEnery's account of his discoveries, and to the incredulous who said that his statements about the antiquity of man as shown by his association with extinct mammals were impossible, retorted that he and his companions 'had not said they were possible, only that they were true'. Rigollet, who had previously disagreed with Boucher de Perthes, immediately associated himself with his unpopular hypothesis after his own discoveries. But for the most part, the learned world before 1858 was content to laugh at a theory which made bones and objects older than the world itself. Indeed, John Frere put the dilemma exactly as early as 1797. He had found flint implements in a brick-earth pit at a depth of twelve feet, and did not hesitate to assign them to a very remote period before the age of metals, 'even more remote than the present world'.[2,3]

[1] Schmerling, *Récherches sur les ossements fossiles découverts dans les cavernes de la province de Liége*, 1833.
[2] W. Pengelly, *Kent's Cavern*, 1876; Alfred C. Haddon, *History of Anthropology*, London, 1934; Marcellin Boule, *Les Hommes Fossiles*, Paris, 1923.
[3] Mr L. W. Kennan has lately called to my attention the opinion of Dr Samuel Johnson, as set out in his *Journey to the Western Islands*. Referring to Rassay, he says: 'A proof much stronger of the distances at which the first pos-

Other valuable archaeological work which prepared the way for the systematic study of the antiquity of man and his early history may be summed up briefly.

'In the early part of the year 1857, a human skeleton was discovered in a limestone cave in the Neanderthal, near Hochdal, between Düsseldorf and Elberfeld. . . . I drew up an account of its remarkable conformation, which was . . . read on the 4th of February, 1857, at the meeting of the Lower Rhine Medical and Natural History Society at Bonn. Subsequently Dr Fuhlrott, to whom science is indebted for the preservation of these bones, which were not at first regarded as human . . . on the 2nd of June, 1857 . . . gave a full account. . . . To this communication I appended a brief report.'[1]

Schaaffhausen noted the unusual size, the narrow, low forehead and flattened dome, and the enormous brow-ridges, which were almost joined so as to form a horizontal eminence, and concluded that 'the human bones and cranium from the Neanderthal exceed all the rest (with which he compared them) in those peculiarities of conformation which lead to the conclusion of their belonging to a barbarous and savage race . . . they may still be regarded as the most ancient memorial of the early inhabitants of Europe'. It remained for the next decade to place the creature where he belonged in the family tree. Virchow, in Germany, declared the specimen to be pathological, in fact the cranium of an idiot. Huxley in 1863 agreed with Schaaffhausen that it was the representative of a primitive race, and in the course of his controversies with the theologians, who objected to the ascent of man from below, and preferred to believe in his fall from perfection, retorted that he preferred a perfected monkey to a degenerated Adam.

In 1806 the Danish government appointed a commission to investigate the geology and natural history of the country. The shell-mounds, with their stone implements and the numerous dolmens, did not fit into any period as revealed by the historians or the earlier sagas. In 1810 Professor R. Nyerup started a collection from these ancient sites, which was later expanded into the Museum of Northern Antiquities in Copenhagen. The first curator was Councillor Christian Jürgensen Thomsen, who served from 1816 until his death in 1865. He arranged

[1] D. Schaaffhausen, of Bonn, 'On the Crania of the most Ancient Races of Man,' Müller's *Archiv*, 1858, p. 453; tr. George Busk in *Natural History Review*, April, 1861.

sessors of the island lived from the present time, is afforded by the stone heads of arrows which are very frequently picked up. The people call them "elf-bolts," and believe that the fairies shoot them at the cattle. They nearly resemble those with the barbs lately brought from the savage countries in the Pacific Ocean, and must have been made by a nation to whom the use of metals was unknown.'

and classified the collections, and established scientifically the sequence of Stone, Bronze, and Iron Ages which Lucretius had assumed. His work was continued and developed by Chamberlain J. J. A. Worsaae. Sven Nilsson's *Skandinaviska Nordens Urinvånare* (Primitive Inhabitants of the Scandinavian North) first appeared in 1838–43, and a second edition in 1862–66.

Between 1839 and 1857 Sir William Wilde investigated forty-six crannogs, or Irish lake-dwellings. He published his first account of these artificial islands in the *Proceedings of the Royal Irish Academy* for 1840. This, and subsequent publications, including his *Catalogue of the Royal Irish Academy*, show that he was fully alive to the importance of these structures in elucidating the early history of Ireland.

In the winter of 1853–54 the unusual drought and long-continued cold caused the lake of Ober Meilen near Zürich to shrink, and disclosed the stumps of piles, and bone and horn and other implements and traces of a bygone culture. Dr Ferdinand Keller, the president of the Antiquarian Association of Zürich, investigated this and other lake-dwellings, discovering pottery, stone implements, bronze, and human and animal bones. The various reports made by him and other investigators were published from the beginning of the work. An English arrangement and translation was made in 1866 and enlarged in 1878 by J. E. Lee under the title *The Lake Dwellings of Switzerland and Other Parts of Europe* (by Dr Ferdinand Keller).

Thus were the foundations of the study of the antiquity of man made ready.

The great event in the biological world, and one which was to revolutionize all the sciences, was the Voyage of the *Beagle* in the years 1831 to 1836. Like the voyage of Columbus, it opened a new world. Charles Darwin, naturalist on board the *Beagle*, visited the Galapos Islands, 600 miles off the coast of South America, in 1835.

This year, 1835, marked the turning point in his career. He had previously observed in Tierra del Fuego how people living under primitive conditions appear to be isolated into a small number of definite groups. In the Galapagos he saw that each island had its own distinctive animal population, although the species in one island were the counterparts of those in another, and nearly all had their counterparts on the continent. It occurred to him that all these corresponding species must have had a common descent.

The importance of this visit to the Galapagos is emphasized in his own words: 'On my return home in the autumn of 1836 I immediately began to prepare my journal for publication, and then saw how many facts indicated the common descent of species. . . . In July (1837) I opened my first notebook for facts in relation to the Origin of Species, about which I had long reflected, and never ceased working for the next twenty years. . . . Had been greatly struck from about month of previous March on character of South American fossils, and species on Galapagos Archipelago. These facts (especially latter) origin of all my views'.[1]

Again, Darwin writes: 'In October 1838, that is fifteen months after I had begun my systematic inquiry, I happened to read for amusement Malthus's "Population" (*Essay on the Principle of Population*, first edition 1798; second edition 1803; four other editions before his death in 1834), and being well-prepared to appreciate the struggle for existence which everywhere goes on from long-continued observation of animals and plants it at once struck me that under these circumstances favourable variations would tend to be preserved, and unfavourable ones to be destroyed. The result of this would be the formation of a new species. Here then I had at last got hold of a theory by which to work'.[2]

It was not, however, until November 24, 1859, that the *Origin of Species* was published. Much happened in the meantime to prepare a wide public to consider, if not accept, the integration of social and biological studies which an evolutionist view of nature implied. The general increase of popular education which the ferment of political and industrial life inspired has already been mentioned.

In 1851 Prince Albert promoted the First International Exhibition, which gave Englishmen an opportunity to compare the industrial and artistic products of the various European countries, and in 1853 organized a Science and Art Department at South Kensington. The Exhibition had a powerful effect in opening the minds of Englishmen to a consideration of achievement other than their own, and moved Tennyson to write of 'the Parliament of Man, the federation of the world'.

In 1853 Harriet Martineau published an English edition of Auguste Comte's *Cours de philosophie positive*, which had been issued at Paris between 1830 and 1842. This, and the *Système de politique*, 1851–54, were works of great importance.

Comte had been powerfully influenced in early life by the ideas of Henri Saint-Simon, especially by his conception of a reformed social order in which all the resources of the state should be used for the benefit of the whole people, this polity to rest on a basis of science. Saint-Simon was a visionary rather than a systematic thinker, and had the optimistic

[1] P. Geddes and J. Arthur Thomson, *Evolution*, London (10th imp.), 1928, pp. 16–18: quoting *Life and Letters of Charles Darwin*.
[2] A. M. Carr-Saunders, *The Population Problem*, Oxford, 1922, p. 34: quoting *Life and Letters of Charles Darwin*, I, 83.

idea that the business of reorganizing society on a scientific basis could be done quickly, given the will to do so.

Comte saw the length of the task ahead of him. First, a new science for studying social phenomena must be founded. Secondly, the sciences on which it was based must be reorganized. For the science of social phenomena, he invented the name 'sociology', and his study of the nature of society embraced the sciences of mathematics, astronomy, physics, chemistry, and biology, the whole leading to the master science of sociology. For him, the science of society was a whole, and not to be studied in compartments.

The development of man was by three stages. 'From the nature of the human intellect each branch of knowledge, in its development, is necessarily obliged to pass through three different theoretical states: the theological or fictitious state; the metaphysical or abstract state; the scientific or positive state.' In the first stage, men explained the universe as the result of the activities of personal gods, moved by human passions. Father Schmidt points out that in his division of the theological stage into three he follows Charles de Brosses's *Du culte des dieux fétiches*, published at Paris in 1760.[1] He traces the development of civilization in this stage from fetishism or animism through astrolatry to polytheism and monotheism, with historical examples from Egypt, Greece, and Rome for polytheism. When the Roman Empire united the Mediterranean world, the stage of polytheism and conquest passed into that of monotheism and defence. During the Middle Ages, the Western world was occupied in the preservation of the Catholic Church and the civilization of the barbarians. Then the Renaissance and contact with the Mohammedans again stimulated intellectual curiosity, and the world entered on a revolutionary period culminating with the eighteenth century.

In the second, or metaphysical state, personified or verbal entities take the place of personal gods. In this transitional period, such metaphysical concepts as those of individual rights and absolute ownership of property are governing forces. This condition of mind corresponds with the current activity of the people. Under previous orders, societies were organized for conquest, and then for defence. Then industry is recognized as the principal activity of mankind, and concepts of natural rights and of freedom are the gods of the people.

The third, or positive state, is the most desirable. In this, men will not trouble about the Absolute, but will confine themselves to investigat-

[1] W. Schmidt, *The Origin and Growth of Religion* (tr. H. J. Rose), London, 1931.

ing and establishing the succession and inter-relations of facts which give the conditions of human actions.

When we consider Comte's law of the three states together with his classification of the sciences in the historical order of their development, we see that in any period all three states will be represented, the simpler sciences being more nearly positive, or exact, and the more complex being still more or less in the metaphysical or theological state. Of all the sciences, sociology is the least positive. The laws of the physical sciences and of biology only give the conditions of social existence, and environment becomes of less and less account as civilization develops. Sociology must follow the example of the other sciences, and discover laws by the direct study of social phenomena, the structure of human society, and the historical development of civilization.

Comte distinguished between social statics and social dynamics, the study of society in development. For the latter, he devised the method of 'historic filiation', first making inductively a generalization from the facts of history, then deducing the same result by showing how the sequence of events could be explained by the known facts of human nature or by what is known of the development of societies. In such a way, Comte arrived at his laws of the evolution of activity, affection, and intellectual development. For example, we have spoken of societies organized for conquest, then for defence, then for industry. To this corresponds a development in the status of workers from slavery to serf-dom, and then to freedom, and a moral progress in the recognition of duties, which are at first considered as owed to family, clan, or tribe, then to the nation, and finally to humanity itself.

Comte believed that the progress of the sciences worked towards the unity of humanity because their results were true for everybody, and all could share them. As the peoples of the earth became more united by these common bonds, the philosophy and religion of the future would be based on the sciences, or at least compatible with them, and as men's energies became more and more occupied in industry, peace would be the normal condition of humanity. The abstract notions of natural rights and ownership of property would give way to those of the accept-ance of social duties and of wealth as social in origin and use.

Comte's great contribution to the social sciences lies in his method of approach. Others before him, like Aristotle, had treated sociology as a part of a scheme embracing all the sciences. Others had studied society statically, or anatomically. He was the first to study it dynamically or physiologically. The English social philosophers and the Encyclo-paedists had taken the study of society as a theory of the state. Comte believed that sociology was the science of the associated life of humanity, based on examining the conditions of social existence. Humanity in his view was an organism with its own laws of development, and the individual an abstraction, meaningless out of the organism which conditioned his thought and life.[1]

Evolutionary ideas were in the air in the thirties and forties. Darwin himself in his preface acknowledges how much other works previous to his own served to remove prejudice, and to prepare the ground for the reception of his views. Among his list of thirty-four authors, he mentions Lamarck, who aroused attention to the probability of all change in the organic world being the result of law and not of miraculous intervention. Chambers's *Vestiges of Creation*, 1844, and the improved edition of 1853, are especially singled out by Darwin as having done much to remove prejudice and prepare for the reception of analogous views. In 1846 the geologist M. J. d'Omalius d'Halloy[2] published his opinion that it was more probable that new species have been produced by descent with modification than by separate creation. In 1852[3] and 1855,[4] Herbert Spencer contrasted the theories of creation and development 'with remarkable skill and force', and applied developmental theories to the study of psychology. Later, in his *The Expression of the Emotions in Man and Animals* (1872), Darwin wrote: 'All the authors who have written on Expression, with the exception of Mr Spencer— the great expounder of the principle of Evolution—appear to have been firmly convinced that species, man of course included, came into existence in their present condition'. As Spencer's work, however, did not reach its full development and recognition until the seventies, it will be treated in the next chapter, rather than here.

Everywhere there was a tendency to synthesize the sciences, and a desire to discover a principle of synthesis. There was also a general understanding of the necessity to collect the relevant facts for biological and social studies, rather than to deduce society and its principles from an accepted theory. A few of these who collected important data bearing on the study of man or attempted to correlate it may be mentioned.

In 1835 A. Quetelet wrote his *Physique sociale*, and between 1837 and 1846 wrote a series of letters to Ernest II, Duke Regnant of Saxe-Coburg and Gotha, on the theory of probabilities applies to moral and political sciences, entitled *Lettres . . . sur la théorie des probabilités . . .*, 1846. These books, published at Brussels, are, so far as I know, the

[1] S. H. Swinny, 'Positivism,' Hastings *E.R.E.*
[2] *Bull. de l'Acad. Roy. Bruxelles*, t. XIII, p. 581.
[3] 'The Development Hypothesis,' *Leader*, March 20, 1852.
[4] *Principles of Psychology*.

first to show the importance of applying statistical methods to anthropological facts. These, and later work of his, are the foundation of the great work of Galton and Pearson, to be described in later chapters.

In 1840 Anders Retzius invented the cephalic index, the proportion of the breadth to the length of the head, and lectured on the classification of cranial shapes to the Academy of Science at Stockholm. He was the first to classify crania as dolichocephalic and brachycephalic, with prognate and orthognate subdivisions in each. In 1836 F. Tiedemann discovered a way to ascertain the internal capacity of the skull by filling it with millet seed and then weighing the seed.[1]

Various catalogues of skulls appeared between 1830 and 1857. In 1830 Sandifort's *Tabulœ craniorum diversarum gentium* appeared, and in 1839, Morton's *Crania Americana*, followed by *Crania AEgyptica* in 1844. The *Atlas de Cranioscopie* by Carus was published in 1845, and the first volume of *Crania Britannica* by Davis and Thurnam in 1856. Von Baer's *Crania Selecta* followed in 1857.[2]

G. F. Klemm's *Allgemeine Culturgeschichte der Menschheit* appeared in ten volumes between 1843 and 1852, and two volumes of his projected *Allgemeine Culturwissenschaft* in 1854–55. The races of man are described consecutively, with no attempt to point out any general stages of the progress of civilization. The work is a great storehouse of facts, and is often quoted by Tylor, especially in his earlier writing.

The greatest of all those who classified and systematized facts about the races of mankind during these years was James Cowles Prichard, whose *Researches into the Physical History of Man*[3] appeared between 1836 and 1847, and *The Natural History of Man* in 1843. He was born in 1786 and died in 1848, and spent the greater part of his life as a physician in Bristol. His earliest work was his thesis for the doctorate at Edinburgh, *De humani generis varietate*, in 1808. In 1810 he went to Bristol, and kept up a regular correspondence with his father, who was very much interested in his work, and had taken great pains to see that he learned as many languages as possible. Bristol was a good place for an anthropologist, and Prichard availed himself of many opportunities to meet sailors of different races. Both father and son were anxious to maintain the orthodox view of the unity of our race. The scope of the first edition of the *Researches* in 1813 appears in Prichard's own words:

The nature and causes of the physical diversities which characterize different races of men, though a curious and interesting subject of inquiry,

[1] Haddon, *History of Anthropology*, 1934.
[2] Paul Topinard, *L'Anthropologie*, Paris, 1876, p. 17.
[3] Third edition, the one usually quoted.

is one which has rarely engaged the notice of writers of our own country. The few English authors who have treated of it, at least those who have entered into the investigation on physiological grounds, have, for the most part, maintained the opinion that there exists in mankind several distinct species. A considerable and very respectable class of foreign writers, at the head of whom we reckon Buffon and Blumenbach, have given their suffrages on the contrary side of this question, and have entered more diffusely into the proof of the doctrine they advocate.

My attention was strongly excited to this inquiry many years ago, by happening to hear the truth of the Mosaic records implicated in it, and denied, on the alleged impossibility of reconciling the history contained in them with the phenomena of nature, and particularly with the diversified characters of the several races of men. The arguments of those who assert that these races constitute distinct species appeared to me at first irresistible, and I found no satisfactory proof in the vague and conjectural reasonings by which the opposite opinion has generally been defended. I was at last convinced that most of the theories current concerning the effects of climate and other modifying causes are in great part hypothetical, and irreconcilable with facts that cannot be disputed. . . .

In the course of this essay I have maintained the opinion, that all mankind constitute but one race, or proceed from a single family, but I am far from wishing to interest any religious predilections in favour of my conclusions. On the contrary, I am ready to admit, and shall be glad to believe, if it can be made to appear, that the truth of the Scriptures is not involved in the decision of this question.

Prichard sets forth the differences of colour, hair, stature, and form, and examines the value of each criterion as evidence of difference in race, and infers from the occurrence of these and similar differences, where identity of race could not be doubted, that they must not be received as evidence against the unity of our species. He brings a good many instances forward to show the permanence of black, brown, and white through many generations in every latitude and climate, and thereby proves that differences in colour are not due to to the influence of the sun acting for many generations on the body. He investigates the production and permanency of the varieties in men and animals, and following an idea of Dr John Hunter, that cultivation helps to produce varieties and to lower the intensity of colour in plants and animals, suggests that civilization was the cause which produced the white varieties of men. Adam and Eve were black.[1]

Professor Poulton is certain that Darwin never read the second edition of the *Researches* which appeared in 1826, for he would have mentioned what Poulton has called 'a remarkable anticipation of modern views of evolution' in the preface to the *Origin of Species*.

[1] Dr Hodgkin, 'Obituary of Dr Prichard,' *J.A.S.*, I, II, 1849, pp. 182 ff. See 1952 edition.

'Varieties of form or colour, as they spring up in any race, are commonly called accidental, a term only expressive of our ignorance as to the causes which give rise to them.' Examples of new varieties occurring within the experience of man are the 'porcupine' skin transmitted through three generations in a particular family, polydactylism, albinos, and other colour variations'. He then describes the sudden appearance of the ancon or otter breed of sheep, with very short legs, desirable because they cannot jump fences. Of the effects of cultivation, he writes, 'Does cultivation actually give rise to entirely new varieties, or does it only foster and propagate those which spring up naturally, or as it is termed accidentally? . . . The artificial process consists in a careful selection of those individual animals which happen to be possessed, in a greater degree than the generality, of any particular characters which it is desirable to perpetuate. These are kept for the propagation of the stock, and a repeated attention is paid to the same circumstances, till, the effect continually increasing, a particular figure, colour, proportion of limbs, or any other attainable quality, is established in the race, and the uniformity of the breed is afterwards maintained by removing from it any new variety which may casually spring up in it'.

So much for the formation of domestic races by artificial selection. As for natural selection, he held that climate was the most important factor. In considering both men and animals, he writes that some of the local varieties he has considered might be specially adapted to 'the circumstances of the countries in which the deviation has given rise', and elsewhere that 'individuals and families, and even whole colonies, perish and disappear in climates for which they are, by peculiarity of constitution, not adapted'.

Weismann, writing over half a century later, argued that inherent characters were blastogenic, and could be inherited, while acquired were somatogenic and not transmitted. Prichard writes, 'Inbred or spontaneous tendencies, governing the future evolution of the bodily fabric, cause it to assume certain qualities of form and texture at different periods of growth. From these predispositions are derived the characteristic differences, and the peculiarities of individual beings. Now it appears that such spontaneous tendencies are alone hereditary, and that whatever changes of organism are superinduced by external circumstances, and are foreign to the character of the structure impressed upon the original stamina, cease with the individual, and have no influence on the race. . . . Whatever varieties are produced in the race, have their beginning in the original structure of some particular ovum or germ, and not in any qualities superinduced by external causes in the progress of its development.'

So far, he has clearly anticipated Darwin and Weismann, but elsewhere his views are more Lamarckian. He considers that local influences 'promote the appearance of those varieties which are best suited to them, or tend to give rise to their production and breed'. He admits that such a conclusion differs from what he had said about the colour of a race not being permanently affected by a change of climate, or in other words, with his contention that acquired characters are not transmitted. His preoccupation with the idea that local influences directly produce adaptation caused him to reject the greater part of what he had previously argued. 'It may, however, be true, that particular varieties, once established in the stock, and transmitted for many generations, though originally resulting in a certain degree from the influence of local causes, will nevertheless continue permanent, even long after the race has been removed from the climate in which they originated.'

It was this theory which Prichard adopted for later editions, and as far as I can make out, no one before Poulton and his friends Davis and Meldola noticed the passages from the second edition which have been quoted. Darwin never saw this edition, and all of Waitz's instances are from the third English edition.[1]

Prichard's immense influence on his contemporaries and on later anthropologists is due to the third edition in five volumes of the *Researches*, and to the *Natural History of Man*, which appeared in 1843. In these, he collected all that was known about the various races of mankind, and it may be said that their synthesis of anatomical, philological, psychological, and ethnological data, form the foundation of ethnology in England.

Another anthropologist who expounded evolutionary doctrines before his time and was not recognized until later, was Sir William Lawrence (1783–1867). His *Lectures* (between 1816 and 1818) *on Comparative Anatomy, Physiology, Zoology, and the Natural History of Man* aroused terrible denunciation, and he was charged 'with the unworthy design of propagating opinions detrimental to society, and of endeavouring to enforce them for the purpose of loosening those restraints, on which the welfare of mankind depends'. As his career was to be that of a surgeon, he yielded to the outcry, and suppressed the work. But the book was steadily pirated, and reached a ninth edition in 1844. He foreshadowed Weismann in his contention that 'in all the changes which

[1] E. B. Poulton, 'A remarkable anticipation of modern views on evolution,' *Science Progress*, New Series, Vol. I, No. 3, April, 1897.

are produced in the bodies of animals by the action of external causes, the effect terminates in the individual; the offspring is not in the slightest degree modified by them, but is born with the original properties and constitution of the parents, and a susceptibility only to the same changes when exposed to the same causes'.

Elsewhere, he anticipated Darwin. 'Racial differences can be explained only by two principles already mentioned: namely, the occasional production of an offspring with different characters from those of the parents, as a native or congenital variety; and the propagation of such varieties by generation.' Domestication favours the production of these congenital and transmissible variations. Lawrence deplored the fact that so much attention was paid to improving the breed of animals, while the breeding of men was left to the vagaries of his individual fancy. Later, Galton was to make headway with this idea.[1]

One of the greatest names in comparative mythology and philology is that of Jacob Ludwig Karl Grimm, whose first edition of *Deutsche Mythologie* was published at Göttingen in 1835, and the second, enlarged, in 1844. The world is familiar with the *Kinder und Haus Märchen* collected by him and his brother, W. K. Grimm, as early as 1812. Mr J. S. Stallybrass in his translation of the fourth edition in 1882 under the title *Teutonic Mythology* has admirably summarized Grimm's contribution:

Jacob Grimm was perhaps the first man who commanded a wide enough view of the whole field of Teutonic languages and literature to be able to bring into a focus the scattered facts which show the prevalence of one system of thought among all the Teutonic nations from Iceland to the Danube. In this he was materially aided by his mastery of the true principles of philology, which he was the first to establish on a firm scientific basis, and which enabled him to trace a word with certitude through the strangest disguises.

The comparative mythology of all nations has made great strides since Grimm first wrote his book; but as a storehouse of facts within his special province of Teutonic mythology, and as a clue to the derivation and significance of the names of persons and things in the various versions of a myth, it has never been superseded and perhaps it never can be. Not that he confines himself to the Teutonic field; he compares it at every point with the classical myths and the wide circle of Slavic, Lettic, and occasionally of Ugric, Celtic, and Oriental tradition. Still among his *Deutsch* kindred he is most at home; and etymology is his forte. But then etymology in his hands is transfigured from random guessing into scientific fact.

There is no one to whom folklore is more indebted than to Grimm. Not to mention the loving care with which he hunted up his *Kinder und*

[1] D. J. Cunningham, 'Presidential Address,' *J.R.A.I.*, XXXVIII, 1908.

Haus Märchen from all over Germany, he delights to detect in many a nursery-tale and popular custom of today the beliefs and habits of our forefathers thousands of years ago. It is impossible at times to forbear a smile at the patriotic zeal with which he hunts the trail of German gods and heroes; the glee with which he bags a new goddess, elf, or swan-maid; and his indignation at any poaching Celt or Slav who has spirited away a mythic being that was German born and bred: 'Ye have taken away my gods, and what have I more?'

Another philologist was Karl Wilhelm von Humboldt, the elder brother of the famous traveller and naturalist. His most important works were *Researches into the early Inhabitants of Spain by the help of the Basque Language*, written in German in 1821; *Über den Dualis*, 1828, about what may be called the metaphysics of language; and his research on the ancient Kawi language of Java. This last was unfinished at the time of his death, but was edited and published by his brother and Dr Buschmann in 1836. The introduction on 'The heterogeneity of language and its influence on the development of mankind' is valuable as one of the earlier attempts at the classification of peoples by languages.[1]

In 1853, Count Arthur de Gobineau exercised himself with the problem of the development and decay of societies, quoting many examples to show that the causes of decay were not religious fanaticism, nor corruption and licentiousness, or luxury, as popularly supposed. The *Essai sur l'inégalité des races humaines*, published at Paris, stated boldly that there were superior and inferior races, and that the majority of races were incapable of civilization. No environmental stimulus can fertilize their organic sterility. Culture is often independent of environment, as may be seen from the fact that certain peoples who are well situated do not advance. Originally there were three different pure stocks, then mixtures. The fundamental factor in development and decay is racial. A people and civilization die out when the fundamental racial constitution is changed or engulfed among other races to such an extent that it ceases to exert the necessary influence.

De Gobineau was probably the first of the selectionists. Lapouge and Ammon and Chamberlain followed him later and had a great effect in Germany, where there was for some time such absurd insistence on a mythical racial purity. Pearson and Galton held that changes in racial stock through selection furnished the most important factor in its rise or fall.

In America in 1857 J. C. Nott and G. R. Gliddon in their book *Indigenous Races of the Earth* maintained the polygenetic theory of the

[1] *Encyclopaedia Britannica*, second edition.

descent of the races of man, and vigorously defended the notion that the Negro was by nature inferior to the white man. Gliddon was an eminent Egyptologist, and Nott was a physician in Mobile, in the heart of the slave-owning southern states, who had received his training in Europe, and at home from Dr S. G. Morton, whose craniological collection at Philadelphia was justly famous, and whose *Crania Americana* was described by Topinard as the best work of its kind. Both Nott and Gliddon were patient in the accumulation of facts without prematurely committing themselves to theories, but their sympathetic bias towards polygeny and the natural subordination of some races were in part the product of their environment and time, as well as of the teaching of Morton, to whom the book was a memorial. Gliddon emphatically denied that the book had any political bearing, but Nott's subsequent writing appears to show that he at least had strong political feelings. Two years after the end of the Civil War in America, when the Negroes were freed, he wrote in the *New Orleans Medical and Surgical Journal* for July, 1866:

> The question then, as to the existence and *permanence* of races, types, species, permanent varieties, call them what you please, is no longer an open one. Forms that have been permanent for several thousand years must remain so at least during the life of a nation. It is true there is a school of naturalists among whom are numbered the great names of Lamarck, Geoffroy St. Hilaire, Darwin and others, which advocates the *development* theory, and contends not only that one type may be transformed into another, but that man himself is nothing more than a developed worm; but this school requires *millions of years* to carry out the changes by infinitesimal steps of progression. With such theories or refinements of science, our present investigation (on the Instincts of Races) has no connexion, as the Freedman's Bureau will not have vitality enough to see the Negro experiment through many hundred generations, and to direct the imperfect plans of Providence.[1]

Theodor Waitz, the first volume of whose *Anthropologie der Naturvölker* was published in 1859, was one of the earliest to realize the full scope of anthropology as a science. This first volume was translated by J. F. Collingwood and published as the first series of translations by the newly founded Anthropological Society of London in 1863 under the title *Introduction to Anthropology*. The Council considered 'that no modern work has so well epitomized the present state of our knowledge on the subject'. Five further volumes, including all the primitive peoples known, were published, the second in 1860, the third in 1862, the fourth and fifth in 1865, and the sixth, edited by Gerland, in 1872.

[1] K. R. H. Mackenzie, Obituary Notice, *A.R.*, VI, p. lxxix.

The author's preface, written in 1858, says that 'scientific problems, which seem to lie between or to embrace the several branches into which we are accustomed to divide human knowledge, are, amongst us, not favoured by fate'. He realized that a great number of sciences were embraced by anthropology, and continues: 'Led to it by psychological studies, I had from the beginning no hope of arriving at a perfect solution of a question which it were desirable should be treated by the united powers of the zoologist and geologist, the linguist, historian, and psychologist. But as such a happy combination may be long in occurring, there remained but the alternative either to leave the question in abeyance, or to try its solution with insufficient means.'[1]

The first volume contains general principles; the later volumes contain the evidence from Africa, America, and the South Seas; and as the description of their external life is better known, it is treated less prominently, and the emphasis is placed on their psychical, moral, and intellectual peculiarities. Waitz's introduction divides the study of anthropology proper into two parts, one embracing the anatomy, physiology, and psychology of man, and the other the history of civilization, or social life in its development. The first great gap in our knowledge is between physiology and psychology, the next is between the physical and the historical parts of the subject. The history of civilization is developed by the collective action of four connected groups of causes. First there is the physical organization of man; secondly the psychical life peculiar to each people; thirdly environment; and fourthly, the sum total of social relations and connexions of individuals and circles of society, externally and internally. The most difficult and valuable task of anthropology would be to form a connexion between the physical and historical part of the subject; but as yet we are 'far from being able, by a philosophy of history growing out of physiology and psychology, to indicate why and wherefore the history of one people has undergone a different process of development from that of another people; why one people has no history at all, and in another the sum of mental performances never exceeds a certain limit; and yet in every case, it is the aggregate of the physiological and psychological facts alone which contains the essential conditions of the historical facts'.[2]

Waitz assigns to anthropology the task of mediating between the physical and historical parts of our knowledge of man, and, great as the claim is, insists that it should be the whole science of the nature of man

[1] Collingwood's translation.
[2] Collingwood's translation.

in every aspect. Ethnography or ethnology he defines as an investigation into the affinities of various peoples and tribes.

The great value of his work lies in his view of the scope and nature of the science of man, and in the magnificent thoroughness with which he presents the ethnological data, and examines with full documentation and dating all the current contradictory views on anthropological questions.

Three great geographers who had a considerable effect on the study of anthropo-geography were Buckle, Ritter, and von Humboldt. H. T. Buckle's *History of Civilization* was published between 1857 and 1861. In attempting to answer the question whether the actions of men were governed by fixed laws or by chance, or by supernatural intervention, he came to the conclusion that environment was the dominant influence, and somewhat overworked his theory.

Karl Ritter published the two volumes of *Die Erdkunde in Verhältnis zur Natur und zur Geschichte des Menschen* in 1817-18, and between 1822 and 1858 completed the volumes on Africa and Asia in *Die Erdkunde*, a work planned on a very large scale. For him, geography was a kind of physiology and comparative anatomy of the earth, the rivers, mountains, etc., being the organs of a country, each with their peculiar functions. As the physical frame is the basis of man, so the structure of each country is the leading element in the historic progress of a nation.

One of the greatest explorers and most prolific writers of any time was the German naturalist, the Baron Alexander von Humboldt, whose scientific work did much to enlarge the imagination of Europe. He travelled widely in the Americas and in Siberia, and among his many contributions to physical geography is the invention of isothermal lines, by which the climatic conditions of different countries may be compared. His *Voyages aux régions équinoctiales du nouveau Continent en 1799-1804* began publication in Paris in 1807. Besides the thirty folio and quarto volumes, there are supplementary works, all containing valuable material. The *Cosmos*, 1848-52, is also valuable as a source. His comparisons between Asiatic, Polynesian, and American cultures influenced Tylor's early work, and that of the later 'culture-circle' and diffusionist writers.

Among travellers' accounts may be mentioned the following works. The Abbé Dubois's *Description of the Character, Manners, and Customs of the People of India* was first published in London in 1817. William Ellis's *Polynesian Researches* appeared in 1829, with an enlarged edition in 1832-34, followed by *Three Visits to Madagascar*, 1858, all published in London. Maximilian, Prinz zu Wied's *Reise nach Brazilien*, Frankfort, 1820–21, was succeeded by *Reise in das Innere Nord-Amerika* at Coblenz in the years 1839–41.

A *Descriptive Catalogue of Catlin's Indian Gallery* was printed at the opening of his Museum of North American Indians in the Egyptian Hall, Piccadilly, in 1840. The first edition of *Letters and Notes on the Manners, Customs, and Conditions of the North American Indians* was published in London in 1841, and there were many other editions. He was an indefatigable traveller, and a good artist, as one of his many works, *The North American Indian Portfolio* of 1844, with its hunting scenes and amusements, shows. The many works of H. R. Schoolcraft, who resided for the best part of a lifetime among the Indian frontier tribes, are of considerable value for their first-hand information, psychological insight, and scholarship. Among them are the *Narrative Journal of Travels through the North-Western Regions of the United States*, etc., Albany, 1821; *Journal of a Tour into the Interior of Missouri and Arkansas*, 1820; *Personal Memoirs of a Residence of Thirty Years with the Indian Tribes on the American Frontiers, 1812–42*, Philadelphia, 1851; and *Historical and Statistical Information respecting the History, Condition, and Prospects of the Indian Tribes of the United States*, under the direction of the Bureau of Indian Affairs, U.S. Act of Congress, March 3, 1847. These six volumes appeared between 1851 and 1860. *A bibliographical catalogue of books in Indian tongues with brief critical notices* was published in 1849.

Other specially good ethnographical works were: John Williams' *A Narrative of Missionary Enterprises in the South Sea Islands*, 1840, by which time 20,000 copies had been sold; E. R. Huc's *Souvenirs d'un voyage dans la Tartarie, le Thibet, et la Chine, pendant les années 1844, 1845, et 1846*, two volumes, Paris, 1850, with an English translation by William Hazlitt in 1852, and finally, David Livingstone's *Missionary Travels in South Africa* in 1857. This last contains an account of over sixteen years' residence in Africa, and of a journey from the Cape of Good Hope to Loanda on the West Coast, then across the continent and down the Zambesi to the Indian Ocean. It is the first of the great explorations of the interior of Africa.

The year 1858 saw a rapid convergence of the studies which bear on anthropology. In that year Pengelly found flint implements associated with Pleistocene fauna in a cave at Brixham, and his evidence was accepted by Lyell, Prestwich, and others. Falconer visited Abbeville, and satisfied himself of the justice of Boucher de Perthes' conclusions concerning the immense antiquity of man, and in the following year, acting on his advice, Lyell, Prestwich, and John Evans, accompanied by his young son Arthur, visited the spot. The boy was the first to discover a flint implement *in situ*, and they were convinced. Thus the way was open for a fresh outlook on the geological succession of organic beings.

The way was prepared for a new outlook on the development of material cultures by Colonel Lane Fox, who took the name Pitt Rivers by royal licence in 1880. The Colonel had long been interested in the development of the service rifle, and in previous years, since 1851, had been collecting weapons at Bethnal Green, and classifying them, and experimenting at Hythe, Malta, Woolwich, and Enfield. He had observed that there were a vast number of contrivances for improvement, of which a few were links in the chain of progress, while many had branched out of the main line, and had contributed nothing of permanent utility. Certain discoveries had no effect until others had prepared the way. His plate showing the gradual development of the rifle bullet and his description of the cumulative effect of many small variations in the rifle and bullet first appeared in the *Journal of the United Service Institution*, No. VIII, Vol. II, 1858, under the title 'On the improvement of the Rifle as a Weapon for general use'. Mr Henry Balfour has told me that it was this work on fire-arms that first turned Lane Fox to collecting and arranging specimens in order of development, and turned his interest towards evolutionary questions and origins generally. The Pitt Rivers Museum at Oxford, with its evolutionary series of different objects, was the ultimate result of his work, and will be treated in the next chapter. For the present, it will suffice to say that by 1858 he had already adopted the plan of arranging each type of weapon or implement in a separate series, with a view to showing its development, and that this principle was entirely different from that of other museums, which employed an arrangement by areas or cultures. Early papers in the *Journal of the United Service Institution* were on 'Primitive Warfare' in XI, xlvii; XII, li; and XIII, lvi.

In 1858 A. R. Wallace, who had been studying the natural history of the Malay Archipelago, sent Darwin a memoir embodying the same general conclusions as those at which Darwin himself had arrived. This memoir he forwarded to the geologist Sir Charles Lyell, who sent it to the Linnean Society. The third volume of the *Journal of the Linnean Society* contains Wallace's paper, together with one by Darwin, printed at Lyell's request.

We have seen how the idea of development inspired the social sciences, with Hegel in the idea, with Marx in the means of production, with Comte in the three stages of intellectual growth. The ethnologists, like Prichard and Waitz, were experimenting with various hypotheses in an attempt to explain how varieties originate, and are perpetuated. The archaeologists were demanding geological epochs rather than Ussher's chronology for the development of mankind. Lane Fox was seeking for the principles governing the origin and development of the arts and industries of men. Bastian in *Ein Besuch in San Salvador, ein Beitrag zur Mythologie und Psychologie* in 1859 was trying, like Herbert Spencer in 1855, to apply developmental theories to psychological study. As Waitz realized, the compartments in which the various studies bearing on man had been confined, were running into each other, and all these studies were seeking for principles governing their development.

The convergence of all these interests was completed by the publication of Charles Darwin's *Origin of Species* in 1859. The evolutionist view of nature implied at once an integration of social and biological studies, and was the tie for which all interested in the study of man were ready. Darwin brought order out of chaos in both. With him the Constructive Period begins.

4

THE CONSTRUCTIVE PERIOD
c. 1859-1900

I. THE ORIGIN OF SPECIES

WITH the publication of the *Origin of Species* in 1859, the Constructive Period of anthropology as a single, though many-sided science, begins. Darwin belonged to his period, as Lamarck belonged to his. The political revolution has its biological interpretation in Lamarck; the industrial has its interpretation in Darwin. To the abandonment of old orders of society, and the movement towards the freedom of the people, correspond Lamarck's doctrines of the effects of use and disuse, and the inward urge of the organism to develop its capacities. To society in Darwin's time, the problem of existence and development was differently presented, and required a different interpretation. The mechanical and industrial revolution had brought very much to the foreground the struggle for existence, both among individuals and among societies. The spread of popular education and the improvement of communications had made it possible for a large number of people to consider with some degree of intelligence the composition and object of society; and when there is general interest, even though much of it is poorly expressed, there is almost bound to be a genius to interpret the tendencies of his time. If the public is prepared, his interpretation has a profound effect. If it is not, his genius will not reach its full fruition for lack of suitable stimulus, nor will his interpretation have a great effect on the life of his time.

The struggle for existence between individuals and ideas at home, and the manifest success of some and the failure of others, the spread of the power of European societies over the rest of the earth with their superior mechanical equipment—these facts seemed to find their justification in the natural law of the struggle for life, and the survival of the fittest. And while the work of Darwin had a far richer content, and far deeper meanings, it was this superficial interpretation in terms of a mechanized civilization that caught the popular imagination, and proved

73

to be the rock on which many eminent social philosophers stumbled for years to come. Men like Huxley and Spencer started with the idea of society as an organism, and were reduced to the idea of its elements warring with each other, and the strongest surviving. Imperial developments appeared to show that the 'lesser breeds without the law' were bound to go to the wall, and that such events were but the working of the law of nature. Success in life, rather than success in living, and mechanical efficiency and progress, became the gods of the people, and Darwin's hypothesis appeared to justify such success and efficiency. So narrow a view of evolution and natural selection was bound to bring people not forward, but back to the old doctrines of utilitarianism and *lassez-faire*. Leave things to take their course, and nature will select the survivor.

After a severe struggle with the old theology, this superficial interpretation found popular favour in the religious and moral life. The idea of perpetual struggle with obstacles, and of turning them into opportunities, suited the temper of an inventive age, which could not but believe that so rapid a change meant that progress on the same lines would go on for ever. The successful were justified in their faith; the failures must realize that inexorable natural law had placed them where they belonged.

The last chapter has shown that these views were all in existence before Darwin wrote. Count de Gobineau and Nott and Gliddon had written of the inequality of races, and the doctrines of Marx had put class against class, while those of Bentham and Mill had resulted in the idea that one person's interest was as good as another's, and that by leaving matters alone, what was best would survive, or, rather, that what survived had better be called the best. The catchwords of 'struggle for existence', 'natural selection', or 'survival of the fittest', appeared to give the sanctity of natural law to the processes that were going on, and by giving a name to them, seemed to explain them.

We must not, then, say that sociologists wrote in the light of Darwin when they use or appear to use some of his terms while still clinging to old ideas which are the result of the mechanical revolution, and are based on urban and mechanical notions. That one nation subdues another or annexes territory because it is superior, or that a man who gains more ease and money for less work than another is therefore the fitter to survive and progress, are ideas begotten not of Darwin but of the competition for mechanical efficiency. The machine was killing the true craftsman; his strength and skill were becoming things of the past; people reduced to fighting for a living wage, or those who contemplated the struggle, must give the palm not to those who could take pride in what they made, or did, but to those who most successfully exploited their fellows.

Darwin's views were very different, and the complete reverse of the urban and mechanical. He was a true farmer at heart, a man of the field and sea, always curious, and quick with the spirit of adventure. You may find his type in the farmers of the remote peninsula of Gower today, where men and women are obliged to exercise all their strength and skill to gain a living from land and sea, and are thrown on their own resources for meeting all emergencies. They are thus independent as kings on their own land, fearless and adventurous, and have a lively curiosity about all that happens round them. There is not one of the caves by the sea that the young men have not entered. A farmer's boy runs away from work and climbs to an owl's nest, bringing down a large handkerchief full of refuse. His father forgets to resent the unfinished work as he pores over the skeletons of mice, and advises his son never to shoot another owl, for mice do much damage to the crops. Another farmer has noticed more than the direct damage, and tells of observing the actions of field-mice, which, he swears, were after bees, and bees fertilize the flowers.[1] Farmers who do their own work and are curious about the world they are in, bring within their view the whole complex of life and its interdependence.

That is the first thing to notice about Darwin. He was no specialist, but like the farmer, interested in everything, and ready to turn his hand or mind to anything. He was a man of the open air, adventurous, and seeing all the complexity and interdependence of the world about him, accepting no theory at secondhand, or without considering the functional relation of his data to the whole complex in which he found it, and testing everything by practical experience. He was the true farmer-naturalist. With so broad a field to investigate, and with so rich an accumulation of facts, he could not possibly accept any facile theory which pretended to explain merely by giving another name to a problem. He saw the whole of life, and his theory must take that whole into account. Geological succession, geographical distribution, embryological and structural relations, all these and other facts were taken into account when he put forward the idea that species were not independently created, but had descended like varieties from other species. The problem was to show how the vast number of species on earth and in the sea today could have been modified so as to acquire the perfection of structure and adaptation which they now display.

[1] A friend has pointed out that my experience in Gower has a likeness to a paragraph in Thomson and Geddes, *Evolution* (11th imp., 1931), p. 153.

The previous chapter has shown from his own life and letters how the visit to the Galapagos Archipelago in 1835 and the reading of Malthus first offered a key to the riddle, the one suggesting the common descent of species, the other, the circumstances governing the preservation or extinction of varieties.

From the first, he saw that the clearest test of his theories of variation and selection would be by controlled experiments with domesticated animals and cultivated plants. He therefore began his work with an account of variation under domestication and the artificial selection which preserves and develops some varieties and rejects others.

Domestic species show a greater range of variation than the wild ones, and this is to be ascribed to the effects of domestication, the principal characteristics of which are increase of food, and changed conditions generally. Some changes appear to bring about definite and regular effects. For example, an increase of food may affect the size of the offspring. But by far the most important effects of these changed conditions are shown in an indefinite variability in all directions, due to the disturbance of the reproductive system, which is very sensitive to external changes. There are no remarkable distinctions between the domestic and wild species, and in a great number of examples, as with the many varieties of pigeons, we can demonstrate that all have a common ancestry. If we can see this unity in so many domestic varieties, we should be willing to admit the possibility of such unity in wild ones.

The domestic races have been produced by the accumulative selection of man, nature giving the variations, and man choosing what he will keep, and breeding from them, often making such great changes that in the course of time the parent stocks are hardly recognizable as the relations of the domestic breeds.

One difficulty in the theory of variation as the effect of the condition of domestication always troubled Darwin. The animals and plants which had been domesticated for the longest time were more variable on the whole than those recently domesticated, or, in other words, those which had been under changed conditions for the longest time appeared to show more variations than those which had been exposed for a shorter time. That fact would seem to show that changed conditions were not the only operative cause of the variability that now exists, for these conditions, once changed, have remained fairly constant for a long time. Another matter that troubled him was that of reversion to the original type, which did not appear to fit his theory of inheritance.

Like other biologists of his time, Darwin accepted the theory that the characters of the parents are blended in the offspring. This means, roughly, that the heritable variance is approximately halved in each generation, and that to explain the continuance of new variations, it is necessary to assume a regular supply of mutations in each generation. As Darwin saw, selection, artificial or natural, must intervene, or constant free crossing would always be counteracting the effect of changed conditions on the reproductive system. He was also of the opinion that these conditions must be capable of acting in a delayed and cumulative manner on the reproductive system, so that variations might continue after the initial effects of the conditions of domestication.

Dr R. A. Fisher in his *Genetical Theory of Natural Selection*[1] has pointed out that Darwin saw the need for an alternative to the blending theory of inheritance as early as 1857, and quotes from one of his letters to Huxley (*More Letters*, Vol. I, letter 57):

Approaching the subject from the side which attracts me most, viz., inheritance, I have lately been inclined to speculate, very crudely and indistinctly, that propagation by true fertilization will turn out to be a sort of mixture, and not true fusion, of two distinct individuals, or rather, of innumerable individuals, as each parent has its parents and ancestors. I can understand on no other view the way in which crossed forms go back to so large an extent to ancestral forms. But all this, of course, is infinitely crude.

Had he adopted this theory of the mixture of hereditary particles, it would have explained the phenomenon of reversion to ancestral types, for there is always the chance that the ancestral combination may at any time be reproduced. It would also have made clear why variations continue under domestication, when the initial effect of the changed conditions on the reproductive system might be supposed to have worn off. The many combinations of hereditary particles would continue under domestication as in a state of nature. But under domestication, mutations could more easily survive, and man is always choosing and preserving new variants which please him, and is thus constantly adding to the possibilities of variation. It is a pity that Darwin never went on with this theory, and that he never saw Mendel's paper of 1865.[2] The world had to wait for the recognition of this particulate theory of inheritance, which Darwin had clearly foreshadowed, until the beginning of the present century. The difficulties in Darwin's theory are here mentioned only to show that he was fully alive to them, and recognized more than his contemporaries or successors for many years, the flaws in

---

[1] Oxford, 1930, p. 1.
[2] G. J. Mendel, 'Versuche über Pflanzen-Hybriden,' *Verh. Naturf. Ver. in Brünn*, Vol. X.

his argument, and the magnitude of the problems on which he worked. Moreover, whenever any new development of his theory occurs, it is more than likely that he himself had realized the possibility of such a development, or has left a place in his scheme for it.

It was the visit to the Galapagos Archipelago which clarified Darwin's views about variation under natural conditions. Each of these islands had a distinctive animal population, but the species in each island were the counterparts of those in the others, and also of species on the continent. With the evidence at hand from the many variations with a common ancestor under domestication, these facts could best be explained by assuming that the species in the various islands and on the continent had a common descent. Again, his large collection of extinct and fossil forms from the interior of South America, and of living animals from the same area, powerfully suggested the same explanation. The structural resemblance between the extinct and the living indicated blood-relationship and common descent. In spite of the imperfection of the geological record in Darwin's time, he foresaw the importance of this likeness, and believed that this class of evidence would in time throw great light on the origin and development of organic beings on earth. The recognition of the immense age of the discoveries of Boucher de Perthes by Sir Charles Lyell and others had already in 1859 opened the minds of scientists to the idea that they must reckon with countless ages rather than with the short period from 4004 B.C., and thus it was now possible for the geologists and palaeontologists to begin to lay out on a large scale the geological succession of epochs and organic beings. Time was needed for the origin and development of so many species, and for their peopling the earth, and the geologists had at last given themselves that time.

Just as artificial selection was responsible for choosing and propagating certain variations and rejecting others, some sort of natural selection must be at work to ensure that certain varieties were perpetuated in one island of the archipelago, and others in another. Otherwise, indiscriminate bisexual reproduction would tend to neutralize the variations.

How was this natural selection to work? Here the principle of Malthus appeared to supply the answer. Organic beings increase by a geometrical ratio, so that in a very short time, a district will be overpopulated with any one species, unless something happens to check the increase. Consequently there is a struggle for life between one individual and another within the same species, or between one species and another of the same genus, or with other species, or with the general conditions of life. It was this lethal selection which was most apparent to Darwin's readers, and had the most effect on the thought of the natural scientists and social philosophers of the time, but Darwin included other factors in the struggle for existence which are no less important.

For one thing, there is the dependence of one being on another, and the various associations into families, societies, flocks, and herds, all of which make for the survival of the individuals within them. The success of the plant, animal, or human being in leaving young was to Darwin one of the most important of all factors in the struggle for life, and he emphasized the association of parents and offspring, and of sexual selection.

To urban philosophers on the whole, the nutritive and individualistic functions bulk larger. But the countryman is more impressed by the processes of growth and by the reproductive functions which make for the preservation of the species, and above all, understands the complex interdependence of people, land, and animals. 'Live and let live' is the fundamental law of his existence, and of his progress. He cannot hire and discharge like the urban employer without thought of issues involved. He knows the relation of his labourer to other people in the village, and understands precisely the results in the general economy of the community of leaving him stranded. He is exercised with compassion at the plight of a landless man, and will help his neighbours' animals as soon as his own if he finds them in difficulties. Nothing touches the countryman more deeply than the dying out of families who have always farmed the land in his community, or a farm falling into the hands of strangers. He knows that if he takes a day's work from a neighbour, he will give one in return, and often the whole village is so organized for reciprocal services that there is no hired labour except that of boys and girls who have no land of their own, but must wait until some relative or friend is in a position to start them in life.

Darwin understood this mutual dependence, and had the countryman's view of the importance of growth and reproduction. In one sense, evolution is a process of the development of parental love, those creatures in which it is most highly developed being most able, and intelligent, and most capable of surviving in a variety of environments. In another, the extension of the law 'Thou shalt love thy neighbour as thyself' has been a powerful factor in the development of civilization, imperfectly as the rule has been applied. Kropotkin's *Mutual Aid, a Factor in Evolution*, published in 1902, is a very valuable account of this imperfectly appreciated side of Darwin's theory, which will be treated in the next chapter. Unfortunately, the popular social thought of the latter part of the nineteenth century was dominated by a consideration of the nutritive and individualist functions, rather than by the reproductive and interdependent factors making for survival, and thus without appreciating the intricate inter-relations of the whole complex of living beings, and failing thereby to understand how very slight differences can be of great moment in determining survival, regarded almost wholly one side only of the theory, that of the lethal struggle for existence, in which the survivors were assumed to be the fittest. Darwin's terminology, as we have seen, was applied to old notions begotten of the mechanical revolution, and people used Darwin's name without being Darwinians, simplifying his theory to a point where it became ridiculous.

The grandeur of Darwin's life was equal to the grandeur of his conception. His friend Huxley[1] rightly speaks of his 'rare combination of genius, industry, and unswerving veracity. [He] earned his place among the most famous men of the age by sheer native power, in the teeth of a gale of popular prejudice, and uncheered by a sign of favour or appreciation from the official fountains of honour; as one who, in spite of an acute sensitiveness to praise and blame, and notwithstanding provocations which might have excused any outbreak, kept himself clear of all envy, hatred, and malice, nor dealt otherwise than fairly and justly with the unfairness and injustice which was showered upon him; while, to the end of his days, he was ready to listen with patience and respect to the most insignificant of reasonable objectors'. It may be added that he displayed the same magnanimous attitude towards those who applied his name and his terminology to unilateral schemes of development which could only be hateful to a man who contemplated the whole rich complexity of organic life on earth. He was not interested in advertisement, but simply in the truth, wherever he found it. Every reader must be struck, not only with his simple, direct and manly style of writing, free from all pedantry or affectation of scientific dogmatism, but by his constant reference to those who have given him information, even in the humblest walks of life.

One of the finest examples of the character of a true man and scientist ever recorded is that of his treatment of his friend Wallace. In 1858, after he had laboured twenty years on the *Origin of Species*, Darwin received a paper sent by Wallace from the Malay Archipelago, of which he wrote to Lyell, 'Even his terms now stand as heads of my chapters',[2]

[1]*Life and Letters of Charles Darwin*, 'On the Reception of the "Origin of Species"', 1887, II, 179.
[2]*Life and Letters*, 1887, II, 116.

and requested Lyell to see to its publication. Sir Charles Lyell and Sir Joseph Hooker, in communicating the paper to the *Journal of the Linnean Society*, added a preface:

So highly did Mr Darwin appreciate the value of the views therein set forth, that he proposed, in a letter to Sir Charles Lyell, to obtain Mr Wallace's consent to allow the Essay ['On the Tendency of Varieties to depart indefinitely from the Original Type'] to be published as soon as possible. Of this step we highly approved, provided Mr Darwin did not withhold from the public, as he was strongly inclined to do [in favour of Mr Wallace], the memoir which he had himself written on the same subject, and which, as before stated, one of us had perused in 1844, and the contents of which we had both of us been privy to for many years. On representing this to Mr Darwin, he gave us permission to make what use proper we thought of his memoir, etc.; and in adopting our present course, of his memoir, etc.; and in adopting our present course, of presenting it to the Linnean Society, we have explained to him that we are not solely considering the relative claims to priority of himself and his friend, but the interests of science generally.[1]

Apart from his life-long and loyal friend Wallace, Darwin thought most highly of the commendation of Lyell, Hooker, and Huxley. On November 25, 1859, he wrote to Huxley: 'I then fixed in my mind three judges, on whose decision I determined mentally to abide. The judges were Lyell, Hooker, and yourself. It was this which made me so excessively anxious for your verdict. I am now contented, and can sing my "Nunc dimittis".'

The first minister of religion to write favourably to Darwin was Charles Kingsley, to whom he had sent an advance copy of the *Origin*. Kingsley wrote on November 18, 1859: 'All I have seen of it *awes* me; both with the heap of facts and the prestige of your name, and also with the clear intuition, that if you be right, I must give up much that I have believed and written. In that I care little. Let God be true, and every man a liar! Let us know what *is*, and as old Socrates has it, ἔπεσθαι τῷ λόγῳ, follow up the villainous shifty fox of an argument, into whatsoever unexpected brakes and bogs he may lead us, if we do but run into him at last. From two common superstitions, at least, I shall be free while judging of your book: (1) I have long since, from watching the crossing of domesticated animals and plants, learnt to disbelieve the dogma of the permanence of species. (2) I have gradually learnt to see that it is just as noble a conception of Deity, to believe that He created primal forms capable of self development into all forms needful *pro tempore* and *pro loco*, as to believe that He required a fresh act of

[1] *Life and Letters*, 1887, II, 115.

intervention to supply the *lacunas* which He Himself had made. I question whether the former be not the loftier view.'[1]

With his life-long friend, the Rev. J. Brodie Innes, sometime Vicar of Down, Darwin had many conversations, and they agreed that the Bible and the book of nature came from the same divine source, and that their lines of truth were separate. 'I do not attack Moses, and I think Moses can take care of himself', was the conclusion of one of Darwin's letters to Innes on the subject.[2]

The best summary of what Darwin's work meant to his more enlightened contemporaries is set out in Huxley's address 'On the reception of the *Origin of Species*':[3]

The publication of the Darwin and Wallace papers in 1858, and still more that of the *Origin* in 1859, had the effect . . . of the flash of light, which to a man who has lost himself on a dark night, suddenly reveals a road which, whether it takes him straight home or not, certainly goes his way. That which we were looking for, and could not find, was an hypothesis respecting the origin of known organic forms which assumed the operation of no causes but such as could be proved to be actually at work. We wanted, not to pin our faith to that or to any other speculation, but to get hold of clear and definite conceptions which could be brought face to face with facts and have their validity tested. The *Origin* provided us with the working hypothesis we sought . . .

The suggestion that new species may result from the selective action of external conditions upon the variations from their specific type which individuals present—and which we call 'spontaneous' because we are ignorant of their causation—is as wholly unknown to the historian of scientific ideas as it was to biological specialists before 1858. But that suggestion is the central idea of the *Origin of Species*, and contains the quintessence of Darwinism.[4]

The *Origin of Species* then provided a scheme which linked together the past and the present, and all forms of life, institutions, and beliefs, as parts of one whole, and in development. Henceforward, anthropology could be the science of man in evolution, following its course not in the light of assumed notions for which there could be no proof, but in the light of a hypothesis which assumed no causes except those which could be proved to be at work. Scientists need no longer start from abstractions arrived at by cogitation. They could now proceed experimentally, unhampered by 'laws' which were not susceptible of proof.

[1] *Life and Letters*, 1887, II, 287.
[2] *Ibid.*, III, 288.
[3] *Ibid.*, II, 197.
[4] *Ibid.*, II, 195.

II. BIOLOGICAL DISCOVERIES AND GENERAL
ANTHROPOLOGY (INCLUDING SOCIOLOGY)

As biological discoveries and theories were the most powerful of all forces in determining the trend of thought in the latter part of the nineteenth century, it will be well to summarize briefly the main developments between the *Origin of Species* and the year 1900, when the rediscovery of Mendel's work gave yet another major turn to the subject. In the course of the summary, various anthropological subjects will be discussed as they are affected by the development of biology.

The first to apply Darwin's hypothesis in detail to the study of man was T. H. Huxley, in a series of lectures first given to working men in 1860 and before the Philosophical Institution of Edinburgh in 1862, and first published under the title *Man's Place in Nature* in 1863.

After a full comparative study of embryology, brains and other organs, bones, and general bodily structure, he concludes:

> Thus, whatever system of organs be studied, the comparison of their modifications in the ape series leads to one and the same result—that the structural differences which separate Man from the Gorilla and the Chimpanzee are not so great as those which separate the Gorilla from the lower apes. . . .
>
> But if Man be separated by no greater structural barrier from the brutes than they are from one another—then it seems to follow that if any process of physical causation can be discovered by which the genera and families of ordinary animals have been produced, that process of causation is amply sufficient to account for the origin of Man. . . .
>
> At the present moment, but one such process of physical causation has any evidence in its favour; or, in other words, there is but one hypothesis regarding the origin of species of animals in general which has any scientific existence—that propounded by Mr Darwin.

In a further lecture, he takes the Engis skull from the valley of the Meuse in Belgium, discovered by Schmerling in 1833 with remains of the mammoth and Rhinoceros tichorhinus, and the Neanderthal skull discovered and described by Schaaffhausen in 1857, and compares them with primitive modern types, remarking that 'though truly the most pithecoid of known human skulls, the Neanderthal cranium is by no means so isolated as it appears to be at first, but forms, in reality, the extreme term of a series leading gradually from it to the highest and best developed of human crania.[1] On the one hand, it is closely approached by the flattened Australian skulls, of which I have spoken, from which

---

[1] In the year 1864 Dr William King, Professor of Anatomy in Galway, classified the specimen as Homo neanderthalensis, a classification which waited about twenty-five years for recognition.

other Australian forms lead us gradually up to skulls having very much the type of the Engis cranium'.

In the course of his investigation, Huxley devised 'a new and precise system of cranial measurements for the detection of racial likenesses and differences—a system which has never been given a rightful trial'.[1] In 1865 in the *Fortnightly Review*, under the title 'Methods and Results of Ethnology', he classifies mankind by hair, as Bory de St Vincent had done in 1827, and by skull-form and colour under those headings. He makes no mention of Pruner-Bey's 'Chevelure comme caracteristique des races humaines' (*Mém. Soc. d'Anthr.*, ii, Paris), published in 1863, the classic paper on the subject, showing that races may be classified not only in accordance with the appearance of hair as straight, wavy, or woolly, but also that the microscopical section of these types is circular, in the form of an ellipse, or in the form of a flattened ellipse, respectively.

By 1870[2] Huxley had come to the conclusion that cranial characters were of subsidiary importance, and classified the principal races by hair and skin-colour. The Australoid type occupied Australia, the Deccan, and a part of Egypt. The Negroid occupied Africa between the Sahara and the Cape, the Bushman, and the Melanesian areas. The Xantho-chroid or fair white type was to be found in Central Europe and Scandinavia, spreading into England and through the Mediterranean region into North Africa and into Asia as far as northern India. The Melano-chroid, or dark white type, extended from England, along both sides of the Mediterranean, into Asia as far as India. The Mongoloid extended from northern Europe, through Asia, into Indonesia and the Americas. Other groups arose by crossing, the Melanochroi themselves probably being the result of ancient crosses between the Xanthochroi and the Australoids.

These papers sum up Huxley's principal contributions to anthropology, though he wrote a great number of papers, including discussions of sociological questions. His opinion of the struggle for existence was that it was the mission of society to control and supersede it.

During the sixties a new tendency started, which was to take the study of biology out of the field into the laboratory, though biologists still continued to go on voyages of discovery to study man and his companions and environment, as on the *Challenger* Expedition in 1872, the Horn Expedition in 1894, and the expedition to the Torres Straits in 1898. This new tendency may be said to have started with Virchow and

---

[1] Keith, *J.R.A.I.*, LVIII, p. 308.
[2] 'On the Geographical Distribution of the Chief Modifications of Mankind' (with coloured map), *J.E.S.*, n.s. II, 1870.

Haeckel. Darwin's observations were on living people, animals, and plants, in their natural surroundings, and his interests were in natural selection, inheritance, variation, geographical distribution and environment, habits, emotions, instincts, mentality. Virchow's opposition, or perhaps it would be better to say, qualified acceptance of Darwin's theory, was due to the type of work he was doing. Virchow[1] was at once a statesman and a scientist, who was not afraid to dictate to governments when it was advisable in the interest of the health of the people. In 1856, after years of work, he put forward his theory of cellular pathology, establishing the fact that every cell originates from a previously existing cell, and that in pathological, as well as in normal physiological processes, the results are the outcome of the interaction of originally normal cells with their circumstances. As all living organisms are made up of living cells, and cells exhibit changes in growth-processes in response to changes in environment, then changes in the growth of the whole organism must be resoluble into changes in the growth-processes of the component cells. Thus individual variability, on which the Darwinian theory depends, is a special and complicated case of cell variability, within the borderland that divides pathology from normal physiology. Thus, until the conditions of cell variability are more exactly determined than they now are (1859), speculations as to origins and transformation of species must be regarded as hypothetical.

Work on cretinism and skull pathology brought him into anthropology, and caused him to consider that Neanderthal man was a pathological case. But more than this, his patriotism, knowledge of biology, and interest in social questions attracted him to the subject. With Bastian he helped to found the Museum für Völkerkunde, and the *Archiv für Anthropologie* (1866). He turned his attention to archaeology and to making a survey of the physical characters of the German people. The pioneer in this work of making exact observations on the physical characters of living men was Dr John Beddoe, who wrote a long series of papers in various languages giving statistics of hair, eye-colour, skin-colour, and other bodily characteristics, between 1861 and 1908. The first paper to attract general attention was 'Sur la couleur des yeux et des cheveux des Irlandais' in 1861.[2] Haddon has a complete bibliography in *Man*, 1911, 93.

Beddoe's census was taken with no political bias, but Virchow's was initiated with a view to making a scientific answer to a Frenchman, who, after the war of 1871, published a villainous account of the composition

[1] See J. L. Myres, *Man*, 1903, 1.
[2] *Bull. Soc. d'Anthr.*, Paris.

of the Prussian race, rather on the style of some of the 'ethnological' statements made during World War II, and of as little value.

Virchow had as much as anyone in Germany to do with organizing the various branches of the science there. His work on cells had a powerful influence on his pupil, E. F. Haeckel, who had so much to do with turning biological studies from the field into the laboratory. Haeckel's *Generelle Morphologie* in 1866 accepted Darwin, but with a difference. Haeckel thought that all the questions of natural selection, inheritance, variation, distribution, and hybridization could be summed up under two headings, those of adaptation and inheritance. All of Darwin except chapter fourteen was so treated. But that chapter on 'Mutual Affinities of Organic Beings, Morphology, Embryology, and Rudimentary Organs' was made a point of departure for his own investigation of these subjects in an evolutionary fashion. He was of the opinion that in morphological study, all the facts concerning anatomy and development are the outcome of forces working according to definite mechanical laws. While such careful studies in the laboratory are of the utmost importance, it is a pity that so many biologists and anthropologists preferred to stay indoors and study the dead, and it is to be feared that a good deal of their work has been influenced by the idea of machinery rather than of growth, and that in their dissections they worked too much in the spirit of a man who takes a watch to pieces. Of course, when he has done so, he can learn the relation of each part to every other, as in the old study of static anatomy. And as it is machinery, he may discover what makes it go. But if it were alive, it is doubtful whether he would have such good fortune.

Among the men whose observations were laying the foundation of what is likely to become one of the most important developments in the future of anthropology, and of the biological sciences generally, Sir William Gull[1] and C. F. Brown-Séquard[2] must be remembered. In the seventies and eighties Sir William Gull was observing that a characteristic group of changes in the body and mind was always associated with atrophy of the thyroid gland, and Brown-Séquard was experimenting on himself with glandular extracts made from dogs. In 1895 Oliver and Schafer discovered certain of the functions of the adrenal glands.[3] The part played by the ductless glands in the economy of the individual body, and in the development of certain physical characters, indivi-

---

[1] *Gull, Sir William, a coll. of the pub. works of*, ed. T. D. Acland, 1894, pp. 315–21; also *Clin. Soc. Trans.*, 1871, *Med.-Chir. Trans.*, 1871, liv. pp. 166, 169; *Lancet*, Dec., 1883.

[2] *Arch. de physiol. et path.*, Sér. 5, Vol. I, pp. 659, 731.

[3] See p. 190.

dually and racially, is lately becoming better understood, and holds as much hope as any kind of investigation for solving many difficult problems.

But these men were far ahead of their time. Pierre Paul Broca was of his time, and one of the ablest of his period. His methods are still in use by many anthropologists, and in their particular field some of them will probably not be superseded. In 1847 excavations in the cemetery of the Celestins turned his attention to physical anthropology. In 1859 he was a founder of the Société d'Anthropologie de Paris, and in 1876 of L'École d'Anthropologie. In a famous paper, 'Instructions craniologiques et craniométriques de la Société d'Anthropologie de Paris', in 1875,[1] he gave methods for collecting and preserving weak and brittle bones, defined exactly the points to be used in taking measurements, and the measurements to be taken, and the instruments to be employed. By such accumulation of accurate measurements, he hoped to be able to discriminate racial types. He also included methods of graphical representation and discussed qualitative descriptive characters.[2]

His technique was used by all French workers until lately, somewhat modified, it is true, but essentially his, and by Belgian, Italian, and Spanish anthropologists. Flower and Turner in England used Broca's method with some alterations, but did not adopt his way of dealing with graphical representation or qualitative descriptive characters. Sir William Flower published a catalogue of the crania in the Museum of the Royal College of Surgeons, and Sir William Turner[3] published a large part of the Edinburgh collection in numerous papers. The large collection in Oxford was measured by Sir Francis Knowles under the direction of Professor Arthur Thomson, one of Turner's pupils, as late as 1910, but has not been published.[4]

The German-speaking countries since 1882 have used the *Frankfurter Verständigung* with various modifications. In that year a conference of German anthropologists met at Frankfort, where Kollmann-Ranke, and Virchow presented a report on craniometric technique which, embodied the results of discussions at previous conferences. This report was printed in the *Archiv für Anthropologie* in 1884[5] under the title 'Verständigung über ein gemeinsames craniometrisches Verfahren', and the agreeement was ratified by sixty-seven anthropologists. Using

---

[1] *Mém. de la Soc. d'Anthr. de Paris*, 2me série, T. II, pp. 1–203.
[2] Account of techniques in measurement follows Buxton and Morant, 'Essential Craniometric Technique,' *J.R.A.I.*, LXIII, 1933, p. 19.
[3] See Keith's bibliography in *Man*, 1916, 42.
[4] Written in 1935. The bulk of this collection was transferred to the British Museum (Natural History), London, S.W.7, in 1946.
[5] Band XV, S. 1–8.

this standardized technique, a catalogue of the crania and other anthropological specimens in the museums of Germany was published between
1877 and 1908 in the *Archiv für Anthropologie* supplements.[1] The
majority of the cranial characters were the same as those outlined by
Broca, but the definitions of the measurements were generally different.
Of the forty-seven measurements described by Broca and the thirty-one
of the Frankfort agreement, only eight can be said to have identical
definitions, and the two techniques differ in the choice of planes in which
the cranium is set up for examination. The Frankfort agreement was
translated and criticized in England by Dr J. G. Garson,[2] who helped
General Pitt Rivers to publish the crania in that museum, and in Germany by Emil Schmidt,[3] whose modifications of the technique were
followed by a few workers in Germany.

The principal critic of methods of measurement and of the indices
derived from them was G. Sergi, Professor of Anthropology in the University of Rome. His contention was that craniometry would demonstrate anything and everything that one wishes, and that many indices
such as the cephalic obscure the important fact that the forms within a
particular group which we call dolichocephalic or brachycephalic may
be very different, and it is these essential forms which distinguish races.
He therefore, like his son, used and still uses photographs and drawings
much more than measurements and indices. I had the pleasure of his
son's company for about a month at Oxford, and he was kind enough to
lay out in groups all of the crania from Kish in Mesopotamia which
Buxton and Rice and myself had published, using craniometric methods.
Like his father, he considers the *norma verticalis*, the view of the
cranium from above, to be of the greatest importance. I was astonished
to see how often a peculiar form which could not be represented by a
measurement or index repeated itself in all ages from 3000 B.C., the
oldest of our present series, up to the present day. He has devised a
series of terms like beloid, pentagonoid, ovoid, ellipsoid, etc., to distinguish these forms, and he also applies criteria of shape to the face in
distinguishing races. Both father and son have had great influence in
forcing the metricians to ask themselves what they are measuring, why
they are measuring, and whether their measurements and indices
obscure or clarify essentials. These ideas were first developed by the
elder Sergi in 'La varietà umane' in 1893,[4] and in *The Mediterranean*

---

[1] *Die anthropologischen Sammlungen Deutschlands.*
[2] *J.A.I.*, 1884, XIV, p. 64.
[3] *Anthropologische Methoden*, Leipzig, 1888.
[4] *Atti soc. romana d' antrop.*, I, 1893. Tr. Smithsonian Misc. Coll. XXVIII, No.
969.

THE CONSTRUCTIVE PERIOD: 1859–1900

Race, a Study of the Origin of European Peoples, in Italian in 1895, German, 1897, and in an enlarged English edition in 1901.

This account of methods of measurement, developing out of Broca's pioneer work, must not obscure the fact that anthropology was far more than a science of measurements to Broca, who played an important part in the foundation of all branches of the science in France. *The Anthropological Review* of London,[1] volumes five and six, contains two papers called 'Broca on Anthropology', translated from the fifth volume of the *Dictionnaire encyclopédique des sciences médicales*, giving Broca's idea of the scope of the subject. The science has for its object the study of the human group in its ensemble, in its details, and in its relation to the rest of nature. In zoological anthropology we determine the place of man in the whole series of creatures. In descriptive anthropology we divide and subdivide the ensemble, and study the groups separately according to their physical and physiological differences, intellectual and social peculiarities. This part may be termed ethnology. In general anthropology we study comparative anatomy, physiology, psychology, and pathology of races, including anthropology, vital statistics, environment, acclimatization, heredity, palaeontology, polygenism and monogenism.

Towards the end of his life Broca was of the opinion that little could be learned from measurements of the brain-case, and devoted his attention to the study of the brain itself. He died suddenly in middle life at the age of fifty-six, leaving his work to be carried on by the brilliant men he had gathered round him in his school.

Of these, Paul Topinard was one of the earliest and most closely associated. He worked no less hard than Broca, but his naturally strong constitution was fortified by a youth spent in the mountains of New York where his father had an estate, and allowed his son to hunt and fish as much as he liked. In 1860 he became a member of Broca's Anthropological Society, and by 1870 decided to give up a promising medical career to enter Broca's laboratory to study the natural history of man. He worked indefatigably in connexion with the society, the school, and the *Révue d'Anthropologie* which he and Broca edited. A fellow-professor at the school was L. A. Bertillon, who was a general anthropologist, but is best known for the Bertillon system of measuring and identifying criminals.[2] Topinard's *L'Anthropologie* was published in 1876, and his *Eléments d'Anthropologie générale* in 1885, and both are classics. The first contains a brief history of the subject, and the two

[1] 1867–68.
[2] A. Bertillon, 'Notice sur le fonctionnement du Service d'Identification de la Préfecture de Police,' *Ann. Stat. de la ville de Paris*, 1887 (1889); *J.A.I.*, 1890, XX, p. 182.

89

develop a scheme by which the subject may be studied. Anthropology proper has a general side, the human species, and a special side, the human races or varieties. Ethnology has a general side in questions relating to every people, and a special, in monographic descriptions of particular peoples. The essential anthropological sciences are human anatomy, embryology, physiology, psychology, and sociology, and the accessory are history, archaeology, linguistics, demography, and comparative mythology.

Like Topinard, Armand de Quatrefages de Bréau was one of the earliest to break away from the sterile old controversy of monogenesis or polygenesis, and to incorporate the ideas of Darwin. In his 'Discours d'ouverture du cours d'anthropologie, professé au muséum d'histoire naturelle' in 1861,[1] he maintained that he would lay great stress on the anatomy and physiology of man. But the natural historian of animals must pay attention to their habits and instincts, and thus it was but right that the biologist who studied man should take account of his habits and instincts and of all the sciences which treated them. The *Rapport sur le progrès d'anthropologie* in 1867 took account of all these accessory sciences, and reduced them to an ordered scheme. Other works are *L'espèce humaine*, 1877, *Les Pygmées*, 1887, *Histoire générale des races humaines*, 1889; and with E. J. Hamy, the *Crania Ethnica*, between 1875 and 1879.

While the French were killing the controversy between the champions of the unity or of the independent origin of the races of mankind, America and England were still in its throes. In the previous chapter the work of de Gobineau and of Nott and Gliddon, who held the polygenetic theory, was noted. But a book which carried far more weight with the American people was Harriet Beecher Stowe's *Uncle Tom's Cabin*, a story which showed the horror of slavery, first published in 1852, and then in innumerable editions. Whether or not the Negro was a separate creation or product of evolution designed for the use of the white man, or better under his care, was an academic question. In 1863, during the Civil War between North and South, Abraham Lincoln set all the Negroes free.

In England James Hunt championed the cause of the South, and in this, as in the Irish, the Celtic, and other European racial questions, and the question of the position of women, he was a firm believer in taking anthropology into politics, and making its problems known to the whole of the people. He thought that the work of the Ethnological Society was too circumscribed, and with his followers, broke away in 1863 and

[1] *Gazette Médicale de Paris*, Sér. 3, Vol. XVI, p. 783.

founded the Anthropological Society. In his opening address[1] he declared that anthropology was the whole science of man, and must include biology, anatomy, chemistry, natural philosophy, and physiology. Ethnology treated only of the history or science of nations or races, while anthropology must deal with the whole matter of the origin and development of humanity, with the aid of the geologist, archaeologist, anatomist, physiologist, and philologist. Thomas Bendyshe in 1865 showed a similar breadth of view, as appears in the opening chapter of this book.

The break with the Ethnological Society was really on the Negro question, and Hunt's declaration that it was the business of anthropologists to discover his place in nature. So great was the enthusiasm he aroused that the society grew rapidly and aroused a wide interest. In 1866 the British Association recognized the subject as a part of biology, and in 1884 gave it a section to itself. In spite of Hunt's breadth of view and his personal qualities, which won him something akin to worship from his followers, the society lost prestige because of its connexion with political and religious questions and the prejudices aroused. Thus many of his plans for raising funds for explorations and for a Government College for Anthropology came to nothing. He died from the effects of a chill at the early age of thirty-six in 1869. After his death the Ethnological and Anthropological Societies united as the Anthropological Institute of Great Britain and Ireland,[2] and the *Journal of the Ethnological Society*, the *Memoirs read before the Anthropological Society*, and the *Anthropological Review* were merged in the *Journal of the Anthropological Institute*, henceforward to be devoted to seeking the truth for its own sake.[3]

Many museums and societies for the study of anthropology were founded from the time of Darwin, hardly a year passing without the foundation of a society which published a periodical. A few may be noticed here. Paris, London, and Berlin have been mentioned. Moscow had a society in 1833, Vienna in 1870, Florence in 1871, Stockholm in 1873, and Washington in 1879, this last being also the date of the foundation of the Bureau of American Ethnology, the first and for a long time the only example of a government department devoted to the systematic study of its native races.

This wonderful achievement was due mainly to the genius and persistence of Major John Wesley Powell, whose first expedition was one

---

[1] *A.R.*, London, 1863, I, pp. 1–20; also *J.A.S.*, 1864, II, lxxx–xciii.

[2] The title *Royal* was added in 1907.

[3] Keith, *J.R.A.I.*, 1917, has the whole history of the Institute.

organized by himself for his pupils to explore the Colorado canyons. He brought back a great deal of valuable data, collected at very small cost, concerning the utilization of water and the reclamation of the desert, and this matter was one which occupied his interest and labours until near the end of his life, when the United States government adopted his plans. The government, however, acted at once on his suggestion that a geological survey would be the most powerful implement that the American people possess for the economy of their heritage, and the Smithsonian Institution founded a geological and geographical survey on the lines that Powell laid down on his first expedition. This trip to the Colorado was Powell's first introduction to Indian life, and resulted n the creation of a separate Bureau for Ethnology of which he became the first director. He had a genius for organization, and for collecting and teaching able men, as well as great financial ability and the knowledge of what could be done and when to ask for it. His output in general anthropology was small and his style and treatment of evidence austere. Under his direction the 'Indian Linguistic Families North of Mexico'[1] were classified, and his contribution 'Anthropology' to Appleton's *Universal Cyclopaedia* in 1900 discusses the subject under the heads of somatology, psychology, and ethnology. But his greatest work for anthropology was the foundation and direction of the Bureau, which gave to the study of native races in America and throughout the world 'a motive and encouragement, a standard of achievement, and a sequel of practical applications of profound significance in the history of anthropological studies'.[2]

We have shown some of the movements which started in the sixties after the publication of the *Origin of Species*. In 1871 Darwin published *The Descent of Man*, and in 1872, *The Expression of the Emotions in Man and Animals*. These two books, and the works which criticized or developed their theories, had a profound effect not only in biological circles but in other branches of science. *The Descent of Man* did not contain as much of Darwin's own observations as the *Origin*, and discussed anthropology, sociology, medicine, and philology and other subjects. It argued that man had gradually evolved from a lower form of life, and that he was akin to the animal in body and mind. He had rudimentary organs resembling those which were functional in lower animals, and was subject to variations. He was a glorified animal even on the spiritual plane. It was true that he was well above the other animals, but let anyone compare the difference in intellect between a dog and a fish.

[1] *B.A.E.*, 7th report, 1891.
[2] J. L. Myres, *Man*, 1903, 10.

Man has the same sort of sense organs as the animals, and must therefore have the same primitive sensations; he has the same impulse to live and increase; with animals he knows mother-love; he feels joy, pain, happiness, misery, as do the animals. Like animals, he has a good or bad temper, is ambitious or the reverse. Even dogs have a sense of shame or modesty; they show the rudiments of worship for their masters. Animals show powers of imitation, concentration, understanding. Thus apart from all homologies and other indications of man's bodily kinship with the rest of animated nature, there are strong indications of his mental and spiritual kinship.

Man may be excused for feeling some pride at having risen, though not through his own exertions, to the very summit of the organic scale; and the fact of his having thus risen, instead of having been aboriginally placed there, may give him hope for a still higher destiny in the distant future. But we are not here concerned with hopes or fears, only with the truth as far as our reason permits us to discover it; and I have given the evidence to the best of my ability. We must, however, acknowledge, as it seems to me, that Man with all his noble qualities, with sympathy which feels for the most debased, with benevolence which extends not only to other men but to the humblest living creature, with his god-like intellect which has penetrated into the movements and constitution of the solar system—with all these exalted powers—Man still bears in his bodily frame the indelible stamp of his lowly origin.[1]

The Expression of the Emotions in Man and Animals carries these comparisons much farther into the emotional and mental life of men and animals, and is a wonderful work of direct observation and common sense, simply expounded. The physiological and psychological causes and effects are carefully examined, and the different chapters consider the expression of all the fundamental emotions in different animals and men, showing the origin and development of these actions through three principles.

The first of these principles is, that movements which are serviceable in gratifying some desire, or in relieving some sensation, if often repeated, become so habitual that they are performed, whether or not of any service, whenever the same desire or sensation is felt, even in a very weak degree.

Our second principle is that of antithesis. The habit of voluntarily performing opposite movements under opposite impulses has become firmly established in us by the practice of our whole lives. Hence, if certain actions have been regularly performed, in accordance with our first principles, under a certain frame of mind, there will be a strong and involuntary tendency to the performance of directly opposite actions,

---

[1] *The Descent of Man*, closing paragraph.

whether or not these are of any use, under the excitement of an opposite frame of mind.

Our third principle is the direct action of the excited nervous system on the body, independently of the will, and independently, in large part, of habit. Experience shows that nerve-force is generated and set free whenever the cerebro-spinal system is excited. The direction which this nerve-force follows is necessarily determined by the lines of connexion between the nerve-cells, with each other and with various parts of the body. But the direction is likewise much influenced by habit; in as much as nerve-force passes readily along accustomed channels.[1]

Following an account of the nervous and muscular actions which express various emotions, Darwin continues 'that the chief expressive actions, exhibited by man and by the lower animals, are now innate or inherited. . . . So little has learning or imitation to do with several of them that they are from the earliest days and throughout life quite beyond our control. . . .'[2]

All these true or inherited movements of expression seem to have had a natural and independent origin. 'But when once acquired, such movements may be voluntarily and consciously employed as a means of communication. . . . . The tendency to such movements will be strengthened or increased by their being thus voluntarily and repeatedly performed; and their effects may be inherited. . . . As most of the movements of expression must have been gradually acquired, afterwards becoming instinctive, there seems to be some degree of *a priori* probability that their recognition would likewise become instinctive.'[3]

While Wallace was in general agreement with Darwin, he differed from him in several respects. For one thing, he did not believe that acquired characters could be inherited. For another, he doubted whether sexual selection had anything to do with the development of varieties, natural selection being sufficient to explain the matter. Domestic animals he regarded as monstrosities, and not analogous to wild ones. He attempted to reconcile religion and science, asserting his belief that God had intervened three times, once when He created life, once when consciousness dawned, and once to give Man a soul.[4]

In Germany, August Weismann[5] followed the tradition of Virchow and Haeckel, studying the same problems as Darwin's in the laboratory,

---

[1] *Expression of Emotions*, 1872, p. 318.

[2] *Ibid.*, 351.

[3] *Ibid.*, 356, 358.

[4] A. R. Wallace, *The Malay Archipelago*, 1868; *Contributions to the Theory of Natural Selection*, 1870; *Darwinism*, 1881.

[5] Lectures from 1881–91 at Freiburg, trans. as *Weismann on Heredity*, 1889, 1892, by Poulton, Schöland, Shipley.

especially the investigation of the individual cells in which he first described the behaviour of the chromosomes in connexion with reproduction. All components of the adult body were hidden in the egg and sperm. The germ plasm was always present in those parts of the body which could produce new organisms. In other parts of the body the somatoplasm had only a few of the components which were in the germ plasm. The germ plasm was immortal and distinct, and what happened to the somatoplasm by way of modification or adaptation to environment did not affect it, at any rate directly. Acquired characters were not then transmitted. In this he agreed with Wallace's surmise, and like Wallace, he came to the conclusion that sexual selection played little if any part in evolution, natural selection being enough to explain the phenomena. But although the germ plasm remained steadily itself in successive generations, Weismann believed that it might be possible for the modifications to have secondary effects on the germ cells, and hence on the offspring.

C. Lloyd Morgan, writing on *Habit and Instinct* in 1896[1] developed Weismann's idea of the plasticity of the germ plasm further:

Suppose that a group of plastic organisms is placed under new conditions. Those whose innate plasticity is equal to the occasion are modified and survive. Those whose plasticity is not equal to the occasion are eliminated. . . . Such modification takes place generation after generation, but, as such, is not inherited. . . . But any congenital variations similar in direction to these modifications will tend to support them, and to favour the organism in which they occur. Thus will arise a congenital predisposition to the modifications in question. The plasticity still continuing, the modifications become yet further adaptive. Thus plastic modification leads, and germinal variation follows; the one paves the way for the other. The modification, as such, is not inherited, but is the condition under which congenital variations are favoured and given time to get a hold on the organism, and are thus enabled by degrees to reach the fully adaptive level.[2]

Thus nurture may play some part, though only a secondary, in human progress, nature being the prime mover, and heredity, rather than environment, the main fact.

This idea harmonizes so well with the older idea of the inequality of races as set out by the Count de Gobineau in 1853, that it is not surprising to find that it found favour with many writers on the Continent,

[1] Also see *Animal Life and Intelligence*, 1890, rev. 1900 as *Animal Life*. In *Habit and Instinct*, p. 315, Morgan states that Mark Baldwin and H. F. Osborn have independently arrived at his conclusions.

[2] Morgan, *Habit and Instinct*, 1896, p. 320: quoted by Thomson and Geddes, *Evolution*, p. 199.

especially in France and Germany. Indeed, the rise of Prussia and the claims of the aristocracy agreed wonderfully well with the idea of the purity of germ plasm and its continuity.

In Germany, Otto Ammon and H. S. Chamberlain developed these theories, and in France, G. V. de Lapouge, Ammon began his work by measuring recruits in the Grand Duchy of Baden, and found the percentage of dolichocephalic recruits from the cities was greater than that from the country. He asked himself whether this was directly due to the city environment or had he a special selection of the city population. A survey of gymnasia and of city recruits with a separation of individuals according to their parents' social position and city or country origin showed the proportion of long heads to be greater in cities, and higher among those who had migrated from the country than among the sedentary population. The upper classes had longer heads than the lower. Ammon could not explain these facts as the direct influence of city life, and supposed that the long-headed people were more migratory than the brachycephals, that the round-heads die out faster in cities, and that the long-headed people climb to a high position better.[1]

When he came to apply his ideas generally to society, he came to the conclusion that human beings were unequal from physical, mental, and moral viewpoints. Genius and ability were due to heredity, and it was in the interest of society to facilitate the production of the best and to get rid of the worst. An ideal society would be one in which all members were appointed to positions suitable to their abilities, and social stratification and avoiding interclass marriages were biologically justified. The machinery for sorting people into classes was social, rather than natural, and had evolved to enable society to survive in its struggle for existence. The upper strata were the dolichocephalic Aryans, the lower were brachycephals. As these latter tended to die out in cities, they were replaced by migrations from the country, mainly of the superior dolichocephals. Thus the good dolichocephalic sap rises in the tree, and we must do all we can to preserve it.[2]

Houston Stewart Chamberlain,[3] an Englishman educated in Germany, declared roundly for superior and inferior races, and insisted on the necessity for good material at the start. The Teutonic stock was the real creator of present-day civilization, and our best hope for the future. This notion later had important political results. So true it is that half-

---

[1] 'Anthropologische Untersuchungen der Wehrpflichtigen in Baden,' 1890. *Samml. gemeinverst. Wiss. Vortrage*, neue Folge, Ser. V, Heft 101, pp. 1-36. *Die Natürliche Auslese beim Menschen*, 1893.
[2] *Die Gesellschaftsordnung und ihre natürlichen Grundlagen*, 1895.
[3] *Grundlagen des Neunzehnten Jahrhundert*, 1899.

baked notions move the world faster than solid truth, though, thank God, with less lasting effect!

Lapouge separated out the three racial stocks of Europe by similar means. The best was the Nordic dolichocephalic Protestant, who is brave, blond and dashing, and likes to do for himself. The next best was the Alpine brachycephalic Catholic, who is brown and quiet, and likes to sit on his own land and obey the government, and hates progress. Then there is the Mediterranean, short, dark, and mesocephalic, who is not as good as the Alpine. Lapouge discusses the struggle for existence in its political, religious, moral, legal, economic, occupational, and urban and rural aspects, and concludes that every form of the struggle tells against the best or Nordic element, which is disappearing. The only thing to do is to create an aristocracy and inbreed.[1]

Meanwhile in both countries the ethnologists were writing without much reference to political issues. It is probable that every German who was not writing an *Allgemeine Culturgeschichte* in ten volumes was writing *Die Völkerkunde* in twenty. Of such kind, the really outstanding classics are O. Peschel's *Völkerkunde*, 1874, and Friedrich Müller's *Allgemeine Ethnographie*. The greatest of the whole is F. Ratzel's *Völkerkunde* of 1885-88, whose second edition of 1894-95 was translated, with a preface by Tylor, as *The History of Mankind* in 1896. Ratzel played so large a part in the history of anthropology that he will be treated more fully elsewhere.[2] Mention must also be made of Thomas Achelis' *Moderne Völkerkunde, deren Entwicklung und Aufgaben*, 1896.

In France, Joseph Deniker, friend and associate of Broca, was collecting data relating to the physical characters of the races of the world from about 1880 onwards. He was of the opinion that no single character, such as the cephalic index, could be the basis of any sound classification, and based his divisions on a large complex of characters. During the progress of his work he brought out the 'Récherches anatomiques et embryologiques sur les singes anthropoïdes',[3] and supported Huxley's contention that the structural differences which separate man from the anthropoid apes are not as great as those which separate apes from monkeys. In 1891, with P. Hyades, he prepared the *Mission scientifique du Cap Horn*, a valuable study of the Yaghan Indians. In 1900 *Les Races et les Peuples de la Terre* and its English translation were published. Deniker recognized at least twenty-nine racial elements in the population of the world.

[1] *Les sélections sociales*, 1896; *L'Aryen, son rôle social*, 1899.
[2] See pp. 177. f.
[3] *Arch. Zool. Expér.*, 1885, Sér. II-III.

Like Deniker, W. Z. Ripley in America used a great number of characters in distinguishing races. *The Races of Europe* was published in New York and London in 1900. With it was bound a complete bibliography of the anthropology and ethnology of Europe, published by the Boston Public Library. Ripley employs all available statistics of the physical characters of the races of Europe, and furnishes many maps showing the geographical distribution of the cephalic index, pigmentation, stature, and other ethnological criteria, and relates these criteria to the physical geography. He discovers three principal race types, the tall, blond, long-headed Teuton in the north, the dark long-headed Mediterranean in the south, and the brownish round-headed Alpine in the middle, pointing out, however, exceptions. After separate chapters on countries and races, he discusses European origins, social problems, acclimatization, and the effect of a change of environment on different races.

Léonce Manouvrier, in addition to many papers on physical characters,[1] in which he did much to perfect the methods of observation and to devise indices, also viewed anthropology and ethnology as a whole,[2] and considered their place in the general scheme of all the sciences, showing the ramifications of anthropology into medical, pedagogical, political, and many other forms.

In England, J. G. Wood's *Natural History of Man* appeared in 1868 and 1870, and A. H. Keane's *Man, Past and Present* in 1899, with a theory of the peopling of the world from one centre by pleistocene man, and an account of the metal ages, historic times and peoples. The African Negro, the Oceanic Negroes, the Mongols, and the American aborigines and Caucasic peoples were all embraced by his scheme.

Arthur Thomson, anatomist, artist, and anthropologist, began a long series of anthropological papers on many bodily characters in the eighties, all notable for their extreme care in the collection and presentation of the evidence, and many of them brilliant in their deductions. A classic paper is 'The Influence of Posture on the Form of the Articular Surfaces of the Tibia and astragalus in the Different Races of Man and the Higher Apes',[3] 1888–90, and a book which has gone into many editions, *Anatomy for Art Students*, was first published in 1896. In 1895 he began to give regular lectures in physical anthropology in connexion with Tylor's lectures on cultural anthropology in the Pitt Rivers Museum at Oxford. The greater part of his work will be treated in a

---

[1] See lists in Martin's *Lehrbuch*, 1914.
[2] 'Classification naturelle des sciences,' in *Ass. francaise pour l'avencement des sciences, Compte rendu*, 2me partie, Paris, 1890.
[3] *J. Anat. and Physiol.*, XXIII–IV.

later chapter. Much of his time before 1900 was given to the development of a school of medicine at Oxford, and to the establishment of anthropological teaching. He found the Department of Anatomy housed in a corrugated iron shed. He left it, with an annexe for anthropology, housed in a modern building.

In 1898 A. C. Haddon published in England and America *The Study of Man*, insisting that anthropology covered the whole science of man, and not physical anthropology merely, as Continental writers claimed. Ethnography was the description of a particular people, and ethnology the comparative study of human groups. This last may be divided into many branches, the most important of which are sociology, technology, religion, and linguistics.

In the same year he led the famous Torres Straits Expedition, numbering among his colleagues C. S. Myers, C. G. Seligman, W. H. R. Rivers, and A. Wilken. This was the first purely anthropological expedition which was organized by a number of scientists, each eminent in his own line, with a view to covering all sides of a people's life by trained investigators, although there had been anthropologists on the Horn Expedition into Central Australia in 1894, when Sir Baldwin Spencer first met F. J. Gillen and became interested in the study of primitive man, and the anthropological evidence from the Challenger expedition of 1872 had been prepared by Sir William Turner in 1886.

One of the immediate results of the Torres Straits Expedition was an important paper by Rivers in the *Journal of the Anthropological Institute* for 1900, entitled 'A Genealogical Method of Collecting Social and Vital Statistics'. While recording after the fashion of Morgan genealogies and terms of address used among kinsfolk, Rivers observed the special behaviour, duties, privileges, and functions connected with the terms, and showed that institutions and their underlying beliefs could be adequately understood only when the inter-relationship of all the individuals concerned was known. While other anthropologists had shown the importance of studying the inter-relations of customs and beliefs to each other within the social fabric, Rivers developed a method by which the study could be placed on a much more exact basis. In the present century Malinowski and his pupils have developed this functional method of investigation, aiming to give thereby an accurate picture of the individual in the whole complex of the society in which he lives.

The psychological work by Myers was mainly confined to experimental psychology of the sense organs and reaction time, and showed that the sense perceptions of the Islanders hardly differed from those of Europeans, and that differences were personal rather than racial.

Although Binet had begun his work on intelligence tests in 1895, his scale was not published until 1905, and his method of measuring intelligence until 1908.[1] Freud had indicated the existence of the subconscious in 1895 in his and Breuer's *Studies in Hysteria*, but these experiments had been done under hypnosis, and it was not until 1900 with the publication of *Traumdeutung* (The Interpretation of Dreams) that his investigations of people in a normal condition arrived at a point where psychologists could understand his methods and begin to apply them.

The Reports on the Expedition have been or are being published during the present century, and have set a new standard for fieldworkers. It must not be forgotten, however, that this type of concerted investigation shows a tendency to become a number of monographs, unless there is a leader like Haddon who can grasp the nature of the whole, and as the best in this kind are but interpretations, there is much to be said for the all-round man like the district officer, missionary, or government anthropologist who has lived a long time with his people and hears what they have to say and sees what they do without asking too many questions, and gives the interpretation of a single mind to the entire complex. Certainly such an interpretation is easier to follow, since we can better make allowance for the personal equation in gaining our picture of the people described, and can more easily see the people as a whole. In the series of monographs on various aspects of the study we see the dissections. In the work of a single interpreter we see the man.

In America, D. G. Brinton in 1886[2] took anthropology to be the study of physical anthropology, and ethnology to be the study of man as a social creature, giving the term ethnography to the collection of facts about peoples. In 1892[3] he elaborated this scheme by placing the various departments of each subject under their appropriate headings, and adding archaeology. In 1890 he published *Races and Peoples*, discussing the physical and psychical elements of ethnography, the beginnings and subdivisions of races, the Eurafrican, the Austrafrican, the Asian races, insular and littoral peoples, the American race, problems and predictions.

In Italy G. Sergi's *Antropologia e scienze antropologiche* was published in 1889, taking anthropology to be the science of the natural history of man, and covers the whole subject, including ethnology, which is made to cover the social side of man, his language, customs,

[1] Seligman, *J.R.A.I.*, 1932, LXII, p. 196.

[2] *Iconographic Encyclopaedia*, Philadelphia, Vol. I, pp. 17–184.

[3] *American Anthropologist*, Washington, 1892, V. p. 263.

religion, and all products of his activity, voluntary and instinctive. Sociology and psychology are to be treated as independent anthropological sciences. *The Mediterranean Race* of 1895 with its method of classification by forms has already been mentioned. The primitive populations of Europe, after Neanderthal man, originated in Africa, and constituted the entire population of neolithic times, the basin of the Mediterranean being the chief centre of movement. From the great African stock were formed three varieties, one peculiarly African, another the Mediterranean, and a third, the Nordic. The name Eurafrican applies to all. The Aryans are a variety of the Eurasiatic species. The Mycenaean civilization had its origins in Asia; the classic Greek and Latin civilizations were Mediterranean.

It will be seen that the ethnologists were in the main more concerned with origins and classification, and that their work, while done in the light of Darwin's hypothesis, did not affect the main stream of thought in civilized countries as much as that of the biologists and sociologists. We have spoken of the trend of sociological work in Germany and France. Let us return to England.

One of the greatest figures is that of Herbert Spencer, who, as we have seen, was applying developmental theories to psychology as early as 1855. In 1858, after experience as a schoolmaster, civil engineer, and inventor, he determined to put all the sciences in their place, and to devote his life to working out a grand scheme which should culminate in a study of society. Two ideas dominated his life, one, that of evolution, which to him meant the survival of the fittest, the other, that of personal freedom as understood by Bentham and Mill. His doctrine of evolution was narrower than that of Darwin, in that he paid attention mainly to the struggle, while Darwin had also emphasized the fact that the growth of parental love and the gregarious impulses resulting in mutual aid had played a very large part in determining the survival of animals and societies. At the end of the whole grand system it would appear that the ideas of Bentham and Mill really triumphed over those of Darwin. But if Spencer failed, it was a grand failure, and worthy of a great place in the history of anthropology, for his system of synthetic philosophy embraces the very subjects which belong to the study of man.

Spencer never got far beyond the views set out in the *Westminster Review* for January, 1860. In the 'The Social Organism' he compares the individual organism with the social. In the individual the lives of the parts must be submerged in the life of the whole, because the whole has a corporate consciousness. But in society the individual units are each conscious, and cannot lose their individual consciousness in a corporate consciousness which does not and cannot exist. Therefore the welfare of individuals must not be sacrificed to some supposed good to the state, but the state must be maintained for the good of its citizens. Whereas then the individual organism must subordinate the parts to the whole, the social organism or corporate life must be subordinated to the lives of the parts which compose it. This early view, while it compares the development of society to that of an organism, is really the old notion of the social contract and the *laissez-faire* ideas of Mill and Bentham in a new dress, and does not really study society biologically.

The first volume of the system of synthetic philosophy appeared in 1862 under the title *First Principles*. Part I, 'The Unknowable', is an attempt to reconcile science and religion by showing that both have a belief in some ultimate cause of phenomena which cannot be known. Part II, 'The Knowable', defines evolution as the process of passing 'from a relatively indefinite, incoherent homogeneity to a relatively definite, coherent heterogeneity', and lays out a scheme of the sciences in their order and proper relation. Astronomy leads to geology, that to biology, which in its turn leads to psychology, on which study sociology may be founded. In several papers[1] he defends this arrangement against that of Comte, who built his sociology directly on biology. Spencer passes over the inorganic sciences rapidly, and really begins his study with the organic world.

Principles of Biology, 1866–68, was a wonderfully acute analysis and arrangement of the biology of the day. It developed as a study of the 'survival of the fittest', and paid far more attention than Darwin did to the inheritance of acquired characters. Environment has a profound effect in modifying individuals, use and disuse of organs leads to development or reduction, and these modifications are inherited. This view he held vigorously against Weismann in the nineties. One of the most interesting views is one that heredity is due to constitutional units, larger than molecules, within the cell, which were possessed of a fixed polarity, and tended to fall into an arrangement characteristic of the structure of the species. In his doctrine of use and disuse, he looked backward to Lamarck; in that of constitutional units he adumbrated the rediscovery of Mendel's theory of particulate inheritance.

The theory of the inheritance of acquired characters runs through *Principles of Psychology*, revised from 1855 to take its place in this series in 1870–72. Expressions of the emotions tended to be inherited and to

---

[1] 'The Genesis of Science,' *Brit. Quart. Rev.*, July, 1854; reprinted with several others on the same subject in all editions of *Essays, Scientific, Political, and Speculative*.

develop into instincts. Out of conflict between various possible responses to situation or conflict of instincts, reason begins to emerge, choice and will are possible, and therefore moral and intellectual life.

Having arrived thus far, we can study the associated life of humanity. In 1867 Spencer started to collect the materials for induction under the heads Uncivilized Societies, Civilized Societies, Extinct or Decayed, and Civilized Societies, Recent or Still Flourishing, and distributed the work among many people. Each great volume of *Descriptive Sociology* begins with tables for each of the groups of people, wherein are set out the inorganic, organic, and sociological environment, and the physical, emotional, and intellectual characters. The main table is divided into two great columns showing the structural and regulative aspects of the particular social organization, and these columns are subdivided under headings which show every detail of their social, religious, political, and economic life. Each of these headings is taken as the title of a chapter, these chapters following the tables and consisting of extracts from books and periodicals exemplifying the headings.

From the data thus accumulated by 1876, 1882, and 1896, he wrote the three volumes of *Principles of Sociology*, developing the subject on the lines laid down in the article in the *Westminster Review* for January, 1860. Societies fall into two main groups, the militant, characterized by compulsory co-operation, and the industrial, characterized by voluntary co-operation, the principal virtues being associated with the latter. The militant type is divided into the purely military and the socialistic, and in both forms we find a wide extension of government power, while in the industrial type we find a great respect for individual liberty. Religion he develops from ancestor-worship, one of the sources described in Tylor's *Primitive Culture*.[1] Again, in spite of the extreme detail in which the analogy between social and biological organisms is developed, he ultimately arrives in this work at the position of Bentham and Mill.

The Principles of Ethics, 1892–93, based on *The Data of Ethics*, 1879, insists that a system of morals must be founded on a doctrine of the evolution of life. The ends of life are furthered by the pursuit of happiness, and, with some exceptions, the pursuit is advantageous to survival, else societies would never have survived. In these concluding volumes Spencer felt that he was facing the same problem that met him at the beginning of his work, the antagonism between the individual who reasons and feels independently, and the social organism of which he is a part. He kept to his opinion that government must be reduced to a minimum, so that every man should be free to do what he likes provided

[1] See pp. 138–139.

that he does not interfere with the freedom of any other man. He noted the slow development of altriuism, and hoped that its further growth would reconcile the differences between the individual and society, so that he might find his greatest happiness in yielding his own interest to the general good when occasion required.

Certain expressions of the emotions and mental qualities were then naturally selected for their survival value. Later, social selection played a part, and by careful nurture developed what was best for a particular society. Spencer's system depends largely on the assumption that what is acquired in one generation can be passed on to the next, and that nurture is therefore little less important than nature. Weissmann's claim that acquired characters are not transmitted appears to destroy Spencer's scheme, though he did allow that the germ plasm is plastic, and that modifications of the body or mind may have secondary effects on it, and this view, as developed by Lloyd Morgan, who allowed useful modifications to work as fostering nurses of natural variations in the same direction, would give some credit to Spencer's system, taking both nature and nurture into consideration.[1] Again, Spencer is not as one-sided in his evolutionary scheme as many suppose. He took account not only of the nutritive and self-regarding instincts in the struggle for existence, but also of the reproductive and other-regarding instincts. From parental and family love, there is a development towards an altruism which takes in larger and larger units. It is a pity that his great plan was practically matured in his mind in the early sixties, and that his cloistered and laborious life did not allow him to take account of the many new discoveries made during his lifetime. He started with the ideas of Bentham and Mill, of leaving things alone as much as possible, with the belief that the best will survive, and while he expounded them with Darwinian terminology, his system remains essentially that in which he was trained as a young man.

Similarly, we have seen how certain of the Continental sociologists began with the ideas of the Count de Gobineau, to which Weismann's discoveries gave some credit, and while marching under Weismann's banner, they were really de Gobineau's army. They would not leave a free field for the struggle, but would choose out the best and breed from that. We have seen how this idea became allied with politics and national pride.

The Count de Gobineau's theory was developed in a different fashion

---

[1] Since speech was invented, each child can become heir to all the experience of the ages. His mind has richer material to use than had his ancestor, and thus has a chance to develop better.

by Sir Francis Galton and Karl Pearson, whose methods depend largely on the work of the Belgian scientist Quetelet, though Galton states that the first idea of using the Gaussian curve came to him from Spottiswoode.

Quetelet's earlier work was mentioned in the previous chapter. In all his studies, astronomical, meteorological, and concerning man's physical and intellectual qualities, he was insistent on the necessity for having a very large amount of data. Quetelet showed that if a series of anthropological measurements either physical or of intellectual qualities were plotted on squared paper, allowing *x* to be the measurements, and *y* to be their frequency, they formed a curve like that representing the expansion of the binomial, or like that formed by plotting the errors of a great number of observers. It was called the Gaussian curve because Gauss had named it as the Normal Curve of Error after experimenting with errors and their frequencies. In the *Physique Sociale*, 1835, and greatly enlarged in 1869, and in the *Anthropométrie* of 1871, Quetelet laid the foundations of all mathematical study of anthropological data. For if the numbers representing the measurements of individual qualities grouped themselves round the numbers relating to the average man as single results of observations grouped themselves round the mean result, then it would seem possible to apply the mathematics of the Gaussian curve to anthropological data, and thus check our data and interpret it more exactly. Is our average a true one? We can compute the average deviation from the average in our series, or 'standard deviation', and by its size tell how far our group is homogeneous, whether our average really is an average, or simply a number. Suppose we were to take another group of the same sort, would our average be the same as the one we have? Here by a simple calculation, we can discover the average deviation of all the averages we might get from their average, a figure called the 'probable error'.

To this method of studying evidence in quantity, Galton and Pearson added the invention of the contingency and correlation tables, the one for immeasurable data, the other for measurable. A correlation table may be made on squared paper by allowing the *x* or horizontal direction to represent, for example, the various lengths of the human femur, dissected out of an anatomical subject. The *y* or vertical direction may represent the statures of the subjects from which the femora were taken. If the femora vary exactly as the heights of their owners, then the dots representing the correspondences on the paper will lie along a diagonal line, the hypotenuse of a right-angled triangle with two equal legs, and the correlation coefficient will be 1. If there is not such exact correspondence, the amount of correspondence can be calculated, and this figure, less than 1 (say .3 or .8) will show how far the one varies as the other. An equation can then be formed on the lines of the one used to turn Fahrenheit into Centigrade readings, so that when we have one of the variables, we can calculate the other. Similarly, in a contingency table,[1] qualities can be plotted against qualities, and a contingency coefficient calculated and turned into a correlation coefficient.

The discovery of the correlation table was made by Galton in 1886, two years after he had founded his anthropometric laboratory at South Kensington at his own expense, for the study of physical and psychological data. His main interests were in the study of psychology and heredity, to which his attention had been turned by his cousin Charles Darwin. His earliest work was in 1865, 'Hereditary Talent and Character', in *MacMillan's Magazine*. *Hereditary Genius* followed in 1869, *English Men of Science* in 1874, *Inquiries into Human Faculty* ... in 1883, and *Natural Inheritance* in 1889.

His general starting point is that of de Gobineau. Human individuals differ in bodily and psychological characters, and are unequal. He develops this by showing that the physical and mental characters in a society are distributed according to the typical curve displayed in the Gaussian 'Normal curve of error'. Great ability is very rare, and there is a vast abundance of mediocrity. Individual differences are due to environment and heredity, but heredity is far more important. The statistical method may be employed in the comparative study of races.

He applied all this to the problems of social reorganization, and founded the study of eugenics. We must labour for the procreation of the best in body, mind, and morals, and hinder the procreation of the rest. But how many of us would assent to the decisions of a committee of selection of the 'best', unless we were members?

As Wundt is the founder of experimental psychology in Germany, so is Galton in England. Wundt is the more patient investigator, while Galton has many brilliant ideas and leaves them to others to develop. In his *Inquiries into Human Faculty*, 1883, he shows the results of his experiments on the relations between the powers of visual imagery and of abstract thought, of the associations between the elements of different sense departments, of the correlation of mental traits, the associations of words, and the times taken in making the associations. One interesting feature of this last series of experiments was the number of aroused ideas that belong to one's childhood or youth. Indeed, how often it is that we find the whole bent of a scientist's mind, the type of his investigation,

[1] Invented by Pearson in 1900. See p. 187.

and even his conclusions, determined by his early life and experiences. Spencer's system developed Bentham and Mill, the work of the Continental sociologists and of Galton and Pearson developed de Gobineau. The very fact that Galton came of a family in which there was so much hereditary genius no doubt played some part in the development of his ideas. Le Play had a happy childhood in his beloved village with its lovable priest, and this determined his sense of values in all his books.

In all his psychological work, Galton laid special stress on individuals, and is the founder of the mental test, from which has arisen so much investigation of aptitude and deficiency, and all the modern study of fitting the man and his vocation in life. Like Darwin, he is one of the most readable of scientists, and the least given to pedantic jargon.

His friend and associate, Karl Pearson, really belongs to our next period, but he began his work in the Galton laboratory, and his *Chances of Death* was first published in 1897, and his 'Mathematical Contributions to the Theory of Evolution' began in 1895.[1] Like Galton he believed that favourable and unfavourable variations are inherited, and that changes in racial stock through social selection furnish the most important factor in its rise and fall. From the first he believed in the importance to the state of a science of national eugenics. Like Galton, he believed that we can know little of a phenomenon until we can measure it and express its relations with other phenomena in quantitative form, and this belief took practical effect in the foundation of *Biometrika* in 1902.

Both he and Galton applied statistical methods to the study of experimental psychology, and Galton is sometimes considered to be the co-founder with Wilhelm Wundt of that science. Wundt wrote his *Grundzüge der physiologischen Psychologie* in 1873, and founded his laboratory for experimental psychology at Leipzig in 1879, a laboratory which has attracted men from all over the world, and has had a greater effect than any other event in the development of the science. But he differs from Galton in the *Völkerpsychologie* of 1900, for example, in that he makes no effort to state the quantitative association between mental and racial characters, and no attempt to show numerically the intensity of association between folk-mentality and folk-customs. His genius lay rather in the direction of finding out the facts and of inventing methods for discovering them, and in long and patient experiment—a discipline which Galton would not endure, he preferring rather to initiate than to continue overlong at the development of one idea.

[1] *Phil. Trans. A.*

While one school of thought was looking at heredity, another looked first at environment as the determining factor in human development.

Frédéric Le Play spent his childhood happily in a French village. His love for his family and village and his early religious training affected his career profoundly. He took the family as the simple and definite unit of social phenomena, and the family budget as the quantitative expression of family life, and as a basis for the quantitative analysis of social facts. The place, or geographical environment, determines the kind of work that people must do to get a living, and the method of getting a living determines the form of social organization. His method, as developed by his pupils, de Tourville, Demolins, and others, is that of the regional survey, taking into account, first, environment of the family, determining its economics, work, property, wages, and savings. These factors in turn determine the organization and functions of the family, its mode of existence and standard of living. Family relations with larger social bodies lead to a consideration of *le patronage*, commerce, intellectual culture resulting from the conditions of life, religion, the parish, the city, the province, the state, then expansion by emigration and colonization, foreign societies, the history of the society, its rank and future.

While still a boy, Le Play went on a walking trip with a friend, the two of them covering over 4,000 miles. He was graduated from the School of Mines in 1832, and from then onward directed the organization of the mining industry in many countries, including Russia. In 1855 he wrote *Les ouvriers européens*, and in the same year started *Les ouvriers des deux mondes* series. *La réforme sociale en France* was published in 1864, *L'organization du travail* in 1870. In 1881, the year before he died, he started a fortnightly periodical, *La réforme sociale*. His walking trip led him to contrast his fortunate village with industrial cities, and his experience in organizing industry strengthened the contrast in his mind. His scientific precision commanded the attention of the intellect; his religion added passion, and thus gave his work a power which few others have possessed.

M. Kovalevsky's main attention was to the size of societies, and directed toward their economic activity. One of the principal motives of economic evolution has been the growth of population, this factor being responsible for the transition from hunting and fishing to agriculture, and from primitive agriculture to intensive, with changes in the system of ownership, and the substitution of a manufacturing system for a domestic. The growth of population called into being the division of labour and social differentiation. The demographic factor may also affect the conduct of society as to certain practices to some extent. As stated, this is too bald an account of Kovalevsky's scheme. He took a great many factors into account, and did not regard historical processes as a simple unilinear development.[1]

Still others of the evolutionary sociologists paid special attention to degeneration and atrophy and to parasitism as products of evolution. In 1890 Ray Lankester wrote 'Degeneration: a Chapter in Darwinism',[2] and in 1895 Émile Vandervelde wrote *Parasitism, Organic and Social*. A most interesting work, *Evolution by Atrophy in Biology and Sociology*, was written in 1894 by Jean Demoor, Jean Massart, and Émile Vandervelde, and translated by Mrs Chalmers Mitchell. The sociologists and biologists of the University of Brussels had formed a society to link the two subjects together, and this was one of the results. In the evolution of organs, parts disappear, and in the evolution of organisms, organs disappear, a fact which may be noted in a study of embryological development. It is the same with societies. We find the rudiments of earlier customs remaining like rudimentary organs, and sometimes we find a whole organism or social organization dying in the interest of a larger or more powerful. All modification of organs or of institutions is attended by retrogression. Degenerate evolution follows no definite path. Artificial selection takes the place of natural in societies. Degeneration must be carefully distinguished from the primitive. Primitive organs or societies or customs have the power to vary. The degenerate or rudimentary may alter, or become a nuisance, but they have not the power of variation and development in any useful direction.

The whole question of the dead or dying branches of Darwin's tree of life, and of the parasites thereon, as applied to social studies, is one of great importance. We may well ask ourselves whether our own development towards greater ease and comfort is not accompanied by the degeneration of many finer qualities, and the growth of parasitism in society. Those who wore leather trousers and lived in a churlish land where there were no figs nor anything else that was good to eat, were at least men, but when they descended into the plains and conquered and adopted the luxuries of the conquered, they became weak and contemptible, and in the end came to nothing.

We have seen sociologists following Bentham and Mill, and de Gobineau, both schools considering society as composed of individuals,

---

[1] *Communal Possession of Land*, Moscow, 1879; *A Study of the Disintegration of Communal Land Possession in Waad Canton*, 1876; 'Evolution du régime économique,' *Le devenir social*, June, 1896; *Coutume contemporaine et loi ancienne*, Paris, 1893; *Die ökonomische Entwicklung Europas*, Berlin, 1908 (begun in Russian, according to Sorokin, in 1898).

[2] *The Advancement of Science*, 1890.

and attending rather to the component parts than to the whole. Another group took its inspiration from Comte, considering sociology to be the study of the associated life of humanity, and like Espinas, believing the individual to be the product, rather than the author of society. A. Espinas developed these views in *Les sociétés animales* in 1878, and in *Les origines de la technologie* in 1898.

In *Der Rassenkampf*, 1883, Ludwig Gumplowicz maintained that the real elements of a social process are not separate individuals but social groups. In history, we must study not the regularities of the behaviour of individuals, but the movements of social groups. In the *Grundriss der Sociologie* in 1885, he says that it is wrong to look for the source of thought in the individual. It is not man who thinks, but a social community. Man's mind and thought are the product of his social medium.

The greatest exponent of these ideas was Émile Durkheim, founder of *L'Année Sociologique* in 1895. *De la division du travail social* appeared in 1893, and *Les régles de la méthode sociologique* in 1895. He believed that it was not in psychology, but in the very nature of social life that we must look for an explanation of social life. Like Gumplowicz, he considered that man's mind and thought are the product of his social medium. There was a collective consciousness and an individual consciousness. These could be distinguished by the objective criteria of exteriority and constraint. Collective representations exist outside of the individual and come to his mind as something exterior in the form of various moral, religious, juridical and logical rules. They are endowed with a power of coercion, which allows them to impose themselves on the individual regardless of his desires. These two characteristics of exteriority and constraint indicate the boundary line between social and purely psychological phenomena. The social mind, collective representations, and society are independent realities and different from the reality of the individual mind and its psychology.

Durkheim arrived at his idea of collective representations from a study of European civilizations, and as evidence began to come in from various investigations of primitive peoples, especially from Australia, it appeared to fit admirably into his scheme, the primitive man seeming to be even more obviously determined in his course by the mob than the European, and his mind more subject to the constraints of its collective ideas.

III. THE STUDY OF PRIMITIVE PEOPLES

As might be expected when ideas of origins and evolution were in the forefront after so great a discovery, the whole atmosphere of social studies in the latter half of the nineteenth century was charged with inquiries into the habits and customs of primitive peoples.

One of the earliest investigators of the beliefs that underlie primitive institutions was P. W. A. Bastian[1] (1826–1905), one of the most indefatigable travellers and writers of any time in the world's history. Up to 1896, the bibliography of his works in the *Internationales Archiv für Ethnologie* shows two large printed pages for titles of books, and fourteen pages for titles of articles and essays. Sir Edward Tylor told Professor J. L. Myres in 1905 that Bastian had written over 10,000 pages, not counting the innumerable articles in the *Zeitschrift für Ethnologie*, and that his works had much profit for students. Their consultation was not easy, and want of references was a drawback, but Tylor's own experience was that Bastian's statements were apt to be confirmed by further study.

Certainly their consultation is not easy. Many of the books have no index, some of them have no chapter divisions, and it is often difficult to separate actual observations from reported facts. The closely printed pages with their vast apparatus of footnotes would repel any but the sternest and most conscientious. But we must not let the too-evident and ever-present example of his incessant industry blind us to the richness of his intellectual wealth, and the vast storehouse of facts and careful observations, nor imagine that he was incapable of seeing the wood for the trees, because of the overwhelming accumulation of material and the frequently involved style. His general position, as developed in his work as a whole, is clear. The similarity of objects used for similar purposes, and of beliefs and practices in similar situations, throughout the world, attest the psychic unity of mankind. Objects, beliefs, and institutions take their peculiar form from their environment, and thus we find differences in form. Through contacts and migrations, we get an infinite hybridization of ideas, and civilization is the product of an infinite number of mixtures, some variations surviving and others perishing in the process.

For the grandeur of his conception, he is Tylor's equal, and both are worthy of the company of Darwin. In one respect only does he rank below Tylor. Tylor was clear throughout in his arrangement of evidence, and the simplicity and beauty of his style were equal to Darwin's. His ideas stand out for all to see. But Bastian's break through the facts with difficulty. He was a man of penetrating insight, but so eager and active in body and mind, that he appeared to find it irksome to sit down and reflect. He must always be moving. A brief account of his life and

---

[1] Th. V. Achelis, *Die Entwickelung der Modernen Ethnologie*, 1889; *Z.E.*, 1896, p. 386; 1905, p. 233; Myres, J. L., *Man*, 1905, **76**.

a bare enumeration of his travels and some of his more important books will give an idea of his equipment and the general trend of his thought, and of the collection of evidence which went to support his conclusions.

He was born at Bremen on June 26, 1826, the son of a well-known merchant whose business and interests were world-wide. He studied law first at Heidelberg, then biology at Jena and Würzburg, where he met Virchow, and finally took the degree of Doctor of Medicine at Prague in 1850. In 1851, he took a post as ship's doctor to Australia, and travelled from then until 1859, visiting many of the Pacific islands, Peru, Mexico, and the West Indies. He then went to China, Malaysia, and India, and returned home by way of West Africa. The only part of these travels to be published in book form appeared in 1859, and was an account of the Congo region of Africa, under the title of *Ein Besuch in San Salvador*. The sub-title, *Ein Beitrag zur Mythologie und Psychologie*, indicates the main trend of all his later work. He often shows very little interest in the environment and physical character of peoples, and little care for their arts and industries except when they specially illustrate racial or national characters. His interest was in the beliefs of peoples, and he was most capable in finding the best people to give him the facts he wanted, and in persuading them to help him. For example, much of the material used in the *Die heilige Saga der Polynesier*, 1881, was collected from Polynesian chiefs, and the groundwork of his study of Buddhism came from a native priest in Mandalay, where Bastian found himself detained for a time.

The first introduction of the terms *Elementargedanken* and *Völkergedanken*, which are always associated with him, was in 1860, in *Der Mensch in der Geschichte; zur Begründung einer psychologischen Weltanschauung*, published at Leipzig. These ideas were further expounded and developed in *Beiträge zur vergleichenden Psychologie: die Seele und ihrer Erscheinungswesen in der Ethnographie*, 1868; *Das Beständige in den Menschenrassen, und die Spielweite ihrer Veränderlichkeit* (*Prolegomena zu Einer Ethnologie der Kulturvölker*), 1868; *Der Völkergedanke im Aufbau einer Wissenschaft vom Menschen*, 1881; and *Wie das Volk denkt*, 1892.

These books show a surprising uniformity of outlook in all the more primitive peoples, and such differences as appear seem to be correlated with observable differences in material surroundings. Bastian was firmly convinced of the psychic unity of mankind, and believed that in philosophy, language, religion, law, art, and social organization, there were a restricted number of elementary ideas and concepts common to all mankind. These he called *Elementargedanken*. The particular form which these elementary and common ideas take is determined by geographical conditions, which impose a peculiar kind of economic organization on the different societies of man. Thus the *Elementargedanken* always find their expression as *Völkergedanken*, or folk-ideas. It was evident to him that similar ideas and cultural traits rose independently in various tribes and regions, and were originally confined to them, the material conditions determining the form, and differences varying with the environment. The folk-ideas were originally confined to their geographical provinces. But isolation is exceptional, and migrations, or contacts along the frontiers of the *Geographische Provinzen*, are continually at work, making the influence of purely geographical conditions more negligible, and introducing ideas and culture traits to environments in which they are not native. Karl Ritter and A. von Humboldt had foreshadowed the idea of geographical provinces, and it was later developed in great detail by Ratzel in 1885-88. This doctrine of geographical provinces is implicit in all of Bastian's work from *Der Mensch in der Geschichte* onward, and is definitely set out in his *Zur Lehre den geographischen Provinzen* in 1886.

To Bastian, then, there was no inherent difference between the mentality of primitive and civilized man. The folk-ideas, originally confined in their provinces, mingled with migrations and by contacts on the frontiers, and civilization was the product of an infinite number of mixtures. Of the hybridization of peoples and ideas, and their consequent development, he writes in *The Ethnology of Civilized Peoples* :[1]

Nothing more strongly characterizes the profound confusion, and the utter want of all elementary principles in ethnography, than the prevailing opinion of the degenerating influence of mixture on race, whilst it is patent that wherever civilized peoples appear in history, they are but the highest product out of an infinite number of mixtures. Generally the primitive roots of their ethnological genesis go back to prehistoric times, which are far removed from our view; the roots become known only by their effects when the race in the light of history has grown into a dominant nationality, but every scientific inquiry is at an end if we then want to consider such nationality as a *deus ex machina*, instead of analysing its organic genesis. We talk of purity of race; breeders consider it of the utmost value to retain the blood of their stock pure, and not to deteriorate it by mixture. So far, so good. But are therefore these thoroughbred races pure races, if by pure is understood primitive and aboriginal? Is the improved English shorthorned breed of cattle the representative of the feral species, or is it not rather a creature grown out of many, and most artificial crossings?

[1] *Das Beständige in den Menschenrassen*, etc. (*Prolegomena zu einer Ethnologie der Kulturvölker*), 1868, pp. 49 ff. Quoted *A.R.*, VII, 99.

In the race of Berkshire hogs, as it now exists, we find English, Tonquinesian, and Neapolitan elements, which compose this valuable breed, as has been proved by Nathusius. The English racehorse is certainly not the progeny of the wild horse of the Steppes or of the Pampas; on the contrary, it is produced by careful crossings out of Arab barbs, and English blood in order to provide it with the requisite qualities. The Arab horse also, will be, according to all probabilities, the product of crossings, its origin dating back into a prehistoric period.

Bastian was so active a traveller, and so rapid a writer, that he did not take time to digest his ideas, or arrange them in a telling fashion, and for that reason, he has not received everywhere the recognition that is his due. While he was not the first to appreciate the importance of the study of *Völkerpsychologie*, he was the earliest of the anthropologists to collect adequate data for such a study, and the first to postulate with adequate evidence the psychic unity of mankind, and to infer the method by which such ideas common to mankind took their particular form under the influence of material conditions in different places. In addition, he recognized the importance of studying culture contacts and the history of institutions and ideas, and the fact that the diffusion of such ideas and the consequent hybridization played a large part in the evolution of cultures. Thus in his work are united two 'schools' of anthropological study, the evolutionary and the historical or diffusionist, which ought never to have been separated, for they are complementary to each other, and any reasonable worker must take account of both.

Bastian's activity was incredible. No sooner had he relieved his mind of its great load of learning in *Der Mensch in der Geschichte* than he must set out for Eastern Asia. From 1861 until 1865 he visited Indo-China, Siam, Malaysia, the Philippines, Japan, northern China, and Central Asia, returning home by way of the Caucasus. In 1868 he published six volumes of *Die Völker des Ostlichen Asiens*. Between 1865 and 1873 he was hard at work organizing ethnological studies in Germany. The Royal Museum at Berlin had two galleries and a workroom devoted to ethnological collections. The transference of these collections to a Museum für Völkerkunde in 1886 was largely Bastian's achievement. Karl Ritter's suggestion that the Berlin Geographical Society should have an ethnographical department was taken up by Bastian, who insisted that there should be an independent society for anthropological studies, like those founded in London in 1843, and in Paris in 1859. With the help of Virchow, the anatomist and archaeologist, the Gesellschaft für Anthropologie, Ethnologie, und Urgeschichte was founded on November 17, 1869, with Virchow as president and Bastian as vice-president. The *Zeitschrift für Ethnologie* was founded in

1868, though Bastian and Hartmann had been editing it as a private venture since 1866. During his presidency of the Berlin Geographical Society, 1871–73, he founded the German African Society and organized the Loango Expedition of 1873. The results were published in *Die Deutsche Expedition an der Loango-Küste* in 1874. As usual, after publishing a book, he set out on new travels, this time to the West Indies and Central and South America, where he spent the years 1875–76. These travels were published in 1878 under the title *Die Kultur Länder des alten Amerika*. The next two years saw him travelling from Persia to Assam and Indo-China, through Malaysia, Australia, and New Zealand, returning home by way of California and Yucatan, and 1881 saw the publication of a new book on the Religious Myths of the Polynesians. His main achievement during the years 1880 to 1888 was the foundation and administration of the Museum für Völkerkunde in Berlin. Between 1889 and 1891 he was travelling again in Turkestan, India, and East Africa, studying Jainism and Buddhism, and the years 1896–98 were spent in examining early Hindu remains in Java and Bali. During the years between 1901 and 1903 he was studying Buddhism in Ceylon, and in 1903 set out on his final journey, visiting Malaysia, which fascinated him most of all, Jamaica, Venezuela, and Trinidad, where he died at Port of Spain on February 3, 1905.

Bastian's main interest was in the beliefs on which institutions are founded. His immediate successors paid more attention to institutions. In 1861, the year after he first expounded the Elementary ideas and Folk-ideas, J. J. Bachofen published *Das Mutterrecht* at Stuttgart, and Sir Henry Maine, his *Ancient Law* in London.

Both authors, unlike Bastian, whose *Ethnology of Civilized Peoples*, already quoted, shows that he had some knowledge of the complexity of the process, assumed that evolution was a simple progress along one straight line. Indeed, this was a weakness of many of the evolutionists of the latter part of the nineteenth century, whose enthusiasm for similarities throughout the world led them to the idea that as men were much the same everywhere, it was a comparatively simple matter to arrange a sequence of varying stages of culture from all parts of the earth and thereby show the origin and development of all human institutions. Darwin himself had given a plain warning to the contrary in the wonderful simile at the end of the fourth chapter of the *Origin*, where he compares the highly complex process of evolution to a great tree.

The green and budding twigs may represent existing species; and those produced during former years may represent the long succession of extinct species. At each period of growth, all the growing twigs have tried to branch out on all sides, and to overtop and kill the surrounding twigs and branches, in the same manner as species and groups of species have at all times overmastered other species in the great battle for life. The limbs divided into great branches, and these into lesser and lesser branches, were themselves once, when the tree was young, budding twigs, and this connexion of the former and present buds by ramifying branches may well represent the classification of all extinct and living species in groups subordinate to groups. Of the many twigs which flourished when the tree was a mere bush, only two or three, now grown into great branches, yet survive and bear the other branches; so with the species which lived during long-past geological periods, very few have left living and modified descendants. From the first growth of the tree, many a limb and branch has decayed and dropped off; and these fallen branches of various sizes may represent those whole orders, families, and genera which have now no living representatives, and which are known to us only in a fossil state. As we here and there see a thin straggling branch springing from a fork low down in a tree, and which by some chance has been favoured and is still alive on its summit, so we occasionally see an animal like the Ornithorhynchus or Lepidosiren, which in some small degree connects by its affinities two large branches of life, and which has apparently been saved from fatal competition by having inhabited a protected station. As buds give rise by growth to fresh buds, and these, if vigorous, branch out and overtop on all sides many a feebler branch, so by generation I believe it has been with the great tree of life, which fills with its dead and broken branches the crust of the earth, and covers the surface with its ever-branching and beautiful ramifications.

Within such a scheme of evolution there is ample room for the historian of ideas and institutions to trace out their genesis and development, noting their extinction, victory, or modification in contact with others, and for the student of function to note the complex inter-relations of the parts within the whole. There is no justification in Darwin's plan, either in the study of natural history or in the study of cultures, for an arbitrary and unilinear scheme of development, which takes no account of the dead and broken branches, and of the ever-branching ramifications. It is surely against this over-simple 'evolution' that other schools of thought have set their faces, and not against evolution.

Both Bachofen and Maine take their evidence from the history of Western civilization, with occasional references to primitive peoples who have not influenced it, the one arguing that our present institutions developed out of a general stage of culture when descent was traced through women and women held authority, and the other, that the beginning of culture appeared at a stage when the father was the head of the family, and descent was traced through him. Both arranged their stages of development typologically, somewhat arbitrarily assuming that those types which appeared the simpler to them, were necessarily the older. This argument from the typological to the chronological order of evolution coloured a great part of the writing of the latter part of the nineteenth century.

Bachofen accepts the evidence of the classics uncritically in setting out his order of development for the family. The first stage is one of promiscuity, to which he gives the name hetairism. The strongest male in the group rules it. Both the Massagetae and the blameless Agathyrsi of Herodotus are the examples of this type of society. Then follows a period of mother-right, when woman's delicacy revolted against loose relations, and she insisted on regular unions on religious grounds. Bachofen's authority for this is taken from Strabo's remark that all men believe that women invented religion. His analysis of Greek cults satisfies him that the beginnings of peace, order, and the ownership of property in place of the previous communism arose when woman founded the family, and all looked to her as the symbol of the fertility of the earth and the creatures on it. The Lycians of Herodotus, who take their mothers' names as family names, are the chosen example. The name of the family descends in the female line, property is inherited by daughters only, and woman rules the family in the early days, and ultimately the state. This gynaecocracy gives way in time to father-right, again for a religious reason. Mother-right involves the worship of a physical principle such as is embodied in the conception of an Earth Mother, symbolizing the connexion between mother and child. For this is substituted the worship of an intellectual principle, symbolized by the Olympian or heavenly type of deity, based on the relation between father and child, which is not understood physically, but legally as the ideal relation. The clash of principles involved in the change from mother- to father-right is shown in the famous Oresteia trilogy of Æschylus. Clytemnestra and her paramour kill Agamemnon, and Orestes, their son, kills Clytemnestra in revenge. The Eumenides, champions of the older order of mother-right, pursue Orestes over the whole world, until he takes refuge in the temple of Athene, champion of the new order of father-right. The Eumenides cannot enter the temple, but wait outside for their victim, until for weariness they fall asleep. Bachofen interprets couvade, a custom by which the father is brought to bed while the mother is in labour, as a legal fiction by which parental status is conferred on the male.

The whole structure is very shaky, as the evidence which forms its foundation is uncritically accepted, and often is no more than a particular interpretation suggested by the theory in view. Such thoroughgoing mother-right as Bachofen postulates has rarely, if ever, been found. When we do find descent traced through the woman for one reason or another, it is generally her brother who controls her family, his property or titles descending to her children, i.e., his nephews and nieces whom he controls, and for whom he is responsible, his own children being controlled mainly by their mother's brother. In such a system a man controls his sisters; in a patrilineal system a husband controls his wife or wives, and his own children. The institution of couvade which occurs in some parts of the world may be due to the natural nervousness of a man when his wife is in childbed, and his feeling that he must do something to help. Such nervousness might take any form, even going to bed with the vague notion of enduring the same ordeal in sympathy with the woman. It is an expression of the same order of feeling as that of St Francis, whose preoccupation with the life of Jesus led him to desire to feel the wounds and endure the suffering of the Christ he loved.

Maine's *Ancient Law* was published in the same year as *Das Mutterrecht*, and displays the same simple unilinear scheme of development, but through a general stage of father-right, rather than of mother-right. His evidence was from the classics, especially Roman law, the Old Testament, and the Indo-European peoples generally. He claims that the study of comparative law establishes the fact that the patriarchal was the primitive type of family. In the beginning was the Cyclopean family, where, as the Odyssey says, 'Each lords it over wife and child, nor reck they of one another'. From the primitive family group arise the gens, by the natural growth of population, assisted by the adoption of strangers by one or another legal fiction, then the tribe, and finally the state. The binding principle of society has been the *patria potestas*, the power of the eldest valid male ascendant, and legal development has been a progress from status, where rights and duties are determined by relationship within a group, to a condition in which the power of contract becomes more and more prominent. *Mulier est finis familiae*, i.e., kinship is limited to agnates, or the male line.

In *Village Communities*, 1871, Maine notices the theories of McLennan and Lubbock, but stands by his own hypothesis. But by 1874, when he published *Early Institutions*, he was bound to take account of Morgan's theories, based on induction from the savage world. He prefers to leave unsettled the question of kinship in the more primitive races, still maintaining that his own plan of development is unshaken, applying as it does to the evolution of the higher races with which history is properly concerned, and challenges anthropologists to show how patrilineal kinship could have developed out of kinship as found among the peoples whom Morgan studied. In *Early Law and Custom* (second edition, 1891), he attacks McLennan's and Morgan's theory of a promiscuous horde out of which the family developed, and quotes Darwin against them. In the *Descent of Man* it is argued that male jealousy would have prevented promiscuity in the beginning and that sexual communism, if it is found, might be a later development when the intellect has advanced and the instincts have correspondingly retrograded. Thus Maine arrives at a new definition of the patriarchal family as the result of sexual jealousy indulged through power. The 'Aryan' race is one of the strongest and most successful branches of human stock, and was probably always patrilineal. McLennan's and Morgan's examples from other races are to be considered as aberrant forms, developed under peculiar conditions which brought about a scarcity of women.

J. F. McLennan's theory of the development of the family was first published under the title *Primitive Marriage* at Edinburgh in 1865, and may be found reprinted in *Studies in Ancient History*, Volume I, 1876. Apparently he had never heard of Bachofen, though he has nearly the same idea of a succession of primitive promiscuity, mother-right, or exogamy leading to father-right, and father-right, based, however, on wholly different inductions. In the beginning was a state of primitive indifference or promiscuity, during which there existed homogeneous 'stock groups' without any organized marriage. These groups were totemic, according to his later articles, 'Totemism', in *Chambers' Encyclopaedia* for 1867, and 'The Worship of Animals and Plants', in the *Fortnightly Review* for 1869. Both these papers may be more easily consulted in *Studies in Ancient History*, Volume II. They are interesting historically because they first introduced the notion of totemism into general anthropology, just as *Primitive Marriage* introduced the terms 'exogamy' and 'endogamy' into the literature. Indeed, these useful terms were invented by McLennan, exogamy as 'the rule which declares the union of persons of the same social group to be incest', and endogamy as the rule by which members of a group are forbidden to intermarry with members of another group, while free to marry among themselves. Totemism may be considered as the mystical connexion between each of these 'stock groups' and some symbol of their unity, such as a plant or animal. It was these symbols that brought about the idea of homogeneity or unity in each of the separate groups, and thus provided the germ from which the idea of kinship and family names evolved.

According to McLennan, then, totemism is prior to exogamy, for exogamy does not begin until his second stage, when a scarcity of women causes marriage by capture. Examples of marriage by capture, or apparent survivals of such a practice, first gave McLennan the idea of investigating the history of the family.

The change to mother-right or to exogamy is due to female infanticide. In primitive societies there is a struggle for food and security, and as female infants are less useful, they are more frequently killed. This brings about a scarcity of women, and has two main results. One is exogamy, the direct outcome of marriage by the capture of women from another group. McLennan does not believe that there is any instinct against the union of kin, since the rule of exogamy so often tolerates the marriage of half-sisters, although in a unilateral system of kinship these will be of a different name or group from one's own and therefore not considered as relations when descent is reckoned through one parent only. He takes the idea of capture from the frequent ceremonies by which the bride is forcibly removed to her new home, or is apparently restrained by her people from changing her abode, ceremonies which may be equally well explained as symbols of her change of status. When men capture women, if they keep them to themselves, we have the beginning of father-right, in which the husband controls his wife and children.

Suppose, however, that there is a scarcity of women, and none is captured. Such a condition results in polyandry, when several men have a wife in common. There are two forms distinguished, the Nair, in which the husbands are unrelated, and the Tibetan or adelphic, in which brothers share a wife. McLennan considers the latter form to be the higher, and argues from the levirate, a custom by which a man marries or inherits his deceased brother's wife,[1] that such adelphic polyandry may once have been general. As brothers shared a wife, the wife may well have lived with her husband's people, and thus again we have the germ of father-right. In the Nair system, as fatherhood is less certain, we find mother-right, or matrilineal kinship. Patrilineal kinship arises when paternity is certain, and such a development is fostered by the growth of private property.

While Maine confined his investigation to one type of people, and based his arguments almost entirely on Roman law, McLennan made a wider induction from a number of primitive peoples. But he assumed too much on too little evidence. Female infanticide and polyandry are

---

[1] When there is no system of state relief, someone must look after the wives of the dead men, since they have left their own people. Among many tribes the son has this obligation; in others, the brother of the deceased.

both rare, and there is no valid reason for making matrilineal kinship generally prior to patrilineal. Both systems have grown up side by side, and both exist today, for a variety of reasons, each of which must be considered on its merits before making an induction. The general argument of all the unilinear evolutionists seems to have been: 'We find ourselves, the best people, counting descent through males, though we recognize kinship on the other side of the family. In ancient times, and among people who are admittedly far beneath us, we find matrilineal kinship. Therefore it must have been prior to patrilineal, and we must explain how one grew out of the other. And, of course, there must have been something before matrilineal kinship, if that came before patrilineal. What could it be except promiscuity?'

Sir John Lubbock, afterwards Lord Avebury, considered the evolution of the family in 1870, in *The Origin of Civilization*, dealing besides with arts and ornaments, religion, law, language, and morals. He is well remembered for a great number of books on many subjects, such as *The Pleasures of Life*, a considerable number of works on insects and plants, and his great industry and ability in the study of prehistory side by side with parallels from modern primitive peoples.

He defines marriage as 'an exclusive relation of one or more men with one or more women, based on custom, recognized and supported by public opinion, and where law exists, by law', and considers that such marriage was preceded by a previous state which he calls 'communal marriage', a condition in which all the men and women in a small community are regarded as equally married to each other. 'Communal marriage' appears to be used in two senses, one, in that of sheer promiscuity, the other, in that of Howitt's 'group marriage' as found in Australia. Howitt had discovered that certain Australian tribes were divided into classes or groups and that men of a particular group were supposed to marry only women who came from another particular group or division of the tribe. It was at first imagined that this division of a tribe began with two groups, or halves, each half sharing spouses in common, and that these two groups were afterwards split into four, and that each of these sections found its mates in one of the other sections which was specially prescribed. A member of any section who travelled was able to find a temporary wife in the tribe he visited provided that she belonged to the section corresponding to his wife's at home. Thus the lucky Australian had, in Lubbock's words, 'a thousand mile of wives'. This curious notion of the evolution of the family from a promiscuous horde is still alive, though scarcely breathing.[1] The argument is that

[1] It was breathing in 1935, but now in 1962 I think it's dead.

there was first promiscuity, then a division into halves, then into quarters, then into eighths, and that ultimately we arrived at the family of today. It was based on the fact that Australian tribes were divided into two, four, or eight classes for the purposes of determining whom a man might marry. It has since been discovered that two named classes always mean four in practice, so that the simple two-class system does not exist. A four-class system develops easily in a small society where cousin marriage is the rule. Remember that kinship in most primitive societies is unilateral, and for the purpose of example, suppose that it is reckoned through the father. Suppose, further, to anticipate Morgan's discovery of the classificatory systems of relationship, that when the men remain at home, and bring their wives from outside, your father and his brothers and cousins are all in the same relation to you as your own father, and perhaps are referred to by the same term. Their sisters will be of your blood, and you cannot marry them. That is one class. Your mother and her sisters and cousins will be another class, and you certainly cannot marry your mother or any of the others whom you class with her. That is a second class. You and your brothers and sisters and all other girls who are the children of the 'fathers' class are a third group, related by blood, and unable to marry. One class only is left into which you can marry. Let us say that your fathers are Smiths, and your mothers are named Jones. Your mother's brother will be a Jones, and his children will be Joneses. You can marry them. In other words, as you cannot marry a mother or a sister, the nearest marriageable girl is a cousin on the other side of the family, or a cross-cousin in technical language. A study of the Prayer Book table of kindred and affinity will show that we ourselves have four classes, the marriageable class being that of cousins and all others less nearly related, or not related at all. Cross-cousin marriage in a small society makes the four classes very evident indeed. Then, if we remember that in a four-class system the children of two brothers may not marry because they have the same name, and that the children of two sisters cannot marry for the same reason, but that the children of a brother can marry the children of a sister, we may ask ourselves whether the children of a brother and the children of a sister (even though their names are different) are not as nearly related as the children of two brothers or the children of two sisters. If we then prohibit the marriage of the children of a brother and the children of a sister, we do not allow cousin marriage, and the nearest relative whom a man may marry is a second-cousin on the other side of the family. This in a small society will immediately make eight classes apparent to everyone's eye. This assumption that the family existed from the beginning and that the classes are the result of cousin or second-cousin marriages is easier to accept than the notion that the family evolved gradually from the promiscuous horde, by a process of division and sub-division.

Lubbock rightly considers polyandry as exceptional, and rejects the idea that it has a place in a universal scheme of evolution. With McLennan, he agrees that the change from communal to individual marriage occurred when marriage by capture started, such marriages being more exclusive, convenient, affectionate, and productive of sound healthy children. Thus by degrees, exogamy became the rule. Various proofs of a previous communal marriage were given by ceremonies of 'expiation for individual marriage', such as ritual defloration and wife lending. As for classificatory systems of relationship, he agrees with Morgan that they represent a previous form of communal marriage, rather than with McLennan, who regarded them as forms of address.

A mention of the classificatory system of relationship brings us to Morgan, its discoverer. Lewis Morgan's 'Systems of Consanguinity and Affinity in the Human Family' was published in Volume XVII of *Smithsonian Reports* in 1871. As early as 1846, while collecting material to illustrate the institutions of the Iroquois, Morgan found among them 'a system of relationship for the designation and classification of kindred, both unique and extraordinary in its character, and wholly unlike any with which we are familiar'. In 1851 he published an account of it in *The League of the Iroquois*. In 1857 he started to investigate the Ojibwa Indians, of the Algonkian stock, and as he suspected, found the classification of kindred to be similar, though every term was, of course, different. He at once prepared a schedule of questions, describing the persons in the lineal, and in the first five collateral lines, which when answered, would give their relationship to Ego, and thus display the whole system of consanguinity and affinity in any nation. This was sent out with an explanatory letter to all the missions and military posts in the United States. The results were so astonishing that Morgan asked the Secretary to the Smithsonian Institution, Professor Joseph Henry, to attempt to interest the government in making inquiries throughout the world. General Cass, the then Secretary of State, thereupon sent out in 1860 letters to every diplomatic and consular representative commending Morgan's investigations to their interest. The several missionary boards in America also co-operated. In all, Morgan was able to present and analyse 139 systems taken from every part of the world.

Some mention of the classificatory method of naming relationships has already been made. Among many peoples it is assumed that all who live together or make up the home circle are related, and it is considered that other groups are related among themselves in the same way. If the men stay at home and wives come from outside, all the men of one's generation will be called by some term which means 'brother', and all the women by a term which means 'sister'. One's own father, his brothers and cousins, and even more remotely related men of his generation will be called by a term which means 'father'. The same thing happens with the other side of the family, the mother, her sisters, cousins on her side, and so on, will be 'mothers'. The simplest and most highly developed system of all is seen in a Maori village, where all the grandparents' generation are grandparents, all of the father's and mother's generation are mothers, all of one's own are brothers and sisters, and all of one's children's generation are referred to as 'my children'. The system goes so far that if two men are in the same generation from a common ancestor, no matter how far back the ancestor, or how far away the men live, they will refer to each other as brothers. In other parts of the world, people belonging to the same marriage class will speak of themselves as brothers and sisters, even though they live miles apart, and have never seen each other. There are various forms of classification in different parts of the world, but in all, the classificatory system expresses the extreme solidarity of the group, and the mutual privileges and obligations of the members. A man's status is determined by his birth into such a group, and he has duties and privileges with regard to every other member of the group. In societies which have no such system, such as our own, contract largely takes the place of status; members of families or social groups need have no concern for each other, and the dole takes the place of mutual aid.[1]

Our own system of nomenclature Morgan called the descriptive. But it is really classificatory. We speak of uncles and aunts and cousins without distinguishing the side of the family, a matter most important to those who have the system which Morgan discovered and named the classificatory system. Nor is the term 'family system' given in *Notes and Queries* satisfactory, as it implies that our small family is the only type, and assumes that its extensions through a wider conception of blood-relationship, or of living together, make it something other than a family. Moreover, the fact that unrelated people at a distance are sometimes classed as relatives because they have the same totem or marriage class is a piece of pure logic, pushed to an Alice-in-Wonderland extreme, and is no more peculiar than our own use of the relationship terms 'aunt'

---

[1] But many of my pupils since 1935 have told me that the classificatory system is a terrible drain on their resources (note in 1962).

and 'uncle' for people who are not related at all, but have simply married our relatives. The system of using relationship terms for distant people is very convenient indeed for travellers, as they find themselves at home immediately, and in the right place, which is more than can be said for all of us when we travel.

Morgan rightly assumed that social reasons were at the root of the system which he discovered, but unfortunately, in *Ancient Society*, 1877, he passed over a magnificent opportunity to relate these terms to active and observable social causes, and proceeded, like the other unilinear evolutionists, to develop the family by a typological series of forms, some of them purely hypothetical. Like the rest, he begins with agamy, a time when there was no marriage. He then has a second stage, which he calls the Malayan or consanguine family. Here the group is promiscuous, but with the limitation that only members of the same generation can intermarry. This type of marriage is admitted to be a pure deduction from the classificatory system of Polynesia, already described, in which each relationship is conterminous with the whole of its generation. It is curious that a system so far removed from the primitive should have been given so early a place in the history of development. The next sort of group-marriage is deduced from the relationship terms of the four-class systems, in which people now marry their cross-cousins. Morgan assumed that the consanguine generation split into two, one of which contained brothers and sisters, and the other the cross-cousins. This further limited promiscuity. The names Turanian—because a good example of a four-class system was found among the Tamils, or Ganowanian, because the American Indians with a four-class system used bows and arrows—were employed for this stage. Our own type of family was termed the monogamian, and proceeded out of group-marriage by way of the syndyasman family, where the union lasted only during the pleasure of the parties concerned, and the patriarchal, at first polygynous, because of the selfishness of men, but ultimately, as the idea of property developed, monogamous. This system corresponds with our own in its relationship terms, and is called the Uralian.

Though Morgan is in the direct line of the more uncompromising of the unilinear evolutionists, his contribution is far greater than that of other students of the marital and filial regulations of society, for besides his discovery of the classificatory system, he is the inventor of a method whereby social structure can be studied as a complex of interacting functions. Since his time, Rivers[1] has developed the genealogical method in

[1] See p. 99.

field-work, and has made clear how valuable an instrument it is for understanding the inter-relations of a society. While his method has been employed only in the investigation of primitive communities, it might well be used with profit in the examination of physical and social conditions in our own villages and rural communities.

Among special studies of questions connected with the family, A. H. Huth's *The Marriage of Near Kin*, 1875 and 1887, should be remembered for its careful treatment of all data bearing on the effects of close inbreeding in men and animals. *Das Weib* by H. Ploss and M. Bartels, 1887, also contains a vast amount of information about the natural history of women in various grades of society, their anatomy and physiology, in health and disease, from cradle to grave, as girls, wives, matrons, and widows.

But the most important study of marriage during the century was Edward Westermarck's *The History of Human Marriage* in 1891. It first appeared in one volume, and has in the present century expanded into three.

By the word 'marriage', Westermarck means a more or less durable connexion of male and female lasting till after the birth of the offspring. He thus follows Darwin's definition, and since such marriage is common to man and some of the lower animals, he distinguishes the matter of his book by calling it a history of human marriage. He will have none of the doctrine of primitive promiscuity, arguing that no tribes of men in a normal state live thus, and that the customs and relationship terms which have been taken as proof of such promiscuity do not, in fact, prove it. Human marriage appears to be an inheritance from some ape-like progenitor, and we find certain of the apes themselves living in families, with the male at the head. While Westermarck admits that in many cases the bond between children and mother has stamped its character on a people and made it matrilineal, as a rule we may say that the father is the protector of the family, and there has been no time in the history of humanity when the family as the fundamental unit of society has not existed. From the evidence at his disposal, Westermarck was inclined to think that the greater apes were unsociable, and that the gregariousness and sociability of men sprang in the main from progressive intellectual and material civilization, while the tie that kept husband and wife and children together was the only, or at least the principal social factor in the earliest life of man.

Tendencies to avoid marriage with near relatives blend through various stages of kinship into exogamy, which bars marriage between members of a clan or village. As to the reason for the tendency to avoid near kin in marriage, Westermarck quotes from Robertson Smith's *Kinship and Marriage in Early Arabia* to the effect that in ancient times in that country, half-brothers and sisters could marry, as they would not be members of the same household under polygamy. 'Whatever is the origin of bars to marriage, they certainly are early associated with the feeling that it is indecent for housemates to intermarry.'[1]

'The objection will perhaps be made that the aversion to sexual intercourse between persons living very closely together from early youth is too complicated a mental phenomenon to be a true instinct, acquired through spontaneous variations intensified by natural selection.' But it 'only implies that disgust is associated with the idea of sexual intercourse between persons who have lived in a long-continued, intimate relationship from a period of life at which the action of desire is naturally out of the question'. 'It must necessarily have arisen at a stage when family-ties became comparatively strong, and children lived with their parents until the age of puberty, or even longer. Exogamy, as a natural extension of this instinct, would arise when single families united in small hordes.'[2]

From a consideration of conflicting evidence, Westermarck concludes that consanguineous marriages are more or less detrimental to the species, and that while there was no doubt a time when blood-relationship was no bar to marriage, variations would arise, and those who bred in and in, would perish, and the others who felt disgust at the idea of union with housemates would survive and pass the idea on to their descendants. Elsewhere and in another connexion, Westermarck takes account of Weismann's theory as to the impossibility of transmitting acquired characteristics, and approves it, so it is plain that he believes that the capacity for such a feeling of disgust is innate, and that living together at close quarters furnishes the necessary experience for the feeling to become active. McLennan's view that marriage by capture introduced the idea of exogamy, the savage seeing how much pleasanter it was to have a woman to himself, or Morgan's, that exogamy arose from a more or less conscious desire to prevent incest between parents and children, brothers and sisters, are more difficult to accept. McLennan's does not explain the dislike, and Morgan's scheme gives no reason why the dislike of such unions could have become general at any one of its stages.

Westermarck had read Darwin more thoroughly and critically than

[1] Robertson Smith, p. 169.
[2] Westermarck, p. 353.

many of his contemporaries, and as Tylor[1] wrote, made a most valuable attempt to work the biological and cultural sides of anthropology into a connected whole. Alfred Russell Wallace wrote an introductory note especially praising Westermarck's views on exogamy and Darwin's theory of sexual selection.

He made a clean break with those who put the family at the end of the series. Writers on the history of law, however, followed Morgan's scheme of development, so that it seemed as though many of them were mainly devoted to showing that his views were correct. Group-marriage went with group-property, group-justice, and group-responsibility. The wretched savage was the slave of custom, without individuality, obedient without understanding his obedience. It is curious that Morgan's discovery of a relationship system which implied reciprocal rights and duties did not suggest sooner a study of the relations between individuals and the rules governing them. Such a collection of rules might be called the civil law of any community. But the emphasis was placed almost wholly on criminal law, and the punishments which followed the breach of custom.

A. H. Post, Franz Bernhöft, and Joseph Kohler were all dominated by Morgan's evolutionary hypothesis, and of these, Post was the most uncompromising in the application of the method, both in his *Afrikanische Jurisprudenz* of 1887, and in the *Grundriss der ethnologischen Jurisprudenz* of 1894.

In the latter, he roundly states that the method of comparative ethnology is different from that of history, and collects the material from a wholly different point of view. While historical investigation tries to get at the causes of the facts of rational life by observing the development of these facts from those which preceded them in separate tribes or peoples, the comparative ethnologist must look for the causes of facts in rational life by collecting identical or similar data wherever they may be found in the world, drawing inferences from these materials to identical or similar causes. We may assume that peoples everywhere will resort to similar expedients in similar situations. Post separates things out of their context, and makes new combinations, ranging over the world in the process, i.e. he takes the different subdivisions of law, and traces them through all the tribes which present any data. For him, the course of evolution is rigorously determined. Parallels in the most diverse peoples are emanations of general human nature. He recognizes four main stages in the development of society. The first organization in which we find the beginning of law is that of matrilineal clans; the next

[1] *The Academy*, Oct. 3, 1891.

is the territorial-associational, determined by the common occupation of a district; the third is the seigneural, where we find relations between overlord and dependants; and the fourth is the social, in which we at length find social intercourse and contractual relations between individuals.

Kohler was a voluminous writer in the *Zeitschrift für vergleichende Rechtswissenschaft*, which he helped Bernhöft to found in 1878. He was Professor of Law at Würzberg and Berlin, and was a versatile scholar, being well-versed in every branch of the law, as well as in poetry, masic, and art. Although he subscribed to the ordinary unilinear theory, as shown in *Zur Urgeschichte der Ehe* in 1897, he took a broader view than Post, insisting that the law of any people could only be understood as a part of the whole culture, and must be studied with the help of history. His monographs on whole areas, such as Germany, France, Babylon, India, German Africa, Australia, and America show that he was more critical than many of his contemporaries, and not so ready to accept a parallel without careful investigation of the whole complex in which he found it.

S. R. Steinmetz also insisted on the necessity for understanding the whole social life of which various laws are a part, both the ancient and the modern; otherwise, the comparative historian of culture will not comprehend the facts he is using out of their context. He takes jurisprudence to be both an art and a science. It is an art of framing rules for social intercourse, and interpreting and applying them. It is a science of investigating these rules, and their conditions and foundations. Steinmetz differs from many of his contemporaries in trying to examine the psychology of the emotional life and character of peoples as well as the intellectual, as for example in his psychological analysis of the feeling of revenge. Like his contemporaries, however, he ignores civil law for the most part, giving his main attention to the study of criminal jurisprudence.

The *Ethnologische Studien zur Ersten Entwicklung der Strafe* was published in 1894, the result of many years of work on the evolution of punishment, during which the author found that he had to cover the whole field of social anthropology. Wishing to follow the law of vengeance back to its ultimate source in human nature, he begins by collecting the opinions of psychologists about human propensities to revenge and cruelty, and finds that the motives for vengeance are blind fury, aggressiveness, pleasure in hurting someone else, a feeling of power and safety while the victim suffers, and a desire to frighten enemies who may attack in future.

E 129

Steinmetz then takes the stages in the evolution of punishment in a similar order, and gives examples from various peoples to illustrate them. First comes the stage of undirected vengeance, corresponding with the feeling of blind fury shown by an Australian aborigine who will hit anyone or anything that comes handy when he or one of his family has been injured. As there is a tendency for such anger to be directed towards an enemy, we find the blood-feud, in which the members of one group will kill any member of another group which has done them an injury, or even kill a stranger to glut their feeling for revenge when one of their own people has been hurt. All the members of a group are responsible for an injury done by any one of them. The blood-feud with collective responsibility is characteristic of the lowest social organizations, likewise of the highest, as may be seen in modern warfare, when nations struggle with nations.

It is clear that unregulated vengeance, especially within a tribe, would soon leave its people in the condition of the Kilkenny cats, who ate each other up. Thus we find such expedients as the regulated duel between the injured man and his aggressor, or expiatory exposure, illustrated by the Australian practice of forcing a paramour to allow the injured husband and his relatives to throw a certain number of spears at him, the victim being permitted to ward them off if he can. Here we find that private justice is somewhat controlled by public authority, as also in cases where composition or compensation is required to settle a dispute. Steinmetz considers at some length the gentleness of many primitive peoples, and brings forward a good deal of evidence to show that punishments are milder among matriarchal than patriarchal societies. As patriarchal societies grow, there is a tendency for punishments to increase in brutality, and for a difference between public and private wrongs to be more sharply distinguished. The chief kills the coward or traitor, the chief or the whole populace wipe out the sinner who practises witchcraft, or commits incest, for these are crimes against all, while offences against particular people are still left to some form of private vengeance or adjustment.

Both at the outset and at the end, Steinmetz discusses the connexion between religion and vengeance, especially as connected with the cult of ancestors or of the dead, who are thought of as inflicting vengeance over and above human punishment on the sinner who breaks the great taboos of the tribe. It is this supernatural vengeance that adds the element of horror to one who breaks a law on which the safety of all depend. The sinner is unclean, and his sin is contagious. Death is his punishment.

At this stage of development, evidence is often taken by divination or ordeal, the first way being a method of asking divine power to reveal the truth, and the second as well, acting on the belief that the innocent will not be allowed to suffer. Out of the ordeal comes trial by torture, resting on the same assumption perhaps, but also on the natural desire to inflict pain. The oath is another form of the ordeal, in which a man invokes a curse on himself if he is not innocent.

Steinmetz pays little or no attention to substantive law, or the application of rules to social relations, but devotes his attention to adjective law, or the procedure by which the regulation is accomplished. Little attention is paid to the law of persons and property, but the main emphasis is laid on criminal law, and within that subject, to the various stages of procedure. Inside these limits, however, he is much sounder than his predecessors in ethnological jurisprudence, and his evolutionary scheme rests on a much firmer basis than that of earlier writers on the development of the family. Dr R. R. Marett has pointed out to me that this is partly due to his application of Tylor's method of investigating social facts, as set out in the eighteenth volume of the *Journal of the Anthropological Institute*, published in 1889.

In this paper, 'On a Method of Investigating the Development of Institutions, applied to the Laws of Marriage and Descent', Tylor showed how the development of institutions might be examined with the help of tabulation and classification. Taking data from all over the world, he arranged in tables the rules of marriage and descent, together with the 'adhesions' of each custom, 'showing which peoples have the same custom, and what other customs accompany it or lie apart from it'. For example, the rules of residence after marriage, with the wife's people, with the husband's people, or beginning with the wife's and ending with the husband's people, were compared with the adhering customs of a man's avoidance of his wife's parents, or a woman's avoidance of her husband's. 'If the customs of residence and the customs of avoidance were independent, or nearly so, we should expect to find their coincidence following the ordinary law of chance distribution.' But, instead of following the law of chance distribution, 'there is a well-marked preponderance indicating that ceremonial avoidance by the husband of the wife's family is in some way connected with his living with them; and *vice versa* as to his wife and the husband's family.'

Two hundred and eighty-two peoples were at Tylor's disposal for this particular example. In sixty-five cases where the husband lives with the wife's family permanently, we find fourteen cases of the husband's ceremonial avoidance of his parents-in-law, and none of the wife avoiding her husband's relations. Were the two customs so distantly connected as to be practically independent, the product of the fractions $\frac{65}{282} \times \frac{14}{282}$ multiplied into the 282 peoples would show that their concurrence might be expected to happen about three times according to the laws of chance. In the seventy-six cases where the couple begin life with the wife's family, but afterwards move, there are twenty-two cases of the husband avoiding the wife's family, instead of the six that we might expect, five of mutual avoidance, and five where the wife avoids her husband's parents. When the wife lives with her husband's people from the first, out of 141 cases there are nine in which the husband avoids the wife's family, three in which there is mutual avoidance, and eight in which the wife avoids her husband's parents.

Thus, 'residence on the wife's side appears earliest, after this the removal stage, and latest, residence on the husband's side. For if it be supposed that the course of society was in the reverse direction . . . avoidance between the husband and the wife's family would be represented as arising in the stage when the husband lived away from it, while avoidance between the wife and the husband's family, which ought on this supposition to continue by survival into the stage of residence on the wife's side, is not found there.'

The rules of residence after marriage are likewise discussed in connexion with teknonymy, i.e. the naming of parents after children, with the levirate, couvade, and marriage by capture, and the evidence, as far as it goes, appears to show that residence with the wife's people is anterior to residence of the wife with the husband.

Tylor was far from being a unilinear evolutionist with a simple and universal scheme of development, and here as elsewhere, he refuses to go beyond his data to mere speculation. 'By this it is not, however, meant to imply that the maternal family as here set forth represents the primitive condition of mankind, but that it is a stage through which the inhabitants of a great part of the world now in the paternal appear to have passed, and which still continues in force over considerable tracts of every part of the globe except Europe.'

Exogamy and the classificatory system of relationships are shown as two sides of the same system, which binds together a whole community with ties of kinship and affinity. The classificatory system expresses the relationship between all the members of a clan, that is, of people who are descended from a common ancestor, or believe themselves to be so descended, or feel their unity and express it by some common symbol, such as a totem. The rule of exogamy requires the members of such a group to marry the members of another particular group, or other groups, within the tribe, and keeps a growing tribe compact. Such marriages very often result in the almost complete endogamy of the tribe, the relationship system emphasizing the solidarity of the different clans, and the system of marriage preserving the solidarity of the tribe.

One great value of the statistical method to Tylor's mind was that it called attention regularly to the nature of the material at his disposal, especially to imperfect or fragmentary data. With Galton, he agreed that in many cases concurrences might arise from transmission, and thus a single character might be counted several times from its mere duplicates, and with Flower, he recognized the difficulty of getting units of comparison[1] of equivalent value when dealing with groups of mankind.

Indeed, this question of diffusion or independent invention was always present in Tylor's mind, and runs from the beginning to the end of his *Researches into the Early History of Mankind*, 1865, 1870, 1878. While his main position was that 'the facts collected seem to favour the view that the wide differences in the civilization and mental state of the various races of mankind are rather differences of development than of origin, rather of degree than of kind', he is extremely careful not to admit the independent origin of similar inventions in different parts of the world until he has exhausted every possibility of diffusion or culture contact. In writing of traditions of a great flood in his account of myths of observation, he maintains that certain features of the story in widely separated parts of the world might easily be due to independent origin, but that others, such as the occurrence of an ark found in so many distant times and places favour the opinion of their being derived from a single source. The geographical distribution of myths, 'after full allowance has been made for independent coincidence', seems 'to warrant some expectation that the American Mythology may have to be treated as embodying materials common to other districts of the world, mixed no doubt with purely native matter. Such a view would bring the early history of America into definite connexion with that of other regions, over a larger geographical range than that included in Humboldt's argument.' From Humboldt's observations and his own in Mexico, especially those on the similarity of calendars, and 'series of names like our signs of the zodiac used to record periods of time . . . combined together, or with numbers, in both countries, in a complex, perverse, and practically purposeless manner', he infers some connexion in the past between the cultures of Asia and Mexico, as such ideas 'can hardly by any stretch of probability be supposed to have come up

---

[1] This difficulty has not been wholly solved in a more recent attempt to apply statistical methods to social anthropology – *The Material Culture and Social Institutions of the Simpler Peoples, an Essay in Correlation*, by L. T. Hobhouse, G. C. Wheeler, and M. Ginsberg, published in 1915.

independently in the minds of two different peoples'. From the form of the bellows used in iron-smelting, he traces a cultural connexion between Madagascar and the Malay Archipelago. His chapter on the Stone Age, past and present, sums up his attitude to the evidence he then had:

How, then, is this remarkable uniformity [of stone artefacts from all over the world at any given period] to be explained? The principle that man does the same thing under the same circumstances will account for much, but it is very doubtful whether it can be stretched far enough to account for even the greater proportion of the facts in question. The other side of the argument is, of course, that the resemblance is due to connexion, and the truth is made up of the two, though in what proportions, we do not know.

So much has been written of late years to the effect that Tylor was a simple unilinear evolutionist, who tore facts from their context and arranged them arbitrarily in a developmental scheme with little regard to their function in their own culture, and often regardless of the possibility of diffusion, that it is, perhaps, excusable to point out that all through his career it is evident that like Darwin and Bastian he kept the whole complex of life with its interdependence in view. Like them he knew the greatness of the task,

'I have, God wot, a large feeld to ere,'

and like them, he realized how little could be accomplished with the evidence then available,

'And wayke ben the oxen in my plough.'

Like them, he left room for development and supplement by his successors, and like them, he refused merely to cultivate a small field, and thereby to sacrifice the largeness of view that comes from attempting great and universal problems.[1]

In some respects, his career is not unlike that of Darwin. Both men found their true interest and future career on a voyage of discovery, both had the leisure to pursue it untroubled by financial embarrassment, and both had large quiet minds aloof from controversy, hospitable to ideas from any source whatever, regardless of academic authority, and adamant against popular fashions or scientific crazes.

Edward Burnett Tylor was born in 1832 and died in 1917. While Darwin went to Edinburgh and Cambridge, getting all his training for the career he was to follow outside the curriculum, Tylor went to no

[1] Cf. *Early History of Mankind*, p. 13.

university, but was apprenticed to the family firm of brass founders. As a young man, he found himself in delicate health, and travelled, like Darwin, with an open and curious mind. After a year in the southern states of North America, he went to Cuba, where in 1856 at the age of twenty-four, a chance meeting decided his career.[1] Hearing the familiar Quaker 'thou' from a passenger in a tram who made some casual excuse to him, he ventured to make further conversation, and discovered that his acquaintance was Henry Christy, the banker, who had for some time been working with Edouard Lartet in the 'bone caves' of Central France. Christy had some thought of going to Mexico, and asked Tylor to accompany him, and it was characteristic of Tylor that he should start at once. The friendship lasted for ten years,[2] during which Christy gave Tylor the benefit of his wide and minute knowledge, both of prehistoric life and ethnology. These conversations and the trip to Mexico made an impression on Tylor which lasted all his life, far beyond the publication of *Anahuac, or Mexico and the Mexicans, Ancient and Modern*, in 1861.

For one thing, he always held to the belief that it was necessary to study geographical distribution and to trace the diffusion of cultures. His earlier views about the historical connexion between Asia and America have been mentioned. Before the British Association at Montreal in 1884, he stressed the connexion, remarking on the physical resemblances between the peoples of the two continents. The Botocudo Indians from Brazil whom he saw in London, to mention one example, could easily have been taken for Siamese or Tibetans, if they were to change their clothes. The Tartars and the Eskimo alike have the composite bow and many other features in common. The calendar, signs of the zodiac, games, and many other things show a connexion between Mexico and eastern Asia. Besides, there are many localized items of culture on the coast of the Americas which point to diffusion from Asia and the islands, probably by sea in fairly recent times.

In 1894 before the British Association at Oxford, he returns to his old love, Mexico, and asserts that culture historians do not sufficiently recognize the importance of the study of culture transmission, pointing out again the many features which show that the nations of America reached a certain level of culture under Asiatic influence, and he makes the geographical province including these culture-traits wider than Humboldt's. He asks for a systematized use of correspondence in culture as a means of tracing connexion and intercourse between ancient and remote peoples. One example is given as an illustration, namely

[1] Information from Dr R. R. Marett.
[2] As long as Christy lived.

the Egyptian stories of what happens to the soul after death. He traces these stories through the Vedic and Zoroastrian regions, and from Eastern Buddhism to Western Christendom, giving also examples from Japan and from the Aztec picture-writing in the Vatican codex.

At the same time, his friendship with Christy introduced him to the discipline of digging up the past, and the problems of the growth and decline of culture, so manifest in Central America, and the study of the development of civilization. The reader of Miss Freire-Marreco's bibliography at the end of the *Anthropological Essays Presented to Tylor*, or anyone who looks at the very varied contents of his library, annotated by himself, and with letters and notes by their authors pasted inside the cover, in every language and on every subject, will see that all the methods, and all the material available for the study of man's body and mental and material culture engaged his attention, and that he took into account all the items of the general life of a people which made its culture, and knew their function within that culture.

Indeed, Tylor was always fully alive to the necessity for examining the function of any particular institution within its own culture before using it in a developmental scheme. His treatment of avoidances as adhesions to rules of residence has already been mentioned. But he insisted that the purposes of these avoidances between relations and relations-in-law were so various in different places that no single reason would account for them all. Again, in his 'Remarks on Totemism' in the *J.A.I.* for 1899, he objects to the very prominent place which totemism has taken in evolutionary studies of religion and sociology. He first points out that there is no such thing as an 'individual totem', the term having arisen from a mistake made by John Long in 1797, who confused the *manitu* or guardian spirit which each Ojibwa Indian possesses with the totem animals of the clans of the tribe, and of the whole story remarks with his usual common sense, 'From an angry bear in the backwoods to a supreme deity of the world is too long a course to be mapped out in merely ideal stages'.

He then continues to show that totems have different functions in different places, and are differently conceived by various peoples. He distinguishes a species of animals allied to a clan from a species of animals inhabited by a god, and thus cuts off sacred animals from totem-animals. Coming to tribes that are divided into totem-clans, he shows that in North America they are social institutions regulating marriage, and that very often a clan considers itself to be descended from the animal. In Central Australia the system has no part in the regulation of marriage, but is based on a theory of re-incarnation and particular sacred areas, while in Melanesia it rests on the idea of the transmigration of souls into animals. Thus a consideration of the functions of totemism in various parts of the world makes it impossible to say much more than that animal worship and the idea of some connexion between groups of men and species of animals are characteristic of many peoples in lower grades of civilization. While allowing full credit to the necessity for studying diffusion and function, Tylor held, like Bastian, to the idea of the psychic unity of mankind. In the *Researches into the Early History of Mankind*[1] he wrote:

The Gesture-Language is the same in principle, and similar in its details, all over the world. The likeness in the formation both of pure myths and of those crude theories which have been described as 'myths of observation,' among races so dissimilar in the colour of their skins and the shape of their skulls, tells in the same direction. And wherever the occurrence of any art or knowledge in two places can be confidently ascribed to independent invention, as for instance, when we find the dwellers in the ancient lake-habitations of Switzerland, and the modern New Zealanders, adopting a like construction in their curious fabrics of tied bundles of fibre, the similar step thus made in different times and places tends to prove the similarity of the minds that made it. Moreover, to take a somewhat weaker line of argument, the uniformity with which like stages in the development of art and science are found among the most unlike races, may be adduced as evidence on the same side, in spite of the constant difficulty in deciding whether any particular development is due to independent invention, or to transmission from some other people to those among whom it is found. For if the similar thing has been produced in two places by independent invention, then, as has just been said, it is direct evidence of similarity of mind. And on the other hand, if it was carried from one place to the other, or from a third to both, by mere transmission from people to people, then the smallness of the change it has suffered in transplanting is still evidence of the like nature of the soil wherever it is found.

Considered both from this and other points of view, this uniform development of the lower civilization is a matter of great interest. The state of things which is found is not indeed that one race does or knows exactly what another race does or knows, but that similar stages of development recur in different times and places.

In a very careful study of 'The Growth and Decline of Culture' Tylor points out that the ethnologist must allow for degeneration as well as progress, and must be prepared to find an uneven development in any given culture, some arts or pieces of knowledge being above the average of the rest. These superior products must be examined to find out whether they have been imported, invented at home, or are relics of a formerly better condition of people. Any particular trait must be

[1] 1870, p. 370.

investigated, or a culture as a whole, to see whether it is really primitive, or a degeneration.

But when all is said and done, 'it would seem that the world, when it has once got a firm grasp of new knowledge or a new art, is very loth to lose it altogether, especially when it relates to matters important to man in general, for the conduct of his daily life, and the satisfaction of his daily wants, things that come home to men's "business and bosoms". An inspection of the geographical distribution of art and knowledge among mankind, seems to give some grounds for the belief that the history of the lower races, as of the higher, is not the history of a course of degeneration, or even of equal oscillations to and fro, but of a movement which, in spite of frequent stops and relapses, has on the whole been forward; that there has been from age to age a growth of man's power over Nature, which no degrading influences have been able permanently to check.'

We have summarized the more important contributions to the study of primitive social organization and law. Tylor's greatest contribution was the study of primitive religion. *Primitive Culture* appeared in 1871, and at once Tylor appeared as the foremost of English anthropologists. For the next thirty years, there was hardly any other theory to hold the field, in England, or in America, or on the Continent. His solid array of accurately attested facts, his common sense in interpreting them, and the beautiful simplicity of his style in dealing with so vast an amount of evidence—a style and power of organization akin to Darwin's—won immediate recognition for his views, and gave them a permanent place in the history of religion. While the students of social organization and for the most part of those of comparative jurisprudence had devoted their attention to institutions, Tylor, like Bastian, dealt with the beliefs that underlie institutions. The approach of both was the psychological. The main difference between the two was in the power of organization and clarity of presentation.

'From survivals in games, proverbs, riddles, and minor superstitions such as those of sneezing, Mr Tylor glides into Magic, as based on the association of ideas; into omens, automatisms, witchcraft, spiritualism, and the doctrine of spirits, "Animism", with its influences on religion and mythology.'[1] Tylor's minimum definition of religion is a belief in spiritual beings, and his scheme of investigation is divided into two parts, first determining how the idea of spirits could have arisen, and then trying to show how from that idea all types of supernatural being could have evolved.

[1] Lang's Preface in *Anthropological Essays Presented to Tylor*, 1907.

There is a difference between the living and the dead. Therefore there must be something in the one that is not in the other. Allied to this, there are the phenomena of sleep, ecstasy, and illness. Then there are the figures of men seen in dreams, or in waking visions, which put into their minds the idea of souls being ethereal images of bodies. As man is the measure of all things, he would attribute souls to animals and plants, and even to inanimate objects, thinking them to be like himself, and knowing that they also appeared in dreams. As they saw the dead in dreams, the idea of survival of the spiritual or phantom part would arise, and with it the tendance of the dead.

Ancestor-worship, the basis of Spencer's theory of religion, grows out of this care for the dead, and from it comes the notion of pure spirit without body. These spirits could be malignant or benign, and could enter into the bodies of living people, or into objects or artificial bodies made for them. Such entry into living people explained the facts of possession, illness, and death. The fetish, the stocks and stones, and the shaped idol were possessed of a spirit.

The idea of spirits was applied to nature, and the worship of nature arose. Spirits inhabited trees, rivers, animals. We find animal worship and totems, and ultimately the deification of a whole species of animal or other natural object of creation, and thus arrive at departmental deities, such as rain-gods, earth-gods, fire-gods, and departmental-gods who preside over certain functions of life.

Monotheism arises out of polytheism by raising one god to primacy. Sometimes there is a stage where the gods are ranked as in an earthly court, with a king and nobility. Sometimes there is the doctrine of the pervasion of the whole universe by divinity.

Tylor's psychological explanation and chronological arrangement were hardly shaken until near the end of the century, when his pupil Andrew Lang wrote *The Making of Religion* in 1898. Lang was a man of many interests, and considered anthropology as one of them, an every-day topic belonging to general culture. He was quite detached from the ordinary current of thought of his time, and was not over-whelmed by the idea of evolution, or by the authority of its exponents. In his earlier work, *Custom and Myth*, 1884, and *Myth, Ritual, and Religion*, 1887, as well as in his article on 'Mythology' in the ninth edition of the *Britannica*, he stood up for Tylor's views against Max Müller's philological school, which treated mythology as a disease of language, but went more deeply into folklore than his teacher, and made more of the study of magic. *The Making of Religion* displays a somewhat sceptical attitude towards a chronological development from lower to higher, showing that gods do not always improve ethically with advancing culture, and that the idea of a high-god, creator and guardian of all, was found among the simplest and rudest races, where European or Islamic influences could be ruled out. In this he relied on the evidence of Howitt and Fison, whose various accounts of the gods Daramulum and Baiamai as found among the South-east Australians were appearing in the *Journal of the Anthropological Institute*. Other fieldworkers like Spencer and Gillen were of the opinion that these tribes had been so long in contact with Europeans that it was difficult to be certain as to which of their ideas were primitive, and maintained that the untouched Central Australians had no notion of a god. The controversy ran on into the next century, especially when a German missionary named Strehlow[1] announced that these same Central Australians had a god. Lang stuck to his guns through it all, maintaining that the high-god faith represented an independent line of development, against the Tylorians, who placed it in the main line. Not only did Lang deny the chronological arrangement of Tylor, but he attacked the psychological explanation. He maintained that the high-god need not be a spiritual being, but simply a magnified, non-natural man. In the twentieth century, Pater Schmidt of Vienna devoted himself to the study of primitive high-gods, and the descent from the original pure faith of humanity to the various perversions which we find today and in historic times.

The high-gods which Lang defended belonged to a stage previous to the animistic, or pre-animistic, to use the term first employed by Dr R. R. Marett, in a paper read before the Folk-Lore Society in 1899, and published in *Folk-Lore* for June, 1900.

Marett was of the opinion that primitive religion was a wider, and in some ways, a vaguer thing than 'the belief in spiritual beings', and without insisting on a chronological scheme, made a new category for 'those residual phenomena which a strictly animistic interpretation of rudimentary religion would be likely to ignore, or at all events, to misrepresent'.[2]

When, to take one of his several examples, 'a Kaffir village, led by its medicine man, will rush to the nearest hill and yell at the hurricane to divert it from its course', awe finds expression in what may be simply personification, with no idea of a directing spirit. He collects many

---

[1] For details of this controversy see: Marett and Penniman, *Spencer's Scientific Correspondence*, p. 95; Spencer and Gillen, *The Arunta*, 1927, II, 594; *Man*, 1933, 96. Strehlow's work is *Die Aranda- und Loritjastämme*, 1907-10.

[2] R. R. Marett, The *Threshold of Religion*, 1909, p. ix. The *Folk-Lore* paper is reprinted in this book.

instances of the savage regarding as living what we class as lifeless, and attributing power or displaying awe in its presence. Over and beyond what can be explained by human intelligence, there is the inexplicable and awe-inspiring, and such events or objects may be treated as though they had personality or will, with no notion that they are directed by a spirit or contain one. While such a condition of mind may be classified under the term 'pre-animism', Marett avoids chronological argument by calling it 'animatism'. To Wundt's statement in *Völkerpsychologie* that his *präanimistische Hypothese* is in opposition to Tylor's theory, he replies that awe in the presence of the inexplicable is a more constant factor in religion than any particular conception of the awful, and that 'before animism, regarded as an ideal system of religious beliefs, can have come into its kingdom, there must have been numberless dimly lighted impressions of the awful that owned no master in the shape of some one systematizing thought'. He is not maintaining that a preanimistic religion as a system of ideas was prior to an animistic, but merely that the indistinct is prior to the distinct, and in that sense the use of the word 'pre-animism', with its chronological implications, was justified in the title of the paper. The new category can take its place as part of the evolutionary scheme in harmony with Tylor's.[1]

After *Primitive Culture*, Tylor wrote no other complete book except *Anthropology* in 1881, in which he displays his characteristic insight and understanding of humanity. To those who would criticize a new subject, he claims that anthropology simplifies the acquisition and understanding of knowledge by showing the simple fundamentals of all human prac-tices, enabling us to disentangle the mystifying growths that have come with later ages.

In 1883 Tylor became Professor of Anthropology in the University of Oxford, and from then onwards, lectured at the Pitt Rivers Museum. For a long period before his death, his health was far from good, and this may have accounted in part for the fact that he wrote no more books. But a great amount of his time was spent in keeping up with all the developments of the subject throughout the world, as an enormous number of reviews and papers testify, and in organizing the subject, and devising methods for its development. Eighteen sections of *Notes and Queries on Anthropology* were drawn up by him for the 1874 and 1892 editions, and he was instrumental in the foundation of many organiza-tions for collecting first-hand evidence, such as the committee appointed at the Montreal meeting of the British Association 'to investigate the

[1] Marett, *The Threshold of Religion*, 1909, preface.

physical characters, languages, and industrial and social conditions of the North-Western Tribes of the Dominion of Canada.'

It was always Tylor's hope that anthropology would develop 'from a derided byway to truth to a time when its help and decisions are sought for by governments', and he often referred with admiration to the Bureau of American Ethnology founded by Powell in 1879 as an example of what governments should do.

There is probably no man who has done more to make the whole European world conscious of the importance of the world outside the public school and university than Sir James George Frazer. By the vast amount of his evidence and the beauty of his style, he has made even governments aware of the interest and value of studying the peoples of their empires, so that now some sort of anthropological training is usually considered desirable or even necessary for those who have any part in the administration of colonies.

Frazer was born at Glasgow on January 1, 1854,[1] and his early education was at the Springfield and Larchfield academies, and at Glasgow University, where he had a sound training in Greek and Latin, natural and moral philosophy, logic and metaphysics, and English literature. To George Gilbert Ramsay, Professor of Humanity, he owed the impulse which directed his thought for many years to the study of the Greek and Roman classics, and to John Veitch, Professor of Rhetoric and of Logic and Metaphysics, he was indebted for an introduction to philosophy, and deeply impressed by the clearness, simplicity and literary finish of his style, as well as by his true poetical feeling. Frazer's own style is simple and pure, free from uncouth jargon, and at times rises to the level of great poetry. Indeed, in one of his later addresses, at a meeting of the Ernest Renan Society, he said, 'Without tenderness, without poetry, one cannot understand man or his creations.' Sir William Thomson, later Lord Kelvin, impressed him with 'a conception of the physical universe as regulated by exact and absolutely unvarying laws of nature expressible in mathematical formulas', a conception which has certainly dominated his whole career. More than any other English scientist, he has a French precision and elegance in the development of his ideas.

He had some hope of competing for a Snell Exhibition to Balliol College, Oxford, but as his family were Presbyterians, they were worried about the High Church tendencies of Oxford, and sent him to Trinity College, Cambridge, where he entered as a scholar in 1874, and gained a

[1] Biographical details in part from 'Presentation of the Freedom of the City of Glasgow to Sir James George Frazer, O.M., April 22, 1932'.

fellowship, which he now holds for life, in 1879.[1] While he was at work on an edition of *Pausanias*, his friend James Ward called his attention to Tylor's *Primitive Culture*, a work which determined the general trend of all the rest of his career.

His lively interest was stimulated to systematic study by William Robertson Smith, a man of great learning and original ideas. He had been expelled from the Free Church College at Aberdeen for his supposed heresy, and had been invited to Cambridge, first as Lord Almoner's Reader in Arabic, then as University Librarian and Professor of Arabic. At the time when Frazer first knew him, he was editing the ninth edition of the *Encyclopaedia Britannica* (1885), and knowing Frazer's interest, asked him to write the two articles 'Taboo' and 'Totemism'. The researches made for these two articles were the beginning of a systematic application to anthropology, and display the thoroughness which has always characterized his work. The writer at one time had the privilege of examining the notebooks from which Sir James Frazer has written his many books. There were about seventy quarto-size notebooks of three to four hundred pages each devoted to various subjects, all filled in Frazer's small regular handwriting with extracts from books and periodicals in every language in which anyone could be expected to write on anthropology, and the remainder of a box the size of a cabin-trunk was filled with notebooks devoted to areas. In spite of the fact that the printed bibliography of various editions of his works by Theodore Besterman in 1934 has eighty-four octavo pages, these notebooks contain systematically collected material for many more books, and now, at the age of eighty-one, with the help of Lady Frazer, he is still publishing.[2]

To the ninth edition of the *Britannica*, Robertson Smith contributed the article on 'Sacrifice'. This was followed by *Kinship and Marriage in Early Arabia*, 1885, and by *Lectures on the Religion of the Semites*, delivered at Aberdeen, which had previously rejected him, in 1888–89, and first published in London in 1889. In these writings he follows the idea of his teacher McLennan, and the earlier views of Frazer, taking totemism as a half-religious, half-social phenomenon, and thinks that he can show it to be at the root of Semitic religion. The names of the tribes are the names of animals. The distinction between clean and unclean beasts suggests the taboos connected with totemism. All leads up to the idea of sacrifice, in which the victim was originally the totem animal of

---

[1] Written in 1935. Sir James and Lady Frazer died within an hour of each other in 1941.

[2] Written in 1935. Sir James and Lady Frazer died in 1941.

the clan, of the same blood as the clan and its god. On ordinary occasions the animal might not be killed or eaten, but on sacred festivals, his kinsmen slaughtered him, and in partaking of his flesh and blood, renewed their unity with each other and with him.

In America at the same time, H. C. Trumbull was delivering lectures on *The Blood Covenant*, which were published in London in 1887. In these he developed the idea of blood brotherhood established by interchange of blood between the covenanters, and of communal meals, in all places and at all times, up to the significance of the Last Supper in which Jesus bade farewell to his disciples, and made them to be of his body and blood.

In Germany, B. Stade in *Geschichte des Volkes Israel*, 1884-87, expressed views similar to those of Robertson Smith, and in England, F. B. Jevons in his *Introduction to the History of Religion*, 1896, adopts the idea of totemism and sacrificial communion as the first stage in religion, preceded by a non-animistic stage of universal personification, which had at first little or no religious character.

The theory of the slaying of the victim as the representative of the god and his worshippers was adopted from Robertson Smith in the first edition of *The Golden Bough* in 1890,[1] as the central idea of the 'essay', which started as a footnote on the custom connected with the shrine of Diana Nemorensis at Aricia. The priest of this shrine had always to watch with drawn sword to guard himself against other candidates for the priesthood, and when he was overcome by a stronger or craftier candidate, the victor became the guardian of the sacred wood until he was in his turn slain by another.

To explain this custom, Frazer set himself to studying primitive superstition and religion throughout the whole world, and especially survivals of primitive superstitions in Europe. The most valuable collection of these had been made by W. Mannhardt,[2] who collected systematically the living superstitions and rites of the peasantry, by oral inquiry, and by printed questions sent all over Europe, devoting himself mainly to the folklore of the woodman and the farmer. Much of his material is yet unpublished, and remains in the library of the University of Berlin. His principal published works are *Roggenwolf und Roggenhund*, 1865-66; *Die Korndämonen*, 1868; *Der Baumkultus der Germanen und ihrer Nachbarstämme*, 1875; *Antike Wald- und Feldkulte*, 1877; and, after his death, *Mythologische Forschungen* in 1884. In all these works, the Rye-wolf and Rye-dog, the spirits of water, corn, and trees, the cults

[1] See Preface to *The Golden Bough*, 1st ed.
[2] *Ibid.*

of wood and field, were displayed as survivals from ancient times, and the origins of later religion. These spirits took their place in Tylor's theory of animism, as well as in *The Golden Bough*, and also in E. Rohde's application of ethnological data to the study of classical civilization, *Psyche, Seelenkult und Unsterblichkeitsglaube der Griechen*, 1891–94. Since 1890 the Folk-Lore Society has been steadily adding to our knowledge of primitive survivals in civilized life.

Among the ethnologists who helped him in his search for material, Frazer singles out G. A. Wilken of Leyden, who put him on the track of the best authorities for the Dutch East Indies in the *Bijdragen tot de Taal-Land-en Volkenkunde van Nederlandsch Indië*, an important Dutch periodical. Wilken himself had made a valuable study of animism in *Het Animisme bij de Volken van den Indischen Archipel* in 1885.

In the two volumes of the 1890 edition, Frazer takes the reader through a study of tree-worship, taboos, the slaying of divine kings, of gods or representatives of gods, and the various survivals represented in harvest customs, etc., explaining that the priest of Diana at Aricia was probably the embodiment of a tree-spirit, and that in earlier times, one of these priests had probably been sacrificed every year as an incarnate god.

The three volumes of the 1900 edition mark many changes. In the earlier[1] he had interpreted the ceremonies observed by European peasantry in spring, at midsummer, and at harvest as survivals of magical rites designed to make plants grow, cattle thrive, rain fall, and the sun to shine. The work of Spencer and Gillen in Central Australia, of J. L. van der Toorn in Sumatra, and of W. W. Skeat in the Malay Peninsula supplied him with parallels in the way of ceremonies designed to assist the operations of nature. The weight of all this evidence, especially the Australian, led him, like Jevons, to separate magic and religion into two different categories, placing magic as everywhere the earlier. At first, primitive man stupidly supposed that his rites automatically controlled nature; then, as he saw that they sometimes did not, he tried prayers instead of spells, sacrifices, and humiliation before powers that he could not compel, and religion began to take the place of magic. Magic is a false science of the working of the universe, which with the development of the knowledge of natural laws, becomes true science.

Father Schmidt[2] points out that Frazer's theory as based on the stages of development of the intellect was preceded by J. H. King's *The Supernatural, Its Origin, Nature, and Evolution*, published in 1892,

[1] Preface to second edition, *Golden Bough*.
[2] W. Schmidt, *The Origin and Growth of Religion*, tr. Rose, 1931, p. 121.

which appears to be one of the few books which Frazer did not read. Indeed, very few people have read it. King distinguishes two kinds of powers, the mental, in men and animals, from which man derives his idea of spirits, and the impersonal, from which he derives his idea of good and bad luck, or of magic. Magical beliefs and practices arise when the usual order of nature is broken, or something unusual happens, and it is felt that something must be done about it. At first, every man is his own magician, seeking to attract good luck and avoid bad; then professional magicians rise from the ranks of the more successful. In purely magical rites there is no notion of spirits or of spiritual power, the rites or objects used working automatically. The universal feeling of good or ill luck, with the corresponding desire or fear, contains also the germ of religion, which develops with the animistic belief in spirits.

Marett's theory of pre-animism, on the other hand, had an emotional basis in feelings of awe and wonder, and the first magical rites treated the Awful as impersonal rather than as activated by a spirit.

Towards the end of the century, É. Durkheim approached the evidence, particularly that from Australia, in a method peculiarly French, and based on the ideas of his countryman, Auguste Comte, who regarded sociology as the science of the associated life of humanity rather than as a study of the individuals composing it. In 1895 he founded L'Année Sociologique, and in the second volume, that for 1897–98, laid down his method of treating the evidence, a method since developed by himself, Hubert Mauss, and Lévy-Bruhl. The article 'De la définition des phénomènes réligieuses' argues that magic is the result of a social agreement translating a social need into action, the universal desire for certain necessities with its hopes and fears keeping up confidence in the methods which have appeared to secure those necessities. These magical rites are often pantomimic representations of what is wanted, and arise spontaneously, the group finding themselves enacting the rite as a whole. This theory of the origin of magic and religion rests on the general notion that we cannot understand the individual apart from his society, which imposes its ideas and feelings on him from the first, and so determines his thoughts and actions.

IV. LINGUISTICS

The study of language played a considerable part in anthropology during the nineteenth century, and at one time enthusiasts thought that it would settle all anthropological problems. It is natural that the subject should receive a great deal of attention. Tylor defined language as 'the expression of ideas by means of articulate sounds habitually allotted to those ideas'. It marks perhaps the most important difference between man and other primates, for they repeat the same cycle of experience in each generation, having no speech by which to collect experience and pass it on to the next generation.

Languages may be divided into four great groups according to their method of expressing a statement. The isolating languages like Chinese range the words representing the parts of the phrase one after another without any change. In the agglutinative languages like the Bantu, the Sibiric, Basque, and others, the principal word in the phrase may have added to it or placed before or after it syllables expressing the relation of the other ideas to it. In the incorporative languages like most of the American tongues, the accessory words are inserted within the verbal members of the sentence, or attached to it in abbreviated forms, so that the phrase appears to be one word (the holophrase). In inflected languages like those of the Indo-European group, the words of the sentence indicate by their own form their relation to the main proposition.

Brinton was of the opinion that the origin of language was to be found in the holophrases[1] of the incorporative languages, and noting the way in which children make up words of their own, believed that in the beginning there were a great many linguistic stocks, rather than the few or one for which many analysts sought as the parent stock.

One method of studying languages comparatively is that of structural analysis. When the tongues of two or more groups do not differ beyond the possibility of understanding each other, they are classed as dialects. When mutually unintelligible languages have consistent similarities in grammatical structure, they are classed as members of the same family. Grammatical structure is more important than verbal similarity, and the serious student must also follow the phonetic laws of the particular groups to which the languages belong. To apply Indo-European phonetic laws, for example, to Polynesian words is absurd, and to take verbal coincidences between an inflected language such as Sanscrit and an agglutinative Polynesian language to prove a case, is to say the least, reckless.

Some of the earliest classifications of primitive peoples by linguistic families were those by Albert Gallatin in 1836,[2] and by Major Powell in

[1] D. G. Brinton, Races and People, 1890; 'The Earliest Form of Human Speech as Revealed by American Tongues,' Essays of an Americanist, 1890; Horatio Hale, 'On the Origin of Language,' Proc. Amer. Assn. Adv. Sci., 1887, p. 279.
[2] Trans. and Coll. Am. Antiq. Soc., Vol. II, 1-422.

1891,[1] whose system of nomenclature for the languages of the New World is the one now generally used.

Other comparative work on the languages of primitive peoples was Robert Caldwell's *Comparative Grammar of the Dravidian or South-Indian Family of Languages*, 1856, 1875; R. H. Codrington's *Melanesian Languages*, 1885; and R. Tregear's *Maori Comparative Dictionary*, 1891. D. G. Brinton's great *Library of Aboriginal American Literature* which he edited, published, and for the most part translated, shows the wide and scholarly basis of his contributions to the general study of languages.

In Europe, and to a considerable extent in America, the main tendency of linguistic studies in the latter part of the nineteenth century was directed towards the 'Aryan' languages and race.[2] In 1786, Sir William Jones, as quoted by Thomas Benfey in *Geschichte der Sprachwissenschaft*, 1869, had shown the affinity of Greek, Latin, Gothic, and Celtic to Sanscrit, and in 1819, Jacob Grimm's *Deutsche Grammatik* had put forward the famous law of the permutation of consonants within the Indo-Germanic group of languages. Franz Bopp's *Comparative Grammar*, 1833–35, established a method of comparing grammatical forms, and so placed comparative philology on a scientific basis. In 1861 August Schleicher's *Compendium der vergleichenden Grammatik der indogermanischen Sprachen* assumed and partly reconstructed a parent speech from which this whole family of languages had descended, and laid down a series of phonetic laws by which the development had occurred. In 1872 Johannes Schmidt,[3] while allowing a parent speech, refused to believe in the family tree of languages constructed by his predecessors, and supposed that in remote antiquity local phonetic disturbances had arisen within the parent language, and that from these centres they had spread until the various dialects met each other. The different languages evolved separately then, and reacted on each other when they later came into contact, thus giving an appearance that one was derived from another, when there was really no more than a collateral relationship. Delbrück followed the same view of independent development, but denied that there was ever any parent language.

For the majority, however, the theory of a parent language and some sort of a family tree held the field, and as it appeared to some students that the more primitive peoples and languages were to be found in Asia, it was assumed at first that the parent stock had lived there. Pictet in

---

[1] B.A.E., 7th report, 1891.
[2] In the account of the Aryan controversy, W. Z. Ripley's account in *The Races of Europe*, 1900, pp. 475–85, has been freely used.
[3] *Die Verwantschaftsverhältnisse der indogermanischen Sprachen.*

1859 was the first to make out a case, and Max Müller in his *Lectures on the Science of Language* in 1861 and in subsequent work made this view widely acceptable to philologists by his scholarship, and popular by his charm of exposition, so that the term Aryan became current both for the language and for the race. But he repented handsomely before the British Association in 1891, saying that the evidence of the philologist was that of language, and nothing else. There must be no compromise between the sciences of ethnology and phonology. Two years previously in *Biographies of Words and the Home of the Aryas*, he had said that an ethnologist who spoke of an Aryan race was as bad as a philologist who spoke of a dolichocephalic dictionary, and A. H. Sayce in the *Science of Language* in 1880 said that language was a help to the historian but not to the ethnologist. Identity of language can prove no more than social contact, nor can relationship of language.

The term Aryan assumes that the parent stock lived in Ariana in Central Asia, and that the other stocks and languages came from there. Opponents of this notion were many, of whom the first is probably d'Omalius d'Halloy, who believed that the ancestors of the modern Europeans did not come from Asia but belonged originally to the continent where they now live. Robert Latham first introduced this idea to England in 1859. In America, W. D. Whitney,[1] and in England, A. H. Sayce[2] and Canon Taylor,[3] showed that several European languages were more archaic in structure than the Sanscrit, and so destroyed all arguments based on the supposed primitiveness of the sacred languages of India and Persia.

This argument found favour among many of the French and German sociologists and ethnologists, who tried to fit the idea of a European cradle-land on to their cephalic indices and hair-colours. Starting with de Gobineau's theory of the inequality of races, and employing Weismann's theory of the unchangeable germ-plasm and the impossibility of inheriting acquired characters, they chose a spot where there was still an archaic language in Europe, and according to national and patriotic inclination, developed the blond dolichocephalic Teuton, or the darker Alpine brachycephalic Frenchman, both superior people. These notions are hardly worth discussing, except for the fact that a history of anthropology is both a history of human progress and a history of human folly. This particular folly is playing a large part in European politics now.[4]

[1] *Oriental and Linguistic Studies*, II, 228.
[2] On the Aryan question in *R.B.A.*, 1887.
[3] *Origin of the Aryans*, 1890.
[4] Written in 1935.

Writing in 1890,[1] Brinton argued that the physical types of the Aryans differed widely, and that the original Aryac tribe was a mixture of blonds and brunettes, with both long and broad heads, and that the language, being an inflected one, was not truly primitive, since grammatical inflexion was the result of a slow growth 'in which the material elements of language are transformed into formal elements, and the "grammatical categories" or parts of speech, gradually assume logical distinctness and independent expression'. Brinton had observed this growth in an imperfect form in the Nahuatl of Mexico, and in the Berber of Morocco, and was inclined to derive his European parent language from the Berber stock. In the same year Canon Taylor[2] had used similar arguments to derive the original from the Finnic stock, inclining however to the theory that the original Aryans were blond.

By the end of the century, the structural analysts confessed themselves to be uncertain about the whole Aryan question. Those who did pronounce a definite opinion were generally influenced by other than strictly philological arguments, and were more often than not dabblers in 'linguistic palaeontology'. Benfey is supposed to have originated this method of the study of root words as symbols of primitive ideas in 1868.[3] The use of this method is shown in Brinton's *Races and Peoples*[4] discussing expressions common to all Aryac languages:

These common ancestors had domestic dogs, cattle, and perhaps sheep; nomadic at times, they at some seasons tilled the soil; they were acquainted with copper, and brewed mead from honey; they had probably even invented a wagon, and milked their cows, and they certainly lived on or near the sea shore, and used boats.

Such a statement, however, tempts one to place the Aryans geographically, and many were tempted on the grounds of such study alone, so to place them. Max Müller[5] showed such attempts in their correct light by pointing out that these root words were common to so wide an area in both Europe and Asia that it was impossible to place the Aryans definitely anywhere. Moreover, many of the roots were probably never words at all, but the mere abstractions of scholars, as Lord Monboddo suggested as early as 1763 in his *Origin and Progress of Language*.

The truth about the whole controversy is between Sayce's view[6] that relationship of languages at least proves social contact, and Keane's[7] that

[1] *Races and Peoples*, pp. 147–49.
[2] *Origins of the Aryans.*
[3] Preface to Fick, *Vergleichendes Wörterbuch*, 1868.
[4] p. 148.
[5] *Biography of Words*, etc., 1888.
[6] *Science of Language*, II, 1880 (also Haddon, 1934).
[7] *Ethnology*, 1896 (also Haddon, 1934).

in some cases, like that of the Basques, language shows the existence of ethnic elements which without its evidence would have been unsuspected.

The progress of linguistic work on the Indo-Germanic languages can be read in Otto Schrader's *Sprachvergleichung und Urgeschichte*, 1883, whose second edition was translated by Jevons in 1890 as *Prehistoric Antiquities of the Aryan People*, and summarized by Canon Isaac Taylor in *Origin of the Aryans* in the same year. Salomon Reinach's *Résumé* of 1892 also has a summary with several additions of French sources.[1]

A useful type of linguistic palaeontology was that devised by Rivers on the Torres Straits Expedition. By the study of fossilized relationship terms, such as 'mother-right' words existing in a patrilineal society, he was able to discover a good deal about the previous condition of the society. This method was worked out in great detail in his work during the present century.[2]

One of the most interesting theories of the origin of language was that of E. J. Payne in the *History of the New World Called America* (1892–99). Like Brinton, he saw the rude foundations of human speech in the American languages, laid in the nature of thought, animal life, and human society. In other linguistic groups, these foundations are obscured by the structure reared above and around them by analytical thought. Here, however, though analysis is at work, we can still see the primitive foundations in the holophrases. Lord Monboddo[3] has best described the nature of the holophrase, in an example describing the action of beating:

There is first the action itself, then the agent or person who beats, then the person or thing which suffers or is beaten, and lastly the manner of beating, whether quickly or slowly, gently or severely, etc. The action and all these circumstances exist together in nature. The savage, therefore considers them all in the lump, as it were, without discrimination, and so forms his idea of the action, and according to this idea expresses it in words. Whereas, in languages formed by rule, all those things are expressed by different words, or by variations of the same word, if that can be conveniently done. Further, there are some necessary adjuncts of the action, such as time. This too, though inseparably joined with it in nature accurate abstraction separates, and expresses either by a different word or by a certain variation of the same word; but this the savage likewise throws into the lump, and expresses all by the same word without variation, or by a word quite different.

[1] Ripley, *The Races of Europe*, 1900, 476.
[2] Rivers, *History of Melanesian Society*, 1914.
[3] *Origin and Progress of Language*, 1763, Book iii, Chap. 7: quoted by Payne, II, 117.

In the American languages, Payne sees the beginnings of speech as it grew out of the imperfectly significant cry of primitive man, utterances at first subjective, but gradually becoming capable of symbolizing objects. Things are roughly classified by the personal relations affecting them, and these personal relations gradually adapt themselves to the moods of wish, question, or command, 'the unit of significance embodying itself in the holophrase, or polysyllabic unit of utterance', Articulation is based on the movements used in the mastication and ingestion of food, the guttural and nasal sounds becoming slowly displaced by increasing oralization, that is, movements of the lips and tongue which bring the sounds forward, and cut them into vocalic and consonantal sounds. When man stood or sat upright to eat, and kept his nose out of his food, he gave up slobbering and mumbling it, and used the muscles of his mouth to better effect. Strenuity gave way to relaxation and adjustment. Originally repetitive ejaculations lost this character through variations to distinguish personality. Gradually the holophrase broke up through its own cumbrousness and the growth of mental analysis and the use of prefixes and suffixes to show the sequence of ideas. General words grew up in holophrases of the third person, and gained their universal character by gradual dispersonalization.

Payne's history is not confined to a study of language, but deals with the whole history of discovery, and every feature of aboriginal life. One of the most interesting parts deals with the animals of the New World, pointing out how few were available for domestication, and how severely this fact limited and arrested the growth of civilization. The Old World animals, on the other hand, could be domesticated, and thus the whole basis of work, leisure, food, and wealth was different, and the history of the Old World was different.

Payne's principal argument is that the advance to civilization is due to the organized provision of the food supply on an artificial basis as distinguished from a natural basis. In America, cultures are built up on indigenous plants and animals, all being utilized. These cultures are therefore native. No small influx of people from abroad could have been responsible. Advance is not imported in single parcels. Communication with any outside influence would have to be regular if it were to have any effect. The ἐκβαρβάρωσις of the newcomers when isolated among savages would invariably occur. Food provision on an artificial basis brings about the need for organized defence against the more barbarous, and the communities in which these combined organizations have been elaborated have extended their boundaries at the expense of the less advanced.

V. TECHNOLOGY

The study of the material cultures of mankind, or of the arts and industries by which man gains a living and adorns himself and his surroundings was no less affected by evolutionary ideas than was the study of the social cultures of the world. Just as Payne built his social structure on the organizations of the food supply and for defence, so had Marx derived his forms of society from their economic organization, and Kovalevsky from increase of numbers interacting with economic factors. Le Play's method of studying the place which determined the method of getting a living, which in turn determined the form of the home circle, has been described.

The first man to study the material arts and industries in an evolutionary fashion was General Pitt Rivers. In a previous chapter we saw the beginning of his work with the service rifle.

During his investigations, conducted with a view to ascertaining the best methods whereby the service firearms might be improved, at a time when the old Tower musket was being finally discarded, he was forcibly struck by the extremely gradual changes whereby improvements were effected. He observed that every noteworthy advancement in the efficiency, not only of the whole weapon, but also of every individual detail in its structure, was arrived at as a cumulative result of a succession of very slight modifications each of which was but a trifling improvement upon the one immediately preceding it. Through noticing the unfailing regularity of this process of gradual *evolution* in the case of firearms, he was led to believe that the same principles must probably govern the development of the other arts, appliances, and ideas of mankind.[1]

In 1851 Colonel Lane Fox, later to become General Pitt Rivers,[2] began his ethnological museum at Bethnal Green. This was later removed to South Kensington, and was finally given to the University of Oxford, where it was housed in a building specially designed for it in 1884, with the help of Moseley, Tylor, Baldwin Spencer, and Henry Balfour, the last of whom was put in charge of the collections, and is still their curator. (Written in 1935. Balfour died in 1939.)

During the years 1867–69 Lane Fox was maturing his ideas in his papers on 'Primitive Warfare' in the *Journal of the United Service Institution*,[3] and in 1874 opened the Bethnal Green Museum to the public, the *Catalogue raisonnée* of the collections being published by the Science and Art Department of the South Kensington Museum in the

---

[1] Henry Balfour, *R.B.A.*, Cambridge, 1904.
[2] This name was taken by royal licence in 1880, when he inherited the Rivers property.
[3] See p. 71.

same year. At a special meeting of the Anthropological Institute[1] at Bethnal Green, he explained the method by which he had arranged his collections, a method entirely different from any other employed in his time, and a method which has been very little used since his day, collections being usually arranged according to the geographical areas from which they come.

He explained that since 1852 he had been collecting not the unique but the ordinary and typical objects in common use by the various peoples of the world, selecting and arranging them in sequence with a view to tracing the succession of ideas and development. Instead of a purely geographical arrangement, he had collected spears together, and so on, going by the form of the object. In each group there was a sub-class for localities, and in each sub-class, or wherever a connexion of ideas could be traced, specimens were arranged according to affinities, the simpler to the left, and successive improvements in line to the right. Such an arrangement, showing that development of specific ideas and their transmission from one people to another, or from one locality to another, was a truly sociological arrangement.

The arts of living races helped to explain what was obscure in those of prehistoric times, as the zoologist helped the palaeontologist to reconstruct the forms of extinct animals from the parts that remained, and ethnological data might be used to illuminate archaeological.

A great advantage of the arrangement by form was that it afforded facilities for tracing the distribution of like forms and arts, so that the connexions between places in former times by spread of race, culture, or commerce may be determined.

Human ideas as represented by the products of industry might be classified into genera, species, and varieties, and the methods of reasoning applied by biology could be used in studying them. The hybridization of ideas was a matter of importance, and caused the rise of new species. When these distinct species had run far enough on distinct lines, so as to create a hiatus, no intercommunication could occur, except in so far as there were simple ideas common to both.

It must not be supposed that the General was unaware of the danger of mistaking accidental resemblances for morphological affinities, that is, of assuming that because two objects from different regions appeared to be similar in form or use, they were necessarily members of one phylogenetic group. On the contrary, he took great care to distinguish between analogies and homologies. Again, with Tylor, he did

[1] *J.A.I.*, 1874, IV, p. 293.

not allow the independent invention of similar forms until he had exhausted the possibilities of actual relationship by diffusion.

The validity of his general views on evolution in the material arts was immediately accepted by many ethnologists who were convinced by his arguments supported as they were by such a volume of striking evidence.[1]

Among those who have followed and developed his method is Henry Balfour, the first curator of the Pitt Rivers Museum in Oxford. Among his earlier work may be mentioned 'The Composite Bow' in the *J.A.I.* for 1890, *The Evolution of Decorative Art* in 1893, and *The Natural History of the Musical Bow* in 1899. The two last named give an indication of his method, and the care he took in collecting his evidence and in drawing inferences from it. In the evolution of decorative art, he dealt first with the appreciation and adaptation of natural or accidental peculiarities as ornamental effects, then the artificial reproduction of natural effects, and the effects of copying and successive copying. The writer well remembers the astonishing results of an amusing experiment which Mr Balfour often makes with his pupils. One draws a picture, and hands it on to another with no explanation. The next man copies the picture and hands it on to yet another. The end of the series is often so different from the beginning that it is extremely difficult or impossible to recognize their relationship without the help of the intervening drawings. Unconscious variation due to successive copying and conscious variation, as well as survivals in symbolic designs were treated, and the adaptation of decoration to the shape and material of the object to be decorated, as well as the persistence of design when the material is changed.

The history of the musical bow makes it clear that the greater part of the probable chain of sequences which led from the simple bow to specialized instruments of the harp family may be reconstructed from types still existing among living peoples, especially in Africa. The native of Damaraland has no stringed instrument specially made, and when he feels like making music, ties a small thong round the bow and bow-string, so as to divide the string into two vibrating parts of unequal length. When lightly struck with a small stick, the string emits a couple of notes. Among other African tribes, bows are specially made for musical purposes, and in some places, to increase the volume of sound, the bow is rested across a hollow resonant body, such as pot or gourd.

[1] See also 'Evolution of Culture,' 1875, *P.R.I.G.B.*, VII, Pt. VI, 496; 'Early Modes of Navigation,' *J.A.I.*, 1875, IV; Collections, e.g., *Papers by General Pitt Rivers, Anthropological, Archaeological, and Other Contributions to Learned Societies up to 1884*; *Evolution of Culture and Other Essays*, ed. J. L. Myres, 1904.

Sometimes the gourd is attached to the bow. Balfour believes that somewhere, probably in West Africa, two or more small bows will be attached to a single gourd. This form has been found in Guiana in South America, and as no indigenous stringed instruments of music have been found in America, and there was a migration of slaves from Guinea to Guiana, it is probably justifiable to place the Guiana instrument in the African series. Such a form would need to be assumed in the series, even were it not found, when we remember the common West African instrument of five little bows each with its string, all of which are fixed by their lower ends into a box-like wooden resonator. This way of fastening the bows to the body of the instrument requires the lower attachment of the strings to be transferred from the bows to the body, so that the bow-like form begins to disappear. In the next type in the series may be seen the substitution of a single stout curved rod for the five little bows, the five strings being attached serially to the upper end of the rod, and their lower ends to the body as before. Rude and inefficient as it is, the instrument has now assumed a harp-like form, and modern varieties and developments of it extend across Africa from west to east, and the harps of ancient Egypt, Assyria, India, and Greece are elaborations of this primitive form. Oddly enough, the fore-pillar, so important a part of the modern harp, does not make its appearance until about the seventh or eighth century in western Europe.

Hjalmar Stolpe[1] also began his studies of the art of primitive peoples in the pioneering days, and early came under the influence of Pitt Rivers. In 1880–81, he made a tour of all the principal European museums, and in 1883–85, he was appointed ethnologist on board the frigate *Vanadis* on her voyage round the world. Though many of the museums were not scientifically arranged, and several of the larger had packed their material in boxes with a view to moving into new quarters, Stolpe found that all were most helpful, even to unpacking boxes. He made a large number of copies, and took a great number of rubbings with paper and black wax, all of which are now in the National Museum of Natural History in Stockholm, where he was director of the ethnographical department. His work was published in Swedish, and there is a bibliography of his many works in the *Nordisk Familjebok*. His paper 'On Evolution in the Ornamental Art of Savage Peoples', the first scientific study of Polynesian art, was published in *Ymer* in 1890 as 'Utvecklingsföreteelser i Naturfolkens ornamentik', and translated by Mrs March in the *Transactions of the Rochdale Literary and Scientific Society*, Volume

---

[1] See *Collected Essays in Ornamental Art by Hjalmar Stolpe*, tr. by Mrs H. C. March, 1927. Much of this information is from the foreword by Henry Balfour.

III, 1891–92; there is also a German translation in the *Mittheilungen der Anthropologischen Gesellschaft in Wien*, XXII, 1892, 18–62. 'Studies in American Ornamentation, a Contribution to the Biology of Ornament', with a folio atlas of South American art designs, appeared in Stockholm in 1896 as *Studier i Amerikansk Ornamentik, ett Bidrag till Ornamentens Biologi*, and was translated by Mrs March for the *Collected Essays* in 1927, together with the previously named paper, to which Stolpe had added an appendix based on Charles Read's 'Origin and Sacred Character of Certain Ornaments of the South-East Pacific' in the *J.A.I.* for 1891, a paper which had independently arrived at similar conclusions.

At the time when Stolpe wrote, students of primitive design were beginning to realize that the early phases of representative art were not art for art's sake, but had their origins in symbolism and religious or magical practices. Thus in 1889 in a paper read by Dr Colley March on 'The Meaning of Ornament' before the Lancashire and Cheshire Antiquarian Society in February, it was maintained that 'zoomorphs took their place in the expectant mind by virtue of some symbolic or mythological meaning, and when this was lost, animal forms were reproduced by the artificer with less attention to detail, and only to satisfy a vague desire for something mystical or auspicious', and this theory was further developed after Stolpe's paper of 1890, in 'Polynesian Ornament a Mythography, or a Symbolism of Origin and Descent' in the *J.A.I.* for 1893. As early as 1881,[1] Stolpe foreshadowed the view that appeared in his paper of 1890, that the conventional patterns had developed from images of gods, and that these highly conventionalized patterns symbolized the primitive image. 'By means of perpetual reiteration of certain ornamental elements, they suggest the divinity to whose service the decorated implement was in some way dedicated.' In 1883 at the Fifth Americanist Congress in Copenhagen, he stated that the linear ornaments on the carved adzes from Mangaia[2] were in the main to be regarded as transformed figures of human or divine figures, mainly divine. The Rev. W. Wyatt-Gill in his *Jottings from the Pacific* in 1885 had pointed out that the adze-handles of the Hervey Islanders, carved with shark's teeth, always displayed in their patterns, however conventionalized to the point of unintelligibility to the European, the figure of a man squatting down, intended to represent Tiki-tiki tangata.

Stolpe recognized that unilinear evolution is a rare phenomenon, and that a given design may be traceable to a plurality of origins, hybridization of ideas being of common occurrence. Another point of great

---

[1] *Collected Essays on Ornamental Art*, 1927, p. 32.
[2] In the Hervey group.

importance with him was the necessity for studying designs in terms of their culture-environment and of the material and technique used in their execution. A problem of interest arising out of his work is that of the great divergence of conventional forms in the different groups of the Polynesian Islands, especially as the peoples are related in blood and have similar primitive notions and images from which the conventional patterns were derived. Probably isolation on the one hand, and culture contacts on the other, are principal factors in bringing about such a variety.

In direct line with the work of Stolpe, Read, and March, is Eugene Goblet, Count d'Alviella's *La migration des symboles* in 1891, a valuable study of the religious value of symbols, and of their migrations. For example, the swastika is traced from Troy to Japan in the one direction, and to Iceland in the other. The psychology and sociology of symbolism were investigated in 1893 by Guglielmo Ferrero in *I simboli in rapporto alla storia e filosofia del diritto alla psicologia e alla sociologia*, and by Yrjö Hirn in 1900 in *The Origin of Art*. Edge-Partington's and Heape's *Ethnographical Album of the Pacific Islands*[1] and Martin's *Photographs of New Zealand Mythographs* of 1890 should also be remembered.

The greater part of this work and much more is admirably worked into A. C. Haddon's *Evolution in Art as Illustrated by the Life Histories of Designs* of 1895, in which the author aims to inculcate the study of decorative art from the biological rather than the aesthetic standpoint. 'Only by the study of the life history of designs, of their origin in some far away field of realistic conception, their evolution and conventional-ization under varying geographic and racial influences, their final assumption of apparently the heterogeneous forms, can the student hope to escape the multitudinous pitfalls with which his path is beset.'[2] After an account of the decorative art of British New Guinea as an example of the method of study, Haddon discusses the material of which patterns are made, treating of skeuomorphs, the forms of ornament demonstrably due to structure, biomorphs, or the representation of living things, and so on. He then passes to a discussion of the reasons for which objects are decorated, including art, information, wealth, magic, and religion, concluding with a statement of his method of study. At the time he wrote, he was Professor of Zoology at Dublin, and this book applies biological deductions to designs and discusses the geographical distribution of animals and designs.

[1] First Series 1890; Second, 1895; Third, 1898. Edition of one hundred numbered copies. Some entries in earlier volumes are corrected in later ones.

[2] *J.A.I.*, XXV, p. 281.

In America the Bureau of Ethnology and the National Museum were devoting a great deal of attention to the arts and crafts, and the writers were legion. Three books by O. T. Mason may be mentioned, *The Origins of Invention* and *Woman's Share in Primitive Culture*, both in 1895, and *Aboriginal American Basketry: Studies in a Textile Art without Machinery* in 1904. In the first book Mason traced 'some of our modern industries to their origins', showing 'how the genius of man, working upon and influenced by the resources and the forces of nature, learned its first lessons in the art of inventing. . . . The term invention is here used in its plain logical sense of finding out originally how to perform any specific action by some new implement, or improvement, or substance or method'. There are chapters on tools and mechanical devices, the invention and use of fire, stone working, the potter's art, the use of plants, the textile industry, war on the animal kingdom, capture domestication of animals, travel and transportation, and the art of war. The second book deals with woman as the food bringer, the weaver, skin dresser, potter, beast of burden, jack-at-all-trades, and as artist, linguist, founder of society, and patron of religion, concluding that all the social fabrics of the world are built around women, the first stable society being a woman and her helpless infant.

VI. ARCHAEOLOGY

Closely allied to the study of arts and industries of now existing peoples is the study of archaeology. On the one hand it shows the origins of cultures and civilizations now existing, and without its help, their history is incomplete. The evidence from excavations may supplement or correct written documents, or it may furnish all the data we have or ever shall have. On the other hand, the evidence furnished by the handiwork of peoples now living, and their beliefs and practices with regard to such objects, may go far towards explaining the work of earlier peoples whose artefacts the excavator uncovers.

In a previous chapter we noted how Councillor Thomsen of Copenhagen first established the succession of Stone, Bronze, and Iron Ages. His pupil, J. J. A. Worsaae, demonstrated it in his field work, and may be called the founder of scientific archaeology. With his collaborators he investigated the Danish peat-mosses.

These accumulations display a well-marked stratification, the layers being distinguished by the species of the principal trees whose remains were buried in the peat. There was at the bottom a layer containing the Scotch fir, a tree no longer found in Denmark; above that was a layer containing oak: over that again, a layer containing another species of oak, with alder and birch: over which grew the beech, this being still the commonest tree in the country. In, and underneath, the lowest stratum were found stone implements; these persisted into the oak strata, but bronze implements, absent from the fir stratum, were there found along with them; while iron implements were for the greater part associated with the beech trees.[1]

This work is described in Sir Charles Lyell's *The Geological Evidences of the Antiquity of Man with Remarks on Theories of the Origin of Species by Variation* in 1863. The idea of careful excavation with special attention to stratification was not entirely new when Worsaae began; indeed Keller[2] was already working on similar principles in Switzerland, but the clear demonstration of three stages of culture for Denmark by such a method, and the influence of geologists like Lyell and biologists like Darwin, together with the insistence of Pitt Rivers on the importance of recording everything, and of ordinary objects rather than a mere collection of curios and works of art, started an entirely new period in the history of archaeology. Indeed, General Pitt Rivers set a wonderful example to the world when he inherited the Rivers property, and began to excavate Cranborne Chase[3] in 1881, continuing to publish the work until 1898, in four great quarto volumes. It was his practice to make accurate models of every excavation so that the evidence could again be reconstructed should occasion require, and to notice everything, for it might well be that later a detail seemingly unimportant at the time would play a much larger part when fresh evidence came to light. The collections and models may be seen at the museum he established at Farnham in Dorset.

Before treating the discoveries of the most ancient men and their cultures, we may summarize briefly the progress of discovery of the more immediate foundations of European civilization and American aboriginal cultures. The first Scythian discoveries were made by Paul Delrux at Kul Oba near Kertch in 1830. Further work in bringing to light these people so fascinatingly described by Herodotus appears in the publications of the Imperial Archaeological Commission of St Petersburg[4] and in Kondakoff, Tolstoi, and Reinach's *Antiquités de la*

---

[1] R. A. S. Macalister, *A Textbook of European Archaeology*, 1921, I, 10.
[2] F. Keller's careful work on the strata of the Swiss lake-dwellings began in 1853, and was published in *The Lake Dwellings of Switzerland and Other Parts of Europe*, 1866; see Chap. 3, p. 56.
[3] Pitt Rivers, *Excavations in Cranborne Chase*, I–IV, 1881–98.
[4] *Antiquités de la Scythie d'Hérodote*, 1866–73; *Compte rendu*, 1859–88 (French). 1889– (Russian). *Bulletin* (Russian), 1901– ; see E. H. Minns, *Scythians and Greeks*, 1913; M. I. Rostovtsev, *Iranians and Greeks in South Russia*, 1922.

Russie méridionale in 1891–92. The second edition of *The Civilization of Sweden in Heathen Times* appeared in 1878 in Sweden, and in Germany in 1885. This valuable work on the neolithic to iron stages in Sweden was revised by its author, Oscar Montelius, in 1888, and translated into English in the same year by the Reverend F. H. Woods. In 1877 Canon William Greenwell and George Rolleston, many of whose collections are in the University of Oxford, published *British Barrows, a Record of the Examination of Sepulchral Mounds in Various Parts of England*, and in 1872 and 1881, Sir John Evans brought out *The Ancient Stone Implements, Weapons and Ornaments of Great Britain*, and *The Ancient Bronze Implements, Weapons and Ornaments of Great Britain and Ireland*. In Italy, Gastaldi,[1] and Stroebel[2] examined *terremara* sites in 1861, and a most valuable examination of the *terremare*, or 'lake -dwellings on dry land', was begun at Castellazzo di Fontanellato in Parma by Pigorini, the first results of the examination appearing in the *Notizie degli Scavi di Antichità* in 1889. T. E. Peet in *The Stone and Bronze Ages in Italy and Sicily* (1909) has a full account of this and subsequent discoveries with a bibliography.

Excavations at Hallstatt[3] in Austria between 1847 and 1864 showed the transition from the use of bronze to that of iron. In this Celtic burying ground, iron is found gradually superseding bronze. First it is used for ornaments, then for edging cutting-tools; then iron objects which are copies of their bronze forerunners are found, and finally iron objects made with a technique suitable to iron. Examples of the Hallstatt period have since been found in Styria, Carniola, Bosnia, Epirus, Spain, and Britain.

The La Tène[4] lake-dwellings at the north end of Lake Neuchâtel were first discovered in 1876, and show a later phase of Celtic work in the Iron Age, succeeding Hallstatt. This stage has been traced through France to England.

Probably the most sensational discoveries in the history of early European civilization were those of Heinrich Schliemann,[5] a shop assistant who read Homer. Through Virchow's help, he was enabled to dig at Troy, and discovered a new period of prehistory and a new field for archaeological research. He was the first man who had the idea of testing literary traditions by archaeological facts. In his day it was

[1] *Atti d. Soc. Ital. d. Sci. Nat.*, III.
[2] *Gaz. di Parma*, No. 169.
[3] Baron von Sacken, *Das Grabfeld von Hallstatt*, 1868.
[4] V. Gross, *La Tène, un oppidum Helvète*, 1886; Vouga, E., *Les Helvètes à la Tène*, 1886.
[5] *Mycenae*, 1876; *Tiryns*, 1886; Schuchhardt, C., *Schliemann's Excavations*, 1892.

generally believed that Greek history began with the first Olympiad in 776 B.C. Schliemann's work at Troy in 1871–73, 1878, and 1889–90, the year of his death, at Mycenae in 1874–76, and at Tiryns in 1884–85, startled the world with the knowledge that Greek civilization was not a unique and startling phenomenon, but was preceded by cultures far older.

A. Milchöfer's *Anfänge der Kunst in Griechenland* of 1883 boldly inferred from the distribution of a kind of seal-stone especially frequent in Crete that this island was the centre of the Mycenaen civilization, which had gradually spread throughout the Aegean Islands, and the results of exploration between 1878 and 1900 generally showed that Crete was really the home of this culture which had spread through the Islands and reached continental Greece. In 1894, Sir Arthur Evans arrived at Knossos, and began excavations which he carried on for many years. In the first year he discovered the Cretan pictographic writing,[1] and by 1900 had started the excavation of the palace of the legendary King Minos.[2] Professor J. L. Myres has summarized all the work in Aegean research in 'The Cretan Labyrinth'[3] with a full bibliography, but two outstanding discoveries may be mentioned.

In 1894 J. L. Myres[4] excavated several cemeteries in Cyprus, as he modestly said, 'to determine special points at small cost'. These special points enabled him to synchronize the Bronze Age culture of that island with those of the Aegean and that of Syria. Between 1896 and 1899, the British School of Athens, working under D. G. Hogarth's direction, excavated Phylakopi[5] in Melos, one of the centres of manufacture of obsidian implements for export among the Cyclades, and found a great deal of pottery and other material which made it possible to equate chronologically the culture of the Cyclades with that of Crete.

During the same period, discoveries in Egypt were furnishing knowledge of the relations of that ancient civilization with the Aegean. The first general interest in Egyptian antiquities began with Napoleon's expedition to Egypt in the years 1798 to 1801. He was accompanied by several archaeologists, and a great deal of material was brought back, including the famous Rosetta stone with its inscription in hieroglyphic and demotic Egyptian and Greek which was deciphered by Champollion

---

[1] 'Cretan Pictographs,' *R.B.A.*, Oxford, 1894: in full (1895–96). In 1952, Michael Ventris discovered that this writing was Greek. See J. Chadwick and M. Ventris, 'Greek Records in the Minoan Script,' *Antiquity*, XXVII, 1953. See also Ventris and Chadwick, *Journ. of Hellenic Studies*, LXXIII, 1953.
[2] 'Excavations at Knossos,' *B.S.A.*, 1900–35.
[3] *J.R.A.I.*, 1933, LXIII, 269.
[4] *Ashmolean Museum Guide*, 1931, 58.
[5] British School: *Excavations at Phylakopi*, 1904.

in 1821. Between 1850 and 1880, Mariette was Director of Archaeology in Egypt, and founded the Museum at Cairo, and in 1881 the Egypt Exploration Fund was started in London, and the Mission Archéologique at Cairo.

The Egypt Exploration Fund was most fortunate from the beginning in having Sir W. M. Flinders Petrie as a field director. He began work at Tanis in 1883. In 1890 he recognized Egyptian imports and examples of Egyptian influence of the Eighteenth Dynasty in objects from the tombs at Mycenae, and in the same year published Mycenaean pottery from Eighteenth Dynasty tombs in Egypt.[1] In the same year he had the good fortune to find Aegean pottery in a Twelfth Dynasty building at Kahun.[2] Further examples were published in *Tell-el-Amarna* in 1894[3] and in the *Royal Tombs of Abydos* in 1901.[4] For earlier Aegean periods a date mark was found by Tsountas[5] in 1898, who discovered a Fourth–Sixth Dynasty type of bead in an early Cycladic tomb. The connexions between Egypt and Crete and the Aegean are especially well shown in the Ashmolean Museum at Oxford, owing to the work of Sir Arthur Evans, Sir W. M. Flinders Petrie, and D. G. Hogarth and J. L. Myres.

While the study of predynastic Egypt belongs largely to the present century, Petrie and Quibell began it with the excavation of Naqada and Ballas in 1895. The type series of objects from this very early civilization is exhibited in the Ashmolean Museum. The publication of his work at Diospolis Parva (Hu) in 1898 brought order out of chaos in the dating of prehistoric Egyptian remains. Petrie devised a system of sequence dates, distributing the objects according to typological methods into periods, to each of which a number is allotted. He began with S.D. 30, foreseeing the possibility of discoveries of yet earlier periods. Discoveries at Badari and Tasa made by Brunton in the present century have justified his belief.

Early excavations in Mesopotamia were inspired by interest in the Bible. Across the Tigris from Mosul rise the great mounds of the ruins of Nineveh, the city to which Jonah was sent to preach. Paul Botta, the French Consul at Mosul, first began excavating these mounds in 1843, and was followed by Sir Henry Layard, Hormuzd Rassam, W. K. Loftus, and George Smith of the *Daily Telegraph*, which has always taken a great interest in Mesopotamian archaeology. Smith's interest

---

[1] *J.H.S.*, XI, 271 (quoted by Myres).
[2] *Illahun, Kahun, and Gurob,* 9, 16.
[3] p. 16.
[4] p. 46.
[5] *Eph.*, 1898–99 (quoted by Myres).

was aroused by fragments of a story of the Flood found in the British Museum, where he had taught himself to read the cuneiform writing by 1858.[1] The ability to read this writing is due mainly to the athletic and learned Major (afterwards Sir) Henry Rawlinson, who in 1835 began copying an inscription commemorating the exploits of King Darius, written in Persian, Susian (or Elamitic), and Babylonian, on a rock at Behistun in the Zagros Mountains of Persia, 135 feet above the village. The Babylonian inscription is on a slanting rock, very difficult to reach, and the inscription partly obliterated by water. Rawlinson began copying the cuneiform or wedge-shaped characters in 1835, and by 1838 was able to send the Persian text with a translation to London. By 1851 he had copied, transliterated and translated the greater part of the Babylonian text. It was a magnificent feat of scholarship and of physical fitness.

The discovery of texts bearing on the Old Testament induced many excavators to take the field. Sir Henry Layard worked at Ashur in 1846, and with Rassam in 1853 and 1878. In 1852 W. K. Loftus worked at Eridu and at Nippur, and in 1854 at Uruk, the Erech of Genesis. Hormuzd Hassam, friend and assistant of Layard, worked at Sippar, one of the cities that were before the flood, between 1878 and 1882, and was followed by Père Scheil in 1891, the same year that Sir E. A. Wallis-Budge worked at Tal ed Deir, at one time supposed to be the city of Agade from which Sargon took his title. E. de Sarzec, French Consul at Basra, worked at Tal Lôh, the ancient Lagash, from 1877–91, and Robert Koldewey began his excavation of Babylon in 1899. An American expedition from the University of Pennsylvania began work at Nippur in 1887. The growth of knowledge about this part of the world may be traced in Layard's *Nineveh and Babylon*, 1853; E. de Sarzec and L. Heuzy's *Découvertes en Chaldée*, 1884 onward; H. V. Hilprecht's *Babylonian Excavations of the University of Pennsylvania*, 1893 onward; A. Winckler's *Tell-el-Amarna Letters*, 1897; and J. P. Peters' *Nippur* in 1897. Among general works are H. Radau's *Early Babylonian History* and R. W. Rogers' *History of Babylonia and Assyria*, both in 1900.

In connexion with the development of knowledge about Mesopotamia may be mentioned that of ancient Elam and of the ancient empire of the Hittites. The first regular work at Susa (in Elam), a ruined city on the Persian border, was done by J. P. de Morgan, whose *Mémoires de la Délégation en Perse* run from 1899 to 1906. In 1861 Georges Perrot was sent to investigate the great inscription of Augustus at Ancyra, and

---

[1] The *Daily Telegraph* paid his expenses to visit Nineveh, where he found other parts of the story in the library of Assurbanipal.

while there, went on to Boghaz-Keui in Cappadocia, where he found a curious sculptured art, not Mesopotamian or Greek. The Reverend Greville Chester collected seals and amulets from this area, and in 1895 D. G. Hogarth sent his first collection of Hittite seals from northern Syria to the Ashmolean Museum,[1] the nucleus of a collection now as good as any in the world, and described by him in *Hittite Seals* in 1920. In 1884 Wright's *Empire of the Hittites* appeared, and in 1906 Hugo Winckler established the fact that Boghaz-Keui was their capital. Since this was written in 1935, O. R. Gurney has published *The Hittites* (Pelican, London, 1952), a most valuable study.

Archaeological discoveries raised new problems of races and migrations. Salomon Reinachs' *Le Mirage oriental* in 1893 argued that the source of inspiration of the early Mediterranean cultures was from the North rather than from the East, and Sergi's *La stirpe Mediterranea*[2] of 1895, and Myres's 'Prehistoric Man in the Eastern Mediterranean'[3] of 1896, using palaeolithic as well as later evidence, supported the view of the spread of a Mediterranean race from Hamitic Africa. They would have nothing of the Aryans as the source of civilization in Europe.

In America archaeologists were studying the antiquities of the aboriginal population. In 1873 Charles Jones wrote of *The Antiquities of the Southern Indians, particularly of the Georgia Tribes*. In 1877 W. H. Dall published a study 'On Succession in the Shell-Heaps of the Aleutian Islands,'[4] and C. C. Abbott wrote *The Stone Age in New Jersey*. A. F. Bandelier's reports on the archaeology of Mexico[5] and the south western United States[6] appeared in 1884 and 1890, and W. H. Holmes dealt with ancient pottery of the Mississippi Valley[7] in 1886, with ancient art in Columbia[8] in 1888, the ancient cities of Mexico[9] between 1895 and 1897, and with stone implements of the Potomac-Chesapeake region[10] in 1897. Cyrus Thomas wrote on 'The Problem of the Ohio Mounds'[11] in 1889, Thomas Wilson on the swastika[12] in 1896, and J. W. Fewkes on Arizona[13] in 1898.

---

[1] *Guide*, 1931.
[2] See pp. 88–89.
[3] *Science Progress*, I–III.
[4] *Contrib. to N. Am. Ethn.*, Vol. I.
[5] *Arch. Inst. of Am., Am. series*, Vol. II.
[6] *Arch. Inst. of Am., Am. series*, Vol. III.
[7] *B.A.E.*, 4.
[8] *Ibid.*, 6.
[9] *Field Columbian Museum*, Vol. III.
[10] *B.A.E.*, 15.
[11] *Ibid.*, 8.
[12] *U.S. Nat. Mus. Rep.*, 1894; Washington, 1896.
[13] *B.A.E.*, 17.

VII. PALAEONTOLOGY

Again we return to the year 1859. When in that year the geologists Lyell and Prestwich, Falconer the palaeontologist, John Evans the archaeologist, and Flower the anatomist visited Abbeville, and agreed with Boucher de Perthes concerning the great antiquity of the flint implements which he had excavated from the gravel terraces, then indeed all these sciences could converge as one in the work of studying the development of man from the most remote antiquity. Before the publication of the *Origin of Species* there had been many, like Lamarck and Geoffroy Saint-Hilaire, who believed that there had been a continuous development which could be shown by the various strata in the rocks, and Edouard Lartet, who had discovered Pliopithecus in 1836 and Dryopithecus in 1850, both in tertiary deposits, announced as early as 1845 that Sansan, the place of their discovery, might well conceal the ancestor of modern man, since it had revealed ancestral forms of present-day apes. Cuvier's great authority generally won the day with its insistence on the immutability of species, and on recurrent catastrophes and recreations. After 1859 it was easier to admit the possibility of tracing the ancestry of living forms back into remote ages. In the year 1859 Sir Joseph Prestwich published 'On the Occurrence of Flint Implements associated with the Remains of Extinct Mammalia' in the *Proceedings of the Royal Society*, and A. Gaudry, the result of his work at Amiens in 'Contemporanéité de l'espèce humaine et de diverses espèces animales aujourd'hui éteintes' in the *Comptes rendus de l'Académie des Sciences*. In 1863 appeared Lyell's *Geological Evidences of the Antiquity of Man*, and in 1865[1] Sir John Lubbock invented the now familiar terms 'Palaeolithic' for the old Stone Age and 'Neolithic' for the later periods or new Stone Age.[2] Roughly speaking the Neolithic period was characterized by implements which were ground or polished in the final shaping process, while the Palaeolithic was marked by the absence of polishing. Palaeolithic implements occur in quaternary deposits, and neolithic only in later deposits.

Since geological evidence is of such great importance in the study of early man, it will be well here to mention briefly the framework within which students work, and the progress made in building it during the latter part of the nineteenth century. The order of formation of the various rocks of the earth may be determined by their fossils. For

---

[1] *Prehistoric Times.*

[2] Polished implements are common in forested areas. In open areas they are much less common, or absent.

example, the Palaeozoic (old life)period displays the fossils of fishes, the first reptiles, and the first amphibians. The Mesozoic (middle life) period is the age of reptiles and birds, and of the most primitive mammals. The Tertiary period of new life (Cenozoic period) is the era of mammals, and displays the first traces of man. The Quaternary or Pleistocene (most new) period is the era of man. As an example of the way in which this framework was made, Lyell's work on tertiary strata in Italy in 1828 may be mentioned. He divided the period into four parts, characterized by the proportion of living to extinct species of shell-fish found in each stratum. His *Principles of Geology*, first published in 1830, embodies these divisions: Eocene (dawn of recent species), Oligocene (a few of the recent species), Miocene and Pliocene (less and more of recent species). The book went through many editions and was always revised to keep in touch with the progress of discovery, as was his work on the antiquity of man.

The principal factor in our present system of determining the chronology of prehistoric man is the geological theory of an ice age including periods of extreme glaciation with milder intervals. The beginning of this study was made by J. L. R. Agassiz, a Swiss geologist and zoologist, who was the first to make a study of the movements of glaciers, their moraines, glacial striations, and roches moutonnées. He came to the conclusions in his *Études sur les glaciers* in 1840 that in a period geologically recent, that is, the Quaternary, Switzerland had been like Greenland, and from a study of glacial deposits it was possible to work out a series of periods of more or less glaciation. James Geikie, a Scotch geologist, in *The Great Ice Age and its Relation to the Antiquity of Man*, 1874, 1894, and *Prehistoric Europe*, 1881, concluded that there were five interglacial periods in Great Britain, and that the palaeolithic deposits of the Pleistocene or Quaternary period were not post-glacial, but pre-glacial and inter-glacial. The great work of Penck and Brückner on the Alpine glaciers belonged to the next century.

As early as 1858[1] Lartet had recognized that the history of men and animals must be placed on a geological basis, and had used the fossil remains of animals in dividing the history of early man into different epochs, such as the age of the reindeer and the age of the elephant and rhinoceros, and 'L'Âge du Renne' still holds the field. In 1860 he began

---

[1] *Sur les migrations anciennes des Mammifères de l'époque actuelle.* Boule's *Les Hommes Fossiles* and Reinach's *Répertoire de l'art quaternaire* have been largely followed in the history of prehistoric archaeology and art.

exploring the caves of Massat (Ariège) and Aurignac (Haute Garonne), and in the former discovered a broken stag's antler, engraved with the figure of a bear's head, which he assigned to the quaternary period. This work was published with two illustrations, that of the bear's head, and that of a horse's head from Chaffaud discovered in 1853, in the *Annales des Sciences naturelles, Zool.*, Tome xv, 1851. In 1862–63 Lartet and his friend Henry Christy, an English banker, began the exploration of the caves and rock shelters in the valley of the Vézère in Dordogne. In 1864 they found the famous piece of ivory engraved with the figure of a mammoth, and published their first article together on the art of the reindeer age in the *Révue Archéologique*, I, p. 233. In the same year Gabriel de Mortillet founded his review *Matériaux pour l'histoire de l'homme*, which was of the utmost importance in systematizing the numberless facts of an infant science. Mortillet was succeeded by Émile Cartailhac as editor in 1869.

In the year 1864 George Busk first reported the Gibraltar female cranium at a meeting of the British Association at Bath, mentioning where it was found, and saying that it resembled the Neanderthal cranium[1] and was obviously of great antiquity. Among living races it most closely resembled the Tasmanian. The cranium had been discovered while blasting at Forbes Quarry in 1848, and had been presented to the Gibraltar Scientific Society, and entered in their museum catalogue by Lieutenant Flint. Busk collected it in 1862, and after exhibiting it to several societies at home and abroad, gave it to the Royal College of Surgeons, where it now is. The British Association was much interested, and voted £150 to Busk and Falconer for examining caves in Gibraltar. Falconer was already a veteran cave hunter and palaeontologist. His work in the Sewalik Hills in India, and in Europe generally, had made him a great authority on extinct mammals, and he had collected all possible information from every excavation, including many that would probably not have been reported in an accessible fashion, like those of Colonel Wood in Gower. Falconer was fully alive to the fact that he had a new species of man to deal with, and proposed the name Homo calpicus, from the name Calpe, the ancient name for Gibraltar. He wrote to Busk of his 'Grand, Priscan, Pithecoid, Agrioblemmatous, Platycnemic, wild Homo calpicus of Gibraltar'[2] and set himself to the work of investigating the bones of the extinct animals from the Gibraltar caves. His and Busk's report to the governor of Gibraltar is on page 554 of the second volume of Falconer's *Palaeontological*

[1] See Chap. 3, p. 55.
[2] Keith, *Nature*, 1911, LXXXVII, p. 313.

Memoirs,[1] and accounts of the work may be read in the *Quarterly Journal of Geological Science* for March, 1865, and in Busk's 'On the Ancient or Quaternary Fauna of Gibraltar' in the *Transactions of the Zoological Society of London*, X, 1879.

Édouard Dupont,[2] working for the Belgian government, had the good fortune in 1865 to discover in the cave of La Naulette on the left bank of the Lesse, the chinless lower jaw of a young adult female. The deposits were undisturbed, and the jaw was at a depth of about fourteen feet of alternate layers of stalagmite and earth. The associated animals were the mammoth, Rhinoceros tichorhinus, and reindeer. In his *Précis de Paléontologie Humaine* of 1870, E. T. Hamy suggested that this massive chinless jaw belonged to the same race as the cranium found at Neanderthal.

Neanderthal remains found at Šipka[3] in 1880, at Banolas[4] in Spain in 1887, and at Malarnaud (Ariege)[5] in 1889, have been noted by Hrdlicka,[6] but the most important discovery in the establishment of the Neanderthal races was at Spy in the province of Namur in Belgium in 1886 by Marcel de Puydt, Julien Fraipont, and Max Lohest. There could be absolutely no doubt of the geological age of the deposits, and the animals were the mammoth, Rhinoceros tichorhinus, and others associated with the period. There were a great number of the kind of worked flint flakes of the type that we now call Mousterian from the type station Le Moustier discovered in 1908. With these were found two adult male skeletons of the Neanderthal type. Fraipont and Lohest's 'Récherches ethnographiques sur les ossements humains découverts dans les dépôts d'une grotte quaternaire à Spy' in the *Archives de Biologie*, VII, 1886, put an end to the hypothesis that previous examples of the same type had been pathological, and confirmed the opinion of those who believed in the existence of a distinct type of man hitherto unknown.

The last Neanderthal discoveries of the century were made at Krapina in Croatia by Professor K. Gorjanovic-Kramberger between 1895 and 1905. Parts of over twenty skeletons, partly calcined, were excavated from the fillings of an old rock-shelter, with the typical

[1] 1868.

[2] 'Etude sur les fouilles scientifiques . . . dans les cavernes de la Lesse,' *Bull. de l'Acad. roy. de Belgique*, XXII, 1866.

[3] Wankel, 1880; Schaafhausen, 1881, 1883; Virchow, 1882; Maška (discoverer), 1886.

[4] Found by Roura: rep. by Cazurro, 1909; Harlé, Pacheco, and Obermaier, 1912.

[5] H. Filhol, 1889: found by Regnault.

[6] A. Hrdlička, *J.R.A.I.*, 1927, LVII, 249 (preceding notes are his).

Mousterian implements, bones of extinct mammals, and the remains of fires. The interesting thing about the discovery was the opportunity it gave to study the children, who had no brow-ridges like their parents, and to notice that the Neanderthal people were both long and round-headed. The various reports are included in the final memoir by the discoverer, *Der diluviale Mensch von Krapina in Kroatien*, 1906.

Meanwhile other types of early man had been discovered, and other evidences of his handiwork in high and far off times.

In the previous chapter we spoke of the discovery of the 'Red lady of Paviland' by Dean Buckland in 1823. Though Quatrefages and Hamy had considered in the *Crania Ethnica*[1] that the bones showed the characters of the Cro-Magnon people, it was not until 1913 that Sollas[2] determined that the bones were those of a man of the Cro-Magnon or Aurignacian period.

The Engis cranium found by Dr Schmerling in 1833, similar to the Neolithic type, was also mentioned. Lyell, among many others, doubted its antiquity at first, as several do to this day. But in 1860 he entered the cavern, which is very difficult of access, and carefully went over Schmerling's evidence.[3] The cranium had been found in breccia five feet down, associated with rhinoceros, horse, and reindeer bones. Lyell agreed with Schmerling that the deposits had evidently been washed into the cave from above, and that there were also bear, wolf, stag, and other bones of animals not extinct. He agreed with Huxley that the Engis cranium approached the Caucasian type, while the Neanderthal cranium of 1857 was much more ape-like. However, Engis was undoubtedly ancient, and he agreed with Pictet that though the bones of both extinct and existent fauna were associated with the cranium, we might well find some early post-pliocene races undistinguished from modern, just as we find many existent mammals which have not changed their bony structure since that remote time. We need not necessarily say that the Neanderthal is earlier because it is inferior, for the inferior need not always be earlier than the superior, and might be co-existent with it, or later.

Lartet's and Christy's work at Aurignac in 1860 established the fact that man was co-existent with extinct animals, and also established the type of flint-implements and culture which we now call Aurignacian, the same culture as that of Engis and Paviland.

In 1866 Ferry and Arcelin, interested in Lyell's work, began the

[1] 1873–82.
[2] *J.R.A.I.*, XLIII, 1913.
[3] *Geol. Ev. of Antiq. of Man*, 1863 (second edition, 1873), pp. 67 ff., 89 ff.

excavation of a site near the village of Solutré, a business which occupied Arcelin until his death in 1904. In 1890 in *L'Anthropologie*, I, he published 'Les nouvelles fouilles de Solutré', describing how at the bottom were Aurignacian hearths, then an Aurignacian midden above them, and above that, a different culture, characterized by the beautiful laurel-leaf-shaped flint implements. The period during which these were made is known as the Solutréan.

In the year 1868 Édouard Lartet's son, Louis,[1] discovered the Cro-Magnon man. Cro-Magnon is not far from Les Eyzies in Dordogne. Workmen building a railway discovered the spot, and Lartet set to work on it. The hearths uncovered displayed the typical Aurignacian flint-implements, and bones of the reindeer period. At the back of the shelter, so disposed as to suggest burial, were the remains of five people, with a number of pierced sea-shells and other ornaments. The skeletons were those of tall, lanky people, like that from Paviland, and the skulls with their flattened vaults, long from front to back, with short, broad faces, were more massive than those of living races, but not unlike those of many alive today. De Quatrefages and Hamy in the *Crania Ethnica* described them as prototypes of the Cro-Magnon race. In 1872 Massénat[2] discovered at Laugerie-Basse a skeleton accompanied by sea-shells, which Hamy assigned to the same race, and Lartet and Chaplain-Duparc[3] at Duruthy, Sordes (Landes), found another Cro-Magnon skeleon accompanied by bear and lion canine teeth, pierced for suspension, and beautifully engraved. Further human remains of the Cro-Magnon type were found at Brünn[4], 1891, and at Předmost[5] and Les Hoteaux[6] in 1894.

About a mile to the east of Mentone, just in Italy, are the red rocks of Grimaldi, rising from the Mediterranean. During the course of the construction of a road along these cliffs from Marseilles to Genoa, Émile Rivière[7] took occasion to investigate the caves and rock shelters just above the road. In 1872, in the Cavillon shelter, he found the

[1] 'Une sépulture des Troglodytes du Périgord,' *B.S.A. de Paris*, III, 1868; also *Matériaux pour l'historie de l'homme*, 1869.

[2] E. Massénat, P. Lalande, E. Cartailhac, 'Un squelette humain de l'âge du Renne à Laugerie-Basse,' *Matériaux*, VII, 1872; Hamy, *B.S.A. de Paris*, 1874.

[3] 'Une sépulture des anciens troglodytes des Pyrénées,' *Matériaux*, IX, 1874.

[4] G. Hervé, 'Le squelette humain de Brünn,' *R.E.A.*, III, 1893; Makowski, A., 'Der diluviale Mensch im Löss von Brünn,' *M.A.G.W.*, XXII, 1892.

[5] Found by Wankel, Maška, and Křiz: Maška, K., 'Vorläufige Berichte über den Fund diluvialer Menschen-skelette in Předmost,' *C.D.G.A.*, 1894, p. 137; 'Nalež diluvialniho človeka v Předmosti,' *Anal. l'Anthr.*, VI, 1895.

[6] Found by Tournier and Guillon: *La Préhistoire*, II, Sect. 2, Chap. 8; *B.S.A.P.*, ser. IV, vol. VI, 1895, 388, 419.

[7] *De l'antiquité de l'homme dans les Alpes maritimes*, 1887.

skeleton of a man just under stalagmite, the l'homme de Menton. In the following year he found three more at Baousso da Torre, and 1874–75 discovered the bodies of two children in the Grotte des Enfants. The culture was Aurignacian, and the skeletons of the Cro-Magnon type. The Prince of Monaco, impressed by these discoveries began work on the caves of Mentone in 1895, calling to his assistance Villeneuve the historian, Boule the geologist and palaeontologist, Verneau the anatomist, and Cartailhac the archaeologist. The magnificent publication of their work belongs to the twentieth century.[1]

Yet another race of fossil man was discovered in 1888 by Féaux and Hardy[2] in a rock shelter at Raymonden in the commune of Chancelade. The skeleton was found lying on the rock beneath three superposed Magdalenian hearths, on its left side, with arms and legs bent, the left hand under the head, and the right under the lower jaw. The body had been covered with red ochre. Hervé[3] classified the skeleton with those from Laugerie-Basse, Duruthy, and Le Placard,[4] and argued for the homogeneity of Magdalenian man, but Testut[5] showed the remarkable likeness of the skull and skeleton to those of an Eskimo. The engraved bone and ivory common to all the caves mentioned and to the type station at La Madeleine, and the discovery of the bones of a Greenland type of seal in one of the Raymonden hearths lent considerable weight to the idea of an Eskimo type of culture in France.

The great gap between the Palaeolithic and Neolithic eras was partly filled by Édouard Piette,[6] who began excavating the cave of Mas d'Azil on the river Arise in 1887, and published his work in 1895. He found a steady succession of layers from Gallo-Roman to Magdalenian, and between the Magdalenian and Neolithic a transitional culture with painted pebbles and harpoons made from stag's antlers. These, though of flattened section because of the larger amount of spongy centre in deer antler than that in reindeer antler, were the successors of the Magdalenian harpoons which had been made from the antlers of the reindeer long since extinct. Thus Piette was able to strengthen the opinion which he had expressed to the Congrès de l'Association Française as early as 1875,[7] that the neolithic industry had developed by stages out of the

---

[1] See p. 197.

[2] M. Hardy, 'La station quaternaire de Raymonden,' *B.S. hist. et arch. du Périgord*, 1891; M. Féaux, *Cat. du Musée du Périgord*, 1905.

[3] 'La race des troglodytes magdaleniens,' *R.E.A.*, III, 1893.

[4] Found by Maret, 1883: E. T. Hamy, 'Nouveaux matériaux pour servir à l'étude de la paléontologie humaine,' *C.I.A.*, Paris, 1889.

[5] L. Testut, 'Recherches anthropologiques sur le squelette quaternaire de Chancelade, Dordogne,' *B.S.A. de Lyon*, VIII, 1889.

[6] 'Études d'Ethnographie préhistorique,' *L'Anthropologie*, VI, 276.

[7] Dates from Reinach, *R.A.Q.*

Palaeolithic. In 1879 very small flint implements were found at Fère-en-Tardenois by Judge Edmond Vielle (*B.S.A.* 4me Sér., i, 959, 1890), and these were assigned to yet another culture between the Azilian and the Neolithic by G. and A. de Mortillet.[1]

Various examples of the art of engraving have been mentioned, wonderful enough for people who had supposed that art began with a high degree of civilization. But more wonderful discoveries were to follow. In 1875 a Spanish nobleman, Marcellino de Sautuola, began examining the cavern of Altamira near his home at Santander, and discovered paintings of animals in black at the back of the cave. In 1879 he took his little daughter into the cave. While he was digging the little girl looked about her. Suddenly her father was amazed to hear her cry 'toros' (bulls). Following her pointing finger he looked up at the roof, and thus discovered the magnificent polychrome frescoes which have made Altamira world-famous. He communicated his discovery at once to the Archaeological Congress in 1879, and in 1880, fortified by the opinion of the geologist Vilanova, published his discovery, *Breves apuntes sobre algunos objetos prehistoricos de la provincia de Santander*. The designs on the roof were shown to the Anthropological Society of Berlin and to the Congrès de l'Association Française in 1882, and were hotly debated, Vilanova defending their antiquity against the general profound scepticism. In the same year Andrew Lang[2] called attention to the similarity of certain modern Bushman paintings to the art of the Magdalenian period, and first pointed out that such art had probably a practical purpose, not only for recording and communicating events, but also for magically ensuring success in hunting. In 1899[3] Reinach suggested that the frequency of animal figures might point to the antiquity of totemism.

Édouard Rivière[4] discovered similar paintings in the cave of La Mouthe in 1895, and François Daleau[5] at Pair-non-Pair in 1896, Daleau also finding the red oxide of iron used for pigment, and the pestles for pounding it up. Rivière met with a most unfriendly reception at the Archaeological Congress in 1897, sceptics being unconvinced even by his statement that many of the drawings had been covered by a thick layer of stalactite, and that the clay floor of the cave covered the feet of many

---

[1] A. de Mortillet, 'Les petits silex taillés à contours géométriques,' *R.E.A.*, 1896.

[2] *Mag. of Art*, V, 305.

[3] *Révue archéol.*, II, 478: Reinach, *R.A.Q.*

[4] 'La grotte de la Mouthe,' *B.S.A. de Paris*, 1897.

[5] 'Les gravures sur rocher de la caverne de Pair-non-Pair,' *Actes de la société archéol. de Bordeaux*, 1897: *L'Anthropologie*, 1898, IX.

of the pictured animals. Marcellin Boule defended him in 1898, demolishing the arguments of those who had attacked Rivière. But the sceptics were not finally convinced until the next century.

The first representation of the human form in palaeolithic art was discovered by a workman at Brassempouy (Landes), the well-known La Poire or Venus of Brassempouy, in 1892. In 1894 Piette and Laporterie discovered in the course of excavations the 'figurine à la ceinture', the 'figurine à la pelérine', and others, carved of mammoth ivory.[1] Shortly afterwards similar statuettes in steatite were discovered in the caves at Grimaldi. These statuettes were poor things when compared with the marvellous representations of animals of the same period, many of them having enormous buttocks and breasts in proportion to the rest of the body. Piette[2] divided his statuettes into two classes, one being modelled from a race unknown, and the other apparently from a race akin to the Bushmen and Hottentots, many of whom are unusually steatopygous. Reinach[3] discussed the statuettes from Grimaldi. The 'negroid' skeletons from there had not yet been discovered.

The problems of chronology and nomenclature exercised the prehistorians from the beginning. The geologists gave the idea of stratification, and the earliest workers were geologists. Geikie established a quaternary series of glaciations and warmer periods. Lartet[4] thought that the evidence from the animal bones might be used to divide the Palaeolithic age into parts, naming each period after the most characteristic animal, and W. Boyd Dawkins, in his valuable and entertaining book *Cave Hunting* in 1874, employed a similar method of division. These methods serve for the larger divisions, but as Gabreil de Mortillet saw, while the flora and fauna can show whether the excavator has to do with a cold or warm period, and can be correlated with the geological evidence of glacial action, they are not enough to distinguish the subdivisions. In the *Matériaux* for 1869, he published an 'Essai d'une classification des cavernes fondée sur les produites de l'industrie humaine', separating the Palaeolithic period into four parts, according to the type of implements found. The first was the Chellean, which he had formerly called Acheulean, named after Chelles, a place where Boucher de Perthes had discovered the *coup de poing* in the river gravels. The next three were called Mousterian, Solutrean, and Magdalenian, in honour of the work of Lartet and Christy, who had discovered a different

[1] Reinach R. A. Q.
[2] *L'Anthropologie*, 1895, VI, p. 137.
[3] 'Statuette de femme nue découverte dans une des grottes de Menton,' *L'Anthropologie*, 1898, IX, p. 26.
[4] See p. 167.

type of implements at Le Moustier, Solutré, and La Madelaine. Their work, which had partly appeared in many papers, was published as a whole by Rupert Jones in 1875 as *Reliquiae Aquitanicae*. M. de Mortillet and his son maintained the same classification in the *Musée préhistorique* in 1881, and in *Le Préhistorique* in 1883. Before the third edition in 1900, the MM. de Mortillet saw the need for filling the gap between the upper Palaeolithic and the Neolithic, and used the discoveries of Chamaison and Darbas at La Tourasse in 1891 to name a new period, the Tourassian, a name which has since been changed to Azilian in honour of Piette's discoveries.

The best paper on chronology was Marcellin Boule's in the *Révue d'Anthropologie* for 1888–89, an 'Essai de paléontologie stratigraphique de l'homme', in which he showed the necessity for employing the geological and palaeontological evidence for fixing the great divisions, and the types of industries for establishing the subdivisions within them.

Mortillet's classification was adopted by John Evans[1] in England, by Rutot[2] in Belgium, and by Morselli in his *Antropologia generale*[3] in Italy. The position of the Aurignacian was not determined until the present century.

Discoveries of rudely worked flint, or of flint apparently worked in tertiary deposits, by the Abbé Bourgeois in 1867 at Thenay, Riberio near Lisbon in 1878, and others[4] caused the MM. de Mortillet to name a new period, previous to the Chellean, as the Eolithic.[5] In 1889 Prestwich[6] published eoliths from Ightham in Kent, and the controversy as to what man can do with flint and what nature can do in the way of stimulating his handiwork is still simmering.

One thing the controversy did do. It pointed to a culture and a type of man far more ancient than any yet discovered. Lartet had discovered Pliopithecus and Dryopithecus, and asserted that as he had found ancestors of present-day apes, so ancestors of present-day men might be found. Darwin's *Origin* had pointed the way to a missing link, and the geological records led people to expect continuity in the development of man as of other creatures.

In 1891 Eugène Dubois[7] discovered in Java a human skull which did

---

[1] *The Ancient Stone Implements*, etc., 1872.
[2] *Conditions d'existence de l'homme*, 1897.
[3] Rome, Naples, Turin, 1888.
[4] Boule, *Les Hommes Fossiles*, 1923, 144.
[5] *Le Préhistorique*, 1883.
[6] 'On the Occurrence of Palaeolithic Flint Implements in the Neighbourhood of Ightham . . .,' *Q.J.G.S.L.*, XLV, 1889.
[7] See G. Elliot Smith, *The Search for Man's Ancestors*, 1931.

not belong to the genus Homo, but had human characters. He gave it the name Pithecanthropus, a name invented by Haeckel for a hypothetical missing link between ape and man.

This startling discovery was the result of a well thought out campaign, and of amazing luck. While he was still a lecturer in anatomy at Amsterdam, Dubois planned to go to the Indo-Malay region. As he could not get the Colonial Department to finance an expedition, he took a post in a hospital in Sumatra, and, against all advice, gave up a promising career in Holland and sailed from Amsterdam in 1887. He had been greatly impressed by two discoveries, first, that of the Neanderthal men at Spy in 1886, which made him believe that there must be some ancestral form not so definitely human, and secondly, Martin's discovery in the same year in the Sewalik Hills in India of fossil ancestors of the apes in the Malay Archipelago. He argued that these tertiary forms in India must have migrated at the time of the first quaternary glaciation of northern India by the then existing land bridge to the hotter climate of the islands, and that in some of these islands, the more generalized and therefore more man-like anthropoid ancestors of the present apes and of man might be found in the quaternary deposits. He expected, as Darwin, Lyell, and Wallace had done, to find ancestral forms of man and ape in the present homes of the anthropoid apes, the gorilla and chimpanzee in Africa, and the gibbon and orangutan in the Malay Archipelago.[1]

Between 1888 and 1891 he sent home a vast number of fossils from Sumatra and Java. In September, 1891, at Trinil in Java, he discovered the skull-cap and tooth of the fossil which he had expected to find. In 1892 he discovered the thigh-bone in the same geological layer. At no time in the history of exploration has there been such a coincidence of luck and judgement.

Before leaving Java Dubois published his account *Pithecanthropus erectus, eine menschenähliche Übergangsform aus Java* in 1894, and on returning home in 1895, exhibited Pithecanthropus at the Third International Zoological Congress at Leyden, at which Virchow, Flower, Milne Edwards, and many other anthropologists were present. In the same year he exhibited the fossils in London and many other European cities, and in 1898, at the Fourth International Zoological Congress in Cambridge, demonstrated on an endocranial cast the transitional nature

---

[1] E. Dubois, 'On the Desirability of an Investigation into the Pleistocene Fauna of the Dutch East Indies,' *Natuurkundig Tijdschrift voor Nederlandsch-Indie*, Vol. XLVIII, part 2, pp. 148–65: quoting Darwin, *Descent*, 1871, VI, 199; Lyell, *Antiquity of Man*, 1863, 499; Wallace, *Malay Archipelago*, 1886, 61. From Elliot Smith, *op. cit.*, pp. 12 ff.

of Pithecanthropus. Nothing so startling was found after 1891 until Mr W. C. Pei found the brain-case of the Peking man in 1929.

VIII. RECAPITULATION

In the course of a long chapter we have seen how the publication of The *Origin of Species* and the recognition of the truth of the contentions of Boucher de Perthes changed the whole outlook of all the sciences that bear on the study of man. We attempted to show how the social conditions of the time acted on the science of biology, and how the development of biological science from Darwin, through Weismann and Lloyd Morgan and Lankester, reacted on sociological theories, their authors usually beginning with the ideas of an earlier period, such as those of de Gobineau, Marx, Bentham, Mill, or Comte, and making a more or less good job of fitting sociological to biological theory. The fact that the majority of the authors fall into schools—selectionist, environmental, *laissez-faire*, sociologistic, and so on—goes to show how often a part rather than the whole of the Darwinian theory was applied to social facts. The whole atmosphere of social studies, whether of material culture or of sociology, religion, and law, was charged with inquiries into the customs of primitive peoples, in an attempt to discover the origins and development of civilization. While it is true that some investigations made the problem too simple and the scheme of evolution unilinear, the better were aware of the evolutionary process as growing like Darwin's tree, and their schemes were large enough to embrace the methods of all schools. The majority of investigators approached their problems psychologically, assuming that the intellect and emotions of the peoples of the earth differed in degree rather than in kind, and that similar things might happen under similar conditions in many places. While they mainly believed in the monogenesis of man, they believed in the polygenesis of his inventions.

Towards the end of the century several writers pointed out the importance of studying the history of the various primitive peoples, especially as shown in their migrations and borrowings. F. Ratzel[1] was of the opinion that there was no necessary spatial limit to the borrowing or migration of single aspects of a culture or of whole culture complexes. In an investigation of the history of the bow in Africa,[2] he first employed

[1] Author of *Anthropo-Geographie*, 1882–91. A standard classic.
[2] F. Ratzel, 'Die geogr. Verbreitung des Bogens u. der Pfeile in Afrika,' *Ber. K. S. Ges. Wiss. Phil-Hist. Kl.*, 1887; 'Die Afrikanischen Bögen,' *Abb. K. S. Ges. Wiss. Phil-Hist. Kl.*, Bd. XIII, iii, 1891; 'Beitr. zur Kentniss d. Verbreitung d. Bogens u. d. Speeres im indo-afrikan. Völkerkreis,' *Ber. K. S. Ges. Wiss.*, 1893; Ankermann on Ratzel, *Z.E.*, 1905, p. 54, n. 2.

the 'criterion of form'. If he found agreement between forms, other than that arising automatically out of the nature, material, and purpose of the objects he was examining, he assumed an historical connexion or borrowing, even though these forms were widely separated and the distribution discontinuous. His pupil, Leo Frobenius,[1] developed out of this a theory of 'culture-circles'. While investigating the cultures of Melanesia and West Africa in 1898–99, he came to the conclusion that a genetic connexion existed not only between single elements of these cultures, but between these cultures as a whole. His examination presented to him a large number of individual agreements. It was he who first thought of taking the number of such agreements between different cultures, and so applying what he called the 'criterion of quantity'. In 1932, Dr van Bulck applied the 'criterion of continuity', i.e. looking for forms in areas between separated areas in which these forms are found.[2]

In previous chapters a list of books in which travellers or explorers had described individual peoples or areas was given. To do the same for this period would make an intolerably long and tedious list. Only a few outstanding books which contributed largely to an improvement in method of investigation, or investigated peoples in a new manner, or added to or changed existing theories, can be mentioned. No better account of the religious experience of a primitive people has been written than Bishop Callaway's *Religion of the Amazulu*, published by the Folk-Lore Society in 1870. Very few works have ever adopted his excellent plan of giving information about his informants, their personality, and aptitude for the work he entrusted to them, their intelligence, and emotional attitude. In *The Melanesians* of 1891, Bishop Codrington introduced a new category into the study of comparative religion, that of *mana*, 'a force altogether distinct from physical power, which acts in all kinds of ways for good and evil, and which it is of the greatest advantage to possess or control'. It is 'what works to effect everything which is beyond the ordinary power of men, outside the common processes of nature'. Whatever has mana is taboo, that is, not to be treated in the ordinary profane way, but as sacred in the sense of the Latin word *sacer*. Such power may work through a spirit, but need not. In 1898 W. J. McGee[3] published an account of the Siouan *wakan*, a word with connotations similar to that of mana, and in 1899 Spencer and Gillen

---

[1] L. Frobenius, 'Der Ursprung der afrikanischen Kulturen.' *Z.E.*, 1898.

[2] Van Bulck, *Beiträge zur Methodik der Völkerkunde*, Vienna, 1932. See Clyde Kluckholn, 'Reflections on the Kulturkreislehre,' *American Anthropologist*, 1938, 157–96.

[3] *B.A.E.*, 15, 182.

published *The Native Tribes of Central Australia*. These tribes had no notion of a god or gods as far as they could discover. Certain of their *churinga* stones and other objects appeared to possess power, but no spirit, and their religion belonged 'to the mana-taboo type, the mana element being the impersonal religious force which is somehow apprehended and manifested in their totemic ceremonies, and the taboo being represented by the penalties which fall on those who approach sacred things without due preparation and precaution'.[1] All of these works had a powerful effect during the present century on the study of comparative religion, offering as they did a convincing hypothesis for the origin of religion, and a category for many phenomena which could not be explained by Tylor's animism.[2] Moreover, discovery by Spencer and Gillen of a highly developed totemism altered Frazer's whole outlook on the subject, and the general belief that they had found an ancient and isolated culture influenced all European and English theories of the origin and development of institutions and beliefs more than any other ethnographical work ever written.[3]

Among valuable works on Africa may be mentioned the admirable studies of *The Tshi-Speaking Peoples*, 1887, *The Ewe-speaking Peoples*, 1890, and *The Yoruba-Speaking Peoples*, 1894, by A. B. Lewis; and Mary Kingsley's *Travels in West Africa*, 1897, and *West African Studies*, 1899. She it was who first noted the importance of the queen-mothers of West Africa.

Dr Franz Boas set a very high standard for all ethnographers in *The Central Eskimo*, published by the Bureau of American Ethnology in 1888. In it he treated the distribution of all the tribes as influenced by geographical conditions, described in minute detail their methods of gaining a living, their manufactures, methods of transportation, trade, habitations, dress, social and religious life, traditions, science, and arts. Few monographs reach this standard. We can see the relation of every feature to every other, and its true function in the whole culture. In addition there is a full bibliography. Ling Roth collected all that was known about *The Tasmanians* in 1899.

Besides the advance of the biological and social sciences, we have seen the rapid development of the study of archaeology and palaeontology from the collection of curios into a science closely linked with the

[1] T. K. Penniman, 'The Arunta Religion,' *Sociological Review*, Jan., 1929.
[2] See p. 138.
[3] R. R. Marett and T. K. Penniman, *Spencer's Last Journey*, 1931; *Spencer's Scientific Correspondence*, 1932.

others, just as the past is linked to the present and is necessary for its explanation.

By the end of the last century then, anthropology was a recognized science, with its biological, sociological, technological, and archaeological parts all working in harmony, and its steady progress seemed assured.

5

THE CRITICAL PERIOD
1900–1935

I. THE SUBJECT OUTLINED

THE period between 1900 and 1935 has been named the Critical Period for two reasons. First, because there was a general tendency to be critical about the large general schemes of the pioneers of the last century, and to examine special problems much more minutely than in the past. This very specialization is the reason also for our naming the period as critical in another sense. For it appears as though there was so much in every branch of anthropology and in the many subsidiary sciences that it would be impossible for any one man to do more than to work intensively in one small part of the subject. Thus the science of man as a whole appears to be in danger of splitting into a great number of independent disciplines, the followers of each often being practically unaware of its bearing on the whole complex of race, culture, and environment. There are various signs, however, that we are in another Convergent Period, like that just previous to 1859, when different sciences were all working towards each other, and that all the intensive work now going on will arrive at a point where some new Darwin will see the relations of many special subjects, and by showing order in the chaos, begin a new Constructive Period, in which all the methods will find a place without disagreement, and to which all the sciences bearing on race, culture, environment, and on man himself, shall contribute. If this book can do no more than to make workers in special fields aware of what is going on in some other fields, it will yet perhaps have served a useful purpose.

To give a general view of the country, it will be necessary to give some idea of the history of the work in the field of biology, with the closely allied work in physical anthropology, palaeontology, and psychology. To study man's culture, we must consider the fields of economics, sociology, religion, law, language, and material arts and crafts, in the present as technology, in the past as archaeology. All these take their place in ethnology, the comparative study of the races of man and their cultures, and must be studied in connexion with geography, or the environment as conditioning man and his activities. No one anthropologist can be expert at all of these subjects, but he must at least be aware of their existence, and have an idea of what each can contribute to the other, for in the study of man one can never be certain what aspect of his life or of his activities will throw light on another.

The work of this period is so diverse, and scattered through so many periodicals and books, that it is difficult to summarize it as was done in the last chapter. Yet there are, after all, only three main divisions under which to treat it all.

First, we shall describe the progress towards understanding what man is, in his physical, mental and emotional make-up. This will include biological, palaeontological, and psychological studies and their development.

Secondly, we shall describe the progress of studies of man's cultures, past and present, as revealed by the sociological and technological sciences, and by archaeology.

Thirdly, we shall deal with the progress in knowledge of the environment, the medium in which man lives and acts.

II. PHYSICAL ANTHROPOLOGY (BIOLOGICAL STUDIES)

First, the problem of what man is. The rediscovery of Mendel's law of inheritance in 1900 turned the attention of everyone to a much more thorough examination of the causes of variation and of their transmission. In a former chapter it was pointed out that Darwin had found it difficult to account for reversions to ancestral types, and for the continuation of variation under domestication, when it would seem that the creatures ought to show less and less variation. He had played with the theory of varying mixtures of characters, but unfortunately gave up the idea in favour of one of fusion or blending of the characters of both parents. He saw, indeed, that the theory of mixtures might allow the ancestral combination to recur, and would allow a great number of variations. In 1865 Gregor Johann Mendel published the result of many years of experiment in his 'Versuche über Pflanzen-Hybriden' with the Natural History Society of Brünn.[1] Nobody appears to have paid much attention to the paper until 1900 when Tschermak in Austria, Correns in Germany, De Vries in Holland, and Bateson in England arrived independently at results resembling Mendel's.

[1] *Verh. Naturf. Ver. in Brünn*, vol. X.

Mendel had crossed tall peas, six or seven feet high, with dwarf peas, nine inches to a foot and a half tall. The offspring of the first generation were all tall. The characteristic of tallness in the first filial generation (F1), he called the dominant character, the character of shortness being recessive. When the tall hybrids were allowed to self-fertilize, which corresponds to close inbreeding in animals, there were talls and shorts in the average proportions of 3 : 1. When the dwarfs of the second filial generation (F2) were allowed to self-fertilize, their offspring, F3, were all dwarfs, or pure recessives, being pure in the character of shortness. When the talls of the F2 generation were allowed to self-fertilize, one-third of their offspring, F3, pure dominants, produced talls only. Two-thirds of them, impure dominants, produced talls and dwarfs in the ratio of 3 : 1. These results may be summarized thus, using D for the dominant character, and R for the recessive: The parents are D and R; F1 is D(R), the parenthesis showing that the recessive character is latent; F2 is 1 D plus 2D(R) plus 1R; in F3, D breeds true. R breeds true, and 2D(R) breeds in the proportion of 1D plus 2D(R) plus 1R.

Mendel explained his results by supposing that the generative cells of the F1 hybrids are of two kinds, each kind bearing only one of the two contrasted characters, and that the two kinds are produced in about equal numbers. If half of this generation, for example, has cells with the dominant character, and half has cells with the recessive character, and fertilization is fortuitous, then a quarter of the fertilized egg-cells will bear the dominant character, male dominant meeting female dominant, another quarter will bear the recessive character, male recessive meeting female recessive, and half will be impure dominants, carrying the latent recessive, male dominant meeting female recessive, and male recessive meeting female dominant. This is the theory of the segregation of the dominant and recessive characters in two different sets of germ-cells, and is known as Mendel's first law.

His second law explained a set of experiments in crossing *Y*ellow and *R*ound peas with green and *w*rinkled, Y being dominant to *g*, and R being dominant to *w*. In the F1 generation, all the hybrids were yellow and round. This generation was allowed to self-fertilize, the F2 generation showing results in the following proportion: *YR* 9, *Yw* 3, *gR* 3, *gw*1. He thus demonstrated that a pair of opposed characters will behave independently of another pair, their manifestation being controlled by dominance and recessiveness, or, in terms of this experiment, that either one of the colour factors might meet equally often with either of the shape factors, and yield results on a numerical basis, as in the previous experiment. The second law, then, is that different factors in combination segregate independently. Later work has shown various limitations on this law of independent assortment.

Naturally this discovery started a period of very active experiment, in which Bateson, Castle, Cuénot, Tschermak, and Punnett, to mention only a few, were especially prominent. The old blending theory of inheritance had led scientists into a great many unprofitable speculations about the causes of variations and their evolutionary effects, and set them to searching for hypothetical agencies which might control the production of variations. They could hardly do otherwise when they were faced with the fact that blending would rapidly produce uniformity, and also with the fact that variability continued. Mendel's discovery of the behaviour of the hereditary particles afforded an entirely new method of considering the whole matter. The possible permutations and combinations of these particles are many in the fusion of eggs and sperms, and will account for the continuance of what may be called quantitative variability.

Besides this variability which may be compared to that shown by the many possible grouping of cards in a pack, and the possible dropping out of a part of the cards, there is what may be called a qualitative variability. In such cases, as Hugo de Vries described in *Die Mutationstheorie* in 1900, there is a sudden, though it may be a minute change in one or more of the hereditary particles of the germ itself, and this sudden leap, or mutation as he named it, continues to breed true. Weismann had shown that the origin of variation was germinal, and Bateson in 1894 had made clear the importance of studying such discontinuous variation. De Vries, however, emphasized the fact that these sudden mutations, with no apparent transitional stages, occurred in the hereditary elements of the germ plasm.

The rapid expansion of the study of genetics after 1900 is very closely connected with the growth of knowledge about the chromosomes, yellow-staining bodies in the nuclei of the cells. When eggs or sperms are to be formed, these bodies come together in pairs, and then separate, so that each egg, or each sperm, has one or the other member of the pair. When the egg has been fertilized by the sperm, the resultant cell of course has the chromosomes of both. Weismann first observed the behaviour of these bodies, and as early as 1887, Édouard van Beneden, working on Ascaris megalocephala, a round worm occurring in the intestines of the horse, demonstrated that the number of chromosomes was the same for each cell in a given body, and was of the opinion that each species of creature would probably have in its cells a number of chromosomes peculiar to itself. In 1901 T. H. Montgomery (*Biol. Bull.*, ii, 342), and in 1902 and 1903[1] W. S. Sutton, worked on grasshoppers, and Sutton showed that the body chromosomes were individually recognizable from cell to cell by their sizes and shapes, and that when eggs of sperms were to be formed, there were eleven pairs and one unpaired chromosome. C. E. McClung in 1901[2] showed that grasshoppers on which he was working had two kinds of spermatozoa, of which one had one chromosome more than the other. In 1905[3] Stevens and Wilson took this work further, showing that when a sperm with the extra chromosome fertilized the egg, a female resulted, and that other sperms fertilizing eggs produced males. That is, a sperm having an X chromosome for determining sex, joining an egg with an X chromosome, would produce an XX fertilized egg which would develop into a female, while a sperm without an X chromosome joining with an egg with an X chromosome would produce an XO (or XY, if as in some species, there is a pair of sex chromosomes, one of which is very much smaller that the other) fertilized egg that would develop into a male, the male having one less chromosome than the female.

It was Sutton's paper on 'The Chromosomes in Heredity' which first stated that the Mendelian characters were factors in the chromosomes, and that all the alternative Mendelian characters in any one chromosome were inherited together, or linked, it being possible for the same chromosome to carry some dominant and some recessive characters. This linkage showed that there was a limitation on the second Mendelian law of independent assortment of the factors, and indicated that the number of freely assorting groups of characters in a species would be the same as the number of chromosomes. Experimental work with a fruit-fly and with the sweet pea showed that this was true. It would take too much space to describe all the work done in establishing the fact that the number of chromosomes is constant in a species, and the curious reader can find it summarized in *Heredity in Man*, published by R. Ruggles Gates in 1929. He states that work by von Winiwarter in 1912, Painter in 1923, as well as Oguma and Kihara, and by von Winiwarter and Oguma in 1925 and 1926, has shown that the number of chromosomes in the white, yellow, and black man is forty-eight, but that it was not

[1] 'On the Morphology of the Chromosome Group in Brachystola Magna,' *Biol. Bull.*, 1902, IV; 'The Chromosomes in Heredity,' *Biol. Bull.*, 1903, IV.

[2] C. E. McClung, 'The Accessory Chromosome—A Sex Determinant?' *Biol. Bull.*, iii, 43.

[3] N. M. Stevens, 'Studies in Spermatogenesis, with Especial Reference to the "Accessory Chromosome",' *Carnegie Inst.*, Washington, No. 36; E. B. Wilson, 'Studies in Chromosomes,' I, II, *J. Exp. Zool.*, II.

agreed whether the sex chromosomes are an XY pair, both being smaller than the others and the Y very minute, or whether the males have an XO arrangement, that is, forty-seven against the female forty-eight.

The fruit-fly Drosophila melanogaster has played a very large part in the study of the mechanism of heredity. Indeed, an enthusiastic biologist once remarked that it was specially made by God for this particular purpose. It was discovered and set to work by T. H. Morgan[1] and W. E. Castle in 1906, and the work has continued under Morgan's direction, with the aid of Bridges, Müller, Sturtevant, and others, ever since. It takes twelve days only for the creature to develop from the egg; it will endure everything; and its four pairs of chromosomes are of different sizes and easily recognizable. Best of all, it is prolific in mutations. A most important part of the work on the fruit-fly has been the localization of the hereditary factors, or genes, as Morgan called them, which, separately or in linkage-groups, act as differentials turning the balance in a given direction, and affecting the various characters which the animal displays. This localization, or mapping of the genes, is the basis of much of the quantitative work in genetics. Morgan was the pioneer in the attempt to make parallel observations on the behaviour of the chromosomes and on body characters and their transmission or alteration, all under controlled experiments. He was also the first to remark the phenomenon of crossing over, when there is an interchange of characters between members of the same pair of chromosomes.

The immediate bearing of such discoveries on the study of heredity in man, both physical and psychological, is apparent. Haldane[2] has also pointed out that Vavilov's genetic studies of crop-plants have shown most of them to have a mountainous origin, thus indicating that the great river-valley civilizations had origins not yet found. His division of species of wheat into three groups, with fourteen, twenty-eight, and forty-two chromosomes, and their distribution, has furnished valuable data for the study of cultural anthropology. The many studies of such organisms as the malaria parasite, or the hookworm which causes anaemia, have a very important bearing on the study of peoples and their accomplishments and outlooks, and work on the various food plants as well, when one considers such deficiency diseases as beriberi from a diet principally of rice, pellagra from maize, rickets from oats, and their effects on the bodies and cultures of mankind.

The foregoing is no more than a rough outline of the discovery of the

---

[1] T. H. Morgan, *The Theory of the Gene*, 1920, with bibliography.

[2] J. B. S. Haldane, 'Prehistory in the Light of Genetics' in *The Inequality of Man*, 1932.

mechanism of heredity, and the reader who desires to understand the main facts of heredity in plants and animals is referred to Punnett's *Mendelism*, Bateson on *Mendel's Principles of Heredity*, and Morgan on *The Theory of the Gene*. In connexion with this experimental work, we must emphasize the great importance of biometric studies of inheritance as developed by Karl Pearson and his colleagues. Pearson's *Grammar of Science* (first edition 1892) of 1900 has an invaluable discussion of the problems of evolution from the point of view of the biometrician, and his mathematical contributions to genetic and other problems in the *Philosophical Transactions, A.*, between 1895 and 1900, and since 1902 in his periodical *Biometrika*, have not only carried on the tradition of Galton, but have added enormously to our ability to investigate physical and psychological data in quantity and exactly. Indeed, there are many characters in which this is the only useful method of analysis. It is now generally realized that experiment and mathematical analysis must work together, and the invention of method owes a very great deal to Pearson. One of his interesting inventions was the coefficient of racial likeness, an attempt to compare the averages of a large number of characters in one race with those of another, and so obtain a figure which will show the degree of likeness or dissimilarity between the two races. Another invention is the contingency table for 'the correlation of characters not quantitatively measurable.'[1]

Specific studies on heredity in man, as well as those on animals, show that the main problem of evolution is still the nature and causes of variation, and that all practical problems of eugenics centre about heredity. The question whether environment or heredity is more important in development is frequently asked. The only way to deal with such problems is by rigorous experiment. Suppose that a new character arises through a variation. The only way to tell whether it is inherited is by breeding from the new type. If it is inherited, then it may be assumed that either a germinal change has occurred, or a germinal reshuffling of characters. If it is not inherited, it may be assumed that the environment has impressed a modification on the individual organism. As to the inheritance of acquired characters, it may be, as Lloyd Morgan and Baldwin pointed out, that regular adaptation to environment by individuals may furnish a favourable medium for germinal changes in the same direction, should they occur. In the meanwhile, the business of experiment is to find out in particular cases whether a variation appearing in an organism is due to environment or heredity. The interaction between the two is far from simple, and the question of their

[1] *Phil. Trans., A.*, 195, 1900.

relative importance is not one for general theory, but for exact and controlled experiment, careful observation, and quantitative analysis. The use of pedigrees is necessary. For human beings, such pedigrees have been collected to show the inheritance of stature, bodily constitution, eye and skin colour, hair form and colour, anatomical features and peculiarities, mental traits and deficiencies, etc., as well as the effects of racial crossing, in which last, it is now known that genetic segregation occurs as in crosses between a normal and abnormal individual, racial characters in the main differing from single abnormalities in that the former are often represented by multiple factors, while the latter are usually represented by single factors.

To mention even authors and titles of the multitude of papers bearing on these important subjects would make a book. Not only studies of man alone would be included, but those of animals and plants, for the mechanism is the same, and all throw light on the problems of heredity. The mention of a few general works in addition to those already given will serve to introduce the reader to the subject. Among such books are Baur, Fischer, and Lenz, *Menschliche Erblichkeitslehre und Rassenhygiene*, 1923; W. E. Castle, *Genetics and Eugenics*, 1916; F. A. E. Crew's *Organic Inheritance in Man*, 1927; C. B. Davenport's *Heredity in Relation to Eugenics*, 1911; H. H. Goddard's *Feeblemindedness, Its Causes and Consequences*, 1914; R. Pearl's *Studies in Human Biology*, 1925; *The Treasury of Human Inheritance, by* Karl Pearson and collaborators, published by the Cambridge University Press; R. R. Gates, 'Mendelian Heredity and Racial Crossing,' *J.R.A.I.*, 1926, and *Heredity in Man*, 1929, this last with long bibliographies on each subject at the ends of the chapters, and with references in the preface to current bibliographies and abstracts.

R. A. Fisher's *A Genetical Theory of Natural Selection*, 1930, devotes the last five chapters to the specific study of man and society. In a statistical study, he shows that variance in the number of offspring produced by civilized man is so great that a considerable fraction must be ascribed to causes other than chance. Temperamental qualities exert great influence in determining celibacy, age of marriage, and production of offspring. The number of children born to women is correlated with the number born to their mothers. Variance in inherited qualities of mind and temperament and the production of children is heritable, and the most powerful selective agency in civilized man is that acting on mental and moral qualities by way of the birth-rate.

Different occupations are distinguished economically by difference in rewards. This fact is biologically important in insensibly controlling selection through public opinion, and opportunity of social intercourse. Thus social classes become differentiated. The birth-rate is higher in the poorer and less skilled in every class. Social selection is of the less fertile, biological of the more fertile, and least likely to win admiration or reward for useful services to society. Constant promotion sterilizes the poorer and least successful classes, they losing their best, and that best as it advances becoming more sterile.

A redistribution of births and a moderate social promotion of fertility would harmonize with our existing economic organization, and is a necessary condition for a permanent and progressive civilization. The composition of existing populations as graded in social ability and effective infertility presents grave difficulties, which only a people capable of deliberate and intentional policy could hope to overcome.

Besides the discovery of the mechanism of heredity, another of great importance to anthropologists was that the blood could be grouped into four types, the blood-grouping being based on whether an individual has one, both, or neither of two chemical substances in his blood. As early as 1899, Shattock[1] discovered that horse serum to which a drop of human blood was added brought about agglutination of red corpuscles. In 1900 Landsteiner[2] found out that the blood of some human beings will cause the red corpuscles in other human beings to clump. This was the beginning of work of the greatest importance in making blood transfusion safe. By 1901 he had divided human blood-groups into three, and it was Jansky[3] in 1907 who discovered the present classification of four, O, A, B, and AB. In O, there is an absence of the chemical substance which agglutinates, and therefore people with this type of blood can offer their blood to anyone. AB has both chemical substances, and is therefore unharmed by receiving blood from anyone. People in the A or B class are more restricted. For example, the serum of A clumps the red cells of B, and the serum of B clumps the red corpuscles of A. In 1910 von Dungern and Hirzfeld[4] showed that the blood-groups were inherited in the Mendelian fashion.

In 1919 the Hirzfelds[5] tested soldiers of many nationalities, and the

[1] S. G. Shattock, 'Chromocyte Clumping,' etc., *Trans. Pathol. Soc., London*, L, 279; *J. Pathol. and Bacteriol.*, VI, 303.
[2] K. Landsteiner, 1900: 'Zur Kenntnis der antifermentativen, lytischen u. agglutinierenden Wirkung des Blutserums,' *Zentbl. f. Parasit, u. Infekt.*, XXVII, 361; 1901: 'Über Agglutinationerscheinungen normalen menschlichen Blutes' *Wien Klin. Woch.*, XIV, i, 132.
[3] Jansky, *Jahresbericht f. Neurol. u. Psychiatrie*, 1907, 1028.
[4] Von Dungern and Hirzfeld, 'Über Vererbung gruppensspezifischer Strukturen des Blutes,' *Z. f. Immun, exp. Therapie*, 1910, VI, 284.
[5] *Lancet*, 1919, II, 675.

results of a vast number of observations has been to show that all races have a high percentage of O. Unmixed Amerindians are pure O, and Australian aborigines are mainly O with some A. The predominance of A over B is most marked in western Europe, and decreases to the east and south. B is the least common among primitive peoples, O generally being the commonest found, and after that, A, while AB is not very commonly found anywhere. Ruggles Gates[1] suggested that O, as it is universal, may be a primitive character, and that A is older than B, as it is more widespread among primitive peoples. In a recent paper in *Man*, 1935-36, he discusses 'Eskimo Blood-Groups and Physiognomy,' showing that in the few cases which could be tested, the pure Eskimo type of face went with the O group, while Eskimos who plainly showed white or Indian admixture, the Indian being half-breed white, had the A group.

Certainly the predominance of certain groups over large areas suggests that the groups have some racial significance, and the fact that only two genes are involved in inheritance opens a great field for the determination of blood-groups in hybrid races. Most interesting was the work of Landsteiner and Miller in 1925,[2] who discovered that the blood of the anthropoid apes has group elements identical with those of man. In recent years, Nuttall, Sudermann and Zuckerman[3] have worked on this subject, and among other matters, have concluded that Old World monkeys are more closely related to man serologically than they are to New World monkeys.

A third subject in which very considerable advance has been made during the present century is that of the endocrine glands, whose functions have gradually become apparent in connexion with certain deficiency diseases. The work of Brown-Séquard, Sir William Gull, and Oliver and Schäfer in the past century has been mentioned, the first for initiating work on the sex glands, the second for initiating work on the thyroid. By the nineties it was known that sheep's thyroid was useful in the treatment of cretinism. In 1895, Oliver and Schäfer[4] discovered that the suprarenal gland attached to the kidneys had the effect of causing a rise in blood-pressure, with a constricting action, especially on the smaller blood vessels. From these glands, Takamine and Aldrich[5] first isolated adrenalin in 1901, a substance of great value in the treatment of

[1] *Man*, 1933, **208**.
[2] 1925, *J. Exp. Med.*, XLII, 841, 853, 863.
[3] *C.I.S.A.E. Compte rendu*, London, 1934, 83; S. Zuckerman, *Functional Affinities of Man, Monkeys, and Apes*, 1933.
[4] *J. Physiol.*, 1895, XVIII, 230.
[5] Takamine, *Am. J. Pharm.*, 1901, LXIII, 528; Aldrich, *Am. J. Physiol.*, 1901. V, 457.

haemorrhages and asthma. Thyroxin was first isolated by Kendall[1] in 1919.

The male sex-hormone was prepared by Butenandt in 1931 from a hormone oil extracted by Schoeller and Gehrke in the same year. Corner and Allen discovered the hormone of the corpus luteum in 1929. The discovery of the follicular hormone was made possible by a method devised by Allen and Doisy in the same year, and was isolated independently by Doisy and Butenandt in 1931. In 1928, Evans, Engle, Smith, and Steinach, and in 1931 Ascheim and Zondek, found that the pituitary gland played a large part in controlling the sex glands, and work by Loeb, 1929, Aron, 1929 onward, Jansen and Loeser, 1930 onward, Junkmann and Schoeller, and Schittenhelm in 1932, demonstrated the part of the pituitary in controlling the thyroid. Schoeller has summed up this work in *The Lancet* for January 7, 1933, page 38, with a useful diagram showing the work of the pituitary gland in controlling the other glands of the body. For example, the anterior lobe appears to control the ripening of the gonads and luteinization, and secretes a growth hormone, which, when too active, produces giantism. It appears to stimulate the thyroid, and accelerate metamorphosis, and has effect in raising or lowering metabolism. One of the functions of the posterior lobe is that of keeping a safety valve on the blood pressure. One of the most important of all discoveries was that of insulin, first prepared from the pancreas as a specific for diebetes by Banting and Best[2] in 1922, and improved by Collip[3] in the following year.

All such work has provided convincing evidence that the growth of the body and racial traits are controlled to a certain extent by these endocrine glands which produce hormones having growth-controlling properties. For example, the testis secretes and sets in circulation a hormone or hormones which affect stature, length of limb, modelling of the face, growth of hair, and general bodily structure, as can be seen by comparing the eunuch with the normal man. A disease of the pituitary causes a general coarsening of the features and giantism on the one hand, or dwarfism on the other. The thyroid secretion affects metamorphosis from youth to maturity, and the growth of skin and hair. Too great an action will produce goitre or age the subject prematurely. Too little, and the cretin is the result. The suprarenal as well has the power to accelerate or retard development.

[1] Kendall, *J. Biol. Chem.*, 1919, XXXIX, 125.
[2] 'The Internal Secretion of the Pancreas,' *J. Lab. and Clin. Med.*, St. Louis, 1922, VII, 251, 464.
[3] *J. Biol. Chem.*, 1923, LV.

E. H. Starling[1] was among the first to enunciate the hormone theory and its application to biological problems in *The Lancet* for 1905 (ii, 339), under the title 'The Chemical Correlation of the Functions of the Body.' Other valuable works have been J. T. Cunningham's *Hormones and Heredity*, 1921; C. R. Stockard's 'The Significance of Modifications in Body Structure,'[2] 'Human Types and Growth Reaction,'[3] and *The Physical Basis of Personality;* S. M. Shirokogoroff's *Process of Physical Growth among the Chinese*, Shanghai, 1925; R. G. Hoskins' *The Tides of Life*, 1933; and J. B. S. Haldane's 'On Being the Right Size,' in *Possible Worlds*, London, 1927. L. Bolk[4] of Amsterdam in a series of investigations dealing with pigmentation and other bodily characters shows how the Negro in embryonic life passes through stages leading from a low to a high degree of pigmentation, and that in the European, this process is arrested at an earlier foetal stage, adult life retaining a stage transitory in the development of other races. Again, the Negro retains in adult life certain infantile characters in the shape of his skull and the hairlessness of his body. Sir Arthur Keith has noted that aberrant action of the thyroid produces Mongoloid features in people of another race, and that achondroplasia, a defect in the formation of cartilage, also reproduces some features of the Mongoloid type. This does not meant that Mongols or Negroes are pathological, but that for some reason certain endocrine glands function in some groups more or less actively than they do in others.[5]

The solution of the question why these glands act differently in different races will probably come from a combined study of nutrition and hormones. A good deal of work has been done in the present century on the chemical constituents of soils, and their result on food, particularly by those interested in dairy cattle. J. R. de la H. Marett made his first attempt to correlate the activities of the endocrine glands with the mineral content of the soil in a paper on 'The Evolution of the

[1] See Keith's bibliography, *J.R.A.I.*, LVIII, 1928, 311, for this and following references.

[2] *Pub. Cornell Univ. Med. Coll.*, 1923–4, X, No. 2.

[3] *Am. J. Anat.*, 1923, 31, 261.

[4] 'On the Origin of Human Races,' *Proc. Konin. Acad. v. Wetensch.*, 1927, XXX, 321; 'On the Characters of Morphological Modifications in Consequence of Affections of the Endocrine Organs,' *ibid.*, 1921, XXIII, 1; 'Anthropogenesis,' *ibid.*, 1925, XXIX, 1; *Das Problem der Menschenwerdung*, 1926. Quoted by Keith.

[5] Sir Arthur Keith, 'Acromegaly,' *Lancet*, 1911, I, 393; 'Progeria and Ateleiosis,' *ibid.*, 1913, I, 305; 'The Differentiation of Mankind into Racial Types,' *R.B.A.*, Bournemouth, 1919; 'Evolution of Human Races in the Light of the Hormone Theory,' *Bull. Johns Hopkins Hosp.*, 1922, 33, 155, 195; 'The Evolution of the Human Races,' *J.R.A.I.*, LVIII, 1928, with bibliography on p. 311.

Jersey Cow' in *The Island Cow* for March, 1932. He then turned his attention to man, and in a more recent book (*Race, Sex, and Environment, A Study of Mineral Deficiency in Human Evolution*, 1935) pointed out that the new information relating to deficiency diseases, and the laws governing the geographical distribution of the various minerals and vitamins, shortages of which may affect mortality or fertility, should be included in any new attempts to understand the relationship of the human or other organism to its environment.

Lieutenant-Commander Marett was in harmony with the general tendency of the time to apply genetical methods to the study of prehistory. For example, J. B. S. Haldane[1] in 1932 from the evidence of the distribution on a world map of the blood-group B, is of the opinion that the distribution corresponds to a migration outwards from Central Asia which never reached America or Australia, and hardly reached western Europe. Hutton in the 1931 *Census of India* thinks that the origin and distribution of the B factor is to be found in the broad-headed Eurasiatic race. As O is found in all races, it may be the most primitive. A is much more frequent than B among primitive people, and may be older. AB is the least frequent of all. Such genetical studies are the speciality of the *Zeitschrift für Rassenphysiologie*.

Palaeontology made considerable advances from 1900 to 1935, though the number of specimens of extinct races is still far from sufficient to allow us to be dogmatic. The reader who desires full accounts of discoveries with a discussion of their place in the general scheme of evolution should consult such works as Marcellin Boule's *Les Hommes Fossiles*, 1923; M. C. Burkitt's *The Old Stone Age*, 1933; Sir Arthur Keith's *The Antiquity of Man*, 1925, and *New Discoveries Relating to the Antiquity of Man*, 1931; H. F. Osborn's *Men of the Old Stone Age*, 1918; R. A. S. Macalister's *A Textbook of European Archaeology*, 1921; Sir Grafton Elliot Smith's *The Search for Man's Ancestors*, 1931; and the lists in Salomon Reinach's *Répertoire de l'art quaternaire*, 1931, and in G. G. MacCurdy's *Human Origins*, 1924. MacCurdy gives a repertory of palaeolithic art, and a full list and bibliography of the stratigraphy of every palaeolithic site up to 1924.

The principal advances in the study of chronology since 1900 have been partly archaeological, and partly geological. In the first sort, the Abbé Breuil[2] has been especially prominent. In 1905, following on

---

[1] See p. 186, f.n. 2.

[2] H. Breuil, 'Essai de stratigraphie des dépôts de l'âge du renne,' *C.P. de Fr.*, Périgueux, 1905, 75; 'Epilogue d'une controverse,' *Révue préhistorique*, IV, 1909, Nos. 8 and 9.

brilliant work done by himself, Cartailhac, Capitan, and Peyrony, he established the position of the Aurignacian period, and from then until 1909 fought and won the general acceptance of the world. The reader can find a summary of the controversy in J. Déchelette's *Manuel d'* *Archéologie*[1] for 1908. By then the present order of the periods was established: Chellean, Acheulean, Mousterian, Aurignacian, Solutréan, Magdalenian, and Azilian.

Among geologists, A. Penck and E. Brückner deserve the first place for *Die Alpen in Eiszeitalter*, published in three volumes between 1901 and 1909, a work which has done as much as any to clarify the problems of Ice Age chronology. On the plains to the north of the Alps they discovered an older and a younger outwash or rubble; and in the valleys of rivers flowing from the Alpine highlands, they found two more outwash formations, one in an upper and one in a lower terrace of the valleys, the upper, of course, being the older, as rivers are continually deepening their valleys. At places, indeed, they found the lower outwash overlying the upper. By a study of shell-content, weathering, and superposition, they were able to arrange the four spreads of glacial outwash in chronological order, and trace each terrace to its respective moraine in the direction of the Alps. The four periods of deposition of the terraces are named from the river valleys in which they observed the phenomena and are, from older to younger, Günz, Mindel, Riss, and Würm. Between these glacial periods were periods of rapid erosion, when the ice was melting freely and the rivers deepening their valleys, leaving the former deposits high up on their banks as terraces. These inter-glacial periods are named Günz-Mindel, Mindel-Riss, and Riss-Würm. Confirmatory evidence of these genial periods has been found by such work as that of R. von Wettstein[2] on the Hötting breccia, which contains many fossil plants which could only belong to a warm epoch. The valley of the Inn shows this reddish breccia clearly, lying between blue boulder clay of the third and fourth glacial episodes. Other pioneer work on the river-terraces was done by Rutot and Commont,[3] who until his death in 1918 studied the four river-terraces of the Somme Valley near Amiens. The loess, or wind-blown deposits of France, were studied by Ladrière and Commont, and in Germany by Penck and Brückner, Wiegers, Bayer,[4] and others, and the marine terraces of the Mediterranean in their rela-

[1] 116–119.

[2] Die fossile Flora der Höttingen Breccie,' *Denkschr. des Kais. Akademie der Wiss.*, Wien, Math. – Nat. Kl., LIX, 1892, 1–48.

[3] G. G. MacCurdy, *Human Origins*, II, 327, s.v., Amiens, etc., for bibliography.

[4] *Ibid.*, 384, s.v., Germany.

tion to the glacial epochs, were studied by General de Lamothe,[1] M. Depéret,[2] Gignoux,[3] and others.[4]

The nearest approach to exactness in chronology, allowing us to count by years to a certain extent even, rather than in epochs alone, is due to a method devised by Baron de Geer. The principle consists in counting the number of layers which the melting ice deposited during its retreat northward in Sweden, the number of layers from the southern coast to a point near the watershed where the ice has almost entirely dwindled away corresponding to the number of summers which passed during the recession of the ice. To discover the number of years which had elapsed since the retreat came to an end, he counted the layers of mud which have been deposited in the lake of Ragunda since it was first uncovered by the ice when it had reached the limit of its retreat. The results of this work were first published before the Geological Congress of 1910, as 'A Geochronology of the last 12,000 years.'

To the English reader there is no clearer or more fascinating account of chronology or of palaeolithic people compared with modern primitive races in a similar stage of culture than that in *Ancient Hunters and Their Modern Representatives* by W. J. Sollas, 1911, 1915, 1924. Geological works of value to the anthropologist are Glinka's *Soil Map of the World*, Beyschlag's *Geological Map of the Earth*, Wegener's *Origin of Continents and Oceans*, and Davidson Black's 'Palaeogeography and Polar Shift,' in the *Bulletin of the Geological Society of China*, Peiping, 1930 (x). Watts' *Geology for Beginners* forms a simple introduction to the subject, especially the account of the fossil animals and plants found in various layers of the earth's surface.

Among discoveries which have added to our knowledge of Neanderthal or Mousterian man are the skeleton of an adolescent male found by

[1] L. de Lamothe, 'Note sur les anciennes Plages et Terrasses du bassin de l'Isser et de quelques autres bassins de lat Côte Algérienne,' *Bull. Soc. Geol. de France*, Sér. 3, Tom. XXVII, 257; 'Les anciennes nappes alluviales et lignes de rivage du bassin de la Somme et leurs rapports avec celles de la Méditerranée Occidentale,' *ibid.*, Sér. 4, Tom. XVIII, 1918, 3; 'Sur le rôle des oscillations eustatiques . . . dans la formation des systèmes de terrasses de quelques vallées,' *Comptes rendus de séances de l'Acad. des Sciences*, Tom. 132, 1901, 1428; 'Les anciennes lignes de rivage du bassin de la Somme,' *ibid.* Tom. 162, 1916, 948.

[2] C. Depéret, 'Essai de co-ordination chronologique des temps quaternaires,' *Comptes rendus de séances de l'Acad. des Sciences*, CLXVI, 1918, pp. 480, 636, 834, CLXVII, 1918, pp. 418, 979; CLXVIII, 1919, p, 868: CLXX, 1920, pp. 159, 212; CLXXIV, 1922, pp. 1502, 1594.

[3] M. Gignoux, 'Les formations marines pliocènes et quaternaires de l'Italie du sud et de la Sicilie,' *Ann. l'Univ. Lyon*, n.s., I, Paris, 1911.

[4] The above and others are quoted and discussed in Sollas, *Ancient Hunters and Their Modern Representatives*, 1924, pp. 29 f.

Hauser[1] at Le Moustier, Dordogne, in 1908, the complete skeleton of a middle-aged male found by A. and J. Bouyssonie and L. Bardon at La Chapelle-aux-Saints[2] in the same year; teeth found in Jersey[3] in 1910; an adult female in 1911 and a child's skull in 1921, found by H. Martin at La Quina,[4] Charente; six skeletons, two male, one female, and four children, found by Peyrony at La Ferrassie,[5] Dordogne, between 1909 and 1912; fragmentary remains from Ehringsdorf,[6] Weimar, found by quarrymen, 1914, 1916, 1925; part of the skull of a young man found in Galilee by Turville-Petre[7] in 1925; and part of the skull of a child about five years old, found by Miss Garrod[8] at Devil's Tower, Gibraltar, in 1926. Miss Garrod[9] has been carrying on work in Palestine since 1929 at Mount Carmel in Palestine, and has done much to establish the sequence of cultures in that country. A large number of skulls and skeletons of men and women have been found belonging to the Mousterian period. In 1929, in gravels near Rome, the Saccopastore skull was found. This is being studied by Professor Sergio Sergi, the son of the famous Giuseppe Sergi.[10]

In 1927 G. M. Morant made a careful biometric study of the Neanderthal race in the *Annals of Eugenics*, concluding that it was remarkably homogeneous, and outside the main line of human evolution. In the same year, in the *J.R.A.I.*, A. Hrdlička collected all of the evidence then available, and preferred to speak of a Neanderthal phase of development, rather than of a species. Buxton and de Beer expressed the opinion in *Nature*[11] that Homo sapiens might be the result of the retention of infantile characters in Neanderthal man, since the five-year-old child from

[1] O. Hauser, 'Découverte d'un squelette du type de Néanderthal,' *L'Homme préhistorique*, Jan., 1909; also H. Klaatsch.
[2] 'La station moustiérienne de la "Bouffia" Bonneval à la Chapelle-aux-Saints,' *L'Anthropologie*, XXIV, 1913.
[3] R. R. Marett, *Archaeologia*, 1911.
[4] 'Sur un squelette humain de l'époque moustiérienne trouvé en Charente,' *Comptes rendus de l'Acad. des Sciences*, Oct 16, 1911; 'Homme fossile de La Quina,' *Archives de Morphologie générale et expérimentale*, 15, 1923.
[5] Capitan and Peyrony, 'Deux squelettes humains au milieu de foyers de l'époque moustiérienne,' *Rév. de l'École d'A.*, Dec., 1909; 'Station préhistorique de la Ferrassie,' *Rév. anthropologique*, Jan., 1912.
[6] Schwalbe, 1914, *Anat. Anzeiger*, XLVII, 337; Virchow, H., 1920. *Die menschliche Skeletreste aus dem Kämpfeschen Bruch im Travertin von Ehringsdorf bei Weimar;* Weidenreich, F., 'Der Schädel von Weimar-Ehringsdorf,' *Verh. Ges. Phys. Anthrop.*, Stuttgart, 1927, II, 34; also in *Korrbl. d.d. Wiss. u. Tech.*, 1927, III, 18.
[7] Keith and Turville-Petre, *Brit. Sch. Arch.*, Jerusalem, 1927, 53.
[8] Garrod, Buxton, Elliot Smith, Bate, 'The Excavation of a Mousterian Rock Shelter at Devil's Tower, Gibraltar,' *J.R.A.I.*, 1928.
[9] *Man*, 1930, 77.
[10] *Proc. First Internat. Congress of Prehistoric and Protohistoric Sciences*, London 1932.
[11] Jan.–June, 1932, CXXIX, p. 940.

Gibraltar, which Buxton had removed from its travertine matrix and mended, was round-headed and had no brow ridges, and the eight-year-old child from La Quina, though long-headed, also had no brow ridges. The evidence from the associated fauna and the type of teeth leave no doubt of their belonging to the Neanderthal race, though the form of the skulls is more like that of Homo sapiens. It is rather difficult to explain how the teeth came to change in form, if Homo sapiens is really in the same line as Neanderthal.

Morant has also studied other prehistoric races in the same manner, the most notable of these papers being on the Upper Palaeolithic periods, in the *Annals of Eugenics* for 1930, treating all of the well-authenticated discoveries of skeletal remains from the Aurignacian, Solutréan, and Magdalenian epochs. Some of the most notable since 1900 may be mentioned.

In 1900 and 1901 M. le chanoine de Villeneuve worked in the Grotte des Enfants at Grimaldi, and found a male and female skeleton of the Cro-Magnon type, and a male and female of a Negroid type, both of the Aurignacian period. These have been described by Dr R. Verneau[1] in one of the magnificent volumes of the series on the Mentone caves, whose excavation and publication are due to the generosity and interest of the Prince of Monaco. The Cheddar skeleton was found in 1903, and has been fully described by F. G. Parsons and C. G. Seligman in the *J.R.A.I.* for 1914. The *Journal* for the same year has an account of the skeleton found at Halling in Kent in 1912, written by W. H. Cook and Sir Arthur Keith.

Professors Boule and Breuil visited the University Museum at Oxford in 1912, and with Professor Sollas examined the 'Red Lady of Paviland' and the associated finds. Boule was much struck by the resemblance of the bones to those of the Cro-Magnon race. Sollas and Breuil then visited the Royal Institution of Swansea, and were greatly impressed by the collections from the Gower caves. They obtained permission from Miss Talbot to continue excavations in Paviland cave, to which they were guided by John Gibbs, a farmer living at Rhosilly, and he and Mr Long assisted Professor Sollas in the excavation. A full account of their work is given by Sollas in the Huxley Lecture[2] for 1913, in which he maintains that the Red Lady is a Cro-Magnon man, and the cave the most westerly of the outposts of the Aurignacian race. It is a pity that the caves of Gower were explored by Dean Buckland, Colonel Wood, Mr. Vivian, and Colonel Morgan in days when so little was

[1] *Les Grottes de Grimaldi*, Tom. II, fasc. I, *Anthropologie*, Monaco, 1906.
[2] *J.R.A.I.*, XLIII, 1913.

known about the antiquity of man. But the discovery of various openings in the cliffs concealed by blown sand and landslides gives hope that not everything has yet been found. The farmers of West Gower have kindly given the writer full rights to search for pleistocene and later caves and deposits and to excavate them. The high, holy, and ancient land of Gower may yet disclose further of her secrets, and add greatly to our knowledge of early man.[1]

The Combe Capelle skeleton was found by O. Hauser in 1909, and described by him and Klaatsch in the same year in the *Prähistorische Zeitschrift*.[2] Verworn, Bonnet, and Steinmann described a male and a female skeleton found at Obercassel near Bonn in 1914 in *Der diluviale Menschenfund von Obercassel*,[3] and descriptions of three female, two male skeletons, and those of two children and a foetus found at Solutré in 1923–24, were published by Depéret, Arcelin, and Mayet in the same years in the *Comptes rendus des séances de l'Académie des Sciences*.[4]

The foregoing account of the well-authenticated discoveries of Upper Pleistocene human remains in Europe is purposely little more than a catalogue, showing additions to our knowledge of Cro-Magnon man gained in the last century. There were two main types in Europe, so far as we know at present, one like the original Cro-Magnon discovery, about six feet tall on the average, with the legs longer in proportion to the arms than in existing races, and a cranial capacity above that of men today. The head is dolichocephalic, the face short and broad, and the nose narrow. The other type, represented by the old woman and boy from Grimaldi, shows a race with Negroid characters, the lower limbs being very long as compared with the upper, the skulls dolichocephalic and Negroid in outline, the nose flat with nasal gutters at the base (a Negroid character), the jaws prognathous, and the palate parabolic with large teeth of an Australoid character. From the anatomical evidence, as well as from certain of the Aurignacian paintings similar to those executed by Bushmen, and from steatopygous statuettes found at Mentone, their form suggesting the Bushman figure, Piette[5] and Sollas[6] among others have argued that there were at least these two races in Europe in the Aurignacian period, one the Cro-Magnon, the other allied to the Bushman.

During the early thirties L. S. B. Leakey has found in Kenya in

[1] This work has long since been the charge of the Royal Institution of Swansea (1962).
[2] Band I, 1909, 273–338.
[3] Wiesbaden, 1919.
[4] Tom. 177, p. 618; Tom. 179, p. 1374.
[5] E. Piette, *L'Anthropologie*, 1895, VI, 137.
[6] Sollas, *Ancient Hunters*, 1915, 386.

East Africa the contemporaries of Cro-Magnon man. His discoveries were the result of a deliberate plan. When he was a boy in Kenya,[1] a cousin in England sent him a copy of H. R. Hall's *Days before History* as a Christmas present, and from that time onward he resolved to find Stone Age man and his tools in East Africa, and lost no opportunity to search, and to familiarize himself with the geology of the country, with a view to knowing what sort of places were likely to have been inhabited by ancient man at different periods. The work of J. W. Gregory[2] who had found the same sort of evidence of glaciations in equatorial Africa as had been observed in the Alps of Europe, was of special value to him, and later he was able to consult with Dr Eric Nillson[3] on the same subject while he was working at Elmenteita in Kenya. Dr Hans Reck[4] of Berlin had discovered a human skeleton at Oldoway in Tanganyika in 1914, tall, long-headed, long-faced, and long-nosed, which he ascribed to the Upper Pleistocene period, though his opinion was not at first accepted.

When Leakey first came to school in England after World War I, he brought a collection of stone implements to the British Museum, which encouraged him to continue the search in Kenya. An accident at Rugby football while he was up at Cambridge prevented his reading for a year, and he took the opportunity of joining C. W. Cutler's expedition to Tanganyika, where he gained much valuable knowledge of the technique of excavating and preserving fossil bones. By 1926 he was able to start a modest expedition of his own, and for the next few years was engaged in work at Nakuru and Elmenteita in Kenya, where a study of old lake-levels and deposits enabled him to work out a general scheme of climatic fluctuations in East Africa, and to formulate provisionally a correspondence between the sequence of pluvial deposits in the Rift Valley with their stone implements, and the glacial deposits of Europe with their palaeolithic implements.[5] Both at Nakuru and Elmenteita, Leakey found burials of people of the same type as the Oldoway Man, tall, with long heads, faces and noses, and powerfully built, contemporaries of Cro-Magnon man in Europe. Sir Arthur Keith considers them to be proto-Hamite, just as Cro-Magnon was proto-European. Leakey's discoveries led to a review of Dr Reck's evidence, especially after Leakey had visited Reck in Berlin, and assured himself that Oldoway and Elmenteita man were of the same type, and opinion was

[1] L. S. B. Leakey, *Adam's Ancestors*, 1934, 3.
[2] *The Rift Valleys and Geology of East Africa*, 1895.
[3] 'Preliminary Report on the Quaternary Geology of Mount Elgon and Some Parts of the Rift Valley,' *Geolog. Foreningens i Stockholm Forhandlingear*, April, 1929.
[4] *Illust. London News*, April 4, 1914.
[5] *Nature*, 1929, Vol. CXXIV, p. 9.

generally in favour of Dr Reck's original views about the age of Oldoway man.[1]

But Leakey was anxious to find the remains of yet earlier man in East Africa, and set about the search with the same thoroughness which characterized his earlier work. He noted that now when the level of permanent snow and glaciers is at 1,400 feet above sea-level, the country above 8,000 feet (or 6,000 feet below the permanent snow level) is cold by night and often by day, and not so densely populated by men or animals. He argued that when the snow-and ice-level was at 10,000 feet, all the country stretching down to about 4,000 feet above sea-level was cold, and unlikely to have been much inhabited by Stone Age man. He decided to search in regions from 4,000 feet above sea-level downwards for sites which had a good water supply at the periods with which he was concerned, this being shown by old lake-beaches, etc., and whose conditions were favourable for the fossilization of bones. Moreover, he hoped for areas where nature had exposed ancient deposits in the sides of gullies and gorges so as to make them accessible. At Kanjera and Kanam in 1931 and 1932, his search was rewarded.[2]

In 1933 the Royal Anthropological Institute[3] appointed a committee at Cambridge to consider the evidence of the age of his discoveries at Kanjera and Kanam. The two Kanjera skulls were considered to belong to the type of Homo sapiens, though the deposits in which they were found belong to the Middle Pleistocene, and the tools were of the Chellean period. The Kanam mandible fragment is very closely related to that of Homo sapiens, and the evidence of the geology and of the fossil animals places it in the Lower Pleistocene, making it of approximately the same age as Pithecanthropus, Piltdown, and Peking man, the first and last of which, at least, are remarkably unlike modern man.

The discovery of this ancient jaw, so human in comparison with other specimens of the same period, has an interesting bearing on such discoveries as the Galley Hill skull and skeleton found near London in 1888. These remains were of so modern a character as compared with Neanderthal that the majority of geologists and anatomists, in spite of

[1] Sir Arthur Keith, *New Discoveries Relating to the Antiquity of Man*, Chap. 10; Reck, 'Prähistorische Grab und Menschenfunde und ihre Beziehungen zur Pluvial-Zeit in Ostafrika,' *Mitteilungen aus den Deutschen Schuzgebieten*, Berlin, 1926, Vol. XXXIV, p. 50; Leakey, *Nature*, 1928, Vol. CXXI, p. 499; Mollison and Giesler, 'Untersuchungen über den Oldoway Fund,' *Verhand. Gesell. f. Physische Anthrop.*, 1929, Vol. III, p. 50.

[2] Leakey, *Adam's Ancestors*, 1934, Chaps 1, 9; *The Stone Age Races of Kenya*, 1935.

[3] *Man*, 1933, **66**.

the evidence of antiquity, were inclined to believe that man of the Chellean period must necessarily be of a type very different from modern man. Sir Arthur Keith accepted the evidence of those who discovered the skeleton, speaking of 'the much greater revelation—the high antiquity of the modern type of Man, the extraordinary and unexpected conservancy of the type'.[1] Leakey's discovery adds weight to this opinion. It is not difficult to imagine many forms, some of which became extinct, others of which are directly ancestral to those of today, and it is not impossible that the type directly ancestral to modern man was contemporary with many odder experiments of nature.

Other discoveries of skulls and skeletons of unknown age are the Boskop[2] skull, found in the Transvaal in 1913, possibly an ancestral form of the present Bushmen, Australoid[3] skulls found in South Africa, a probably Capsian (Aurignacian in Africa) skeleton from Asselar[4] in the Sahara, a pleistocene skull at Talgai[5] in Queensland, Australia, and two skulls from Wadjak[6] in Java, found in 1890, but not described until 1920. Hrdlička[7] has carefully examined all of the ancient skeletons which have been found in America and attributed to a very early date, and has come to the conclusion that so far, palaeolithic man has not been found in the New World.

Among types which are human, yet very different from modern man, is the famous Mauer jaw, the most massive of all yet found, discovered by Otto Schoetensack in 1907, so far removed from our own kind in age and type that its discoverer gave it a new genus and species in his memoir of 1908, *Der Unterkiefer des Homo heidelbergensis*. This discovery, according to Sir Grafton Elliot Smith, stimulated Charles Dawson to search for similar remains in Sussex.

While he was attending a land court near Piltdown, he noticed that workmen were repairing a road with flint, and wondered why they were taking the trouble to bring such poor material from a long distance, for he supposed the nearest flint was over four miles away. On inquiry, however, he discovered that flint was used because the road crossed a small patch of gravel in which it occurred, a patch so small that it had been overlooked by the geological survey. He told the workmen to keep

---

[1] Keith, *Antiquity of Man*, 1916, 192.
[2] Haughton and Pycraft, *J.R.A.I.*, LV, 1925, 179.
[3] Boule and Vallois, *Arch. Inst. Paléont. humaine*, *Mém.* 9, 1932; Keith, *New Discoveries*, 140.
[4] Boule and Vallois, *ibid*.
[5] S. A. Smith, *Phil. Trans. Roy. Soc.*, Ser. B., Vol. CCVIII, 1918, 351.
[6] Dubois, *Proc. K. Akad. van Wetench. te Amsterdam*, XXIII, part 7.
[7] *Smithsonian Inst. Bull.*, 33, 1907; 52, 1912; 66, 1918; cf. also Boule, *Les Hommes Fossiles*, 1923; Keith, *New Discoveries*.

a lookout for fossil remains, and regularly visited the spot from 1908 onward.

On one visit, a workman showed him a very thick[1] human parietal bone, and in 1911 Dawson himself recovered the frontal part of the same skull from the spoil heap of the gravel pit, and other fragments. In the summer of 1912 he recovered the greater part of the right half of the mandible, the ascending ramus being intact, except for the top of the articular condyle which fits into the glenoid cavity on that part of the base of the skull formed by the temporal bone just in front of the ear. The horizontal part contained two molars, the first and second, the third having dropped out after death, and the lower part extended nearly to the chin, which was ape-like in that there was no prominence but a rounded slope, while there was the well-marked beginning of the simian plate or shelf on the inside, a plate which unites the lower borders of the right and left halves of the jaws of apes on the inside, and strengthens the union, its place in man being taken by a thickening of the lower border of the jaw and a pushing forward of the bone into a prominent chin. This ape-like chin[2] may be seen in a modified form in some modern specimens of man, but is rare.

By the end of the summer of 1912, the right half of the mandible, a large part of the frontal bone, the whole of the parietal, and the temporal had been found for the left side of the skull, and a piece of the occipital and a part of the right parietal had been found, and Sir Arthur Smith Woodward had begun his reconstruction. In 1913 Father Teilhard de Chardin discovered in the same deposits a canine tooth, more like that of a female chimpanzee than of a human being. It was a tooth similar to that which Smith Woodward had assumed for the mandible in his reconstruction. Dawson had been doubtful about the inclusion of a large canine, for as he pointed out, the two molars were ground down very flat.[3]

Now to my mind, this is a very important point. In the first place, the glenoid fossa and what little remains of the articular condyle in Piltdown form a joint entirely human, and quite unlike the same joint in an ape's skull. If the reader will watch any animal like an ape or a dog with large projecting canines, he will notice that they lock when the mouth closes, and that the animal has only an up and down motion in his jaw. If he notices himself in the act of chewing, he will observe that

---

[1] Much has been made of this thickness. But Mr E. T. Leeds has shown me several skulls from the neighbourhood of Oxford as thick as, or thicker than, the Piltdown.

[2] I have seen this sort in a modern Melanesian mandible in the Department of Human Anatomy at Oxford.

[3] *Quart. Journ. Geol.*, 1913, LXIX, 151; *ibid.* LXX, 1914, p. 85.

his jaws have a rotatory motion, with a consequent grinding action on the molars. In Piltdown, as in many primitive peoples today who chew hard and rather gritty food, the cusps are worn down, and the molars present a flat smooth surface. The Piltdown grinders show that he had a rotatory motion when chewing, and such a motion would have been impossible if he had four large canines of the type included, for they lock, and prevent all except an up and down motion.

It might be argued that he had lost some of his canines during life, and that his back-teeth then became ground down. To test this point, I asked two of my pupils, Mr and Mrs Culwick, to send me some baboon skulls from Tanganyika. I noticed as the old males lost their canines, their molars became worn down, but that these molars did not wear with a flat surface, but tended to wear down on the inside and to hollow out. The baboon, of course, has an ape's type of articulation, and no rotary motion of the jaw. The lack of canines would allow his jaws to meet unevenly, and so cause uneven wearing. But he would not have the rotary motion, by which alone his molars could have been ground down to a flat surface.

The inclusion of the canine makes the mandible long and ape-like. This necessitates bringing the face out to enable the lower and upper jaws to meet, and produces a monstrous degree of prognathism. The area of attachment of the temporal muscle would hardly allow so big a jaw. Now in the apes and in primitive men with great jaws, there is generally a massing of bone over the eyes, and a more slanting forehead than in modern man. The force of the bite is greatest at about the region of the second molar, and in ordinary men this force comes against the malar bones and is ultimately against the arch of the frontal bone of the skull. If the frontal bone is on the slant, so that the arch does not take the force of the bite, we generally find a heavy massing of bone at the brow-ridges taking the force of the bite, rather than the arch as in cases where we have a dome-like head with the jaw tucked underneath. There is no sign of this massing of bone over the eyes in the piece of the Piltdown frontal which is preserved.[1]

At the time of discovery, it was felt that Piltdown was so different from other species of men that a special genus and species were given to it, Eoanthropus dawsoni. The late Arthur Thomson reconstructed the cranium, and produced a result very different from that of Smith Woodward. His reconstruction, which has never been published, is very like the Eurafrican type common among the ancient Egyptians, and the

[1] Cf. Arthur Thomson, 'Facial Development,' *Dental Record*, London, 1924, XLIV, 3, p. 119.

Bedouin of today. Professor Ramstrom[1] of Upsala has also attempted to show the resemblance of Piltdown man to the Combe Capelle skull, which is a prototype of the modern Eurafrican. If the bones had their original edges intact and unrolled, one would have more confidence in one or other of the various attempts to fit them together. As it is, a tilting outward of the temporal bone can make an ape-like spread at the base, while bending it inward will make the result more human. The piece of occipital also may be tilted outward so that the foramen magnum would come towards the back, as in an ape which does not walk upright, or it can be tucked inward, so that the foramen magnum comes underneath, and we get a man who would walk upright.

The controversies about Piltdown would fill a book,[2] and the reader who desires to know about the literature and the arguments of experts may find what he wants in Boule's *Les Hommes Fossiles*, 1923; Hans Weinert's *Menschen der Vorzeit*, 1930; Smith Woodward's *Guide to the Fossil Remains of Man in the British Museum*; Keith's *Antiquity of Man*, 1926; and Elliot Smith's *Essays on the Evolution of Man*, 1927.

The two last mentioned have done a good deal of work on casts of the interior of the skull, believing that the central problem of man's evolution is the development of the size and capacity of the brain.[3] Other workers in the same field have been Dr Ariëns Kappers[4] of Amsterdam, Dr Tilly Edinger,[5] and Eugene Dubois.[6] When Elliot Smith first saw the brain-cast of Piltdown, he regarded it as 'the most primitive and simian human brain so far recorded.' He supports Smith Woodward's reconstruction. Keith is inclined to 'make the Piltdown type spring from the main ancestral stem of modern humanity,' and finds close affinities between it and the London skull of the Chellean-Acheulean period.[7]

The discovery of Peking man was the culmination of a well-organized search extending over a number of years. The first hint was given as long ago as 1903, when Professor Max Schlosser of Munich reported on a quantity of 'dragon's bones' from an apothecary's shop in China. One of the fossil teeth he assigned to a new genus and species, which might be

[1] 'Der Piltdown-Fund,' *Bull. Geol. Inst. Upsala*, XVI, 1919.
[2] What probably is the final book is Weiner's *The Piltdown Forgery*, Oxford 1955. I have left this account as a matter of history, to record our doubts long before the final exposure occurred.
[3] Keith, *New Discoveries*, 'The Interpretation of Brain Casts.'
[4] *Proc. Roy. Acad. Sci. (K. Akad. van Wetensch.) Amsterdam*, 1929, 32, 2; 32, No. 5.
[5] *Die Fossilen Gehirne*, Berlin, 1929.
[6] 'On the Endocranial Cast of Pithecanthropus,' *Proc. Roy. Acad. Sci.*, *Amsterdam*, 1924, 27, Nos. 5, 6.
[7] Keith, *New Discoveries*, 1931, Chaps. 29, 30.

the remains of a very ancient human type with simian affinities, and recommended a search for a new fossil anthropoid, or for a Tertiary or Early Pleistocene human being.[1] In 1912, at the instance of Sun Yat Sen, the new Chinese government began the project of a geological survey of China, and in the course of time, realizing the importance of the study of fossils for the elucidation of the geology of the coal fields and other problems, began a series of memoirs, the *Palaeontologia Sinica*. In 1921 Dr J. G. Andersson, adviser to the survey, found a piece of quartz in a bone-bed near Peking, which he knew must have been brought there by ancient man. Two more human teeth were found at Choukoutein in 1926 and one in 1927, which caused Dr Davidson Black,[2] Professor of Anatomy at Peking, to create a new genus and species of human-being, Sinanthropus pekinensis, the name being suggested by Dr A. W. Grabau. In the following year, C. C. Young and W. C. Pei found two human jaws with simian characters. The Rockefeller Foundation, which had been sponsoring the work for the past two years, was so impressed that in 1929 they renewed their grant, and founded a special department under Dr Davidson Black for further research. Almost immediately after the new appropriation had been made, on December 2, 1929, W. C. Pei[3] found an almost complete and uncrushed brain-case of Peking man. The cranium has a frontal region with brow-ridges like Pithecanthropus, but is much more expanded, and the whole is more voluminous. According to Elliot Smith, there are distinct likenesses to Piltdown, but 'the brain-case of Sinanthropus reveals many features which are unknown either in the Ape-Man of Java or in the Piltdown skull, and throws a great deal of light upon the characters of the common ancestor of the human family, from which all these genera had been derived.[4] This first discovery of an adolescent male skull was followed in July, 1930, by that of the brain-case of a woman about twenty-five or twenty-six years old. Fragments of two other skulls of the same kind have been found. Accounts of the work and descriptions are published regularly in the *Bulletin of the Geological Society of China*, the *Memoirs of the Geological Survey*, and the *Palaeontologia Sinica*. A complete account to date may be read in 'Fossil Man in China,' by Davidson Black and others.[5]

[1] *Abhandl. der Königl. Bayerischen Akad. Wissensch, Math. – Phys. Klasse*, Band XXII, 1903, pp. 20. 21.
[2] *Pal. Sin.*, VII, 1927, p. 21.
[3] W. C. Pei, *Bull. Geol. Soc. China*, VIII, 3, 1929, Peiping; also Davidson Black, *ibid.*
[4] Elliot Smith, *The Search for Man's Ancestors*, 1931, 41; *Antiquity*, V, 1931, p. 21.
[5] *Geol. Memoirs*, Ser. A, No. 11, *Geol. Survey of China*, 1933.

A clear and fascinating account of the discoveries of the Java, Piltdown, and Peking man is given by Elliot Smith in *The Search for Man's Ancestors*, 1931, with an illuminating discussion of the cradle of mankind, and the possible wanderings of early man and apes. By the beginning of the Pleistocene period, we find these earliest remains of man as far apart as England, Java, and China. Then too, there is the jaw found at Heidelberg, and in Africa, the curious skull found at Broken Hill in Northern Rhodesia,[1] unfortunately undatable, with brow-ridges far larger than those of Neanderthal man, huge orbits, and high upper jaw, so big that the huge Heidelberg jaw is too short and narrow to fit it, and the man-like ape, Australopithecus africanus,[2] found by Professor Dart at Taungs in Bechuanaland. Very likely, the much more human Lloyd's skull of London[3] belongs to the same period, though there is doubt in the minds of some people about its age. Certainly man and ape-like Man had travelled far in those early times, and these types must have had ancestors in yet earlier times. They are all so different, and there are so many conflicting views on the subject, that one is inclined to agree with Osborn,[4] that the final solution of the problem of man's descent will be found only when we have a continuous series of fossils from modern man to his Eocene ancestors.

W. K. Gregory[5] considers that men and apes alike were derived from a more generalized type of common ancestor such as Dryopithecus. Elliot Smith[6] suggests that the Miocene beds of the Sivalik Hills north of Delhi, in which the remains of Dryopithecus and several kinds of apes of both living and extinct varieties have been found, were the centre from which the apes wandered, as far east as Borneo and Sumatra, as far west as Spain and France, and all over Africa. These wanderings occurred in the Miocene and Pliocene periods. By the beginning of the Pleistocene, man had wandered all over the Eurasiatic and African areas, and anywhere in this vast land mass might have been the original home of the human family.

According to the same author, Professor Joseph Barrell, Dr David-

---

[1] Found in 1921. Keith, *The Antiquity of Man*, II, XX, XXI, 1924; *Rhodesian Man and Associated Remains*, Pycraft, Elliot Smith, Yearsley, Carter, Smith, Hopwood, Bate, Swinton, British Museum, 1928.

[2] Found in 1924. First reported in *Nature*, Feb. 7, 1925, p. 195; Keith, *New Discoveries*, 37–104.

[3] Keith, *New Discoveries*, 433–68.

[4] H. F. Osborn, 'Recent Discoveries Relating to the Origin and Antiquity of Man,' *Proc. Amer. Phil. Soc.*, Philadelphia, Vol. 66, 373–89.

[5] (and M. Hellman), 'The Dentition of Dryopithecus and the Origin of Man,' *Anthrop. Papers, Amer. Mus. Nat. Hist.*, XXVIII, Pt. 1, 1926.

[6] *Search for Man's Ancestors*.

son Black, and Dr Grabau[1] have argued that the raising up of the Himalayas in the Miocene period provided the circumstances by which certain anthropoid apes were forced to adapt themselves to new conditions which promoted the beginning of change in the human direction. Apes to the south of the mountain ranges could continue their arboreal habits and frugivorous diet, while those left on the north side might be compelled to walk on the ground and eat meat.

This may have been so. On the other hand, the Taungs ape, which seems to have shown some of these changes beginning in its face, brain, and teeth, was found in South Africa, a circumstance which calls to mind Darwin's theory that Africa, the home of the gorilla and chimpanzee, was also the cradle of mankind. The truth is that there is no decisive evidence as to the place or the time of origin of the human kind.

Two very valuable books on primate palaeontology are Othenio Abel's *Die Stellung des Menschen im Rahmen der Wirbeltiere*, 1931, probably the most complete book of reference on primate palaeontology, and W. E. Le Gros Clark's *Early Forerunners of Man*, 1934, which is a morphological study of the evolutionary origin of the primates, dealing fully with anatomy, palaeontology, and embryology, the last of which subjects has yielded rather disappointing results in this branch of study. Le Gros Clark insists that 'all anatomical characters must be taken into account in assessing affinities', and that in evaluating 'genetic affinities, anatomical differences are more important as negative evidence, than anatomical resemblances are as positive evidence.' In discussing the development of certain characters, he makes a very strong argument for evolutionary parallelism.

A great deal of intensive work has been done on the soft tissues of the body, but little to connect it with the very extensive work on osteology. In 1904 W. L. H. Duckworth's *Morphology and Anthropology* collected what was known of the comparative anatomy of the apes and of the different races of man, including in its scheme the comparative anatomy and morphology of Eutherian mammals, embryology, osteology, the comparative morphology of the soft tissues and central nervous system, and a study of fossil primates. In 1931 Edward Loth's *Anthropologie des parties molles* collected such material as was available for the study of the comparative anatomy of the different races of man. The material at his disposal was limited, as few if any accurate dissections had been done on some of the races of man. In a preface, Sir

[1] 'An Outline of the Geological History of North China,' *Peking Nat. Hist. Bull.*, 1929–30, Vol. V.

Arthur Keith drew attention to the immense possibilities for comparative and co-operative work of this sort within the British Empire. At present the material available permits only the crudest grouping. The great value of the book is that it suggests what may be a new trail in physical anthropology. As Duckworth foresaw near the beginning of the century, the whole of the ape or man ought to be considered in making racial distinctions, and not merely his bones.

Lately Dr S. Zuckerman has approached the relations of man to the other primates from a comparatively fresh point of view, departing from the usual morphological method of assessing degrees of affinity by similarity of anatomical structure. He has collected physiological and bio-chemical evidence, and has done an enormous amount of work on the physiology, etc., of the primates. In general, he appears to find that their functional characters tend to confirm the evidence of comparative anatomy. For example, the lemurs show themselves aberrant in structure, and their reproductive habits, visual processes, and serum precipitin reactions of the blood show them to be very different from the other primates. The functional differences between New and Old World monkeys are also very marked, especially in the menstrual cycle and character of the blood. The anthropoid apes, like ourselves, have the four blood-groups with similar reactions, and in this point are unlike the monkeys. Similarities in the menstrual cycle, vision, blood, and other features between man and the anthropoids are treated carefully and fully in the *Functional Affinities of Man, Monkeys and, Apes*, 1933. The reader interested in the far-reaching sociological implications of these likenesses should turn to *The Social Life of Monkeys and Apes*, 1932, by the same author, which is discussed on page 220 of this book.

It is the fashion now to deprecate the old hard and fast division between anatomy and physiology, and for anatomists today to call themselves functional anatomists, meaning that they keep function in mind as well as structure. But many of the older anatomists always had the dynamic view, and for that reason I have spoken of Zuckerman's outlook as comparatively new. One of the older anthropologists who always studied the relation of structure and function was the late Arthur Thomson, whose work along these lines began in the eighties. Among his more notable contributions in the present century are 'A Consideration of Some of the More Important Factors Concerned in the production of Man's Cranial Form,'[1] 'Facial Development,'[2] and a study with L. H. Dudley Buxton of 'Man's Nasal Index in Relation to Certain

[1] *J.A.I.*, 1903, XXXIII, 135.
[2] *Dental Record*, London, XLIV, No. 3, March 1, 1924, 119.

Climatic Conditions,'[1] this last showing that the nasal index, dependent on the width of the nasal aperture, 'is to be interpreted largely as evidence of the habitat occupied,' though there are areas, as in India, where it has ethnic significance. In 1905, with D. Randall-MacIver, he wrote *The Ancient Races of The Thebaid*, a work based on the anthropometric examination of over 1,500 ancient Egyptian crania.

The principles of anthropometry, together with the method of observing external characters, were laid down in the last century, and during the present have been subject to considerable scrutiny. Many efforts have been made to secure uniformity of technique as far as possible. All methods have been described and illustrated by Rudolf Martin in his monumental *Lehrbuch der Anthropologie* of 1914. A. Hrdlička's handbook *Anthropometry*, 1920, besides instructions, gives the Monaco agreement of 1906 and the Geneva agreement of 1912. In 1933 Buxton and Morant published in the *J.R.A.I.* 'The Essential Craniological Technique,'[2] defining the points from which measurements were to be taken. Various attempts have been made to standardize other kinds of observations, as, for example, those of skin-colour. Miss Blackwood has summarized them and made her own contribution in 'Racial differences as recorded by the colour-top' in the *J.R.A.I.* for 1930.[3] A great number of observations of external characters together with precise measurements have been collected by various people all over the world. Some examples of such work are that by Buxton on Cyprus,[4] Malta and Gozo,[5] the Romano-Britons,[6] and the Eastern Mediterranean,[7] of Bryn and Schreiner in Norway,[8] and of Baron von Eickstedt[9] in Southern Asia, to mention only a few, apart from the great amount of work published in *Biometrika* since 1902.

The question arises whether the various characters employed are constant racially, or subject to rapid modification. Franz Boas[10] is of the opinion that various round-and long-headed immigrants to the United States tend to change their head-shape within a period of about ten

---

[1] *J.R.A.I.*, 1923, LIII, 92.
[2] LXIII, 19.
[3] LX, 137.
[4] *J.R.A.I.*, L, 1920, 183.
[5] *J.R.A.I.*, LII, 1922, 164.
[6] *Journal of Roman Studies*, 1935.
[7] *Biometrika*, XIII, i, 1920.
[8] H. Bryn, *Der Nordische Mensch*, 1929; Bryn and Schreiner, *Die Somatologie der Norweger*, 1929; A. Schreiner, *Die Nord-Norweger*, 1929.
[9] See Egon Freiherr von Eickstedt, *Rassenkunde und Rassengeschichte der Menschheit*, 1934.
[10] *Immigration Commissions*, Washington, 1910, 1911; *American Anthropologist*, 1912, 532; *Changes in Bodily Form of Descendants of Immigrants*, 1912; *Proc. Nat. Acad. Sci.*, II, 1916, 713; VI, 1920, 489.

years, and to approach an uniform type, but his conclusions have not generally been accepted.

The work of Pearson and his colleagues has already been noted elsewhere. It should be remarked that Pearson's biometric interests go far beyond the ordinary measurements taken by physical anthropologists. Before the British Association at Cardiff in 1920, he insisted that we wanted not so much physical measurement of dark and white, but vigorimetry and psychometry. He has always been connected with the Eugenics Laboratory in University College, London, which publishes the *Annals of Eugenics* (1909–). The *Eugenics Review* deals with 'the study of agencies under social control that may improve or impair the racial qualities of future generations, either physically or mentally.' All this work is of course intimately connected with the study of genetics, whose progress was noted earlier in this chapter, and which is an increasingly important part of the study of physical anthropology. Such studies as Shrubsall's 'Physical Characters and Morbid Proclivities,' 1903,[1] and 'The Incidence of phthisis in Relation to Race-Type and Social Environment in South and West Wales' in 1928 by E. G. Bowen,[2] show how the methods of physical anthropology can be applied to the study of the physical and mental reactions of people to the conditions in which they live. In the preface to A. T. and G. M. Culwick's *Ubena of the Rivers*, 1935, Dr Dudley Buxton stressed the necessity for applying such methods to the problems of our own civilization, and not reserving them solely for distant foreigners.

III. PSYCHOLOGY, THE LINK BETWEEN PHYSICAL AND CULTURAL ANTHROPOLOGY

The study of psychology should go hand-in-hand with that of physical anthropology, since man's body and mind are so closely linked together. Moreover, since psychology deals with beliefs, and beliefs underlie institutions, it could be the study which links physical and cultural anthropology. For that reason, we have given it this transitional place between the study of race and culture.

In the previous chapter it was pointed out that Wilhelm Wundt, the father of experimental psychology, realized the necessity for the study of folk-psychology as well. His *Völkerpsychologie* of 1900 and *Elemente der Völkerpsychologie of* 1912 played a very great part in bringing cultural

---

[1] *St. Bartholomew's Reports*, XXXIX.

[2] *J.R.A.I.*, LVIII, 1928, 363; and for Central Wales, *ibid.*, LXIII, 1933, 49. Both the above quoted by Haddon, *History of Anthropology.*

anthropology and psychology together for mutual aid. For him the psychological foundations of culture were not to be found in individuals, but in the group, which always co-operates actively in the production of activities and ideas, for the group is the carrier of habit and tradition, and constrains the individual to the pattern historically transmitted by it. For example, the study of the individual alone could not explain language, religion, or art. The social factors must be taken into account as well as the interchange of ideas between individuals, and diffusion of ideas is a dynamic factor in cultural growth.

Émile Durkheim, in *Les Formes élémentaires de la vie religieuse* in 1912, insisted that social facts are of a special order, and require their own method of study and explanation. In early society, and in primitive society today, there is a solidarity in the feelings, thoughts, and actions of men as members of a social group which gives them a specific character, and these are not actuated by motives of the same order as those which actuate the individual. Indeed, as we showed in the last chapter, Durkheim's theory, like that of MM. Hubert and Mauss, as set out in the volumes of *L'Année Sociologique*, places the individual in a medium whose collective representations compel his thinking, feeling, and acting according to a definite pattern.

C. C. J. Webb's *Group Theories of Religion*, 1916, argues that the individual cannot be transcended by these collective representations without at least recognizing himself as being transcended. Certainly there is a good deal of truth in Durkheim's idea of the compulsive power of the social medium in which the individual develops. But Webb's reminder of the part played by the individual is a necessary corrective. I well remember one cold day in Llangennith when about a dozen children between the ages of five and ten got off a bus which had brought them from school. One child, feeling the cold, began to cry in a forlorn fashion. Immediately all began to cry on the same note, and were all howling. Then one little girl, strung to nervous tension by the uproar, began to giggle. In a few moments all were giggling. Then a small boy, noticing a pair of wheels and an axle by the road, rushed to it and started to push it down the hill. All of the children followed him, and began to push the wheels about and sing. Soon all were happy and busy. Each time there was an individual who began to interpret the general feeling. And at the last, the one with the most initiative set the pace in the play which followed.

For myself I think that the primitive rituals spontaneously arising out of the whole group, which, under stress of hunger, for example, enacts in pantomime the successful hunting, killing, and eating of an animal, and feels good after having let off steam instead of moping, furnish the experience which actualizes the capacities of the individual. Someone will start an action which interprets the general feeling, and all will follow. Then some individuals will be better than others in developing the experience, either in harmony with the group, or sometimes, a little in opposition to it. In this way only could progress come. Certainly it seems impossible to imagine a group in which individuals do not sometimes take the lead.

Lévy-Bruhl has made the study of primitive mentality especially his own, and is of the opinion that savages have prelogical minds, differing in kind rather than in degree from our own. This is a doctrine hard to accept. It is true that some of their categories are different from our own, and that these categories differ widely from people to people. For example, those whom a man calls his relations in one tribe, will form quite a different group from those considered as relations in another. But there is always a definite set of rules for mutual obligations and privileges between relations, however they may be grouped. Again, cause and effect may be put together in many different ways, one people supposing that the ghost of a dead man has magically caused smallpox in others, another people considering that 'germs' from the one have infected the other. In both cases, precautions are taken. The reasoning differs in degree rather than in kind, and the false collection of unrelated things in categories may be compared with our own progress in the sciences, where we are constantly revising our categories. Consider, for example, the category *Primates* in Linnaeus, and today. Some creatures have been taken out, and others put in, with an increased knowledge of facts.

According to Lévy-Bruhl, primitive minds have no clear idea of individuality, apprehending a connexion or participation between the separate parts of what was once a whole, imagining that actions performed on hair or nail-parings can affect the man of which they were once a part. Apparently, too, they mingle their feelings and thinking, themselves, and the object of their thought in complete confusion, being in the state of mind of one who has for example done something indecent in church, and cannot for the moment separate himself, his surroundings, his feelings, and his thoughts from a general welter of misery. In this, they are not unlike ourselves. Again, their thinking is not subject to the law of contradiction, and they can easily hold opinions incompatible with each other without realizing the fact.[1] Thus a man

---

[1] L. Lévy-Bruhl, *Les fonctions mentales dans les sociétés inférieures*, 1910; *La mentalité primitive*, 1912; *L'Âme primitive*, 1927; translated by L. A. Clare, *How Natives Think*, 1926; *Primitive Mentality*, 1923; *The 'Soul' of the Primitive*, 1928.

may be at once himself and a kangaroo, or like a small friend of mine, at once Mary and the Ginger Cat. But Mary, and probably the savage, knows when she must act as Mary, and when as Ginger Cat. In this she is less confused than a former teacher of mine who fought nobly in the class-room for the freedom of the ancient Greeks, and sturdily resisted any effort for freedom on the part of the less fortunate wage-earners of his own city and time.

In the 1934 Congress, C. S. Myers,[1] the veteran of the Torres Straits Expedition, declared that primitive man was not radically different in mind or body from ourselves, and that differences were due to environment and tradition. There was no such thing as a social mind. The basis of social psychology lay in the fact that when persons are associated with one another in society, their experiences would be different from those when they were isolated. The sociologist studies social products and actions and the social psychologist examines such products and actions for the conscious and unconscious mental processes underlying them.

Before treating of the unconscious, the study of which has made so important a contribution to anthropology, we may mention another train of investigation, also started in 1912, by M. Wertheimer, whose classic paper 'Experimentelle Studien über das Sehen von Bewegungen'[2] was published in that year, and placed the *Gestalt* theory on a firm foundation. Wertheimer began his experiments with the forerunner of the modern motion picture projector, and by slowing it down or speeding it up, was able to study the conditions under which the perception of movement arises. The older associationist school would analyse the perperception of movement into an association or combination of space and time perceptions, which are of course implied in the perception of movement. But Wertheimer believed that his perception was of the whole situation, and that it could not be analysed into a sum of sensations. The whole pattern, *Gestalt*, or configuration, was grasped at once. It is of no use to consider the parts in isolation, and a change in one changes the whole. W. Köhler's *The Mentality of Apes*, 1927, and *Gestalt Psychology*, 1930, show that animals similarly have an insight into a whole situation, grasping a new configuration, embracing all of the complicated means to a desired end, suddenly and as a whole. Others who have made very important contributions to the literature of this school are Spearman and Koffka.

[1] *C.I.S.A.E.*, *Compte rendu*, London, 1934.
[2] *Z.P.*, 1912, LXI, p. 161.

Wertheimer's work was not entirely new. In his *Analytical Psychology* of 1896, G. F. Stout had said that 'noetic synthesis owes its peculiarity to the introduction of a distinct kind of mental factor, the apprehension of the whole, which determines the order and connexion of the apprehension of parts', and many of the associationists had had some apprehension of a similar kind, as for example, C. von Ehrenfels in 1890, in his 'Über Gestaltqualitäten' in *Vierteljahresschrift für wissenschaftliche Philosophie*, XVI, 249. But it was Wertheimer who really grasped the full implications of the value of the study of phenomena as wholes, and gave impetus to the study. J. C. Flugel's *A Hundred Years of Psychology* in this series gives a full history and bibliography of this school.

A most interesting application of the *Gestalt* method to the study of whole societies was made by Ruth Benedict in her *Patterns of Culture* in 1935. She has taken three cultures which have been very thoroughly studied, the Pueblo, Dobu, and Kwakiutl, and has shown that

a culture, like an individual, is a more or less consistent pattern of thought and action. Within each culture, there come into being characteristic purposes not necessarily shared by other types of society. In obedience to these purposes, each people further and further consolidates its experience, and in proportion to the urgency of these drives, the heterogeneous items of behaviour take more and more congruous shape. Taken up by a well-integrated culture, the most ill-assorted acts become characteristic of its peculiar goals, often by the most unlikely metamorphoses. The form that these acts take, we can understand only by understanding first the emotional and intellectual mainsprings of that society. . . . The whole . . . is not merely the sum of all its parts, but the result of an unique arrangement and interrelation of the parts that has brought about a new entity.[1]

As Dr Franz Boas writes:

Dr Benedict calls the genius of culture its configuration . . . This treatment is distinct from the so-called functional approach to social phenomena in so far as it is concerned with the discovery of fundamental attitudes rather than with the functional relations of every cultural item. It is not historical except in so far as the general configuration, as long as it lasts, limits the directions of change that remain subject to it. In comparison to changes of content of culture the configuration has often remarkable permanency.[2]

Just as configuration was opposed to associationism, so was behaviourism opposed to the earlier methods of introspection. The study

[1] Pp. 46–47.
[2] Benedict, *op. cit.* p. xiii.

of behaviour has been largely experimental and physiological, and two of its great classics are I. P. Pavlov's *Conditioned Reflexes*, 1927, and V. M. Bechterev's *La Psychologie objective* of 1907. Bechterev, working on dogs, discovered that if a particular stimulus is applied, there is a well-marked reflex action to it, and moreover, that if another stimulus of quite a different kind is applied always at the same time as the first, in time the second associated stimulus will alone be sufficient to induce the reflex, though previously this second stimulus would have produced no such effect, Pavlov, also working on dogs, found normal reflexes could be artificially conditioned by almost any stimulus which he associated with the normal stimulus. Among those who have applied such physiological studies to human behaviour are J. B. Watson and W. B. Cannon, the latter of whom in *Bodily Changes in Pain, Hunger, Fear, and Rage*, 1915, has shown the close connexion between the action of the endocrine glands and the emotions. While all such able work has enormous possibilities, the enthusiastic reader would do well to read not only Watson's *Behaviourism*, 1924, on the practical effect of conditioning in moulding human character, but also Aldous Huxley's *Brave New World*.

A most important work in the neurological field is Sir Charles Sherrington's *The Integrative Action of the Nervous System*, 1906, on the interaction of reflexes. He has shown among a great number of detailed studies of interaction the many important changes which occur in a nervous impulse when it crosses a synapse. This word is a term applied to the anatomical relation of one nerve-cell with another, which is effected at various points by contact of their branching processes. The state of shrinkage or relaxation at these synapses is supposed in some cases to determine the readiness with which a nervous impulse is transmitted from one part of the nervous system to another.

According to Flugel the earlier work of William McDougall was largely concerned with this subject of nervous energy. In 1905 in *Physiological Psychology* and in various succeeding papers, McDougall developed the theory that the synapse was the seat of consciousness, and that inhibitions were not a mere prevention of what would otherwise occur, but due to a redistribution of energy over the nervous system, on a physical analogy with the redistribution occurring in the water system of a house when the stream of water from the tap of a hand-basin is lessened by turning on the tap of the bath. As Flugel points out, his theory fits in with the displacement and sublimation doctrines of the psycho-analysts, and with Pavlov's theory of the conditioned reflex.

But McDougall is by no means a behaviourist with a purely mechanistic theory. His mechanistic views are firmly linked with a purposive view of life and mind. This first became evident in his *Introduction to Social Psychology* in 1908, a work intended to provide a psychological basis for the social sciences. His analysis of instinct, emotion, and character is so much more in touch with real life than the generality of books on psychology, that the book has gone into a great number of editions.

Instincts are psycho-physical dispositions, or hereditarily determined channels for the discharge of nervous energy. They are studied in three aspects: the afferent or perceptual, the tendency to pay attention to objects of a certain class; the central, affective, or emotional, the tendency to experience particular emotional excitement at the perception of such objects; and the efferent or motor aspect, by which we have a tendency to react to such objects in a particular manner.

Both in this book and in the *Outline of Psychology* in 1923, he develops the idea that each instinct has its characteristic emotion, and in the latter, the theory that instincts vary in the complexity of bodily adjustment needed to fulfil them, and that their corresponding emotions therefore vary in specificity. Those which are very simple in their bodily expression have the least specific and least easily recognizable emotions.

Instincts are often of so generalized a character that they may be expressed in a variety of ways. They may become canalized in a particular direction, and organized by means of sentiments in relation to particular objects. Such an organization of instincts brings consistency into our orectic life, all being organized round the idea of self in a well-integrated personality.

In *The Group Mind*, 1920, McDougall deals with group loyalties and ideals, and in *National Welfare and National Decay*, 1921, he applies his system to various practical problems.

J. Drever's *Instinct in Man*, 1917, advances the theory that emotion is aroused only when an instinct is obstructed and the organism thrown out of psychic equilibrium. This would appear to be in harmony with Herbert Spencer's view that mental activity is the result of tension, and the effort to restore equilibrium, and is not out of line with McDougall's theory. William James was of the opinion that man had so many instincts that they got in each other's way, and so compelled choice and reason. All of the schools have some version or other of Spencer's or James's theory of the development of reason.

Wundt's *Völkerpsychologie* and Wertheimer's theory of *Gestalt* both appeared in 1912. The third great influence of that year which has had a profound effect on the study of anthropology was Freud's *Totem and Taboo*, first published in *Imago*. He compared such savage institutions as totemism and exogamy and taboo and avoidance with the facts revealed by a study of neurotic patients at his clinic in Vienna. All of these institutions display an ambivalent or double attitude of hate and love, fear and desire, such as that exhibited in neurotic phobias and obsessions. Taboo, for example, exhibits both fear and desire, love and hate, trembling in the balance. The great taboos of totemic peoples against eating the totem and marrying within the clan are explained as two aspects of the Oedipus complex, the wish to kill the father and marry the mother.

Sigmund Freud may be compared with Darwin in one way. Like him, he opened up a whole new territory for exploration, that of the unconscious, as revealed by neurotics, in dreams, in fatigue, in slips of the pen, tongue, or memory, and developed a method for bringing the unconscious to light, displacing an affection from one idea to another, sublimating a harmful desire. His studies of the development of the sexual instinct from a number of component instincts, oral, anal, genital, etc., at first seeking their satisfaction independently, and ultimately becoming integrated under instincts connected with the sexual organs and reproduction in normal people, have had a profound effect in helping us to understand the reasons and treatment for various forms of perversion, neurotic condition, and types of character.[1]

As an example of a study in character, Ernest Jones's remarkable paper 'Anal-Erotic Character Traits' may be mentioned. He discusses the role of sublimated infantile anal interests in character formation and social institutions, these interests ultimately displaying themselves in individualism, determination and persistence, love of order, power to organize, reliability, generosity, miserliness, tyranny, irritability, obstinacy, etc.[2]

Among anthropological studies which have owed a great deal to Freud's influence may be mentioned those of Bronislaw Malinowski, in such works as 'Mutterrechtliche Familie und Oedipus Komplex,' *Imago*, 1924, X, 228; *Crime and Custom in Savage Society*, and *The Father in Primitive Psychology*, both of 1926; *Sex and Repression in Savage Society*, 1926; and *The Sexual Life of Savages*, 1929.

[1] S. Freud, *Traumdeutung*, 1900; *Der Witz und seine Beziehung zum Unbewussten*, 1905; *Drei Abhandlungen zur Sexualtheorie*, 1905; 'Zur Einführung des Narzissmus,' *Jahrbuch für Psychoanal. u. Psychopathol. Forschungen*, 1914; vi, i; *Vorlesungen zur Einführung in die Psychoanalyse*, 1917; *Massenpsychologie und Ichanalyse*, 1921; *Das Ich und das Es*, 1923; *Collected Papers*, 1925; *Das Unbehagen in der Kultur*, 1930.

[2] *J. Abn. Psych.*, Vol. XIII; reprinted in *Papers on Psychoanalysis*, 1920.

An example of his method may be taken from *Sex and Repression in Savage Society*, in which he varies Freud's explanation of totemism to suit a matrilineal people in Melanesia. In such a society the ambivalent attitude of love and hate for the father is split into two elements, love for the real father, who has no authority and tends to become a friend and playmate, and hate and respect for the maternal uncle, whose business it is to exert authority and bring up the child in the way he should go.

G. Róheim's *Australian Totemism*, 1925, is worthy of study.

Studies of sex by Freud and Havelock Ellis[1] have done much to free us from the conspiracy of silence and from the wrecking of lives through ignorance. But there are other aspects of life besides sex. As we say in Gower, 'First, we must earn our living.' The psychoanalysts, like other psychologists, are not unaware of this very important side of life. Abraham's[2] study of the oral stage of the libido, when love and hate are expressed by activities connected with the mouth, may be mentioned.

Three first-rate studies of the part that food and methods of gaining a livelihood play in the whole social organism are Audrey Richard's *Hunger and Work in a Savage Tribe*, 1932; A. T. and G. M. Culwick's *Ubena of the Rivers*, 1935, in which economics is given its due place in one of the ablest and most sympathetic studies of a primitive people in transition that I have ever read; and Raymond Firth's *Primitive Economics of the New Zealand Maori*, 1929, a valuable foundational study prerequisite to the understanding of the whole of Maori culture, integrating economics with other features.

Since anthropology deals with civilized as well as with uncivilized peoples, we must not forget the many works on criminology, penology, industry, and education which have lately been written, and the light which studies of primitive people can throw on our own problems. For an account of recent work on such applied psychology, the reader is referred to Flugel's[3] book in this series, and for the interaction of psychology with anthropology, to C. G. Seligman's admirable papers on 'Anthropology and Psychology' and 'Anthropological Perspective and Psychological Theory' in the *J.R.A.I.* for 1924 and 1932 respectively. For a valuable criticism of methods of mental testing, read Miss B. M. Blackwood's 'A Study of Mental Testing in Relation to Anthropology' in *Mental Measurement Monographs*, Serial iv. for December, 1927. Rivers insisted in his *Psychology and Ethnology*, 1926, that 'the final aim

---

[1] *Studies in the Psychology of Sex*, 1897–1928.

[2] 'Untersuchungen über früheste prägenitale Entwicklung der Libido,' *Intern. Z. f. arztl. Psychoanal.*, 1916, Jahrg. IV, 71.

[3] J. C. Flugel, *A Hundred Years of Psychology*, 1934.

of the study of society is the explanation of social behaviour in terms of psychology,' and Karl Pearson's[1] address before the British Association in 1920 on 'The Science of Man, its Needs and Prospects,' spoke of the Treaty of Versailles as ethnologically unsound, saying that if the science of man had been as far developed as the physical sciences, there would probably have been no war. The great need of our generation was the study not only of individual, but of folk-psychology, to be studied with the precision set out by Galton in the previous century: 'Until the phenomena of any branch of knowledge have been submitted to measurement and number, it cannot assume the status and dignity of a science.'

A work which links closely with that of Tylor and Bastian is C. J. Jung's 'The Psychology of the Unconscious' in *Collected Papers on Psychoanalysis*, 1916. He deals with the personal unconscious, embracing all the acquisitions of the personal existence, forgotten, repressed, or subliminally perceived, and with the collective unconscious, all personal acquisitions which originate in the inherited possibility of psychic functioning in general, or in the inherited brain-structure. All primitive thought, and much of our own, is at bottom conditioned by this collective unconscious. Such theories as these, and the general equation of the primitive, the neurotic, and the immature mind, recall the ideas of Tylor and Bastian on the general psychic unity of mankind, the monogenesis of man, the polygenesis of his inventions.

IV. CULTURAL ANTHROPOLOGY

In our summary of sociological work since 1900, it will be well to treat three different groups, those who approach the subject psychologically, and, on the whole, from an evolutionary standpoint, those who follow the diffusionist and historical method, and those who employ the functional. It is a pity that any of them should ever be at loggerheads with each other, for their work is strictly complementary, and all sides are needed to make a complete picture. The true business of the psychologist is to attempt to understand the beliefs that underlie institutions, and to do this, he must certainly take account of the history of peoples and of the diffusion of ideas and objects, and also of the function of each element of a society in relation to the rest. The diffusionist will recognize the fact that no people will accept an idea from another source unless it is psychologically capable of doing so. Both must have some common meeting ground, mentally and emotionally, and must have

[1] *R.B.A.*, Cardiff, 1920, p. 140.

travelled along somewhat the same road if the one is capable of assimilating the idea of the other. Anyone who argued for the world-wide distribution of certain traits from a common source should be prepared to admit that Tylor and Bastian were not so far wrong in assuming the psychic unity of mankind. Such an assumption, employed with the precautions which the newer schools have insisted on, is necessary if we are to continue to study man, rather than confine ourselves to inventories of men.

While the study of origins is not carried on in the same blithe and carefree way that was somewhat common in the past century, it yet holds an important place, and rightly so. And it is not as far removed from practical life as many would have us believe. To discover that the beginnings of a cherished institution are not as noble as we should like to believe, in no wise detracts from its present value. In the first place, there is a better hope for humanity if it has climbed upward from poor beginnings, than there is if it has descended from a high estate. To the religious-minded, it might seem a better argument for the goodness of God to suppose that he made his creatures to advance rather than to fall from a pristine perfection and to continue to descend.

In the second place, a study of the origins of institutions and beliefs may do for societies what psychoanalytic treatment has done for some individuals. By discovering the springs of action, it may be possible to heal disorders by beginning at the source. Once we know and face a fact, even an unpleasant one, we can start to deal with it, and by knowing ourselves, become free from slavery to misunderstood half-truth. Believing that men are fundamentally the same the world over, we can use the knowledge gained in one place for the good of another.

Psychological investigation of primitive peoples, and even of apes, is beginning to throw light on our own problems. For one thing method can be more easily developed in working on a simpler society where the salient features are more apt to be apparent than in our own complex societies. With such investigations before us it is hoped that we can more easily see where to begin with ourselves.

In the second kind the most valuable and scientific work on ape and monkey society has been begun by Zuckerman in *The Social Life of Monkeys and Apes*, 1932. Although a good many previous writers had made assumptions, Zuckerman's is the first adequate attempt to interpret simian society. Since apes differ from men in having no culture or speech, such social groups as they have must necessarily depend on physiological characters, and as these are similar to those of human beings, they separate men and apes completely from the lower mammals, and in this respect put them into a class by themselves.

In the lower mammals as a rule, there are special breeding seasons interposed between seasons of complete celibacy. The female accepts the male only during periods of heat, and this intermittent character of the sexual interest is reflected in the transitory nature of the social union. The apes, however, unlike the lower mammals, have regular menstrual cycles, that of the Hamadryas baboons which Zuckerman watched for seventy-two cycles being about thirty-one days long on the average. The apes and monkeys have both eyes in front, so that the two fields of vision overlap, and both eyes can concentrate on the same object. Man and the sub-human primates then, both have the same stereoscopic vision. Moreover, their eyes are capable of distinguishing colours, whereas the lower mammals for the most part appear to be colour-blind. Like man they have hands which can grasp an object, and they take pleasure in grooming each other.

These facts separate the sub-human primates physiologically and anatomically from the lower mammals, and have far-reaching effects in giving continuity to simian as to human society. In the first place the female ape is always more or less ready to receive the attentions of the male, and in the second, the allurements of the eye are capable of arousing desire, which in the lower mammals is excited only by physiological changes which occur in connexion with the periodical ripening of germ cells. The pleasure too, that they take in grooming and picking over each other's fur is another powerful factor in keeping the group together. This action may precede or follow or take the place of direct sexual activities.

The unit in the simian society described by Zuckerman is the family group, made up of a male overlord with his female or females, and this is held together by the interest of the male in his females, and theirs in him, and by the interest of the females in their young. One or more young bachelors are frequently attached to the family group, and watch their chances to get at the females, usually a difficult thing to do, as the more attractive females, that is the ones whose sexual skin is swollen, keep very close to their overlord, constantly grooming him or being groomed, and frequently presenting themselves and being mounted. Should a bachelor cover a female who has moved a little away from her overlord, and he turn round to look, the female will promptly run to her overlord, presenting herself sexually, and threatening her seducer. This may cause the overlord to pursue the seducer, or threaten him, or, if he be tired or not as strong as he was, to vent his anger on one of his females or some smaller ape. The chief wife is always the one whose skin is most swollen, and she always keeps very close to her mate. If there is only a limited supply of food, she is allowed to eat some of it, though her mate would attack her or any other if she were to attempt to share his food when her sexual skin was quiescent.

Social relationship within these groups appear to be governed by the inter-relationship between each ape's dominant characteristics and those of his fellows. Dominance determines the number of females that a male may possess, and except when there is an abundance of food, determines how much an ape can get to eat. If a limited amount of food is given to a baboon family, the dominant male will eat all, or guard what he cannot eat, and his females will not eat nor attempt to touch the food, even when they have young, unless their sexual skin be swollen. Closely connected with the practice of dominance is the practice of prostitution, as a means by which weaker apes manage to survive. Any member of a social group, old or young, male or female, will stimulate sexual responses of some sort in another; other animals and various objects may be used for sexual purposes, homosexual and autoerotic behaviour being common. This diffuse sexuality, due partly to the possession of hands and stereo-scopic and colour vision, allows sexual behaviour to become conditioned, and adapted to a social life based on a system of dominance. To mention a few cases only. A weaker animal secures some food, and immediately presents himself sexually to a more dominant fellow. This act of submission may be followed by the more dominant fellow covering, grooming, or otherwise examining it, and the sexual opportunity presented usually serves to inhibit the dominant animal's anger at the loss of food. An animal may attract the threats of another and stronger, and reacts by running away, or by presenting its hindquarters to the aggressor. Sometimes the two parties ignore each other after the presentation, and sometimes the aggressor mounts his fellow or grooms him. An animal may present sexually to gain the alliance of another, or even to attract an enemy which he wishes to bite. In these and other ways, sexual behaviour may be adapted to suit the situation.

The remaining bond in the group is that between the females and their young. During the lactation interval in the Hamadryas baboon, which lasts for five months, the mother's sexual skin does not swell, and she is not an object of sexual interest to the males. Should the baby die, however, the swelling will begin again within ten to twenty days, and the female is again an object of interest. During these five months the baby is carried by the mother and relies on her for protection. Its first reaction is to her fur, and it finds the nipple by trial and error, the mother making no effort. The father displays no more interest in it than in any other young baboon, such attention being displayed by picking over its fur. At the end of five months the little baboon is more independent, and wanders about among the rest, all of which manifest their interest by smacking their lips, or touching it as it passes, this smacking being the usual preliminary for various of their diffuse sexual activities. By the age of nine months the young baboon is as active as any in sexual interests, and presents sexually in a variety of situations, some of which contain an element of fear.

Imitation, or 'the relatively instantaneous regrouping of old habits,' apparently plays no part in the development of their social order. What looks like imitative behaviour is probably no more than the same response made by the same kind of animal in the same situation, and while the experience of one ape is shared by all its fellows within the group, it does not seem to result in true imitation, by which advance might come.

Many interesting questions arise out of Zuckerman's work. For example, can the gap between the behaviour of apes on the physiological plane and that of men on the cultural plane ever be bridged? Future studies, linking up physiology and psychology, both for apes and men, may bring us nearer to understanding how it is that minds of varying power, working on the emotions involved in the reproductive and parental, as well as in the gregarious instincts on the one hand, and on the other, on the emotions such as anger, fear, wonder, etc., involved in the self-protective, self-assertive, and self-sustaining instincts, may modify them under various circumstances, or given various experiences.

In the words of William James, 'Man appears to lead a life of hesitation and choice, an intellectual life, not because he has no instincts, but because he has so many that they block each other's path.' We have already seen how the self-protective and self-sustaining instincts, as well as the self-assertive, have conflicted with the sexual impulses, and have been modified among the baboons, which, if they cannot run away or otherwise obtain food, will present sexually to a dominant fellow, and if a female is in heat, will allow her food out of a limited supply. The emotion of wonder, closely allied to fear, and often conflicting with it, involved in the instinct of curiosity, would be a powerful factor for development, given a large brain, and a body which could fulfil the message sent from it.

The personality of an animal or man, or that which causes him to act as a whole and with purpose, appears to use the brain and members of the body as its tools, and while it can only express itself by their aid, to be something different from any of them, for the separate parts can be kept alive and stimulated to various actions when the co-ordinating personality is gone. It must be that in this co-ordinating personality are all the capacities which, given a suitable bodily mutation, and then experience or necessity, will develop the body or organ of the body for its use, and that such development, as of brain or hand, enables the personality with its better equipment to continue its development without limit. It seems reasonable to suppose with Lloyd Morgan[1] that times occur when favourable individual developments coincide with favourable mutations, and thus make progress possible.

It is admitted that no experience or necessity, however great, would cause any group of apes now living to start an age-long development towards anything like the rudest human societies alive today. Like the lower animals, they have continued too long in one way, and have become specialized. For a very long time, then, men and apes have been moving on different lines, men in an environment profoundly influenced by the lives of pre-existing people, and apes in an environment unaffected by the lives of animals which have been before them, for they have no speech in which to collect experience and hand it on, as Zuckerman has pointed out.

Admitting generalized ancestors common to apes and men, let us suppose that some of them were forced to rely on their wits to gain a living in a variety of manners.[2] If Dr Robert Broom[3] is right, both the little Taungs ape[4] and the Rhodesian man[5] ate meat as well as fruit and vegetables. Being weaker than the other animals, these early forerunners of man must have been obliged to co-operate with their fellows in bringing down the quarry, and to stand by each other to protect themselves from the more powerful beasts.

The one thing necessary for the beginning of culture would be the possession of speech, and this may, as Sir Richard Paget[6] has suggested, have begun from an emotional cry shaped by the mimetic action of suitably shaped jaws, lips, and tongue, into articulate speech. Once language was born, its possessors would be for ever different from all other animals, and development could begin, for each generation could profit by the experience of past generations, and the emotions which

[1] See p. 95.
[2] See p. 206 f.
[3] *The Coming of Man*, 1933, p. 137.
[4] See p. 206.
[5] *Ibid.*
[6] Sir Richard Paget, *Human Speech*, London and New York, 1930; *This English*, 1935.

were before individual could be universalized, and become matter for thought.

Concerted mimetic action foreshadowing the good to come when all are hungry, or expressing the grief or uneasiness felt at the loss of a fellow, might awaken emotions which would add richness to life, or afford food for reflexion. In the common ritual, if so we may call it, experience is provided which actualizes the capacities of the individuals who participate. The mass action stirs up the emotions necessary for the attainment of good, and at the same time those which lead to evil, and by stripping them of their purely personal content and emphasizing them, makes them matter for thought and choice, rather than mere matters of perception, and so makes possible a life in which thought and moral behaviour can play a part. Such concerted action, while rousing emotions of which the individual by himself would not be capable, yet actualized the capacity of the individuals, so that one a little better than his fellows might become a leader, and enrich the life of the group which brought his powers to birth.

It is not necessary to consider again the old theory of the inheritance of acquired reactions as a condition of progress. Language itself universalizes emotions, forcing a choice from the welter of bewildering emotions and instincts which would condemn us to an age-long repetition of the manner of life followed by our remote forebears. Supposing that we inherited the same reactions mentally and emotionally in each generation. Even then, once language has appeared, each generation starts with the accumulated experience of past generations, and is so much the better off.

It seems impossible to explain or account for the varieties of human social structure except on Prichard's[1] assumption that the convictions which hold it together imply for their validity the prior capacity on our part, and that different varieties of environment and experience have actualized the capacity. In other words, Tylor and Bastian, and the old evolutionary school generally, were right in assuming that all human beings everywhere have within themselves the possibilities of originating the basic elements of civilization. It is often argued that though emotions may be the same the world over, customs are very different, and that explanations must be sociological rather than psychological. But the ultimate explanation must always be psychological, because any sociological arrangement must satisfy the emotions and mind of man if it is to endure.

---

[1] H. A. Prichard, *Duty and Interest*, Clarendon Press, 1929.

Various authors have been mentioned as emphasizing the importance of a change from a frugivorous to a meat diet, and of the consequent compulsion on our early ancestors to associate together for mutual aid and protection.

Among the earliest to emphasize the factors of mutual aid and parental love as important in evolution, factors which Darwin had stressed, but many of his followers practically ignored, were the Russians. As early as 1880 Professor Kessler of St Petersburg University wrote in the *Memoirs of the St Petersburg Society of Naturalists* (Vol. XI.) 'On the Law of Mutual Aid,' a development of ideas suggested by the *Origin of Species* and *The Descent of Man*, and in 1881 appeared J. L. Lanessan's *La Lutte pour l'Existence et l'Association pour la Lutte.* Louis Buchner's *Liebe und Liebesleben in der Thierwelt* was published in 1882 and 1885. P. Kropotkin,[1] influenced by the general tendency of evolutionary studies in Russia, began collecting material in 1883. It happened that he was spending a part of his youth in eastern Siberia and northern Manchuria, and noticed how the animals crowded together in their migrations before the snow and flood to cross the Amur where it was narrowest. He was impressed by their consciousness of kind, and general instinct of solidarity, the same sort of vague instinct which would make him rush with a bucket of water to the burning house of a neighbour whom he did not know. To his mind the struggle for existence against such difficulties as a scarcity of food weakened even the strongest, and was a drawback, rather than a potent factor in evolutionary advance. His work goes on to treat of the solidarity of the clan among the barbarians, of the mediaeval city, in Labour Unions, in strikes, etc., and of mutual aid in villages and slums, all this solidarity and mutual help being powerful factors in the development of society, and in survival.

Anyone who knows a village well will recognize that it is like a very solid family, with all the love and dissension that characterize a family, and anyone who has had experience of poverty-stricken areas in cities during a crisis or time of poverty-stricken areas in cities during a crisis or time of depression will be struck by this same solidarity among the unfortunate. One who has read of or seen primitive communities, again, will have noticed the solidarity of the clan, extended family, village, or whatever other unit makes up the home-circle. So close is it, indeed, that the usual marriage is with a cross-cousin. That is, the primitive man marries as near to the home-circle as possible without

---

[1] *Mutual Aid, a Factor of Evolution*, 1902.

breaking into it. There can be little doubt that such solidarity has played a most important part in racial survival.

The study of primitive communism has taken a powerful hold on Russia since the October revolution of 1917, the principal work in the U.S.S.R. being mainly directed to three problems, first, the social structure of pre-class society, second, the nature and genesis of primitive religion, and third, the ethnography of the many primitive peoples within their own vast territory. Professor E. Kagarov[1] of the Institute of Anthropology and Ethnography, Academy of Sciences, U.S.S.R., has summarized the development of these studies since the revolution.

The study of pre-class society splits up into a number of separate questions, such as the nature of primitive communism, the laws governing the development of pre-gens society, the nature of pre-gens society and its decline, and the history of various forms of the family. The practical value of such studies to the present government is found in Karl Marx's idea, 'The new system which modern society is approaching will be the re-emergence of the archaic social type in its highest form' (*Arkhiv Marksa i Engelsa*, T. 1, 1928, p. 278).

Of all the legacies of classical ethnology, the most highly valued are the works of L. H. Morgan, which were greatly esteemed by Marx and Engels. *Ancient Society* has been translated by the Academy of Sciences as a work of fundamental importance. While the majority of Soviet ethnologists consider that the historical existence of primitive communism has been confirmed beyond a doubt, there are yet a few, like Professor P. Kushner,[2] who deny it, maintaining that in such primitive communities as the Australian and the Fuegian, the methods of gathering food prevent the man and woman from being much together, and there is a tendency for people to consume food on the spot when they have gathered it, so that the distribution of food is based on the animal rather than the communistic principle, each one receiving such food as has been obtained by his or her help. As such theories exist, a large number of Soviet ethnographers have taken part in a discussion, the net result of which, according to a work edited by N. M. Matorin, is to show that communism was the earliest stage of social development.[3]

The general evolution of society has been traced by S. P. Tolstov in *Sovietskaia Etnografia* for 1931, Numbers 3-4, pages 69-103. In his

[1] 'The Ethnography of Foreign Countries in Soviet Russia.'

[2] 'On Primitive Communism,' *Records of J. M. Sverdlov Communist University*, Vol. II, Moscow, 1924. 'O pervobytnom kommunizme,' Zapiski kommunisticheskogo Universiteta im. J. M. Sverdlova.

[3] N. M. Matorin, (ed.), 'Primitive Communism,' 'Primitive Society,' Moscow, 1932, 5-26. 'Pervobytnyi Kommunizm' v sbornike 'Pervobytnyi obschchestvo.'

view the earliest stage was the hunting of big game, after the ape had somehow changed into a beast of prey. Man, being weaker than the animals, had to herd together and share all things in common. Totemism arose as the ideological reflexion of the productive differentiation existing within the groups, and was at first of a temporary nature, but later led to the splitting of the community into groups consisting each of a more or less permanent body of individuals who specialized in hunting and breeding their totem animal. The division of labour on the sex principle led to the formation of male and female productive totem groups, and a further differentiation within the sex totem groups served as a basis for the formation of the prototype of a punaluan[1] family by establishing marriage relations between two totem groups, the male and female. Later, the accumulation of surplus agricultural supplies and herds of cattle necessitated the organization of groups to guard these supplies, and thus arose the gens. The increasing rôle of the individual producer led to the formation of the paired family, which became the basic social and economic unit.

A. M. Zolotarev[2] considers that the earliest stage was one of food gathering, with no chiefs or leaders, all matters being settled conjointly. When improved tools made big game accessible to man, the chase became man's work, and gathering women's. According to the locality and the prominence of one or other of these occupations, man or woman dominated in social life. Somewhere between the Chellean and Mousterian epochs the division of labour led to the economic and social isolation of the male group, and the struggle between the sexes to the formation of secret unions with initiations to which the opposite sex was not admitted. While the young and strong were hunting, the old men stayed at home and made tools and took counsel with each other. This led to gerontocracy, for the old men had superior technique and experience and knowledge of animals and life generally, and thus were gradually able to concentrate power in their own hands. The gradual improvement of tools led to their being individually used, and ultimately private property was recognized. In the primitive herd there was promiscuity. With the division of labour, since men hunted and women gathered, each sex found itself in need of the other's services, and this resulted in more or less constant marriages between groups. Zolotarev emphasizes the fact that the best bourgeois ethnologists, such as Frazer, Rivers, and Briffault, all believe in the former prevalence of

[1] A Hawaiian word. See L. H. Morgan, *Ancient Society*, under chapter 'The Punaluan Family.'

[2] In above work, cited on p.227, ed. Matorin, Moscow, 1932, 77-104.

group marriage, as established by Morgan, Spencer, and Gillen. Apparently, Bronislaw Malinowski and N. W. Thomas are included in the category of those who have established the same form of marriage, but in the discussion of pirrauru and piraungaru as described by Howitt[1] and by Spencer and Gillen[2] respectively, Thomas[3] finds neither the features of an actual group marriage nor the traces of such a previous state of things. Malinowski, in *The Family among the Australian Aborigines*, 1913, quotes him with approval in his own discussion of pirrauru, and in the addenda to his book on page 308, associates himself with Andrew Lang's criticisms in *The Secret of the Totem*, 1905, and with Ernest Crawley's in *The Mystic Rose*, first published in 1902. The result of Malinowski's examination of the tribes which were studied by Howitt, Spencer, and Gillen, and others is summed up at the end of the book:

The individual family was shown to be a unit playing an important part in the social life of the natives and well defined by a number of moral, customary, and legal norms; it was further determined by the sexual division of labour, the aboriginal mode of living, and especially by the intimate relation between the parents and children. The individual relation between husband and wife [marriage] is rooted in the unity of the family. Moreover, it is expressed by a series of facts connected with the modes in which marriage is brought about and in the well-defined, although not always exclusive, sexual right the husband acquires over his wife.

In the *Sovietskaia Etnografia* for 1929 (Vol. VII, No. 1, pp. 23–54), S. A. Tokarev argued that the Australian relationship terms referred originally to the group, and not to blood-relationship, such terms acquiring an individual meaning at a later period. In the same year, in the *Sociological Review*,[4] the present writer attempted to show by an examination of genealogies that marriage with a cousin on the other side of the family within a small society always made four classes apparent, and that the prevention of marriage between the children of a brother and those of his sister, in addition to the usual prevention between the children of two brothers or the children of two sisters, made second-cousin marriage the nearest allowable, and made eight named classes apparent, the names for the classes being an extension of the terms expressing blood-relationship.

The discoveries of Sir Baldwin Spencer and Mr F. J. Gillen, as set

[1] A. W. Howitt, *The Native Tribes of South-East Australia*, 1904.
[2] W. B. Spencer and F. J. Gillen, *The Native Tribes of Central Australia*, 1899.
[3] N. W. Thomas, *Kinship Organizations and Group Marriage in Australia*, 1906, 136.
[4] January, 1929.

out in *The Native Tribes of Central Australia*, 1899, *The Northern Tribes of Central Australia*, 1904, and *The Arunta, a Stone-Age People*, 1927, have had a very powerful effect on European, and especially English, anthropology. From 1897 until his death in 1929, Spencer corresponded regularly with Sir James Frazer, and *Spencer's Scientific Correspondence*[1] shows the warm regard which the two men had for each other. Frazer arranged with Macmillan for the publication of the first work of Spencer and Gillen, and wrote:

Works such as yours (I wish there were more of them than there are), recording a phase of human history which before long will have passed away, will have a permanent value so long as men exist on earth and take an interest in their own past. Books like mine, merely speculative, will be superseded sooner or later (the sooner the better for the sake of truth) by better inductions based on fuller knowledge; books like yours, containing records of observation, will never be superseded.

Spencer influenced Frazer profoundly, and the influence is especially apparent in *Totemism and Exogamy*, published in four volumes in 1910. The inclusion of the original essay of 1885 on *Totemism* serves to show how far a knowledge of the subject had developed since Frazer began to write. The bulk of the four volumes is taken up by full accounts of totemic and exogamic organization throughout the world, and is, of course, the most complete work of its kind in the whole world, comparable only with the third edition of *The Golden Bough*, 1911–15, in twelve volumes, the most comprehensive account in existence of the magico-religious ideas of primitive man, whether in savage life, or surviving in our midst. The charm of the style, and the vast accumulation of evidence, have probably done more than any other work to advance the study of anthropology, and to make governments and churches realize the necessity for studying the peoples among whom they work.

Frazer bases his theories of totemism and exogamy on the Australian evidence collected by Spencer and Gillen, believing that certain customs are a survival of a former state of group-marriage, and that the eight marriage-classes among the southern Arunta are the artificial result of the bisection of the promiscuous horde, and then of further bisection. The curious method by which totems are determined leads him to argue that totemism orginated in the sick fancies of pregnant women, who thought that their children were to be attributed to some external and non-human object. In the introduction to *Spencer's Last Journey*,[2] 1931, he emphasizes the fact that totemism in Australia has yet another

---

[1] Ed. Marett and Penniman, 1932, p. 22; quotation dated July 13, 1898.
[2] Ed. Marett and Penniman, p. 6.

aspect as an industrial organization, the natives having divided the whole of nature into totems, each clan having the duty to maintain and increase its totem for the benefit of the rest.

Knowledge of the elaborate intichiuma ceremonies performed by the Arunta for the increase of their totem animals or plants led to a great deal of controversy and the development of a great many theories among European anthropologists. These ceremonies, in Frazer's view, were a kind of sympathetic or contagious magic, a misapplication of two fundamental laws of thought, the association of ideas by similarity, and the association of ideas by contiguity in space or time. The mistaken association produces magic, the legitimate association, science. Magic precedes religion, which is a propitiation or conciliation of powers superior to man, and religion in its turn is gradually withdrawing from provinces of action in favour of science, as people come to learn the true laws governing the universe.

Marett's theory[1] of a pre-animistic or animatistic stage of religion, already alluded to, was greatly strengthened by the addition of the Australian evidence, which appeared to show magical or religious ceremonies performed by a people who had no notion at all of a god or gods, and were in awe of many churinga objects, which had no soul or spirit part associated with them, but yet had power. Marett, like Durkheim, preferred to consider any social attempt to get into touch with power over and above ordinary human ability as religious. The cult of the sacred—using 'sacred' in the ambivalent sense of holy and unclean, or set apart and powerful for good if rightly approached and for evil if wrongly approached, as in the Latin word *sacer*—whose end is infinite good for all, is religion, according to Marett, and this appears to be Durkheim's view as well. Magic, according to both, is individualistic, and as a rule, antisocial.

K. T. Preuss in his article 'Der Ursprung der Religion und Kunst' in *Globus*[2] for 1904 and 1905, followed Marett's lead, and made the term pre-animism current in Germany, and placed magic and primitive stupidity (*Urdummheit*) first in the order of man's development. In later work, notably 'Die geistige Kultur der Naturvölker'[3] and 'Die höchste Gottheit bei den kulturarmen Völkern,'[4] he takes Lang's and Schmidt's evidence into account, and admits that in some cases high gods are not the latest stage in development, but may be an early religious testimony.

[1] See p. 140.
[2] Vol. LXXXVI, 321–27, 355–63, 375–79, 388–92; LXXXVII, 333–37, 347–50, 380–84, 394–400, 413–19.
[3] No. 542 of *Aus Natur u. Geisteswelt*, Leipzig, 1914.
[4] *Psychol. Forschungen*, Berlin, II, 1922, 161.

Durkheim's *Les Formes élémentaires de la vie religieuse: le système totémique en Australie* of 1912 has already been mentioned several times with reference to sociological theories of the origin of religion and magic. He finds the beginning of religion in totemism. While the Australian would attribute to an external power in the form of an animal or plant the exaltation and increase of vitality he feels in performing his rites, the error is only in the symbol, the reality being the society, which inspires him, and the symbol being necessary to the consciousness of belonging to that society.

The totemic emblem then stands for the collective religious power which is to be found in man, all that he was, and is, and may be, and in his plant and animal relatives. Man and his environment depend on each other, and the same sacred power is in both, mighty for good if rightly approached and handled, mighty for harm if lightly or irreverently approached. Its symbolic representations enable it to be apprehended, and turned to the use of men.[1]

In the previous chapter Codrington's introduction of the Melanesian words *mana* and *tabu* to European notice was mentioned, as well as the discovery of Amerindian words like *wakan* and *orenda*, all of them signifying personal or impersonal power and beyond ordinary human ability and comprehension. In *The Threshold of Religion*, 1909, Marett writes:

I conclude, then, that *mana*, or rather the *tabu-mana* formula, has solid advantages over animism, when the avowed object is to found what Dr Tylor calls 'a minimum definition of religion.' *Mana* is co-extensive with the supernatural power, differing in intensity—in voltage, so to speak— but never in essence; animism splits up into more or less irreducible kinds, notably 'soul', 'spirit', and 'ghost'. Finally, *mana*, whilst fully adapted to express the immaterial—the unseen force at work behind the scene—yet, conformably with the incoherent state of rudimentary reflexion, leaves in solution the distinction between personal and impersonal, and in particular does not allow any notion of a high individuality to be precipitated. Animism, on the other hand, tends to lose touch with the supernatural in its more impersonal forms. . . .[2]

A valuable paper on the same lines as Marett's 1900 paper on pre-animistic religion was Hewitt's '*Orenda* and a Definition of Religion' in the *American Anthropologist*, N.S., Vol. IV., 1902. A. Goldenweiser's *History, Psychology, and Culture* of 1933 approaches religious problems similarly, using the word 'thrill' to express the complex of feelings in the face of the supernatural which Marett called 'awe,' and considers that

[1] Penniman, *Sociol. Review*, Jan., 1929, 25.
[2] p. 137.

magic ultimately divested itself completely from the religious thrill. Hartland has summed up the whole case brilliantly in his 'Address to the Anthropological Section of the British Association' at York in 1906.

Anthropology owes a great deal to the lucidity and analytical skill of the French authors who have contributed to *L'Année Sociologique*, and not least to H. Hubert and M. Mauss. In Volume VII their 'Esquisse d'une théoric générale de la Magie' displays Durkheim's attitude that religion and magic are the social expression of social needs, but affirms Marett's view of the common participation of magic and religion in notions of the mana type. In volume II the same authors have an admirable essay on sacrifice,[1] in which they display three distinct phases. In the first, the sacrificer gains an entry into *le monde sacré*, and so is removed from *le monde profane*, a dangerous proceeding because a wrong approach to the supernatural is hazardous. In the second phase the sacrificer is a part of the sacred world, and effects the purpose of the rite. The third phase is that of desacralization, which enables the sacrificer to return to the profane world and to pursue his ordinary duties among ordinary people, rid of the superior sanctity which would make him a danger to himself and others in ordinary life.

In *Les Rites de Passage*, 1909, A. van Gennep takes us from cradle to grave, through all the seasons of the year, showing how such rites as those at birth, marriage, and initiation are intended to effect a similar transition from one stage of life to another. In general, these *rites de passage* have a threefold structure, of *rites de séparation, rites de marge*, and *rites d'agrégation*. To a member of one social stage, the next stage in society is a part of *le monde sacré*, to which the transition is potentially dangerous. The girl who has reached puberty, for example, undergoes rites of separation which sever her from *le monde asexué*, of transition, and finally of aggregation to womanhood, when she puts on outward and visible signs of her change of status. Another work largely concerned with initiation is Hutton Webster's *Primitive Secret Societies* of 1908, dealing with the discipline, training, and ritual observances characterizing initiation into adult life, and showing how tribal societies with political, religious, and judicial functions arise on the basis, for example, of original puberty organizations.

The old question as to the priority of mother-right over father-right has survived into this century, though to many it is a barren question. Two works on this subject are E. S. Hartland's *Primitive Paternity*, 1909, and Robert Briffault's three great volumes on *The Mothers*,

---

[1] Reprinted in H. Hubert and M. Mauss, *Mélanges d'histoire des Religions*, 1909.

published in 1927. Hartland has also written a valuable book on *Primitive Law* (1924).

A great number of books have been published on special subjects since the beginning of the century. Before discussing movements that begin in the present period, a few of the outstanding special studies mainly on lines laid down in the previous century may be mentioned.

First there is Hasting's *Encyclopaedia of Religion and Ethics*, a work of lasting value, its subjects being treated by masters in their kind.

Among outstanding studies on primitive marriage is Ernest Crawley's *The Mystic Rose*, first published in 1902, and edited by T. Besterman in 1927. Crawley rightly attempted to consider marriage in relation to the whole complex of primitive thought. 'Men and women at marriage, women during menstruation, pregnancy, and childbirth, boys and girls at puberty, infants, not to mention other critical conditions and circumstances, are regarded by early man as being in that mysterious religious state which necessitates the imposition of restrictions and safeguards, of taboos, in a word.' People in such conditions are charged like the Ark of the Covenant with a sort of spiritual electricity which may bring harm or good, according as it is rightly or wrongly approached. Crawley points out that one sex feels a natural nervousness towards the other. In one respect woman is regarded as weaker than man, and her weakness may infect him. In another, owing to such facts as menstruation, childbirth, and sexual solidarity, she is mysterious and dangerous. Marriage ceremonies are supposed to neutralize the danger inherent in union between the two sexes. Both these fears seem to imply that we start with the full-grown male, who has had no sexual experience previous to adult life, a condition not always found. If there has been prenuptial unchastity, why should the marriage ceremony be needed to neutralize danger? Is not the marriage ceremony rather a social recognition of the fact that two people are going to live together? Again, if the male fears that he will contract the female's weakness, why is this not counterbalanced by the female's belief that she will gain the strength of the male by contact? Crawley is very difficult to follow when he maintains that the sexual taboo is on all intercourse primarily, and that the taboo on incest is the general taboo intensified. He is right in saying that the horror of incest has a magico-religious basis, for such a sanction alone could explain the horror. But it is hard to see from his argument why, since all unions are dangerous, some can be made safe and others not.

In a penetrating study of the various ambivalent emotions which are the raw material of religion and ethics, Marett[1] has made the valuable suggestion that the primary rules of the home-circle, his expression for what many writers call the incest-group, are 'blood for blood against the rest of the world', and 'no killing or unchastity within the home-circle'. He emphasizes the solidarity of these primitive groups and shows the consequences of sexual jealousy and strife within them, if such were allowed. It is clear enough that though men may be afraid of women, they do marry them. It is also clear that the home-circle is the one place where a man has a refuge in a dangerous world, and that disharmony must not enter it. Now suppose that a man breaks that harmony by killing one of his own people, or by possessing a kinswoman. If he is not at once killed in anger, he escapes to live alone. A Maori once told me how awful it was to be alone, saying that the sacred inner life principle was exposed to all the evil spirits. Cut off from the companionship and solidarity which is life itself, such a one is indeed dead in spirit, and far from shunning the punishment of his outraged kin, he welcomes the blow that puts him out of his misery. Occasional infraction of either of the great primary rules would make the sinner and his people realize how dreadful it was to break the concord, and spoil the only permanent sanctury in a world full of unknown evil.

In *Jocasta's Crime*, 1933, Lord Raglan amusingly, and often convincingly, demolishes most of the theories invented to explain the horror of incest, but develops theories of his own which are quite as amusing as his criticisms of others. He is not right in supposing that incest-groups are artificially formed. The nucleus of such a group is always the blood-relations, and this may be extended by the inclusion of other more or less related people who live with them and share the same life, and are considered to be related, or by the sort of false logic that counts an aunt by marriage with an aunt by blood, or a godparent with a parent, or Panunga in Alice Springs with Panunga in Hermannsburg. Nor is he right in supposing that because some people have no abstract word for incest, they have not the idea. The moment that a savage prohibits a mother and a daughter and a sister, all different women, he has made the abstraction.

Among books dealing with marriage laws and their history, the fifth edition of Westermarck's *The History of Human Marriage*, 1921, in three volumes, is noteworthy. Among the principal additions are increased attention to economic conditions, especially as influencing the development of monogamy or polygyny, and to divorce. Also much greater attention is paid to the evidence from folklore.

One of the best books on the method of studying folklore is G. L.

[1] R. R. Marett, *Faith, Hope, and Charity in Primitive Religion*, 1932.

Gomme's *Folklore as an Historical Science*, 1908, in which he attacks
the problem how best to utilize tradition in the interests of history. In
The Village Community in Britain and in *Ethnology in Folklore*, he had
argued for the possibility of finding an ethnical element in folklore and
of reaching important historical conclusions by analysing and comparing traditions, ritual, and institutions. In this book, too, he protests
that historians have not sufficient regard for tradition, and that students
of folklore do not carry their researches into the field of ethnology and
correlate them with those of historians. The book is an attempt to show
how such work may be useful to historians.

Two great works on ethics appeared in 1906, Westermarck's *The
Origin and Development of the Moral Ideas*,[1] and L. T. Hobhouse's
Morals in Evolution.[2] The first examines the emotional origin of moral
judgements, the nature and origin of the moral emotions, the principal
moral concepts, customs and laws as expressions of the moral ideas,
the general nature of the subjects of enlightened moral judgements, the
will as the subject of moral judgement and the influence of external
events, agents under intellectual disability, motives, character, moral
valuation and free-will, and then goes on to map out human conduct
into provinces, and within each province to select various outstanding
forms of practice, as for example, homicide, or of institution, e.g.
slavery, as nuclei about which are collected facts exemplifying the influence of ethnical norms. The survey is thus more sociological than
psychological in scope. Hobhouse's work approaches the theory of
ethical evolution 'through a comparative study of rules of conduct and
ideals of life . . . the results of classification when seen in the light of
evolutionary theory acquire a wholly new significance and value. They
furnish us with a conception of the trend of human development based
not on any assumption as to the underlying causes at work, but on
a matter-of-fact comparison of the achievements reached at various
stages of the process itself. . . . For the study of development the ethics
of civilization are not less, but, if anything, more important than those of
savagery, and have therefore received closer attention in this work. But
the complexities of civilized ethics, interwoven as they are with religious
and political doctrines, can only be treated within the limits of a general
sketch by keeping to what is distinctive and fundamental in each system,
and of this only so much is selected for discussion as is deemed to have a
bearing on ethical development.'[3] It is part of the plan of the work to

[1] Second volume in 1908.
[2] Two volumes.
[3] Hobhouse, *Morals in Evolution*, preface.

estimate critically the place of each system in the line of development. To do this the author has made an attempt to put aside preconceived notions and bias, and to examine the ethics of Christendom and modern thought on the same footing, and in the same spirit, as the others, as phases of development to be impartially examined.

So much for a general summary of some of the work being done by the evolutionary school. The last chapter showed the rise of another method of dealing with anthropological problems, the historical and diffusionist.

As the last chapter showed, this school of thought took its rise naturally among students chiefly interested in material culture, the earliest exponents being Ratzel and Frobenius,[1] who invented between them the criteria of form and quantity, the first showing that agreement in form of two objects, other than that arising out of the nature, material, and purpose of the objects, meant historical connexion or borrowing, even though these objects were widely separated in space. The criterion of quantity, showing the number of agreements between different cultures, indicated a more or less close connexion between the two. In 1905 two members of the staff of the Museum für Völkerkunde published their first work of this kind under the titles 'Kulturkreise und Kulturschichten in Ozeanien,'[2] and 'Kulturkreise und-Kulturschichten in Africa,'[3] respectively, and in 1913 Father Schmidt published 'Kulturkreise und Kulturschichten in Südamerika.'[3] In all these papers they worked out a number of spheres of culture in the areas they studied, and displayed their relative chronology as culture-strata. N. C. Nelson,[4] Franz Boas, Clark Wissler, and others developed the culture-area concept in America. This was the result of many detailed studies of a considerable number of tribes which appeared to show that cultures could be grouped round various centres. In each of these centres was a specific group of culture-traits, these traits diminishing in number and new ones appearing as we go farther from the centre. The new ones gradually increase in number until we find ourselves at a new centre. Wissler's The American Indian, 1917, 1922, shows the method fully applied. For some of its limitations and dangers, R. B. Dixon's The Building of Cultures, 1928, may be consulted. Perhaps the best effort to establish a method for determining the relative chronology of culture-strata was made by E. Sapir in his Time Perspective in American

[1] See pp. 177, 178.
[2] Z.E., XXXVII, 1905, 28 (Graebner), 54 (Ankermann).
[3] Z.E., 1913, 1014.
[4] In 1919, 'Human Culture,' Natural History, XIX, No. 2, New York.

Aboriginal Culture, A Study in Method,[1] which offers a series of criteria based on the inward connexions and outward extensions of the various culture elements. The Americans were among the first outside Germany to break away from the evolutionary school and to insist on historical analysis. As early as 1910 Boas took this attitude in his lecture 'Ethnological Problems in Canada,[2] and reaffirmed it in 1920 in 'The Methods of Ethnology,'[3] In France, Father Pinard de la Boullaye's *L'Étude comparée des Religions* adopts the historical method, and in Sweden, Baron Erland von Nordenskiöld's[4] *Comparative Ethnographical Studies* (Göteborg, Vols. 1–9), between 1919 and 1931, are mainly on the lines of historical and geographical methods, though the brilliant and independent author was far from going all the way with the German historical school, or indeed with any other.

The most uncompromising exponent of the method in Germany is F. Graebner, whose *Méthode der Ethnologie* appeared in 1911. For him the history of humanity is not one great story of evolution, in which some peoples have progressed more than others. It is rather a collection of stories of the origin and growth and interaction of many cultures arising in different centres and from different causes, and thence diffused through adjacent areas, and indeed, in some cases, all over the world. Bastian's *Elementargedanken* do not exist for him. The psychology of one people differs from that of another. To trace similarities to a common element in human nature is mysticism, and not science. For example, if a member of the evolutionary school were to find designs transitional between realistic and geometrical designs, he would say that in such transitions there was evidence for an evolutionary process which has led man everywhere in the world to the conventionalization of realistic forms, so that in time they become geometrical designs. To Graebner, Foy, and others of the German historical school, however, these transitions are examples of the blending of two cultures, one of which employed realistic designs, the other of which used geometrical forms in decoration.

Every cultural phenomenon is an integral part of the whole culture, and cannot be separated from it. Its existence anywhere in the world apart from its own home indicates the diffusion, though perhaps in an attenuated form, of the whole culture in the direction in which it is found. The two main criteria for discovering the historical connexion between cultural elements and complexes are those of form and quan-

---

[1] Canadian Dept. of Mines, Ottawa, 1914.
[2] *J.R.A.I.*, XL, 1910, 529.
[3] *Amer. Anthropologist*, N.S., XXII, 1920, 311.
[4] See *Man*, 1933, **35,** for obituary and bibliography.

tity, as described above. Every people is regarded as being stratified, or in other words, has received a series of cultural deposits. If two cultures touch each other and overlap, they will produce crosses. If they merely touch there will be signs of the contact. Forms arising out of a crossing or contact will be older than the parent forms, and again, when forms due to mixture or contact show the different components clearly, they will be younger than types where the components are more blended.[1]

Two questions may be asked. First, if the psychic unity of mankind be denied, how is diffusion possible? Or, in other words, why are not the elements of one culture meaningless nonsense to another? Secondly, since Graebner claims that his method is objective, and that the evolutionary is subjective, is he not making a purely subjective assumption in postulating that striking similarity of form shows historical connexion, and that independent invention is unthinkable? When the method is applied to social phenomena it is possible to be quite as subjective as in the evolutionary method, for often on the evidence available, to say that a custom is historically prior to another is as much a matter of personal opinion as to say that it is psychologically more primitive.

The method has yielded its most valuable results in the study of material cultures, but has been applied with some success to sociology. In 1911 W. H. R. Rivers, one of the ablest sociologists and psychologists of our time, spoke on 'The Ethnological Analysis of Culture' before the British Association at Portsmouth. In that address he announced that he had been led independently to much the same general position as the German historical school. In a previous chapter[2] his use of the genealogical method of collecting statistics was mentioned. By this means he was enabled to record a vast amount of sociological data with a readiness and accuracy not hitherto possible. His method has done as much as any to bring precision into social anthropology. In 1910, while going over material so collected in Melanesia, he was led by the facts to see how much in the past he had ignored considerations arising from racial mixture and the blending of cultures.

To take one example of his method. A study of relationship terms showed that they fell into two main classes. One class was generally diffused throughout Melanesia. The other class differed considerably in different cultural regions. The terms of the first class denoted relationships which his comparative study of the forms of the systems had shown to have suffered change, while the terms which varied greatly in different parts of Melanesia denoted relationships, such as those of

[1] See also p. 178 for the criterion of continuity.
[2] See p. 99.

the mother and mother's brother, which had apparently suffered no great change in status. From this he inferred that at the most primitive stage of Melanesian society which he could discover, there had been great linguistic diversity which had been transformed by a general immigration from without into the relative uniformity he now found. Following this clue he found much other evidence to support this theory. The first volume of *History of Melanesian Society*, 1914, is written on evolutionary lines, the second on historical.

Rivers was not confined to any one aspect of social life, nor to any one method of study. Perhaps his greatest work lay in his effort to integrate the studies of ethnology and psychology into one discipline. Among the works of this sort are *Instinct and the Unconscious*, 1922; *Conflict and Dream*, 1923; *Psychology and Politics*, 1923; *Medicine, Magic, and Religion*, 1924: and *Social Organization*, 1924. In the last named, he wrote at the beginning: 'I am one of those who believe that the ultimate aim of all studies of mankind, whether historical or scientific, is to reach an explanation in terms of psychology, in terms of the ideas, beliefs, sentiments, and instinctive tendencies by which the conduct of man, both individual and collective, is determined.' Generally his works show that ethnological studies should contribute to a better understanding of man and his culture and to the solution of the problems with which humanity is confronted. By a comparative study of beliefs and customs, we may be enabled to construct a history of human progress, showing the struggle with material and social environment, and the movements of thought which led up to them, displaying how minds, once adapted to a rude and savage existence, have developed so as to cope with the complexity of modern civilization. Ethnological facts will supply valuable material for the study of psychology, and in its turn, psychology will aid in their interpretation, and, it is hoped, will increasingly contribute its part in disclosing the origins of human actions and in giving direction to them. Thus, as our knowledge increases, we shall have more opportunity of consciously working for the best, instead of merely hoping for it.

The outstanding protagonist of the historical school in the study of religions is Father Wilhelm Schmidt. In *The Origin and Growth of Religion, Facts and Theories*, translated by H. J. Rose in 1931, he has given a very full history and bibliography of all the theories ever put forward by the various schools of comparative religion. His greatest work is *Der Ursprung der Gottesidee* (The Origin of the Idea of God). The first edition was published at Münster in 1912, and the second in 1926, both of Volume I only. In the second edition there are detailed special studies of the South-East Australian Supreme Beings and of the religion of the Tasmanians. Volume II, Münster, 1929, studies America; Volume III, 1930, Asia and Australia; IV, 1933, Africa; V, 1934, contains supplementary material for volumes II and III. Of future volumes, VI will be entitled *Zusammenfassende Vergleichung der Religionen aller Urvölker*, and volumes VII and VIII will be *Die Religionen der Nomadenhirtenvölker* for Africa and Asia respectively. No one has ever arranged so much evidence in so masterly a manner except Sir James Frazer, but there the resemblance ends. Frazer follows the universalistic and comparative method. Father Schmidt is historical in his treatment of the data, and writes with the object of establishing with certainty and by objective means the ethnological age of the high gods. Considering the nature of much of his evidence, it is hard to believe that some of his decisions as to ethnological age are not on as subjective a basis as those of the psychological school, when they assert, for example, that the idea of *mana* is psychologically prior to that of animism.

Instead of a slow development upward to the realization of a high god, Schmidt pictures a sort of primitive Eden in America and Africa, for example, with a Supreme Being, this happy state of affairs being later overlaid by naturism, fetishism, manism, animism, totemism, magism, these *isms* coming with higher forms of civilization. Father Schmidt's high gods are thus rather better creatures than Lang's magnified non-natural man.[1]

Apart from his theory, Schmidt's analysis of the *Kulturkreise* and general methodology are highly illuminating, as well as the knowledge he displays of a vast number of obscure tribes and cultures, and his collection and presentation of evidence will be as lasting a possession as the *Golden Bough*.

As for his theory, it is doubtful to me whether all the labour that he has expended on it will prove it to be any sounder than the theory of the archaic culture diffused from Egypt according to Elliot Smith[2] and W. J. Perry.[3] Father Schmidt says that 'their lack of any real method is so complete that it can bring only discredit on the new movement.'

Of late years there have been two sorts of reaction against these quantitative treatments of culture, due, no doubt to the feeling that all these great studies of religion, sociology, and the like, both in the comparative and the historical method, presented static pictures which even when put together did not give a full picture of a living society. One

[1] See p. 140.
[2] *Human History*, 1929.
[3] *The Children of the Sun*, 1926.

school has attempted to describe specific cultures as configurations, following the method of the *Gestalt* psychology. In this kind, Ruth Benedict's *Patterns of Culture*,[1] with an introduction by Franz Boas, who first introduced the concept of 'pattern' in the description of cultures, has already been mentioned earlier in this chapter.

The second school attempts to describe cultures as integral wholes, with regard to the proper inter-relations of all the parts. In England, Bronislaw Malinowski has set out this method in *Argonauts of the Western Pacific*, 1922, and especially in the foreword to *The Sexual Life of Savages*, second edition, 1932. A. R. Radcliffe-Brown has taken much the same position in his address on 'The Present Position of Anthropological Studies' before the British Association in 1931. Raymond Firth,[2] R. F. Fortune,[3] Margaret Mead,[4] and Audrey Richards[5] follow Malinowski's methods, and Richard Thurnwald is often placed in this school, but to my mind he takes so wide a view and is cognizant of so many methods that he cannot be labelled. It is remarkable that while the functional method is so admirably adapted to portray the whole life of a people with all its inter-relations, the bulk of the work done by this school is on special subjects. No one of them, since the school first received a name, has given a better functional account of a people than H. A. Junod's *The Life of a South African Tribe*, 1912, 1913.

In *Papuans of the Trans-Fly*, 1936,[6] F. E. Williams discusses the limitations of the functional method, saying that the culture of a people is only an approximation to a condition of unity or integration. There are inner disagreements, cross-purposes, congestion, and cultural rubbish to consider. Force of habit and imitation lead to an easier and truer interpretation of survival than ingenious efforts to relate features to the whole of a culture as an integral or necessary part.

Accounts of the various ethnological theories are given in the introduction to Paul Radin's *Social Anthropology*, 1932, the same author's *The Method and Theory of Ethnology*, 1933, and in Richard Thurnwald's *Die Menschliche Gesellschaft in ihren Ethno-Soziologischen Grundlagen*, Volume I, 1931. The same author has also published in English an account of *Economics in Primitive Communities*, 1932, on the evolution of the economic organization from the most primitive cultures

[1] See p. 214.
[2] *Primitive Economics of the New Zealand Maori*, 1929.
[3] *Sorcerers of Dobu*, 1932.
[4] *Growing Up in New Guinea*, 1930.
[5] See p. 218.
[6] The Clarendon Press.

to the more complex societies of the ancient world. He declares that he adheres to the functional theory, but it is hardly possible for him to adhere to it and at the same time maintain his thesis that the development of economic skill alone determines every other element of a culture.

The previous chapter showed the development of the evolutionary school in technology, the study of the material cultures of peoples, and the beginning of the historical school.[1] The present chapter has already mentioned the development of the historical school[2] by such men as Graebner, Ankermann, and Foy, and the most conspicuous successes of the school have been made in this subject. In the functional school, Malinowski has shown in *Argonauts of the Western Pacific*, 1922, that a relation between social organization, religion, magic, commercial interests, and much besides, occurs in the *kula* system in the archipelagos off South-East New Guinea, and Raymond Firth and Audrey Richards have treated certain features of material culture functionally in *Primitive Economics of the New Zealand Maori*, 1929, and *Hunger and Work in a Savage Tribe*, 1932, respectively.

A few more or less general works, mainly in the evolutionary school, may be mentioned. O. T. Mason, *The Origins of Invention*, 1901; P. T. H. Grierson, *The Silent Trade*, 1903; A. H. Lane Fox Pitt Rivers, *The Evolution of Culture and other Essays* (ed. J. L. Myres), 1906; L. Hooper, *Hand-Loom Weaving*, 1910; L. Franchet, *Céramique Primitive*, 1911; C. Sachs, *Handbuch der Musikinstrumente*, 1920; S. Culin, *Games of the North American Indians*, in Number 24 of the reports of the Bureau of American Ethnology; R. B. Dixon's *The Building of Cultures*, 1928; E. Nordenskiöld, *Comparative Ethnological Studies*, 1–9; R. U. Sayce, *Primitive Arts and Crafts, An Introduction to the Study of Material Culture*, 1933. In addition, there are the ethnographical handbooks of the great museums, reports of expeditions such as the Jesup North Pacific Expedition, and accounts in various books and papers on special peoples or areas.

In all these schools, much of the most important work in this kind is printed in papers in various ethnological journals. Merely to name the journals would take up a good deal of space, and the reader can find the principal ones in the list of abbreviations. It is unfair to suggest, as some have done, that the evolutionary school follows a simple unilinear scheme, or takes no account of diffusion. For example, a very large part of Henry Balfour's work at the Pitt Rivers Museum has been concerned with geographical distribution, and in all of his many papers in

[1] See p. 177.
[2] See pp. 237–238.

the *J.R.A.I.* and elsewhere, he has never admitted the possibility of independent invention until every possibility of diffusion has been exhausted. Attacks on the evolutionary school as it exists today are like flogging a dead horse. The best members of that school welcome the emphasis which the others have placed on a fresh outlook on the evidence, and refuse to be labelled. They simply keep an open and a critical mind, refusing to allow any one method to be enthroned as the only one.

Prehistoric archaeology is technology in the past tense, and must be closely linked with it in any general study of man's handiwork, the means by which he gains a living, and adorns himself and his surroundings. Accounts of the various excavations where palaeolithic man has been found have been given elsewhere,[1] and the monographs and books there quoted give full descriptions of the evidences of their culture. The establishment of the principal Palaeolithic epochs during the Pleistocene period has been mentioned.

A great addition to our knowledge about man in the Pliocene period was made by J. Reid Moir[2] in 1910, who collected flints from the Red Crag near Ipswich (Upper Pliocene). Ray Lankester agreed with him that these rostrocarinate flints were tools made by man, though others disputed this. But in 1920 Reid Moir found an undoubted artefact in the Red Crag, and his work in the Foxhall pit has established his main contentions as to the existence of pre-palaeolithic man.

For the Lower Palaeolithic, or Early Pleistocene period, Professor O. Menghin of Vienna in *Weltgeschichte der Steinzeit*, 1931, has described uniface flake-tools extending over the whole of Eurasia, from southern England in the west to northern China in the east, as made by Piltdown and Peking man respectively. In western Europe this developed through pre-Chellean and Clactonian to Mousterian, whose Levalloisian branch developed in North Africa and spread down through East to South Africa. The biface core-tools appear to be the oldest in India and Africa, and are also found in southern England and in western and southern Europe as the familiar *coups de poing*. Presumably they spread to Europe from northern Africa. Their sequence in Europe is Chellean, Acheulean, and Micoquian. The uniface is associated with an arctic climate and fauna, the biface with interglacial or milder conditions. The Upper Palaeolithic tools are blade-tools in the main. One branch of the Aurignacian apparently spread from Asia into Europe and America;

---

[1] See p. 195 ff.
[2] J. Reid Moir, 'Discoveries at Foxhall,' *Proc. Prehist. Soc. E. Anglia*, I, 1911, 17, 24; II, 1915, 12; III, 389; *Prepalaeolithic Man*, 1920; *The Antiquity of Man in East Anglia*, 1927.

another, known as the Capsian, from North Africa to Spain in one direction, and into South Africa in another.

Three investigators have described Mousterian and Aurignacian types of tools found together, indicating that the two types of artefacts were made at the same period. Among the extinct Tasmanians, Mr Balfour[1] has found both types, Mr Leakey[2] has found the same in Kenya, and Miss Garrod in Palestine.

The main additions to our knowledge of Palaeolithic man during the present century have been that he certainly made tools during the Pliocene epoch, and that Pleistocene man had wandered all over Eurasia and as far as South Africa.[3] The chronology of these periods has been better worked out and the different phases of his culture have been more sharply defined by much more intensive and careful work[4] than was possible during the pioneer days of the last century.

Up to 1900 Piette's discoveries as Mas d'Azil and Judge Vielle's at Fère-en-Tardenois had helped to fill the gap between the Palaeolithic and Neolithic period. In that year G. F. L. Sarauw[5] explored a peat bog on the island of Zealand in Denmark, and found remains of a culture which he termed the Maglemosian (great swamp). The harpoons resembled the Azilian, while the microlithic flints were Tardenoisian. Certain of the knives and picks looked like those of the later Campignian, an early stage of the Neolithic period characterized by large chipped but unpolished tools, and perhaps contemporary with the Danish kitchen-middens (Ertebolle). This station had been described by A. de Mortillet[6] in 1899. The Azilian-Tardenoisian phase has been found in Europe, Asia, and Africa, while the Maglemosian and Kitchen-midden are mainly North-European cultures.

Since 1900 there has been an ever-increasing interest in the study of the later periods, the Neolithic, Chalcolithic, Bronze, and Iron Ages, for with the Neolithic come the beginnings of civilization, agriculture,

[1] 'The Status of the Tasmanians among the Stone-Age Peoples,' *Proc. Prehist. Soc. E. Anglia*, 1925. The Westlake collection in the Pitt Rivers Museum shows many other types, all apparently contemporary, as there seems to be no stratification.

[2] *The Stone Age Culture of Kenya Colony*, 1931.

[3] H. Breuil, 'L'Afrique préhistorique,' *Cahiers d'Art*, 1930; M. C. Burkitt, *South Africa's Past in Stone and Paint*, 1928; *The Prehistoric Period in South Africa*, 1912; N. Jones, *The Stone Age in Rhodesia*, 1926.

[4] Some works on areas or places in Europe: H. Obermaier, *El Hombre Fósil*, 1916 (*Fossil Man in Spain*, tr. C. D. Matthew, 1924): É. Cartailhac, H. Breuil, D. Peyrony, *La Caverne d'Altamira près Santander*, 1906; L. Capitan. H. Breuil, D. Peyrony, *La Caverne de Font de Gaume aux Eyzies* (*Dordogne*), 1910; Miss D. Garrod, *The Upper Palaeolithic Age in Britain*, 1926.

[5] 'Sur les trouvailles faites dans le nord de l'Europe datant de la période dite de l'hiatus,' *Congrès préhist. de France*, 1905 (Périgueux), 244.

[6] *B.S.A.*, 4e Sér., X, 36.

domestic animals, and pottery. To see how wide the field is, glance at the Proceedings of the First International Congress of Prehistoric and Protohistoric Sciences held in London in 1932. There has been a tremendous expansion of work done in Europe, Crete and the Aegean, Egypt, Syria, Mesopotamia, and the East as far as North-West India. This is easy to understand, for such work is illuminating our own beginnings, explaining the life of men like ourselves and a civilization closely bound up with that of today.

Three main features characterize the work of the years from 1900 to 1935. One is that excavations on a large scale are often the result of international effort, such as the Oxford-Field Museum Expedition to Kish in Mesopotamia and the British Museum and University of Pennsylvania Expedition to Ur of the Chaldees. Sometimes a government will undertake such work on a large scale, as did the Government of India at Mohenjo-daro in Sind. Here Sir John Marshall, Ernest Mackay and others have uncovered a great new civilization.[1] Many of the great museums with the help of public subscriptions keep expeditions in the field. The countries whose lands are rich in buried civilizations are waking up to their importance, and are more and more insisting on keeping the evidence of their own past in their own museums. This is all to the good provided that they are willing and able to excavate scientifically and to make their results available to the world which shares in their civilization.

In bringing about a scientific technique in excavation and recording and interpreting the work done on these large sites, probably no one has done more than Sir Flinders Petrie. No longer is there exploitation of sites, taking objects of art, tablets, or other chosen material, and throwing the rest away on the dump. Though the main object may still be to solve definite problems, every part of the site is carefully excavated and recorded, and many different sciences are called upon to solve the different problems of the excavator and to make the picture of the past as complete as possible. General Pitt Rivers also had a profound effect on archaeological technique. It was his custom to build models of his sites, so that the whole excavation could be reconstructed from the beginning. These models are exhibited in the museum founded by him at Farnham in Dorset. The late M. L. Ch. Watelin, chosen by Professor Langdon as field director at Kish in Mesopotamia, caused a model to be made of the enormous site which he had excavated at the Harsagkalama mound, copies of which are in the Ashmolean Museum at Oxford and in the Field Museum in Chicago.

[1] *Mohenjo-daro and the Indus Civilization*, Probsthain, London, 1931.

A third interesting and valuable feature is the use of air photography, first thought of and put into practice by O. G. S. Crawford of the Ordnance Survey. Many air photographs revealing details that would otherwise be unseen are published in his journal *Antiquity*. He and A. Keiller have also published *Wessex from the Air*, 1928.

The very fact that a more austere standard in excavating and recording prevails nowadays has made it much more difficult to generalize than it was in the past century. Again, the fact that in some areas there has been really scientific excavation while in other intervening areas very little scientific work has been done, or was done in the past before the present standard of accuracy was in vogue, makes the problem harder. Moreover, we find each area more or less adopting its own chronology regardless of others, and the attempts to correlate them differing so much that it seems almost impossible to gain any general picture.

One great change there has been. In the last century for the most part, race, language, and culture tended to form part of one concept. In the present, the word 'race', as scientifically used, means a group of persons sharing measurable physical characters that can be inherited. I omit, of course, differences in colour, hair, and eyes, for we are dealing with archaeological material only; except in Egypt, and Peru, where mummification was practised, we have only the bones to study.

At the beginning of the century the generally accepted classification of races in Europe by physical characters had three main divisions. In the north were the tall, blond, blue-eyed, long-headed Nordics, and in the south, the short, dark, brown-eyed, long-headed Mediterranean people, while the people of the central highlands were the stocky, round-headed Alpines. Prehistorians then, and to a certain extent now, were inclined to suppose that these races originally existed in a pure state, and had cultures, and that the task was to disentangle the races and cultures, and put them in chronological order.

But it has constantly been found in the present century that round heads are found where long heads should be, and long heads where round heads should be. For example, Gordon Childe mentions round heads found in some numbers in Neolithic deposits in Sardinia, Sicily, Spain, Sweden, and Denmark, which upsets somewhat the theory that Neolithic long heads came first, then Bronze Age round heads, and that their mixture perhaps produced Iron Age mesocephals. Again, Leeds has not seldom found long-headed people buried with Bronze Age beakers, though this might of course be interpreted as a survival, and Dingwall's and my own work at Culver Hole Cave, Llangennith,

Gower, has shown an almost entirely long-headed population in the Bronze Age, and this again, might be interpreted as a survival into a new culture phase. In Mesopotamia it was at first thought that there would be long-headed people entering with one culture and round-headed with another, and that the problem was to determine the succession. But lately, Buxton,[1] and later, myself,[2] on even more ancient material, determined that as far back as we could go, there was a completely mixed race in Mesopotamia, such as exists today.

This mixture of races within a given culture and period has shown that we must treat race as one thing, going by physical characters, and culture as another, meaning by culture groups of material traits, and such spiritual traits as we can infer from burials and styles of decoration. Taking culture and language together, for example, we might speak of a Sumerian people. To speak of a Sumerian race as far as we know at present would be a misnomer, for the people of the Semitic culture which overlies them are of exactly the same mixture at Kish, to name one place.

The task of the archaeologist today, then, is to investigate peoples, that is groups of cultures and languages as revealed by excavation, and the task of the physical anthropologist, who works with him, is to investigate races, whose existence in a 'pure' form can only be determined satisfactorily by statistical methods.

In the first kind may be mentioned Henri Frankfort's *Archaeology and the Sumerian Problem*, 1932.[3] By a comparison of culture traits at various sites during the Chalcolithic period, he postulates an Iranian culture, using the evidence of Sir Aurel Stein, Sir Leonard Woolley, and others, stretching from the border of the Indus Valley across Persia into Mesopotamia, overlaid by an Anatolian-Transcausian culture stretching from Anau in Turkestan to Hissarlik (Troy), and downward all over eastern Mesopotamia. Northern Mesopotamia shows the influence of the Syrian province.

Probably the most far-reaching work in cultural analysis is that developed by V. G. Childe in *The Dawn of European Civilization*, 1926, and especially in *The Danube in Prehistory*, 1929. Here we have a vast amount of material well documented, published in all the languages of Europe, and scattered in many museums, giving the evidence for the foundation of European civilization 'as a peculiar and individual manifestation of the human spirit.' No one before him had brought the

[1] *J.R.A.I.*, LXI, 1931 (with Talbot Rice).
[2] *Kish*, IV.
[3] Oriental Institute of the University of Chicago, Studies in Ancient Oriental Civilization, No. 4.

whole field of European prehistory from the fourth to the middle of the second millenium B.C. together with an attempt to interpret it together with the neolithic and urban revolutions in western Asia. The first few pages of his preface to *The Danube in Prehistory* show the fundamental principles on which we must all work.

In the second kind may be mentioned the various studies of ancient European races which appear from time to time in *Biometrika*. To discuss the literature of all the provinces would make a book in itself. A list of a few more or less general works is therefore put in a footnote.[1]

V. ENVIRONMENT, THE MEDIUM IN WHICH MAN AND CULTURE DEVELOP

The study of race and culture is incomplete without a study of the environment, the medium in which they develop. The French and the Germans, who have devoted themselves more especially to geographical conditions, have gone on somewhat different lines, the French more or less following Le Play's formula, place, work, social organization; and the Germans, the idea of Ratzel that geography is the science of the co-

[1] Childe, V. Gordon, 'Races, Peoples, and Cultures in Prehistoric Europe' (to which the writer is indebted for a part of the foregoing), *History*, October, 1933 (called to my attention by Mr L. W. Kennan); Frankfort, *Archaeology and the Sumerian Problem*, 1932, gives a good introduction to work in Mesopotamia; for further east: Sir Aurel Stein, 'An Archaeological Tour in Waziristan and Northern Baluchistan,' *Archaeological Survey of India*, Memoir 37, 1929, and 'An Archaeological Tour of Gedrosia,' *ibid.*, Memoir 43, 1931; Sir John Marshall and others, *Mohenjo-daro and the Indus Civilization*, 1931; R. Pumpelly, *Explorations in Turkestan*, 1908; for Egypt: Sir Flinders Petrie, *Prehistoric Egypt*, 1920, and G. Brunton's work at Badari and Tasa; for the Aegean: J. L. Myres, 'The Cretan Labyrinth,' *J.R.A.I.*, LXIII, 1933, 269; Sir Arthur Evans, *The Palace of Minos at Knossos*, 1921-35; for Europe, V. Gordon Childe, *The Dawn of European Civilization*, 1926, and *The Danube in Prehistory*, 1929, the first with a bibliography for each area, and the second with a list of authorities; Nils Åberg, *Das Nordische Kulturgebiet in Mitteleuropa wahrend der jüngeren Steinzeit*, 1918; *La civilization énéolithique dans la péninsule ibérique*, 1921, and *Studier ofver yngre Stenaldern i Norden och Västeuropa;* O. Montelius, *Die vorklassische Chronologie Italiens*, 1912; T. Zammit, *Prehistoric Malta*, 1930; Hans Reinerth, *Chronologie der jüngeren Steinzeit Süd-deutschlands*, 1924; Carl Schuchhardt, *Alteuropa*, 1921; J. L. Myres, introductory chapters in *Cambridge Ancient History*, Vol. I; V. Gordon Childe, *The Bronze Age*, 1930; H. Peake, *The Bronze Age and the Celtic World;* Lord Abercromby, *The Bronze Age Pottery of Great Britain and Ireland*, 1912; R. A. S. Macalister, *The Archaeology of Ireland*, 1928; E. T. Leeds, 'A Neolithic Settlement at Abingdon,' *Antiquaries' Journal*, VII, VIII; Sir Cyril Fox, *The Personality of Britain*, 1932 (National Museum of Wales); for America: A. V. Kidder, *An Introduction to South-Western Archaeology*, 1924; T. A. Joyce, *South American Archaeology*, 1912, *Mexican Archaeology*, 1914, and *Central American Archaeology*, 1916. For general archaeology, palaeolithic, neolithic, etc.: J. Déchelette, *Manuel d' Archéologie*, 1908-; M. Ebert, *Reallexikon der Vorgeschichte*, 1924-.

relation of distributions. The German ethnologists like Graebner, Foy, Frobenius, Ankermann, and others who developed the culture-area and culture-strata methods are geographers in this kind. In America Miss E. C. Semple made an adapted translation of Friedrich Ratzel's *Anthropogeographie* in 1911 under the title *Influences of Geographic Environment*. Two other of her works are *American History and Its Geographical Conditions*, 1903, and *The Geography of the Mediterranean Region*, 1931. The work of Nelson, Boas, and Wissler, in developing the culture-area theory in America, Sapir's contribution to chronological method, and Dixon's criticism have already been mentioned.[1] Clark Wissler's study of *The American Indian*[2] pays special attention to the food areas, pointing out how culture areas tend to group themselves according to bison, salmon, manioc, acorns, etc. So far, then, environment plays its part. But he notices, too, that environment plays little part in the development of many arts and ceremonies, which are as distinctive as the food areas and as localized. Again, people of a given area have chosen only a few out of the many possibilities of making a living, and have specialized in those, leaving the rest alone. Apparently, when a people has worked out a method of getting a living, it establishes social habits which resist change, and the successful adjustment of one tribe to a locality will be followed by neighbours, 'to the inhibition of new inventions, or adjustments'. The origin of a culture seems to be due to ethnic more than to geographical factors. Once located, however, environment tends to keep it stable.

The Le Play method of studying the environment, methods of earning a living, and the consequent organization of peoples, was followed in this century by E. Demolins in *Comment la route crée le type social*, in two volumes, 1901–03. His general idea is that the cause of the diversity of peoples is due to the road they have travelled, that is, to the environment. Change the road, and you change the type. Two examples of his idea may be quoted. The steppes, for example, produce grass, and a uniform type of labour, that is, herding. All operations can be carried on successfully by the extended family with the patriarch in charge, and property is in common, as there is no cultivation.

Since the large family is self-sufficient there is no integration of families into a larger society. On the other hand hunters in Africa and South America, because of the exigencies of the pursuit of game, lead a less stable life, and break up into small groups.

Henri de Tourville explained how environment had played a part in

[1] See p. 237.
[2] 1922, 370–74.

developing the type of family characteristic of Europe, the British Empire, and the United States in *The Growth of Modern Nations, a History of the Particularist Form of Society*, 1907. Life on the fiords of Norway made large family groups impossible. Each adult son had to look for a new place to live in, as there was little room to spare, and do without the help afforded by the association of individuals, and to depend on self-help in the development of his new estate. Qualities so developed led to the spread of such people over a large part of the globe.

Ellsworth Huntingdon's *The Pulse of Asia*, 1907, *Civilization and Climate*, 1915, *The Character of Races*, 1924, and *The Human Habitat*, 1928, all deal with the effect of climate and geography on the races of man, past and present. He has an interesting theory that the great fluctuations of the weather within narrow limits, such as we find in the British Isles, for example, have had a powerful effect in making the British energetic and progressive.

A. J. and F. D. Herbertson on *Man and His Work*, 1909, have written a very readable short introduction to the whole subject, and J. Brunhes' *La géographie humaine*, 1910 (2nd edition, 1912), is a valuable work to consult. Griffith Taylor's *Environment and Race*, 1927, has a most ingenious 'migration-zone theory of race evolution,' with a very interesting map.

VI. GENERAL ETHNOLOGY AND ETHNOGRAPHY

Throughout this book we have maintained that ethnology was the comparative study of peoples by any or all three of the methods of anthropology, i.e. physical anthropology, technology (past and present), and social anthropology. Sometimes a work will consider them all, though it is more usual for the ethnologist to use one of these methods only. Once any branch of anthropology is used in this way, that is, comparatively, it becomes ethnology. Thus all branches of anthropology, the science of man, partake in the study of ethnology, the comparative study of races and cultures. When any or all of the methods of anthropology are applied to the study of a particular people or area, we have ethnography.

So enormous is the literature, both in books and papers, that we can mention only a few examples. Many of the works which have been under review in this book are ethnological or ethnographical according to our definition, but our main interest has been in the different anthropological methods which have been applied to the comparative studies of race and culture.

As far as the development of these subjects in the present century is concerned, there has been a steady improvement in field method and in the quality of the data as more and more men and women are sent from the universities with special training for this work. Every teacher of anthropology has but to think of his own pupils who are district officers, missionaries, or special investigators all over the world. To have taught a Spencer or a Rattray[1] is honour enough for any teacher. To attempt a list of works on the different peoples of the world would be invidious. The various schools of anthropology make their own bibliographies of such ethnographical works for the use of beginners and research students. In a recent preface,[2] Dr Dudley Buxton has expressed the conviction that it is no less important to study the peoples of our own countries by the excellent methods employed by the authors of the book. He has little patience with those who must rush a 'trained anthropologist' to study a small and remote group before it is 'too late.' If our main interest is to study such barren and ancient questions as whether mother-right preceded father-right, or whether the most primitive men were promiscuous in their marriage relations, no doubt it is always too late. If we are interested in people as they are, it is never too late. The most important and pressing work is the study of peoples in transition, who are being forced to adapt themselves to changed conditions, and this sort of study should be applied not only to peoples in Africa, India, America, Asia, or the islands of the sea, but to our own. The depressed areas in the north of England or in South Wales are no less necessary and worthy objects of our attention. Durkheim's *L'Année Sociologique* carries its task of investigation through from savagery to civilization, and rightly so. As Marett has said, anthropology must not be allowed to sink to mere barbarology.

A few general works on ethnology are: J. Deniker, *The Races of Man*, 1927; H. J. Fleure's *The Races of Mankind*, 1927; A. C. Haddon, *The Races of Man*, 1924, and *The Wanderings of Peoples*, 1912; A. H. Keane, *Man, Past and Present*, 1920; R. B. Dixon, *The Racial History of Man*, 1923; V. Giuffrida-Ruggeri, *Homo Sapiens*, 1913; Egon Freiherr von Eickstedt, *Rassenkunde und Rassengeschichte der Menschheit*, 1934.

On special areas there are: W. Z. Ripley, *The Races of Europe*, 1900; L. H. Dudley Buxton, *The Peoples of Asia*, 1925; *The Census of India*, 1901, 1931; C. G. Seligman, *The Peoples of Africa*, 1930; Clark Wissler, *The American Indian*, 1915, 1922.

Much of the most valuable work on special areas is in papers, and

---

[1] Author of the classic works on the Ashanti.
[2] To *Ubena of the Rivers*, 1935, by A. T. and G. M. Culwick.

nothing short of a catalogue would summarize it. With more and more data scientifically collected, ethnology has become a more rigorous discipline than in the past. Generalizations tend to become fewer, and better founded. As ethnology is in a sense the application of anthropology, there is less to say about its history. Our concern has been with tendencies and their development. And when we have described how methods arose and how they developed, we have done all that we could in a book of this size and scope.

At this point in the 1935 edition we ended this chapter with the question. 'What of the future?' and followed with a chapter entitled 'The Future' in which tendencies and possibilities of the years to come were discussed. We suggested that there would be a new convergence and consolidation in the coming years. The 1952 edition perhaps appeared to show more consolidation than convergence. By now, however, enough has happened to show some of the convergence in the sciences and arts comparable to that of 1835 to 1859. Accordingly, our final chapter is entitled 'Convergence and Consolidation.'

6

CONVERGENCE AND CONSOLIDATION
1935—

I. TRENDS TOWARDS A NEW CONSTRUCTIVE PERIOD

DURING the Critical Period between 1900 and 1935 the general tendency
was for the several sciences and parts of them to go their own way and to
develop separately in depth rather than in breadth, but there were yet
signs of efforts to meet at border lines and to cross into each other's
territories, as well as to consider large areas or subjects and to get out of
compartments. One recalls Gordon Childe's *The Dawn of European
Civilization*, now in its sixth edition of 1957, in 1926, and his *The
Danube in Prehistory* of 1929, with a new method of cultural analysis
covering European civilization and its roots in western Asia; J. B. Orr
and J. L. Gilks on *The Physique and Health of two African Tribes* in
1931, dealing with the social habits, nutrition, and physique of the
Masai and Kikuyu; and E. G. Bowen's 'The Incidence of Phthisis in
Relation to Race-Type and Social Environment in South and West
Wales,' and later in Central Wales (*J.R.A.I.*, 1928 and 1933), as a few
examples. I personally remember the old Committee for Anthropology
at Oxford, which had professors from every faculty on it, and it was my
pleasant duty each term to prepare a list of the times at which each of
these professors would be at home to our diploma or research students to
discuss problems relevant to their subjects. This ended in 1938 after
thirty years, and we were the poorer.

Now we see again two great tendencies which marked the Constructive Period. One is the synthesis and evaluation of material covering a large area or subject. Another is the co-operation with the
physical and biological sciences, and with other faculties than our own.

One notes especially such studies as that of J. G. D. Clark in *World
Prehistory, an Outline*, published at Cambridge in 1961, and his *Pre-
historic Europe, the Economic Basis* (London 1952). For China, we have
Cheng Te-Ku'n, who is publishing from Cambridge his great work on
Archaeology in China in eight volumes, covering the long period from

the prehistoric through to the end of the Ming Dynasty. Two volumes have appeared, *Prehistoric China* in 1959 and *Shang China* in 1960. A work of great magnitude is Joseph Needham's seven-volume *Science and Civilization in China*, again from Cambridge. He is assisted by Wang Ling, and so far three volumes have appeared, in 1954, 1956, and 1959. It is hard to overestimate the importance of these volumes for anyone wishing to understand the interaction between inventions and the development of civilization in the Eastern world.

Some of the contents of this work remind us of a marked tendency to shift the emphasis from cultural analysis towards an economic and technological approach to development, and towards a greater under-standing of the part that the sciences have taken in the history of civilization. Through the enlightened generosity of Imperial Chemical Industries and the active collaboration of the Clarendon Press at Oxford, the great five-volume *History of Technology*, edited by C. S. Singer, E. J. Holmyard, and A. R. Hall (1954–58), gives an account of the principal inventions on which our Western civilization rests, their development, and their interactions with our social life. Both this work and Needham's give us a deeper respect for the peoples of the world, who started from savage beginnings, and made it possible for the most naked and weak of the animal creation to become the strongest in their power for good or evil. For when we find what we can do, that may be opposed to what we ought to do, and from time to time our hard-won civilization is attacked by evil, and on occasion almost perishes. But so great a treasure is it that men do not willingly let it die, and natural goodness restores what was spoiled. It survives the ages, and triumphs over the injuries of time.

Previous to the publication of Volume I of the *History of Technology*, the Pitt Rivers Museum at Oxford had started in 1944 to publish a series of *Occasional Papers on Technology*, some of which have developed into substantial books, on the techniques of Stone-Age peoples, textiles, metallurgy, ivory, bone, and antler, music, etc., following the principle *nullius in verba*, and proceeding by observation and experiment in such a way that every point could be verified by other workers in the same fields. The series has now reached nine volumes and is continuing. In March, 1955, the University of Oxford inaugurated the Research Laboratory for Archaeology and the History of Art, largely inspired by Professor C. F. C. Hawkes and the late Lord Cherwell, which is devoted under the guidance of Doctors E. T. Hall and M. J. Aitken to improving present scientific techniques and to discovering new techniques. As the Statute says, 'The work of the Research Laboratory . . . shall be to make examination of archaeologically and historically significant material by such methods, especially of physical science, as may cause knowledge of the history of human activity to be advanced; and to set out the results from time to time in a manner suitable for publication.' Besides publishing in various other journals, since 1958 the Laboratory has published its own journal, *Archaeometry*, in which one can read its contribution to field-work in prospecting by physical techniques, such as resistivity and magnetic surveys, and to new or greatly improved laboratory methods of dating and analysis. A good account of this work and much besides is to be found in M. J. Aitken's *Physics and Archaeology*, published in New York and London in 1961.

This valuable book and F. E. Zeuner's indispensable *Dating the Past*, first published in London in 1946, and now in its fourth edition (1958), bring us to a consideration of the great advances made in chronological studies by radioactive decay methods, such as uranium and potassium argon for the Pleistocene and earlier ages, and radiocarbon or carbon 14 for the last 50,000 years'[1] These methods depend on the fact that the time-rate at which the disintegration of a radioactive mineral proceeds is constant and determinable, and so we have a method for the measurement of time. Zeuner describes the technical details clearly and at some length so that the archaeologist can gain an idea of the work involved and grasp the sense of a scientific report. Attempts at a summary here would be misleading.

Of all these methods, radiocarbon (carbon 14) dating has had the greatest impact on the archaeologist. Its pioneer is W. F. Libby, whose *Radiocarbon Dating* was published in Chicago in 1955. Aitken's chapter on 'Radiocarbon Dating' in *Physics and Archaeology* gives a full account of developments of the method up to 1961, and of the publication of dates produced by laboratories all over the world with current lists of dating laboratories, as well as a full bibliography. I can well remember when we all had enormously ancient dates, then the gradual development of a reduction of these dates to times nearer our own; now we are pushing them backward again, as the accumulation of radiocarbon dates appear to force us to realize, for example, the great antiquity and long duration of the Neolithic in the Near East and Europe.

Among biological methods, one may mention developments in pollen analysis. The climate of a region is reflected in the types of trees which flourish there. Knowledge of past climates may be gained by microscopic identification of tree-pollen found in stratified peat bogs.

[1] For fluorine studies, see Dr J. S. Weiner's mention on p. 294, also Aitken and Zeuner.

J. G. D. Clark has brilliantly shown how this method, linked with the older work of de Geer on varves, studies of the moraines of former glaciers, work on old coast lines, stratigraphy, etc., can reconstruct the succession of environments from the end of the Upper Palaeolithic to historical times. His *Mesolithic Settlement of Northern Europe* was published in 1936. Zeuner's 1958 edition of *Dating the Past* gives a full account of the application of pollen analysis.

Present work on Pleistocene marine shells is very promising. They are being collected from various places to see whether they can be used to date fossil men and their implements generally. This method is in addition to the more conventional ways of dating by climatic changes, fossil plant remains, and fossil mammals. In the first stages of this work, the shells were found to belong to grades which were intermediate between the ancient Pleistocene fauna and those of today, thus confirming the work of earlier geologists (Searles Wood, etc.): the method was based partly on the extinction of ancient forms of shells and by the gradual arrival of more modern forms. Tests were then done to support this work by collecting from places where the shell-beds occur with glacial deposits and with other beds, like those at Clacton in Essex, which contain Palaeolithic implements. The sequence of shell-beds was found to agree well with the glacial and palaeolithic sequences, and the results were summarized by D. F. W. Baden-Powell and R. G. West in 1960 in the *Proceedings of the Geological Association*, LXXI, p. 62. In the meantime, the work has been extended to include the Mediterranean area and to correlate this with Britain, and again the shell-beds were found to agree with each other and with archaeological sites such as those studied by Breuil and many others along the coastal districts of Portugal, France, Italy, and Morocco. The correlation between Britain and the Mediterranean was summarized by D. F. W. Baden-Powell in 1955 in *Proc. Geol. Assoc.*, LXVI, p. 285. An attempt is now being made to extend the work to cover the coastal areas of parts of Asia and Africa, in the hope of throwing new light on the geological age of *Australopithecus*- and *Pithecanthropus*-beds, but it is not yet known how far this will be feasible. In addition to its value to archaeology, this work is also helping with certain geological problems, especially those connected with the study of relative changes of land- and sea-level.

Another of the methods of scientic aid to archaeology and ethnology, mentioned in the earlier part of this book, is the increasing aid given by aerial photography. Here I will mention the work of a former member of my staff, J. S. P. Bradford, and his comprehensive

I   257

and valuable book, with a great amount of original work, *Ancient Landscapes, Studies in Field Archaeology*, London, 1957. Another useful book, *Science in Archaeology*, London, 1962, is edited by two Cambridge men, E. S. Higgs and D. R. Brothwell.

II. PREHISTORY AND TECHNOLOGY IN THE OLD WORLD

A very large part of the story of man's rise from savagery to civilization has been uncovered in what used to be called the Near East, and is now usually spoken of as the Middle East. Following on the Chellean and Acheulean artefacts of the high deserts of Arabia and Egypt, we have the stratified caves of Mount Carmel, so admirably excavated and reported by Dorothy Garrod, formerly Disney Professor of Archaeology in the University of Cambridge. These show an unbroken series of occupations from the Lower Palaeolithic Acheulean to the Natufian or Mesolithic. At Jericho[1] Professor John Garstang in 1935 found what is apparently a Natufian or Mesolithic industry of microliths under a Neolithic stratum with sickles, arrowheads, querns, mortars and pestles, and mud houses with red plastered walls and grain bins, followed by a stratum with copper. The uncivilized had invented civilization.

Writing in 1952, it appeared to me that Garstang's report indicated a Natufian or mesolithic below the neolithic at Jericho. In 1957, Dorothy Garrod's important lecture to the British Academy on *The Natufian Culture* indicated that this culture of the Mount Carmel caves was found to a considerable extent over Palestine, southwestern Syria, and the Lebanon, and even at Heluan, twenty miles south of Cairo. This mesolithic culture at the end shaded into the Tahunian at el-Khiam, with arrowheads, domestic goats, and a small ox, as well as the dog, which had been domesticated in the Middle Natufian. This period, though without pottery, appears to be neolithic. In *Archaeology in the Holy Land*, London, 1960, Kathleen Kenyon writes of a Natufian settlement at the base of the very deep Jericho excavations which she made between 1952 and 1958; a record of this work is being published in London for the British School of Archaeology in Palestine. Volume I of *Jericho* appeared in 1960. This Natufian culture is overlaid by a neolithic period without pottery in which there is evidence of agriculture. The charcoal of the Natufian period gives a carbon 14 dating early in the eighth millenium B.C., and that of the succeeding neolithic gives a date early in the seventh millenium.

While Europe and the Far East were still in the mesolithic stage of

---

[1] Liverpool *Annals of Archaeology and Anthropology*, Vol. XXII.

hunting and gathering, the peoples of western Asia and Egypt began to give up this wandering life, and to settle in communities, sowing seeds and reaping the harvest, domesticating animals for food and traction, and invented the plough and the wheel, metallurgy, textiles, wheel-made and kiln-fired pottery, orchestral music, and writing. This complex of inventions represents the greatest and most important revolution that humanity has seen in material development. All that has happened since depends on it. Everything invented since could disappear from the world, and the good life would still be possible.

Much of the work that went to the telling of the long history of mankind in this area had of course been done before the thirties, and some of it has been described earlier, but it is since the thirties began that the details and sequences took their place in the most orderly scheme yet known. I well remember the excitement of being in the field at Kish with the Oxford University and Field Museum Expedition in 1929 when we at Kish, Woolley at Ur of the Chaldees as director of the British Museum and Pennsylvania University Expedition, and Jordan at Warka, the Uruk of the Sumerians, the Erech of the Book of Genesis, all reached virgin soil, ourselves after digging through sixty feet of buried civilizations, and passing downward through more than 5,000 years of history. Thus, for the first time we were in a position to establish the main succession of events from the beginning of civilization in the Valley of the Two Rivers, the Tigris and Euphrates. In 1931 the International Conference of Orientalists at Leiden, in view of the evidence, agreed on the sequence in southern Mesopotamia of three periods previous to the Early Sumerian Dynastic, the Al 'Ubaid, flourishing early in the fourth millennium, the Uruk, about 3500 B.C., and the Jemdet Nasr, about 3200 B.C.

The most ancient of these periods, the Al 'Ubaid, showed the essentials of material civilization, including the use of copper, already established on the alluvium brought down from the northern mountains. To go back farther in time, we must examine the more northerly settlements, founded while southern Mesopotamia was still below the waters of the Persian Gulf. Speiser at Tepe Gawra near Khorsabad, and Mallowan at Arpachiyah near Nineveh, found pottery of a chalcolithic culture like that earlier found by von Oppenheim at Tell Halaf in the Mosul area, and by Herzfeld in work at Samarra, under an Al 'Ubaid layer, and thus took the prehistory of Mesopotamia back into the end of the fifth millennium. Then Campbell Thompson's wonderful stratification at Kuyunjik from Assyrian through Babylonian, Akkadian, Sumerian, Jemdet Nasr, Uruk, Al 'Ubaid, and Halafian, found pottery yet earlier at the bottom of his seventy-foot shaft which he called neolithic. At Tell Hassunah, south of Nineveh, in 1943, Seton Lloyd and Sayyid Fuad Safar (*J.N.E.S.* IV, No. 4) discovered a settlement of pre-Halaf times with pottery the same as that found by Campbell Thompson at the bottom of his deep shaft at Nineveh. It would appear then that Speiser's paper in *Antiquity* for 1941, proposing to precede the Al 'Ubaid period by the Halaf-Samarra and the neolithic, can be generally accepted.

It is clear from the Garrod-Bate Dama-Gazella curve[1] that from the Mesolithic period onward, the climate of the Near East was dry and dependent on irrigation as it is today. The constant silting of the Euphrates and overflow towards the Tigris, with its mixture of lagoons, swamps, dry, and fertile land, presented to the early dwellers in the dessicating hills a lesson and an opportunity. Water could be taken where it was wanted and away from where it was not wanted. The early tablets of ancient Sumer show the beginning of law, at first regulation of water between persons, then between cities. That the beginning of agriculture in the Valley of the Two Rivers was in the hills and high ground is shown in the extensive work of Professor Robert Braidwood. In his and Bruce Howe's *Prehistoric Investigations in Iraqi Kurdistan*, published by the Oriental Institute of the University of Chicago (Studies in Ancient Oriental Civilization, No. 31) in 1960, there is an account of expeditions of the Institute led by Professor Braidwood from 1947 onward. Caves and open sites in the piedmont and foothill zones of Iraqi Kurdistan have been examined, with a time range from the Middle Palaeolithic to the Late Neolithic. Special attention has been paid to the transitional period between the Mesolithic and the Neolithic, when cave sites were gradually abandoned for open villages, and an economy of food collecting gave way to one of food production. Three sites straddle this vital period: Zarzi, a cave first occupied about 12,000 B.C., with a culture corresponding to the Natufian of Palestine; Karim Shahir, an open station of the ninth millennium, where there is evidence of agriculture, though no trace of pottery; and Jarmo, dated about 7000 B.C., a settlement with a full neolithic culture, where pottery makes its first appearance. The Jarmo culture overlaps that of Hassuna, discovered by Seton Lloyd and Fuad Safar, and thus provides a link with the earliest occupation levels in the Mesopotamian plains. The Expedition has paid close attention to evidence bearing on the climate, fauna, and flora of the sites examined with a view to discovering whether the great cultural transition to the

[1] *The Stone Age of Mount Carmel*, vol. I, 1937.

Neolithic corresponded to any marked environmental change. This same interest in the earliest appearances of village farming communities has characterized the work of Jean Perrot in Israel ('Palestine, Syria and Cilicia' in R. J. Braidwood's and G. R. Willey's *Courses toward Urban Life*, Viking Fund Publications in Anthropology, 32, Chicago, 1962), Kathleen Kenyon in Jordan, and James Mellaart in Anatolia (*Anatolian Studies*, 1961), to mention only a few. Ralph Solecki and Arlette Leroi-Gourhan in 'Palaeo-climatology and Archaeology in the Near East' (*Annals of the New York Academy of Sciences*, 95, 1961) have extended their interest in the Pleistocene antiquity of Kurdistan to the first phases of incipient cultivation and domestication.

It would appear then that with Dorothy Garrod's Mount Carmel sequence from Lower Palaeolithic to Mesolithic, and this work on later periods, we can gain a fair picture of the long history of man in the Near East from about 500,000 years ago to historic times, starting the Neolithic in the seventh millenium B.C., and the Mesolithic about 12,000 years ago, according to area.

This brief outline of recent progress in the Near East has been given because the story is so complete that it forms an outline within which we can discuss special events and with which we can compare progress in other areas.

A most important event was the publication in 1937 of *The Stone Age of Mount Carmel* by D. A. E. Garrod and D. M. A. Bate. Miss Garrod saved everything, and labelled it, and for each layer gave a table which showed the numbers of each type of implement. An important result of this laborious work was that the whole disclosed the fact that core, flake, and blade tools were all found together in the Lower Palaeolithic, and throughout, but that the all-purpose core implement of the Lower Palaeolithic became gradually less dominant, yielding to a dominance of more specialized flake tools in the Middle Palaeolithic, while the most specialized blade tools slowly increased until they became dominant over other types in the Upper Palaeolithic. This enables us to examine afresh the older ideas of sequence of types in the Dordogne, and helps to free us from the old-fashioned idea of judging the sequence in the world by that in the remote tip of the Eurasiatic Peninsula. Her classical paper on 'The Upper Palaeolithic in the Light of Recent Discovery,' based on her Presidential Address to Section H of the British Association at Blackpool in 1936, appeared in *Proceedings of the Prehistoric Society* for January-July, 1938.

A most valuable part of the book is the part on animal bones by Miss Bate, and the diagram by the authors known as the Dama-Gazella curve, made by counting the bones in each layer of Dama mesopo-tamica, a woodland deer, and of the gazelle, a desert animal. The proportions of each, graphically shown, display a regular rhythm of wet and arid periods during which the various cultures of the Palaeo-lithic and Mesolithic flourished. With this for western Asia, and L. S. B. Leakey's Pluvial Curve, based on high and low lake shores in which artefacts of different periods were found, we also have the Milankovitch solar radiation curve, showing the amplitude of solar radiation at 65 degrees north for the last 600,000 years. This was fitted to the classical Günz-Mindel-Riss-Würm glaciations by F. E. Zeuner in Volume 72 of the *Geological Magazine* in such a way that one seeing, e.g. the curve during a glacial rising to 75 degrees north, would note that it was 10 degrees colder at 65, and that we who live at 51 degrees north would have a climate similar to that of southern Norway and Sweden. On the other hand, if we see the curve during an interglacial period descending to 55 degrees, we can say that as it is 10 degrees warmer at 65, we at 51 degrees would have a Mediterranean climate. With these three curves compared, we can see a similarity in the rhythm of climates and in the rhythm of types of artefacts over three great con-tinents for a vast period of time. The Pluvial Curve, as well as a valuable table of sequences for the African continent, appear in Leakey's *Stone Age Africa*, published in 1936.

For southern and eastern Asia, H. L. Movius has put down a good comparative study of 'Early Man and the Pleistocene Stratigraphy in Southern and Eastern Asia,' published by the Peabody Museum of Harvard University in 1944 as Volume XIX, No. 3, of their Papers. It sums up work by Teilhard de Chardin in China, Hellmut de Terra in India and Burma, von Koenigswald in Java, and the work of the American South-east Asiatic Expedition of 1937–38, with comparative stratigraphies. The industries of chopping tools and coarse scrapers accord well with O. Menghin's summary in his *Weltgeschichte der Steinzeit* of 1931, showing two main provinces of industries in the Lower Palaeolithic, the flake province embracing eastern Europe, China, and South-east Asia, and the core province including western Europe, Africa, and southern Asia as far as South India. Much of this work had of course been done by Breuil and Obermaier. Useful summaries of Russian work on prehistory were published by Field and Prostov in the *American Anthropologist* btween 1936 and 1938, and by Zolotarev in 1938. A good bibliography of Russian work in ethnology and prehistory appears in the *Biennial Review of Anthropology* in 1959, edited by Ber-nard J. Siegel and published by the Stanford University Press of

California. The principal authors publish in *Sovetskaya arkheologiya* and *Sovetskaya etnografia*, and works such as that of S. P. Tolstov on Central Asia and of S. V. Kiselev on Southern Siberia are indispensable to those who wish for information on the great amount of work done in these fascinating regions. Other periodicals which will inform the reader about Eastern and Central Europe are *Acta Archaeologica*, *Acta Ethnographica*, and *Acta Linguistica*, published by the Hungarian Academy of Sciences in Budapest, and the *Archaeologiké Rozhledy*, published in Prague since 1949. Valuable studies of archaeology and anthropology have appeared in 'Studies in the Anthropology of Oceania and Asia,' *Papers of the Peabody Museum*, Vol. 20, 1943, published in memory of Roland Burrage Dixon. For Oceania alone, we have Te Rangi Hiroa's *An Introduction to Polynesian Anthropology*.[1]

For the Palaeolithic in Europe, we have Karl Absolon's eight volumes of the *Palaeoethnologische Serie* in the *Studien aus dem Gebiete der allgemeinen Karstforschung, wissenschaftlicher Höhlenkunde und den Nachbargebieten*, published at Brünn from 1933 to 1945, dealing with Eastern Europe. In Western Europe there was the exciting discovery of Lascaux on September 12, 1940, by five boys digging to find their lost dog. The main hall of this great cave is about sixty feet long and thirty feet broad, and all parts of the cave are covered with brilliant frescoes of animals with some human figures, preserved by a thin covering of calcite. They appear to be mainly Late Aurignacian, though some of them have been called proto-Magdalenian. They are sumptuously published under the title *Lascaux* by Fernand Windels at Montignac-sur-Vézère, Dordogne, in a limited edition of 500 copies. An introduction by the Abbé Breuil is dated 1948. The English edition of Windels's book, translated with a preface by Professor C. F. C. Hawkes, will be most useful, as few copies of the French are likely to be available. Professor Hawkes's *The Prehistoric Foundations of Europe*, the best general study for the student who needs a comprehensive survey, was published in 1940. This has an extensive bibliography. MacCurdy's *Human Origins* still has the best list of sites with stratifications and bibliographies up to 1924, but its value is extended by Denis Péyrony's *Le Périgord Préhistorique* which carries on this good work to 1949. It is published at Périgueux. A good general introduction is W. B. Wright's *Tools and The Man*, 1939.

Leakey's *Stone Age Africa* has already been mentioned as a general summary of Africa Stone Age cultures. Among special studies are T. P. O'Brien's *The Prehistory of the Uganda Protectorate* of 1939,

---

[1] *B.P. Bishop Museum Bull.*, 187, Honolulu, 1945.

following on earlier work by J. W. Gregory and E. J. Wayland, the four volumes of full and detailed survey of palaeolithic man in the Nile Valley by K. S. Sandford and W. J. Arkell[1] for the Oriental Institute of the University of Chicago, and *The Stone Age Cultures of South Africa*, by A. J. H. Goodwin and C. van Riet Lowe, published as volume XXVII of the *Annals of the South African Museum* in 1929. Later works are J. D. Clark's *Stone Age Cultures of Northern Rhodesia*, 1950, and *The Prehistory of Southern Africa*, 1959. Since 1945, the South African Archaeological Society at Cape Town has issued *The South African Archaeological Bulletin*, and since 1938 the Bureau of Archaeology of the Union of South Africa has issued an *Archaeological Series*. Valuable material is collected in the *Pan-African Congresses on Prehistory*, Oxford, 1952, Paris, 1955, and London, 1957.

Recent works on later periods of prehistory include *The Desert Fayum* by G. Caton-Thompson and E. W. Gardner, published by the Royal Anthropological Institute in 1934, *Early Khartoum*, 1949, by A. J. Arkell, G. Brunton's *Mostagedda and the Tasian Culture* of 1937, all on excavations of early periods, and E. J. Baumgartel's *The Cultures of Prehistoric Egypt* of 1947, a reasoned and highly critical examination of the prehistoric material from Egypt. This had a revised edition in 1955, and a second volume was added in 1960.

Two very useful books are the three-volume *History of East Africa* by A. G. Mathew and R. Oliver, to be published by Oxford, and the *Mediaeval History of the Tanganyika Coast*, by G. S. P. Freeman-Grenville, again from the Oxford University Press. Following work by the Rev. A. G. Mathew, James Kirkman, Eric Lanning, Peter Shinnie, and G. S. Freeman-Grenville in Kenya, Tanganyika, Uganda, and Somaliland, came the visit of Sir Mortimer Wheeler and the foundation of the British Institute of East African History and Archaeology with headquarters at Dar-es-Salaam and Kampala. Dr Merrick Posnansky, curator of the Kampala Museum and assistant director of the Institute, has worked especially on early pottery, carried out excavations in Uganda, and collaborated with Dr Roland Oliver in his study of oral history in the same area. As usual, prehistory and ethnology are part of one continuous process, and not in separate compartments. The present director of the Institute, Nevill Chittick, is at work on excavations on Kilwa Island, off the coast of Tanganyika, and these are proving to be

---

[1] Sandford and Arkell, *Palaeolithic Man and the Nile-Fayum Divide*, 1929, and *Palaeolithic Man and the Nile Valley in Nubia and Upper Egypt*, 1933; Sandford, *Palaeolithic Man and the Nile Valley in Upper and Middle Egypt*, 1934; Sandford and Arkell, *Palaeolithic Man and the Nile Valley in Lower Egypt*, 1939.

of outstanding interest as late as mediaeval times and for earlier Stone Age times.

Among the most important work in Asia was that by Claude F. A. Schaeffer at Ras Shamra (Ugarit) in Syria. The site was occupied from neolithic times until its destruction at the beginning of the twelfth century B.C., and is especially interesting for its relations with Mesopotamia, Egypt, and the Aegean. Its archaeology is being published by Paul Geuthner of Paris as *Ugaritica I*, 1939, *Ugaritica II*, 1949, *Ugararica III*, 1956, and *Ugaratica IV* (in process of publication). Schaeffer has also published with the Griffith Institute of the Ashmolean Museum at Oxford the monumental *Stratigraphie Comparée et Chronologie de l'Asie Occidentale (IIIe et IIe millénaires)*, a book dealing with the sites in Syria, Palestine, Asia Minor, Cyprus, Persia, and the Caucasus. This appeared in 1948. In 1946 appeared a small book by T. Burton-Brown covering the same vast area, and including Mesopotamia, with brief summaries of important sites and their stratifications, entitled *Studies in Third Millennium History*. Among the principal sites are those described by Sir Leonard Woolley in *Ur Excavations, I* being on *Al' Ubaid*, in 1927, with H. R. Hall, and *II* being on *The Royal Cemetery*, in 1934. Woolley's work on Atchana-Alalakh has been appearing in *The Antiquaries Journal* since 1938. He died on February 20, 1960, and the entire 1960 volume of *Iraq* was devoted to his contributions to Near Eastern archaeology, the most considerable of any. The first five parts of Jordan's *Uruk-Warka*, in German, appeared between 1930 and 1934, and Parts 6–10 came out in 1935–39. Ernest Mackay's 1931 *Report on Excavations at Jemdet Nasr, Iraq*, was published by the Field Museum of Chicago, and S. Langdon's *Kish I, III, IV*, by Geuthner in Paris. For earlier periods, the reader may consult E. A. Speiser's *Excavations at Tepe Gawra*, 1935, M. E. L. Mallowan's and J. C. Rose's *Prehistoric Assyria: The Excavations of Tall Arpachiyah*, 1933, Baron Max von Oppenheim's *Tell Halaf: A New Culture in Oldest Mesopotamia*, 1933, and R. Campbell Thompson and R. W. Hutchinson on *A Century of Exploration at Nineveh*, 1929. Campbell Thompson's later work appeared in the Liverpool *Annals of Archaeology and Anthropology*. H. Frankfort's *Cylinder Seals*, 1939, is of great use for comparative study and for understanding ancient institutions, and useful books for gaining a view of the whole area are the *Guide to the Iraq Museum Collections*, Baghdad, 1942, and André Parrot's *Archéologie Mésopotamienne*, 1946. For Mallowan's work at Nimrud, 1949–59, the reader may consult the periodical *Iraq* (published in London), founded in 1934 and continuing. This covers all of the archaeology of the country. The most important work on chronology in Iraq has been that of fixing the date of the first Babylonian Dynasty, the pivot of Mesopotamian chronology. In 1928, the epic work of Professor Stephen Langdon and of Dr J. K. Fotheringham at Oxford, had fixed this date at 2169 B.C. in their book on *The Venus Tablet of Ammizaduga*, (who reigned for twenty-one years as tenth king of that dynasty). Tablets discovered at Kish preserve astrological observations on the morning and evening appearances and disappearances of the planet throughout his reign, and working on these and on harvest tablets which gave dates based on lunar months, they arrived at a date in Ammizaduga's reign which satisfied the conditions of a particular observation of Venus. Work by Sidney Smith and Brigadier-General Sewell on material discovered by Sir Leonard Woolley at Alalakh in Syria, allowed them to place the occurrence of this particular behaviour of the planet in her next cycle, 275 years later, thus fixing the foundation of the first Babylonian Dynasty in 1894 B.C. *Alalakh and Chronology* by Sidney Smith appeared in 1940.

Anatolia has long been recognized as a centre of early developments in civilization, and as a bridge between Asia and Europe. Of the later work in that region, one recalls T. H. Bossert's *Altanatolien* in 1942, H. Z. Kosay's *Ausgrabungen von Alaca Höyuk* in 1944, published at Ankara, and John Garstang's *Prehistoric Mersin*, Oxford, 1953, which covers the long period from Lower Neolithic to about A.D. 1500. Since 1951, this area has been served by the periodical *Anatolian Studies*, published in London, and containing the regular reports on such key sites as Polatli (Seton Lloyd and N. Gökçe), Beycesultan (Lloyd and J. Mellaart), and Hacilar (James Mellaart). This last excavation has been reported in *Anatolian Studies*, VIII–XI, 1958–61; it shows a rich and extensive neolithic and chalcolithic culture, beginning with an aceramic or pre-pottery neolithic, and appears to have affinities with the Sesklo culture in Thessaly on the Gulf of Volo, which extends into the Balkans and Greece, and links with the neolithic and chalcolithic of Cilicia and North Syria. Much valuable work appears in the index and bibliography in Volume X, 1960, both by Turkish and other scholars, and a good deal of work is published at Ankara, sometimes with summaries in English. Of these one might mention Tahsin and Nimet Özgüç, *Kültepe-Kanis*, Ankara, 1959. Another valuable publication is Hetty Goldman's *Excavations at Gözlü Kule-Tarsus*, Princeton, 1956.

Noteworthy among Persian sites is Sialk, excavated and published by R. Ghirshman as *Fouilles de Sialk près de Kashan* in 1938 and 1939, and Tepe Giyan, published by Ghirshman and G. Contenau as *Fouilles de Tépé-Giyan* in 1935. Important reconnaissances by Sir Aurel Stein are *Old Routes of Western Iran*, 1940, and *Archaeological Reconnaissances in North-west India and South-eastern Iran*, 1937. His many journeys, now unhappily over, have opened a wider territory of the past than those of any other man. A most valuable book for pulling together the many sites in Persia, and for comparison with Iraq, is Donald E. McCown's *Comparative Stratigraphy of Early Iran*, published in 1942 by the Oriental Institute of the University of Chicago. *Iran in the Ancient East*, 1941, by E. Herzfeld, is also most useful.

In the Indus Valley, Ernest Mackay's last work was at Chanhu-daro in 1935–36 for the American School of Indic and Iranian Studies and the Boston Museum of Fine Arts, and was published as *Chanhu-daro Excavations* by the American Oriental Society of New Haven, Connecticut, in 1943. Previously he had published in 1938 two volumes on *Further Excavations at Mohenjo-daro*, and in 1935 a small book entitled *The Indus Civilization*, of which a new edition by Dorothy Mackay was issued in 1948. Civilization in the Old World began in four great river valleys, the Nile, the Tigris-Euphrates, the Indus, and the Yellow River Valley, and he had worked in all except that of the Yellow River, as well as in Palestine. Since the war, Sir R. E. Mortimer Wheeler has worked as Director-General of Antiquities, and accounts by him and others have appeared in *Ancient India*, the Bulletin of the Archaeological Survey of India, founded and edited by himself since 1946. He has also written an archaeological outline called *Five Thousand Years of Pakistan*, 1950. A later work is *Early India and Pakistan to Ashoka*, 1959. W. H. Gordon's *The Prehistoric Background of Indian Culture* is a valuable work published at Bombay in 1958.

Work in the Yellow River Valley has also progressed. In 1942, Carl Whiting Bishop published a brief handbook on the *Origin of the Far Eastern Civilizations* in the War Background Studies of the Smithsonian Institution which forms a valuable summary and general introduction to the subject. H. G. Creel's *The Birth of China*, 1936, and *Studies in Early Chinese Culture*, 1938, carry on the pioneer work of J. G. Andersson, whose 'An Early Chinese Culture,' published in 1923 as No. 5 of the *Bulletin of the Geological Survey of China*, and *Children of the Yellow Earth: Studies in Prehistoric China*, 1934, are still indispensable, as is T. J. Arne's account of 'The Painted Stone Age Pottery from the Province of Honan,' published in 1925 in *Palaeontologia Sinica*, D. 1, 2. For the great nomad empires of Asia, René Grousset's *L'Empire des Steppes*, 1948, is a standard work, and the histories of India, China, and South-east Asia, and Japan to the fifteenth century are given in *L'Asie*

Orientale, des Origines au XV Siècle, première partie, *Les Empires*,[1] 1941, by R. Grousset, J. Auboyer, and J. Buhot. Tsui Chi's *Short History of Chinese Civilization*, 1942, covers the time from Peking man to the present with a table of emperors and dynasties, another of main events, and a bibliography of Chinese sources. Probably the most important work still proceeding is that which began in 1929 at Anyang in Honan on the Mounds of Yin, the ancient capital of the Shang Dynasty (1766–1122 B.C.). *The Preliminary Reports on Excavations at Anyang*, 1929–33, have been extended and summarized in Creel's books, already mentioned (page 267), and results show that all of the inventions of early civilization, including the use of bronze and writing, had already reached China and were flourishing. Cheng Te-K'un's eight-volume work on *Archaeology in China* was mentioned on page 254.

For European prehistory since the Palaeolithic, we mention a few outstanding publications. For a mesolithic site there is J. G. D. Clark's *Starr Carr (Yorkshire)*, 1954. H. Shetelig and H. Falk wrote a good book on *Scandinavian Archaeology* which appeared in 1937, translated by E. V. Gordon, and Brøndsted's *Danmarks Oldtid*, 1938–40, is a most important contribution. Ernst Sprockhoff's series the *Handbuch der Urgeschichte Deutschlands* began appearing in 1938. W. Lamb's *Excavations at Thermi in Lesbos* was published in 1936. For the British Isles, *The Irish Stone Age* by H. L. Movius appeared in 1942, and V. Gordon Childe's *Prehistoric Communities of the British Isles* in 1940. The important site of *Maiden Castle, Dorset*, was excavated by R. E. M. Wheeler, and published by him in 1943 as Report XII of the Research Committee of the Society of Antiquaries of London. What amounted to re-excavation of Cranborne Chase was most valuably done by Professor C. F. C. Hawkes and printed in the *Archaeological Journal* (CIV) for 1948. Owing largely to the principles expounded by General Pitt Rivers late in the last century, comparative knowledge is now far greater than it could be in his lifetime. Accordingly, Professor Hawkes re-examined the work recorded in *Excavations in Cranborne Chase* (1881–98). In Hawkes's own words in 'Britons, Romans and Saxons round Salisbury and in Cranborne Chase,' the General 'recorded it so well, and preserved his finds so carefully, that this process can really amount to re-excavation of his sites'.[2] The American School of Pre-

---

[1] *Histoire Générale. Histoire du Moyen Âge.* Tome X.

[2] It is sometimes the fashion for able young archaeologists who have discovered the General, as each generation is bound to do, to cavil at what they deem the faults of those of us who excavated vast dusty mounds in the East. With two or three Europeans, a couple of skilled foremen, sometimes about a thousand unskilled men, and a railway, we happily ranged over sites three-quarters of a mile long and went down sixty to seventy feet over areas about three hundred yards on

historic Research returned to its activities in 1948 with *Bulletin* 16, which carried the grievous news of the death by accident of its veteran founder, George Grant MacCurdy, and of the death in war by torture of James Harvey Gaul, whose last work, 'The Neolithic Period in Bulgaria,' is printed in this issue. *Bulletin 20* (1956) contains Part I of 'The Prehistory of Eastern Europe' by Marija Gimbutas. Students can keep up with work on European archaeology through *Antiquity*, 1927–, *The Antiquaries Journal*, 1921, *Proceedings of the Prehistoric Society*, 1908–, and other journals.

From the foregoing, it becomes apparent that the last few years have done much to give us a clearer idea of the origins of civilization and the main sequence of events. We can see the Mesolithic coming to an end in the Near East in the eighth millennium, and the Neolithic with cultivation of the ground, domestic animals, pottery, and textiles coming on through the seventh. Then, in the fourth millennium, we find the use of copper together with stone, and writing, people are living in villages, and laws about the management of water are necessary. About 3500 B.C. we find the complex coming into the Indus Valley, and by about 1800 B.C. into the Yellow River Valley, and also well established in western Europe. A very simple diagram will give a general idea (p. 270).

Some brief account of advances in the study of the technology[1] of our forerunners can now be given. During the Palaeolithic or Old Stone Age, which lasted over half a million years, mankind learned to make tools of stone, bone, and antler, which enabled them to pound, cut, saw, drill, gouge, plane, scrape, and sew materials. Their greatest discovery was that of making fire at will by friction or percussion. In western Europe and South Africa their development of graphic and plastic arts, of painting and engraving, partly for their own sake, and partly to aid them to control the incalculable in life, has never been surpassed.

The study of the methods by which our ancestors and modern peoples living in the Stone Age made their implements has been going on for a long time, and in this country we have had practical illustrations

---

[1] *Technology*, used with the original meaning of τέχλη, an art, skill, or craft, means here the comparative and analytic study of arts and industries.

---

each side. I thought of the General's barrows and villages during the race to virgin soil at Kish, Uruk, and Ur, when our expeditions tied in a comparative stratification for Mesopotamia, and am convinced that we did right to discover the main sequences first, and later, in other areas, to tackle the details with the meticulous care for which British archaeology is justly famous. Whether the General would have done what my masters and colleagues in the Eastern field did, I do not know. But the old General was a strategist of the first order, and met the situations that faced him, and I am certain that he would not have attacked a Tell after the manner of a Round Barrow, nor used a tablespoon when a railway truck was better.

CULTURAL PERIODS OF EARLY MAN[1]

Period	Time
PALAEOLITHIC	
Lower Palaeolithic. Abbevillean (Chellean), Acheulean, Clactonian, Early Levallois.	*c.* 550,000–250,000 years ago.
Middle Palaeolithic. Late Acheulean and Clactonian, Levallois, Mousterian.	*c.* 250,000–100,000 years ago.
Upper Palaeolithic. Aurignacian, Solutrean, Magdalenian.	*c.* 100,000–12,000 years ago.
MESOLITHIC	*c.* 12,000–5,000 years ago.

Later Periods

Western Europe	Western Asia and Egypt	China	
Mesolithic	Neolithic	Mesolithic	7000–4000 B.C.
Mesolithic	Chalcolithic[2]	Mesolithic	4000–3000 B.C.
Neolithic	Chalcolithic Bronze	Neolithic	3000–2000 B.C.
Bronze	Bronze, then Iron	Bronze	2000–1000 B.C.
Iron	Iron	Iron	1000–500 B.C.

in our own generations from Snare, Spalding, and Edwards in the Coach and Horses Gun-Flint Works at Brandon, which still exports gun flints. The problem of getting good flakes across from both sides to meet and of making a thin section exercised Sir John Evans, Sir Edward Tylor, Professor Henry Balfour, and many others. Snare and Spalding could do some work as well as Stone Age people, but kept their secret. The first literate presentation of the method of 'turning the edge' so as to form a suitable striking-platform was by Sir Francis Knowles, in 1944,

---

[1] Table prepared by the author for Dr F. G. W. Knowles in *Man and Other Living Things*, George G. Harrap & Co., 1945. Palaeolithic 'dates' follow C. F. C. Hawkes, *Museums Journal*. Sept., 1941.
[2] A period when copper and stone were both used for tools.

in 'The Manufacture of a Flint Arrowhead by Quartzite Hammerstone,' published by the Pitt Rivers Museum as the first of its *Occasional Papers on Technology*.[1] Professor A. P. Elkin of Sydney had noted that H. Basedow in *The Australian Aboriginal* of 1929 had mentioned rubbing and rasping the edge to clear away small chips, and on receiving a copy of Sir Francis Knowles's paper, sent two observers among the aboriginal stone workers to watch them at work. They, of course, found that the makers of stone and glass lance-heads turned the edges to prepare striking-platforms precisely as Sir Francis Knowles had done in making flint implements.[2] Professor A. S. Barnes's valuable paper on 'The Differences between Natural and Human Flaking of Prehistoric Flint Implements' appeared in the *American Anthropologist* for January-March, 1939, in the same year that his 'De la manière dont la nature imite le travail humain dans l'éclatement du silex' appeared in the *Bulletin de la Société Préhistorique Française*. Beatrice Blackwood's 'The Technology of a Modern Stone Age People in New Guinea,' published as the third *Occasional Paper on Technology* by the Pitt Rivers Museum in 1950, describes fully with illustrations how present-day people make and use stone implements and the other things that go with a Stone Age economy.

MacCurdy's *Human Origins* of 1924 is still the best book I know for its account of fire-making and light in the most ancient world, and Miller Christy's *Catalogue* and *Supplement* of the *Bryant and May Museum of Fire-Making Appliances*, published in 1926 and 1928, is the fullest and most accurate modern account of the methods of making fire. In 1939, F. W. Robins published *The Story of the Lamp (and the Candle)*, an account of all types of lighting appliance with indications of their history. A point one notices in all of the lamps is the small container and rather feeble light, but when one notes that the oil or fat used was edible, it is not difficult to understand why good oil lamps were not available until the coming of cheap paraffin after 1860.

The discovery of Lascaux in 1940 with its Late Aurignacian to Early Magdalenian frescoes, and its publication by Fernand Windels in 1948 with an introduction by the Abbé Breuil, formed a worthy successor to the earlier great publications of *Altamira* (Cartailhac and Breuil), *Font de Gaume* (Capitan, Breuil, Péyrony), *Les Cavernes de la région Cantabrique* (Alcalde del Rio, Breuil, Sierra), and *La Pasiega* (Breuil, Obermaier, Alcalde del Rio), and it is pleasant to think that the

---

[1] This was followed by Knowles in 1953 by 'Stone-Worker's Progress,' No. 6 in the same series, including this and much more material.

[2] *Man*, 1948, **130**.

late Abbé Breuil, the pioneer, had taken an active part in all of this magnificent work over so long a period of time. His four volumes of *Les Peintures Rupestres schématiques de la Péninsule Ibérique* appeared between 1933 and 1935, and in 1929, he had collaborated with M. C. Burkitt in *Rock Paintings of Southern Andalusia*, these last being of the Neolithic and Copper Age.

Work like that of A. Leslie Armstrong in the *Journal of the Royal Anthropological Institute*, January-June, 1931, on the Rhodesian Archaeological Expedition, showed in the Bambata Cave a beautiful series of paintings corresponding with coloured pencils of ochre in the layers beneath[1] from Upper Palaeolithic to Bushman. In 1930, Dorothea Bleek published *Rock Paintings in South Africa Copied by George William Stow* between 1867 and 1882, and in the same year Hugo Obermaier and Herbert Kühn brought out *Buschmannkunst*, both in colour, like the Altamira and other European volumes. *Bushman Paintings*, copied in colour by M. Helen Tongue, with a preface by Henry Balfour in 1909, forms a beautiful album. Other books on African art include four splendid volumes of *Centres de Style de la Sculpture Nègre Africaine* by Carl Kjersmeier, published between 1935 and 1938, the most comprehensive work of its kind, *Arts of West Africa (excluding music)*, 1935, edited by Michael E. Sadler; *African Negro Art*, edited by James Johnson Sweeney, and published by the Museum of Modern Art in New York in 1935; and the portfolio *Les Arts Sauvages—Afrique*, by A. Portier and F. Poncetton in the Editions Albert Morancé. *The Art of Ancient Egypt*, with an introduction by Hermann Ranke, published by the Phaidon Press, Vienna, in 1936, and presented in Great Britain by George Allen and Unwin, has all the beauty and quality that one expects from a Phaidon book. Earlier books are Sir E. Denison Ross's *The Art of Egypt through the Ages*, 1931, and Hedwig Fechheimer's *Die Plastik der Ägypter*, 1920, and *Kleinplastik der Ägypter*, 1921.

Publications on Oriental art include the journal *Oriental Art*, 1948-51, and 1955-, edited by the Department of Eastern Art, Oxford; Werner Speiser's *Die Kunst Ostasiens*, 1946; Ernst Diez's *Iranische Kunst*, 1944; Chiang Yee's *The Chinese Eye*, 1935; William Cohn's Phaidon Press (London) magnificent *Chinese Painting*, 1948; the splendid *Catalogue of The Chinese Exhibition* in London, 1936; Ludwig Bachhofer's *Short History of Chinese Art*, the London Batsford edition being dated 1947; and H. F. E. Visser's *Asiatic Art in Private Collections of*

---

[1] For a critical examination of Armstrong's stratigraphy, see Neville Jones in *Occasional Papers of the National Museum of Southern Rhodesia*, No. 9.

Holland and Belgium, 1947. Two useful books are Benjamin March's *Some Technical Terms of Chinese Painting*, Baltimore, 1935, and *Chinese Jade Carving* by S. Howard Hansford, 1950. This last is a most admirable book, one of the all too few books on an art or craft in which a reader who wants information on a particular point can look and not be disappointed, and given the skill, can carry out the process described. A series that will never be superseded is that of *Die Kunst des Ostens*, edited by William Cohn, and a book of the utmost value is the very rare *Ko-ji Hô-ten* in two volumes, a dictionary and encyclopaedia of Chinese and Japanese art, fully illustrated, by V.-F. Weber, privately printed by the author in Paris in 1923. Recent publications are *The Scythians* by Tamara Talbot Rice, 1957, and James Mellaarts' account of Catal Hüyük, with the earliest neolithic frescoes known. These are in the *Illustrated London News* for June 9 and 16, 1962. This paper is the best medium for keeping up-to-date with principal excavations and discoveries.

Oceanic arts include *Arts of the South Seas*, 1946, by Ralph Linton, Paul S. Wingert, René d'Harnoncourt, and Miguel Covarrubias; *Dance and Drama in Bali*, by Beryl de Zoete and Walter Spies, 1938; *Melanesian Design* in two volumes, by Gladys A. Reichard, 1933; and the three volumes of Karl von den Steinen's *Die Marquesaner und ihrer Kunst*, 1925–29.

It is impossible to enter the field of sophisticated European art; it is too large a subject, and has too many sides to fit in here. It seems possible to present the arts of other ages and places as part of their general history and culture, and thereby to gain an insight into the nature and development of a people. So far as I am aware, the *Oxford History of English Art*, edited by T. S. R. Boase, whose volumes are still appearing, is the only work on a large scale to attempt such a study, though a one-volume book by D. Talbot Rice on *Byzantine Art*, published in 1935, gives a good general outline of what it stood for, led to, and of what it was derived from, a model of what such books should do. Three outstanding books on long periods of European art are Herbert Kühn's *Die vorgeschichtliche Kunst Deutschlands* of 1935, covering German art from the Old Stone Age to about A.D. 1000, E. T. Leeds's *Celtic Ornament in the British Isles down to A.D.* 700, published in 1933, and Paul Jacobsthal's two volumes on *Early Celtic Art*, 1944, which give as well a conspectus of Continental Celtic art and culture. Raymond Bloch's *The Etruscans* appeared in 1958. Peasant arts of Europe are dealt with in *The Studio* series, which brings out volumes for each country. A large and comprehensive folio volume by H. Th. Bossert on *Peasant Art in*

Europe is valuable for comparative study and identification. Handsome books for the study of peasant art are Max Tilke's *The Costumes of Eastern Europe*, Berlin, 1925, and Emma Calderini's *Il Costume Popolare in Italia*, Milan, 1934. Then, too, there is Estella Canziani's earlier work, illustrated lavishly by her own paintings, in *Costumes, Traditions and Songs of Savoy*, 1911, and the French version, *Costumes, Moeurs et Légendes de Savoie*, Chambéry, 1920; *Piedmont*, with Eleanor Rohde, 1913; and *Through the Apennines and the Lands of the Abruzzi*, 1928. In *Art and Society*, 1937, Herbert Read makes an attempt to examine the nature of the relations which subsist between society and individuals responsible for the creation of works of art. A valuable contribution to the comparison of the arts, the beginning of comparative criticism, is the *Paragone*, a comparison of the arts by Leonardo da Vinci, with an introduction and English translation by Irma A. Richter, published in 1949.

General comparative works are Joseph Gregor's *Masks of The World*, 1936–37, ranging from savagery to sophistication, Leonhard Adam's small Pelican book of 1940 on *Primitive Art* (revised and enlarged edition, 1949), and Herbert Kühn's *Die Kunst der Primitiven* of 1923.

So far we have spoken of arts and industries with a palaeolithic beginning. Earlier, we described the inventions following the neolithic revolution when men turned from hunting and gathering to agriculture and domesticated animals in the great river valleys. While we do not find writing before the advent of copper, nor any great variety in musical instruments or sign of the development of music,[1] it seems well to consider them here, as they are, like sculpture and painting, methods of expressing human ideas and emotions.

Much has happened of late years to throw light on the history of writing. Falkenstein's *Archäische Texte aus Uruk*, 1936, and Langdon's *Pictographic Inscriptions from Jemdet Nasr*, 1928, (*O.E.C.T.*, *VII*), show pure pictographs, and pictographs which represent sounds rather than ideas in Mesopotamia. The dates of this ancient writing run from about 3500 to 3200 B.C. Further evidence of the origins of writing comes from the oracle bones of the Shang Dynasty (*c.* 1766–1122 B.C.) at Anyang in the province of Honan. We have already referred to the publication of the excavations (page 268), and to Creel's *The Birth of China* and *Studies in Early Chinese Culture*. In the notes to H. G. Creel's *Literary Chinese*, Vol. I, 1938, the reader can note how pictures of ideas become pictures of sounds, and how writing evolves from that

---

[1] It is true, of course, that whistles made from reindeer phalanges are known as early as the Magdalenian period, and bone flutes are found from the Neolithic.

on the oracle bones through that on the Chou (1122–256 B.C.) stone drums and bronzes, to the Shuo Wên Dictionary of the Han Dynasty, published in A.D. 121. The same process can be seen in the notes opposite each of the Jemdet Nasr signs already mentioned. In his Schweich Lectures to the British Academy published in 1939 as *The Cuneiform Texts of Ras Shamra-Ugarit*, C. F. A. Schaeffer describes alphabetic inscriptions using twenty-nine cuneiform signs, their date being the fifteenth-fourteenth centuries B.C. The people of Ugarit, living at a cross-roads on the Syrian coast, had found the need of something less cumbrous than the syllabic system. Two French scholars, Éd. Dhorme and Charles Virolleaud, unravelled the secret of the Ras Shamra alphabet, and Virolleaud deciphered and published the majority of the alphabetic texts recovered during nine years of excavation (see 'Le déchiffrement des tablettes alphabétiques de Ras Shamra' in *Syria*, XII, 1931). In 1948, Dr David Diringer first published an important work on *The Alphabet, A Key to the History of Mankind*, which appeared in a revised edition in 1949. This book contains extensive bibliographies and summaries of all known scripts and the people who have worked on them, e.g. the work of Sir Alan Gardiner in the Egyptian field and of Maurice Dunand on Byblos in Syria. It was published too soon to include the most important Schweich Lectures of 1944 on *Semitic Writing* by Professor G. R. Driver,[1] in which he traces the developments of writing from the time of the first Sumerian pictographs to the development of alphabetic writing. On general linguistics, *Les Langues du Monde*, Paris, 1924, by A. Meillet and Marcel Cohen, still remains the most comprehensive survey of the subject. A new edition, greatly enlarged and improved, appeared in 1952. Dard Hunter's *Paper Making, the History and Technique of an Ancient Craft*, appeared first in 1943 and in a revised and enlarged edition in 1947.

The technical study of musical instruments and of systems of music is of the greatest value to the anthropologist. The forms of instruments require such skill and understanding, and the forms of musical expression so much more, that the study of comparative musicology becomes a crucial test for the origin, development, and diffusion of ideas.

For musical instruments throughout the world, Curt Sachs gives most comprehensive descriptions and histories for all types in *The History of Musical Instruments*, 1942, and in *The Rise of Music in the Ancient World*, 1943, with a suggested system of classification in the first; an earlier work of his is the *Geist und Werden der Musikinstrumente* of 1929. Karl Geiringer is especially good at explaining the

[1] Oxford, 1950.

acoustics of instruments in the Western world, in his *Musical Instruments*, 1943, with a second edition in 1945. Professor Rosario Profeta's *Storia e Letteratura degli Strumenti Musicali*[1] is useful and wide ranging. For English and European instruments, Canon F. W. Galpin is incomparable in his *Old English Instruments of Music*, 1910 and 1932, and in *European Musical Instruments*, 1937, 1944, 1946, and 1956. His glorious collection left England for the Boston Museum of Fine Arts, and we have from them Nicholas Bessaraboff's splendid catalogue of it, so well prepared that instruments could be made from it, and one can learn precisely what the instruments can do. This is entitled *Ancient European Musical Instruments*, and was published in 1941. In his book on English musical instruments, Canon Galpin proposed one of the most reasonable classifications of instruments extant; much is to be said, too, for the classification made by Henry Balfour for *Notes and Queries on Anthropology* in 1929.[2] Other books mainly on instruments are the 1888 *Musical Instruments* of A. J. Hipkins and William Gibb, a de luxe affair with a second edition in 1945; Anthony Baines, *Bagpipes*, 1960, published by the Pitt Rivers Museum, Oxford, as No 9 of its series; A. Chapuis and Ed. Gélis, *Le Mondes des Automates* in two splendid volumes, Paris, 1928; and A. Chapuis and Ed. Droz, *Les Automates*, Neuchâtel, 1949.

Among works which deal with all aspects of music either for the world or for an area are Percy Scholes's *Oxford Companion to Music*, an indispensable book in dictionary order first published in 1938, and several times since. H. G. Farmer's *History of Arabian Music*, 1929, A. H. Fox-Strangways on *The Music of Hindostan*, 1914, and Louis Laloy, *La Musique Chinoise*, are all classics for their areas. Books which would be difficult to praise too highly are Jaap Kunst's two-volume *Music of Java*, The Hague, 1949, Kathleen Schlesinger's *The Greek Aulos*, 1939, and *A History of Byzantine Music and Hymnography*, 1949, by Egon Wellesz, with a revised and enlarged edition in 1961. For South Africa, we have the authoritative work by P. R. Kirby on *The Musical Instruments of the Native Races of South Africa*, 1934, and for the Hawaiian Islands, Helen H. Roberts on 'Ancient Hawaiian Music,' *Bulletin 29* of the Bernice Pauahi Bishop Museum, Honolulu, 1926. Her *Form in Primitive Music*, 1933, is also most useful. Canon Galpin's last important book was *The Music of the Sumerians*, 1937, in which he used the method of copying the ancient instruments, and playing on them, and so pushed the history of civilized music back into

[1] Casa Editrice Marrocco, Florence, 1942.
[2] Rev. ed., 1951.

the third and second millennia. It is good to know that the Galpin Society has been formed to commemorate his genius, and to carry on his wonderful researches into the history of music. The *Galpin Society Journal* began publication in 1948. Indispensable are two volumes of the *Encyclopédie de la Musique* by Albert Lavignac and L. de la Laurencie, *Histoire*, 1931, and *Technique*, 1925. Also of great value is Friedrich Blumes' great alphabetical *Allgemeine Encyclopädie der Musik: Die Musik in Geschichte und Gegenwart*, Basel, London, New York begun in 1949 and continuing. These cover the world. Some valuable collections of gramophone records of recent years are the 'Two Thousand Years of Music,' chosen by Curt Sachs, and 'Music of the Orient,' chosen by one of the greatest of comparative musicologists, Erich Maria von Hornbostel. Both have commentaries, and von Hornbostel has valuable analyses; they are issued by Parlophone. There is also the Columbia 'History of Music', the text written and records chosen by Percy Scholes. We must add *The New Oxford History of Music*, planned in eleven volumes (first volume, 1957), with the attendant albums (H.M.V. and Oxford), *The History of Music in Sound*. Other useful works to the comparative musicologist are H. Panum's *Stringed Instruments of the Middle Ages*; Gustave Reese on *Music in the Middle Ages*, 1941; Harold Gleason's *Examples of Music before 1400*, Crofts and Co., New York, 1946; and Arnold Dolmetsch on *The Interpretation of the Music of the XVII and XVIII Centuries*, 1916 and 1946, the text published at Oxford, and the appendix with twenty-two illustrative pieces by Novello and Co. Among books on special subjects or areas are *Dances of England and France from 1450–1600*, with music and the authentic manner of performance, by Mabel Dolmetsch, 1949; *The Lures of the Bronze Age*, 1949, by H. C. Broholm, William P. Larsen, and Godtfred Skjerne; *Introduction to the Study of Musical Scales* by Alain Daniélou, The India Society, London, 1943; *Musical and Other Sound Instruments of the South American Indians*, Göteborg, 1935, by K. G. Izikowitz; Gilbert Chase's *Bibliography of Latin-American Folk-Music*, compiled for the Library of Congress in 1942; and the Royal Empire Society bibliography of *African Native Music*, compiled by D. H. Varley in 1936. Readers wishing to study African music should know of the African Music Society, whose postal address is P.O. Box 6216, Johannesburg, Union of South Africa. This society is actively engaged in research and in recording under the supervision of Hugh Tracey, and many long-playing records have already been made and distributed with a catalogue from the International Library of African Music, P.O. Box 138, Roodepoort, Transvaal, South Africa.

For a general introduction to all aspects of the development from savagery to civilization, the student cannot do better than begin with the nine volumes of *Corridors of Time* by Harold Peake and H. J. Fleure. The series began in 1927 and ended in 1936, and the titles themselves, *Apes and Men, Hunters and Artists, Peasants and Potters, Priests and Kings, The Steppe and the Sown, The Way of the Sea, Merchant Venturers in Bronze, The Horse and the Sword, The Law and the Prophets*, give a good outline of the steps in the growth and diffusion of civilization. We see how technological stages mark archaeological ages, to reverse the order of the title of Gordon Childe's Huxley Memorial lecture for 1944,[1] and advances in techniques bring social changes. Dr John Murphy's *Lamps of Anthropology*, 1943, shows the process as one of widening horizons, the cultural horizons being 'all that a man can see when he looks out upon his world as he knows it, his group, his tribe, his nation, or his civilization'.

The primitive horizon is that of the simplest groups of hunting and gathering peoples, past and present, with their mainly semi-instinctive perceptual, and concretistic way of thinking. The larger and more closely organized tribal societies show a more developed imagination, and are deeply involved in custom, which is their law and ethics, and held by the solidarity of the group. Out of this in the great river valleys of antiquity develop the beginning of the civilized mind, when people begin to realize their power over what they have accomplished, to organize their resources, and in specialization of work to realize individuality. The necessity to share water in irrigation, not only between neighbours but between cities, sees the beginning of law. The pauses in steady work which occur in an agricultural civilization give opportunities for thought about directions and values which the older hand to mouth life denied. Finally, the growth of great civilizations, trade, and commerce, the increase in power of the nomads of the steppes, getting in each other's way, and consequent wars and hybridization of cultures bring about the great period of the last millennium before Christ, when the Confucians in China, the Buddhists in India, the prophets in Israel, and the scientists and philosophers in Greece lay the foundations of freedom of thought, and of ethical and religious values. The questions arising from conflict of customs and ways of life are no longer 'What is done?' but 'What is right?' No one has put more vividly the impact of the horse riders of the steppes on the horse drivers of the river valleys than Carl Whiting Bishop in his classic paper on 'The Horses of T'ang T'ai-Tsung' in *The Museum Journal* of the University of Pennsylvania

[1] 'Archaeological Ages as Technological Stages,' *J.R.A.I.*, 1944.

in 1918. Three valuable recent studies of ancient religion inspired by recent discoveries are Henri Frankfort's *Kingship and the Gods*, 1948, a 'study of ancient Near Eastern religion as the integration of society and nature', S. H. Hooke's Schweich Lectures of 1935, published in 1938, on *The Origins of Early Semitic Ritual*, in which he relates the ritual practices of the Hebrews to the larger field of those of Mesopotamia and what is known of the early ritual of Canaan, and C. J. Gadd's Schweich Lectures for 1945, published in 1948, on *Ideas of Divine Rule in the Ancient East*, which are concerned 'to observe in what different forms and institutions the universally assumed divine governance was conceived to be exercised over them by the various peoples of the ancient world down to about the time of the Persian dominance'.

The great excavations of the Near East have helped to open the earlier history of agriculture and domestication of animals. The Old World was fortunate above the New in having domesticable animals and cereal grains, which allowed a rhythm of ploughing and sowing and harvesting with periods of leisure between, during which people had time to develop the arts which amuse and educate as well as those which improve the material conditions of life. A. E. Watkins wrote an excellent paper in *Antiquity* for 1933 on 'The Origin of Cultivated Plants,' with a map based on his own and on N. I. Vavilov's work for the *Bulletin of Applied Botany* in 1926, 1927, and 1931, as well as Vavilov's 'The Problem of the Origins of the World's Agriculture in the Light of the Latest Investigations,' published by Kniga (England), Bush House, Aldwych, London. This shows the centre of dispersal of the wheats, barley, millet, and rice. On the Uruk tablets (Falkenstein, *Archäische Texte aus Uruk*) of 3500 B.C. and on the Jemdet Nasr tablets (Langdon, *O.E.C.T.*, VII) of 3200 B.C., appear the symbol for bales of wool, proving domestication. Sign 125 at Jemdet Nasr shows a plough, and work at Uruk shows that oxen were used for traction by 3500 B.C. Pigs, cattle, sheep, and goats were domesticated early when increasing desiccation drove men and animals together in the still-green areas, and the relation of the chase gave way to that of more or less peaceful co-existence. The valuable hen of course is a native of India. Horse bones were found by the chariots in the graves of the middle to late third millennium, and on the palace walls at Kish were inlaid shell and limestone figures showing animals being milked. These were later in the third millennium than the chariot graves. The student desirous of working up any one or more of these subjects has a large amount of material in the reports on ancient sites, and can aim at good technological histories or comparisons such as those of Sir Flinders Petrie's splendid book on *Tools and Weapons*, 1917, or Axel Steensberg's valuable publication on *Ancient Harvesting Implements* in 1943. André Leroi-Gourhan has taken the whole technical apparatus of primitive peoples for illustration, comparison, and discussion in two volumes of *Évolution et Techniques*, one entitled *L'Homme et la Matière*, 1943, and the other *Milieu et Techniques*, 1945. Albert Neuburger's *Die Technik des Altertums* was translated into English as *The Technical Arts and Sciences of the Ancients* by Henry L. Brose in 1930, and is a useful book with a large amount of information. One error on page 79, figure 130, should be corrected in a second edition. It is not a picture of leather working, but a reproduction of Plate VII in Part III of F. Ll. Griffith's *Beni Hasan*, and shows the chipping of flint knives. A most important work is *Ancient Egyptian Materials and Industries*, by A. Lucas, 1926, 1934, and 1948. Among books which deal with agriculture and domestication of animals are E. C. Curwen's *Plough and Pasture*, 1946. Among books which deal with agriculture and domestication of animals are E. C. Curwen's *Plough and Pasture*, 1946; F. H. King's *Farmers of Forty Centuries*, dealing with the Far East, first published in 1926, and reprinted in 1933 and 1939; and R. N. Salaman's *The History and Social Influence of the Potato*, 1949.

Since the classic work of William Gowland on the ancient use of metals and metallurgy, a most important work has been that of T. A. Rickard, whose two-volume *Man and Metals* appeared in 1932. Listing of earlier work need not be attempted here, as it is all found in Rickard's bibliographies. This work is most comprehensive for all metals. Other books are Andreas Oldeberg's *Metallteknik under Förhistorisk Tid*, Lund, 1942; A. K. Hamilton Jenkin's *The Cornish Miner*, 1927 and 1948; R. J. Forbes, *Metallurgy in Antiquity*, 1950; and Notes on the Prehistoric Metallurgy of Copper and Bronze in the Old World' by H. H. Coghlan, 1951. This book contains chapters by Dr E. Voce on 'Examination of Specimens in the Pitt Rivers Museum' and 'Bronze Castings in Ancient Moulds,' as well as contributions by T. K. Penniman on 'Furnace Bellows' and 'Cire Perdue Casting,' and is No. 4 in *Occasional Papers on Technology* of the Pitt Rivers Museum.

Since the year 1950–51, when we last went to press, there has been considerable increase and development all over Europe in research directed towards the problems of ancient metallurgy. This increased development is due to the fact that it is now realized that the metals hold an important place in cultural history. Most excavations had for some time published analyses, and some of them had been evaluated, but it is only lately that we have generally adopted the idea that a metal-using culture cannot be fully understood unless we can find out the geographical source from which the metal has been smelted, how the smelting was done, and how the metal was cast, or worked into shape in the stages of manufacture. To the archaeologist or anthropologist it may be of vital interest to know the place of origin of a metal which may have been found many hundreds of miles away from its parent mineral. Again, there are many problems of importance in the assessment of the technical level of a culture which relate to the casting, forging, fabrication, and finishing of metallic artefacts. As a whole, the problem is not of easy solution, and calls for collaboration of the geologist, mining expert, metallurgist, metallographer, foundry chemist, and mechanical engineer. For long, metallurgical study was a sort of poor relation of archaeology, and pioneers like C. H. Desch with the old Sumerian Copper Committee, in the reports of the British Association from 1928 onward, were few and far between. But now much is being done, and collaboration with the sciences is more usual.

At the present time the major activity of the Ancient Mining and Metallurgy Committee of the Royal Anthropological Institute is directed towards research to investigate the origin and development of the earliest copper metallurgy known in the British Isles. This research is not too difficult because the cultural area is relatively limited. Also, the number of early copper artefacts is not too great; but on the other hand, we meet the problem of correlating ore to metal, and also the practical difficulty of discovering where in fact ancient mining was carried out, so as to obtain representative specimens of ore for the purpose of analysis. Among papers by this Committee are 'The Early Metallurgy of Copper in Ireland and Britain' by H. H. Coghlan and H. J. Case in the *Proceedings of the Prehistoric Society*, Vol. XXII, 1957, and a considerable number of reports in *Man*, mainly by Coghlan, 1950, No. 4, 49, 199, 236; 1951, No. 6, 65, 234; 1952, No. 124; 1953, No. 150; 1954, No. 21; 1955, No. 4; 1957, No. 84. Papers done by request of the Committee are F. C. Thompson's 'The Early Metallurgy of Copper and Bronze' in *Man*, 1958, No. 1, and 'Ancient Metallurgical Furnaces in Great Britain to the End of the Roman Occupation' in *Sibrium* (Varese, Italy), IV, 1958–59, by T. K. Penniman, I. M. Allen, and A. Wootton.

The Pitt Rivers Museum is also actively engaged in the field of technology and scientific research, and besides publication of Coghlan's book on copper and bronze, already mentioned, has issued Coghlan's *Notes on Prehistoric and Early Iron in the Old World* as No. 8 of its

Occasional Papers on Technology in 1956, with contributions by I. M. Allen, and 'A metallographic and Metallurgical Examination of specimens selected by the Pitt Rivers Museum' by courtesy of the Director of Research and Technical Development of Messrs Stewarts and Lloyds. Its main work in metals at present is the preparation, in its own laboratories, with the help of that of the University Laboratory for Archaeology and the History of Art, of No. 10 of the same series, *A Metallographic Examination of British Bronze-Age Implements in the Pitt Rivers Museum*. In connexion with the work of C. F. C. Hawkes, the University Laboratory has published extensive research on metals and important hoards of metals, e.g. in *Archaeometry*, Vol. II (Supplement). The general work of this laboratory is mentioned on pp. 255–256.

Since 1950, a leading position in research in ancient metallurgy must be granted to Austria. Here, R. Pittioni and his colleagues have carried out a valuable programme of metallurgical research into the correlation problems between Austrian minerals and metal artefacts. In the course of this work some 6,000 analyses have been made. One might mention Pittioni's 'Beiträge zum Problem des Ursprunges der Kupferzverwirtung in den alten Welt,' in *Archaeologia Austriaca*, Heft 12, 1953, 'Urzeutlicher Bergbau auf Kupfuerz und Spurenanalyse', *ibid.*, Beiheft 1, 1957, and with H. Neuninger and E. Preuschen, 'Das Kupfer der Nordtiroler Urnenfelderkultur', *ibid.*, Beiheft 5, 1960. A considerable German work by H. Otto and W. Witter is the *Handbuch der ältesten vorgeschichtlichen Metallurgie in Mitteleuropa*, Leipzig, 1952; another major work is Otto Johannsen's *Geschichte des Eisens* (third edition), Düsseldorf, 1954. *Metallanalysen kupferzeitliche und frühbronzezeitliche Bodenfunde aus Europa*, Berlin, 1960, by S. Junghans, E. Sangmeister, and M. Schroder is a work on the scale demanded by research on large quantities of material.

In Italy, study centres have been established at Varese, publishing in *Sibrium*, and in Milan, publishing in the *Associazione Italiana di Metallurgia*, and Russian, Polish, and Czechoslovakian material is published in *Archeologiké Rozhledy* at Prague.

Big general books are L. Aitchison's *A History of Metals* in two volumes, London, 1960, and C. Stanley Smith's *A History of Metallography*, University of Chicago Press, 1960. We have already mentioned the great *History of Technology*, p. 255, and Needham's *Science and Civilization in China*, p. 255. While waiting for the volume on metallurgy, there is his Dickinson Memorial Lecture to the Newcomen Society on 'The Development of Iron and Steel Technology in China,' London, 1958. For the Indian area we have D. H. Gordon's 'The Early

Use of Metals in India and Pakistan,' *J.R.A.I.*, LXXX, Parts I and II, 1950.

The study of pottery naturally receives a great deal of attention, because it is so useful for defining periods of occupation and areas of diffusion. Apart from what may be learned from the publications on various sites already mentioned, we may name a few books devoted to the study of pottery. H. Frankfort's classic *Studies in Early Pottery of the Near East* is in two parts, the first in 1924 dealing with 'Mesopotamia, Syria, and Egypt and their earliest Interrelations,' and the second in 1927 with 'Asia, Europe and the Aegean, and their earliest Interrelations.' Earlier in this chapter (page 267), we mentioned McCown's work on Iran and Mesopotamia, and Arne's work on Chinese pottery. For the technology of pottery, L. Franchet's *Céramique Primitive* of 1911 is still good, and Bernard Leach's *A Potter's Book* of 1940 can be recommended for its practical value. William Bowyer Honey's *Ceramic Art of China and Other Countries of the Far East*, 1945, is especially important for both its historical and its technical information, and another useful work is the *Chinesische Frühkeramik* by Dr Oscar Rucker-Embden, published in 1923. R. L. Hobson's *Handbook of the Pottery and Porcelain of the Far East*, published by the British Museum in 1937, has the qualities that one would expect of the author of *Chinese Pottery and Porcelain*.

Evidence of the textile art is very ancient. Apart from spindle whorls in neolithic sites, we have already linen in the neolithic Fayum in Egypt, the symbol for bales of wool appears in the Uruk and Jemdet Nasr tablets of *c.* 3500 and 3200 B.C., traces of cotton fabric are found on a silver vase at Mohenjo-daro in the Harappa period in the third millennian, and in the Shang Dynasty in China, silk was already in use sometime between 1500 and 1122 B.C., according to Sylwan in the *Bulletin of the Museum of Far Eastern Antiquities* for 1937 (Vol. IX, p. 119). For technical accounts of all processes in the production of silk the reader is recommended to *The China Journal* for May, 1928, and to the *Silk* volume published by the Maritime Customs at Shanghai in 1917. For general technical studies of the fabrics of different areas, ancient and modern, and for the looms on which they were woven, one cannot do better than consult the *Bankfield Museum Notes*[1] published at Halifax (England) by H. Ling Roth and by Laura E. Start. They are all done in such a way that the reader can repeat the work given the

[1] Ling Roth: 'Ancient Egyptian and Greek Looms,' 1913; 'Studies in Primitive Looms,' 1950, 1934, 1917–18 (and in *J.R.A.I.*, 1916–18). Start: 'Coptic Cloths,' 1914; 'Burmese Textiles,' 1917; 'The Durham Collection . . . from Albania and Yugoslavia,' 1939.

materials and equipment. More recent work by Miss Start has been the publication with A. C. Haddon in 1936 of *Iban or Sea Dayak Fabrics*, and 'The McDougall Collection of Indian Textiles from Guatemala and Mexico,' this last being the second of the *Occasional Papers on Technology* published by the Pitt Rivers Museum in 1948. An important contribution is that of R. B. Sergeant on 'Material for a History of Islamic Textiles up to the Mongol Conquest' begun in Volume IX of *Ars Islamica* in 1942, and still continuing. A good general introduction to the art of weaving and spinning is Luther Hooper's *Hand-Loom Weaving*, 1910, and more recent work, such as *The Weaver's Craft*, by L. E. Simpson and M. Weir, 1932, and *Weaving for Amateurs* by Helen Coates.

Cylinder seals of the Jemdet Nasr period in predynastic Naqada in Egypt, and the Indian chank-shell and white-etched cornelian beads from India in Mesopotamia in the third millennium suggest the early development of land and water transport, and as we have already mentioned, chariots are found in the third millennium. Commandant Lefebvre des Noettes may be consulted on animal transport in *La Force Motrice Animale à travers les Âges*, published by Berger-Levrault in Paris, and for water transport there is James Hornell on *Water Transport, Origins and Early Evolution*, 1946, and *British Coracles and Irish Curraghs*, 1938, this last containing an account of the Mesopotamian coracles. Hornell's work on boats is so important that any student of the history of navigation should get his *Bibliography of Scientific Publications* published by the Cambridge University Press in 1938. *The Mariner's Mirror* is also of great use for all aspects of navigation. For studies of shipbuilding, Sir Westcott Abell's *The Shipwright's Trade*, 1948, and John R. Stevens' *An Account of the Construction and Embellishment of Old Time Ships*, 1949, are valuable for the Western world. For the Eastern, we have G. R. G. Worcester's *Junks and Sampans of the Yangtze* in two volumes, published by the Maritime Customs at Shanghai in 1947-48, and an earlier volume on the *Crooked-Bow and Crooked-Stern Junks of Szechwan* in 1941. For Oceania, consult the three volumes on *Canoes of Oceania* by A. C. Haddon and James Hornell, published by the Bernice Pauahi Bishop Museum at Honolulu between 1936 and 1938.

So far in this account of prehistory and technology in the Old World we have confined ourselves to that side of ethnology which deals with arts and industries, all of which begin in an archaeological context and continue into modern times, omitting anything accomplished by mass-production. On the whole, we have quoted books or papers which deal with one art or one industry. Many ethnological or ethnographical books have a chapter or chapters on the material culture, i.e., arts and industries of the peoples described. Such general books we shall notice briefly in the section on general ethnology and social anthropology beginning on page 361. Here we will mention a few ethnographical books or papers which deal with the whole of the arts or industries of a people. Among these are Margaret Trowell and K. P. Wachsmann on *Tribal Crafts of Uganda*, London, 1953, and Margaret Trowell's *African Design*, London, 1960, which is an ethnological, i.e. comparative work considering many kinds of art throughout the continent. A valuable work covering a very large area is Rudolf Hommel's *China at Work*, New York, 1937, one of the most informative of books on this subject, from which one can gain a real insight into processes involved. Two long and detailed books are by Sir Peter Buck (Te Rangi Hiroa) on *Samoan Material Culture*, published as *Bulletin 75* in 1930 by the Bernice Pauahi Bishop Museum in Honolulu, and *Arts and Crafts of Hawaii*, Special Publication 45, 1957, published by the same museum. Here I might mention as an aside one of the most helpful books I know, William T. Brigham's *Index to the Islands of the Pacific Ocean*, published by the Bishop Museum Press at Honolulu in 1900. Each island is listed alphabetically by each of the names it has held throughout its known history, with cross-references, maps, history, and description. It is difficult to imagine how any ethnological museum can function properly without it.

III. PHYSICAL ANTHROPOLOGY: A SURVEY OF DEVELOPMENTS[1]

by J. S. Weiner, M.Sc., M.A., Ph.D., M.R.C.S.

INTRODUCTION

Today the term 'physical anthropology' signifies a range of study which embraces several cognate, yet rather specialized disciplines, as is evident from the books by Harrison, Weiner, Tanner and Barnicot (1964),[1] Ashley-Montagu (1960),[2] Hooton (1946), Howells (1959),[3] Barnett (1957),[4] and Comas (1960).[5] As Penniman has recorded elsewhere in this 100 years' survey, this situation is the natural outcome of the ever-increasing pace of application to anthropology of advances in theory and method in the biological and medical sciences. No slackening in this process, in the aggregate, is discernible in the period since

[1] References in this section are grouped together at the end of the section, pages 316–320.

1935. Reference, for example, to the admirable Viking Fund Year Books in physical anthropology and to the Cold Spring Harbor Symposia (1950, 1955, 1959)[6] and to *Excerpta Medica*[7] will reveal the abundance of current literature. Much of the work noticed in this review is therefore cited only as illustrative of particular trends or topics of major interest.

The achievements in physical anthropology during this period afford ample justification for claiming that substantial advances have been made, amounting to a complete reorientation in some aspects of the subject. This is outstandingly the case with regard to the study of racial differentiation. At the present time, through the application of genetics —a prime result of the discovery of new blood-group gene systems— the analysis of racial affinity is undergoing a far-reaching revision. This has already gone on to an extent which makes necessary the re-interpretation of the conceptions and classifications of 'race' built up over the last 100 years. The recent works by Stern (1960),[8] Boyd (1950), Garn (1961),[9] and Mourant (1954)[10] give excellent accounts of this important development.

In a second field of interest, that of human evolution, striking advances can also be recorded. There have been finds of new fossil material on an impressive scale, and improvements in geological dating have been introduced. A notable event was the exposure of the Piltdown forgery (Weiner 1955,[11] Weiner, Oakley, and Le Gros Clark, 1953).[12] Our picture of the course of human evolution and of the primate ancestry of man has accordingly become more definite and coherent, as may be seen from the books by Le Gros Clark (1955,[13] 1960[14]), Boule and Vallois (1957),[15] and Howells (1959).[3]

These developments in our understanding of the course and outcome of human differentiation have served to draw greater attention in recent years to what may be termed the ecological and adaptive aspects. More emphasis is being placed on studies of the interrelation between man and his environment and on the nature and limits of human adaptability. Of the various possible approaches, a particularly fruitful technique for distinguishing between hereditary endowment and environmental modification is that based on the comparison of twins. The work of Newman (*Twins*, Chicago, 1937, *Twins and Super Twins*, Hutchinson, 1940), P. J. Clark (1956),[16] Osborne and De George (1959),[17] and their colleagues has been noteworthy. Boas's pioneer investigations of the alterations in the bodily features of the descendants of immigrants have also been successfully followed, particularly by Shapiro (*Migration and Environment*, Oxford, 1939) and Lasker (1952, 1954).[18] Lastly, there is a growing realization of the pertinence and feasibility of investigations of bodily fitness, nutritional status, and climatic adaptation, in either a biotic or social context. Here, physical anthropologists stand undoubtedly to gain from accomplishments in the science of animal ecology (Elton, *Animal Ecology*, London, 1949; Allee *et al.*, *Principles of Animal Ecology*, London, 1949). The treatment of ecological dynamics and equilibria appertaining to a variety of animal situations may well provide valuable pointers to the human context.

A feature of the recent period to which attention is directed is the general advance in technique and the accession of new methods. Improved palaeontological dating has already been instanced; notable, too, is the greater refinement and precision of statistical methods (Mahalanobis *et al.*, 'Anthropometric Survey of the United Provinces', *Sankhya* IX, 1949; Penrose, 1953;[19] Ashton *et al*, 1957)[20] and the appraisal for anthropological purposes of such bodily properties as growth and physique, fitness for work, and adaptation to climate.

While emphasis has been placed, at the outset, on the progress which can be justly claimed during this period since 1935, there has nevertheless been some anxious and repeated examination of the aims and methods of the subject. Before World War II, disquiet was aroused by the perverse use made of anthropology by Fascist countries and the association of a few professional workers with inhuman and unscientific Nazi race doctrines. Scientists in non-Nazi countries did much to counter this abuse of anthropology, in works such as those of Morant (*Biometrica* XXXI, p. 72, 1939), Dahlberg (*Race Reason and Rubbish*, New York, 1942), and Ashley-Montagu (*Man's most dangerous myth*, New York, 1945). The irresponsible use to which eugenics and racial genetics had been put by 'racists' is discussed by Dunn (1962).[21] The Russian viewpoint on racism is given in a series of essays published in an English translation in the *International Journal of American Linguistics*, Vol. XXVII, No. 3, July, 1961.

At the same time the feeling grew that physical anthropologists were unduly restricted in their interests to the pursuit of a somewhat artificial taxonomy of race, and that much of their work was conducted on a narrow and even questionable basis both as to method and material (Fisher, *J.R.A.I.*, LXVI, p. 57, 1936). There was an over-emphasis on skeletal material to the neglect of the genetics and ecology of living communities. Thus Haddon, the doyen of racial studies, pleaded in 1934, for 'a wider study, that of Human Biology, which would also embrace the physiological study of Man as a living organism.' And Fleure (*J.R.A.I.*, LXXVII, p. 1, 1947) has spoken in a similar spirit.

The wider perspectives open to physical anthropology were outlined by Fisher (1936) and Le Gros Clark (*R.B.A.*, 1939), amongst others, in the years before the war. Since then, a large measure of re-orientation and re-definition has undoubtedly occurred (Washburn, 1951;[22] Weiner, 1957;[23] D. F. Roberts and Weiner, 1958).[24]

An allied question also much discussed, though so far without a satisfactory outcome, concerns the relation of the physical to the social, cultural, and archaeological branches of anthropology. Penniman elsewhere in this book, on historical and other grounds, argues strongly for the essential unity of the subject; and, no doubt, the different branches of anthropology could appear as aspects of a unified discipline as long as the general outlook remained predominantly evolutionary or Darwinian. That the evolutionary analysis of social phenomena continues to exercise a strong attraction for the biologist is evident from the writings of Joseph Needham (Herbert Spencer Lecture, Oxford, 1937) or Huxley (*Evolution*, London, 1942). There are of course many fields in which the sociological and biological aspects must be considered together as in studies on nutrition, the relation of mating systems to genetic constitution of populations (Li, 1955),[25] the relation of physical type to culture (Coon, *Races of Europe*, 1939; Fleure, *J.R.A.I.*, 1937, Hooton, LXVII, in *Custom is King*, ed. Buxton, 1936; Herskovits, *Man and his works*, New York, 1949).

Anthropological research nowadays wears a piecemeal and compartmentalized appearance. Radcliffe-Brown (*Nature*, August 26, 1944), for example, recognizes only a formal or pedagogic congruity between the different branches. On its side, physical anthropology has been lamentably slow to recognize the cogency of biological analysis of a 'functional' kind complementary to that of the social anthropologist. Malinowski's (1944) proposals for resolving culture into a series of 'institutions' subserving fundamental human needs, though containing much of value, do not meet the case as they entail the subordination of sociological analysis to a rather vague and arbitrary biological scheme. Although there are signs of an interest in ecological analysis, it still remains for the physical anthropologist to demonstrate in the field how the well-being, the fitness, the output of physical work, the reproductive capacity, and the health and morbidity, that is, the biological properties, of a community and its social organization are interrelated. An aspect which it is generally recognized might be profitably pursued is that of the interaction of nutrition and social status. The field studies of Platt (*Roy. Soc. Emp. Sci. Conf.*, 1946, *Trans. Roy. Soc. Trop. Med. Hyg.* XL, p. 4, 1947), of the Fortes (*Africa* IX, No. 2, 1930), Richards (*Hunger and*

Work in a Savage Tribe, 1932, *Proc. Nutrition Soc* V, 1946), Fox (1953),[26] and the classical investigations of Orr and Gilks (*The Physique and Health of two African Tribes*, H.M.S.O., 1931) may serve as suggestions of what such an integrated functional analysis might involve.

Though more clearly defined aims and a wider scope may be claimed for physical anthropology today, the distribution of effort, judged from the period under review, appears ill-balanced. The field-work is still too often concerned with 'racial' characters, and these mainly non-genetic and usually limited to adult males. There is still insufficient attention given to the underlying physiological or adaptive significance of the traits observed, and specially to such biological characteristics of the community as the state of fitness or nutritional well-being of its members. When the overall activities in physical anthropology are considered, the relative dearth of field work and its restricted nature (in contrast to the exhaustive and long-term studies of the 'functionalist' social anthropologist) become apparent; the major effort is still concentrated on work conveniently done in the laboratory and on urbanized European and American subjects. In fact, the accumulation of anthropological data for Europeans, not only of bodily dimensions but also on growth, development, physique, fitness, and even on responses to heat and cold, has now reached the stage where comparable inquiries on aboriginal peoples would be immediately enlightening. There are signs of progress in this direction from the work of recent years (Barnicot, 1959). An ill-balance of activity exists, in a sense, also in regard to evolutionary studies. The present vigorous state of interest in human palaeontology should not obscure the fact that the material collected has accrued from the activities of a comparatively few individuals, in this recent period, notably Broom, Robinson, Leakey, von Koenigswald and Elwyn Simons.

The account given below is sufficient, it is hoped, to reveal the great potentialities which exist for valid anthropological work, whether evolutionary, morphological, genetic, functional, or ecological; though one must insist that the full realization of its value requires a wider application to aboriginal communities. Today the resources exist for bringing even specialized equipment into the field, and material can be sent rapidly back to base laboratories. It is paradoxical that the paramount question has become, not what physical anthropology should do, but whether, in the face of growing nationalism and industrialization and the diminishing access to aboriginal peoples, the technical possibilities will be applied in time to secure a more complete biology of still-existing simple communities of different race.

THE EVOLUTION OF MAN

Man's Primate Ancestry

In his monumental classification of the mammals, Simpson (*Bull. Am. Mus. Nat. His.* 85, 1945) has provided a detailed and documented appraisal of the taxonomic relations of the Primates. Here the reader will find the now fairly generally accepted allocation of the ancestral and modern forms of Primates totwo hierarchical levels or sub-orders—the Prosimian and the Anthropoid. The prosimians comprise the lemurs, lorises, and tarsiers, which in a general evolutionary sequence (expounded by Le Gros Clark, 1960a[12]) lead on to the anthropoid suborder containing the Old and New World monkeys and the Hominoids (the 'super-family' of apes, man, and their allied fossil forms). This classification by Simpson provides us with a clear perspective of the general lines of human evolution and, along with the recent reviews by Strauss (*Quart. Review of Biology*, XXIV, 1949), Le Gros Clark (1949), and Zuckerman (*Biological Review*, XXV, 1950), presents a quite impressive picture of the Primates from their first beginnings in the Palaeocene some sixty million years ago, according to Zeuner's (*Dating the Past*, 1950) provisional estimate. A more general account will be found in Le Gros Clark's *History of the Primates*,* in Romer (1949), and in J. Z. Young (*Life of Vertebrates*, Oxford, 1950). A Russian account is available (Nesturkh, 1959).[28] For the specialist primatologist the handbook *Primatologia*[29] and the magnificent series in course of publication by Osman Hill (1953, 1955, 1957, 1960)[30] are indispensable.

The prosimian phase of primate evolution is still imperfectly known, but despite the little new fossil evidence of the last twenty years its interpretation has been generally clarified (Le Gros Clark, 1949), Simons (1960).[31] Wood Jones's (*Hallmarks of Mankind*, London, 1948) hypothesis of a tarsioid ancestry for man along a line from which he excludes the apes, has remained generally inacceptable (Gregory, *Man's Place among the Anthropoids*, Oxford, 1934; Strauss, *Quarterly Review of Biology*, XXIV, p. 200, 1949).

It is the apes which have been placed in a new evolutionary perspective as a result of the work of the past few years. Whereas the older generation of anthropologists stressed inordinately the similarities— and they are numerous—(Schultz, *Archive de Julius Klaus Stiftung*, XXIV, p. 197, 1949; Yerkes and Yerkes, *The Great Apes*, Yale, 1945) between man and present-day apes, in support of the doctrine of common descent, this undoubtedly obscured the very large divergencies

* British Museum (Natural History), 1958, 6th edition.

between them. Today, the belief in a common anthropoid ape ancestry for the living hominoids is more securely based on the evidence of fossil remains. The great apes of the present are in many ways divergent from man, particularly in their specialization to a 'brachiating' mode of progression, though the largely terrestrial mode of life of the gorilla has brought about, by parallel modification, certain resemblances to man. Zuckerman (*Functional Affinities of Man, Monkeys and Apes*, 1933) Le Gros Clark (1949, 1960a),[14] and above all Schultz (1949, 1956)[32] have expounded this more balanced view of the relations between the living Anthropoidea. The tally of recognized resemblances between man and the great apes continues to mount and, indeed, indications of the probable existence of identical genes have been forthcoming. For example, the genes underlying the antigenic blood-group substances A and B, and M and N, can be detected in apes as in man (Wiener, *Blood Groups and Transfusion*, Springfield, Illin., 1943), as also the gene underlying tasting (or non-tasting) detection of phenylthiocarbamide (Fisher, Ford, and Huxley, *Nature*, CXLIV, p. 750, 1939). The resemblances between the human foot and that of an arboreal anthropoid have been the subject of illuminating studies by Elftman and Manter (*Am. Journ. Phys. Anthr.*, XX, p. 69, 1935) and by Morton (*The Human Foot*, N.Y., Columbia, 1935). The employment in experimental neurophysiology of chimpanzees has brought to light the basic similarity to man of many of its cerebral properties, as shown, for example, in certain consequences of damage to the motor cortex (Fulton, *Physiology of the Nervous System*, Oxford, 1949).

The present-day view of the apes as specialized has not hindered the continued belief that man's possession of a limb structure conferring mobility and dexterity, and many features of his brain and his sense organs, especially of vision, are attributable ultimately to a primate arboreal heritage. The 'arboreal hypothesis' of Elliot Smith (*Essays on the Evolution of Man*, 1927) may be said in principle to be still generally acceptable. But the view is now gaining ground from fossil evidence (and in conformity with the divergencies of modern apes) that the common hominoid ancestor may not have been exclusively adapted to a tree habitat. The former existence of generalized apes appears to be the outstanding inference to be drawn from the remarkable finds in the last few years of Miocene apes in East Africa by Hopwood, Leakey, and MacInnes (Leakey, 1946; Le Gros Clark, 1949). These discoveries include amongst many specimens of teeth and jaws, for the first time a fairly complete cranium with face, as well as parts of limb bones. These Early Miocene fossil apes, considered with those of the later Miocene and the Early Pliocene discovered in the Siwalik Hills by the Yale-Cambridge India Expedition of 1935 (Gregory, Hellman, and Lewis, Carnegie Inst., No. 495, 1938) indicate a profusion and wide, evolutionary radiation of apes giving rise, as there are many reasons for suspecting, to forms ancestral to the modern hominoids. Forms such as Limnopithecus and Proconsul foreshadow the gibbon and the chimpanzee respectively, and there are other forms leading perhaps to the gorilla. More important, there are grounds to support the claim of certain of them as perhaps not very far removed from the hominid line. 'The limb structure may possibly have provided a basis for the development of limbs of human type,' writes Le Gros Clark (1949), and the face and jaws (e.g. Ramapithecus) appear in some particulars to have escaped the specialization typical of later apes.

That the hominoid stage gave rise to the hominid line in Pliocene times is supported by the important fossil Oreopithecus, which in some characters of the face and pelvis is close to the hominid, and in some dental and limb characters resembles the Pongid or even the cercopithecid-condiiton (Hürzeler, 1958, 1960;[33] Schultz, 1960,[34] Straus, 1961).[35]

From such discoveries—and new material is still forthcoming—it is clear that we must be prepared for large changes in our evolutionary vista; a conclusion reinforced by the South African fossil finds of Broom and Dart and their colleagues in the period since 1935, and more recently by Leakey.

It will be recalled that in 1925 Dart put forward the claim that the newly discovered infant ape-like specimen from Taungs exhibited in its skull and dentition features which linked it closely to man and that this claim was dismissed nearly unanimously by anthropologists at the time. However, from about 1935, the veteran palaeontologist Robert Broom, well known for his work on Karroo fossil reptiles, uncovered a truly amazing assemblage of new australopithecine material which in many respects substantiates Dart's claims. The story of these controversies and discoveries has been told recently in characteristically vigorous autobiographies by Broom (*Finding the Missing Link*, London, 1950) and Dart (1959).[36]

The Australopithecinae are now known by cranial and skeletal (including limb) fragments of at least twenty-five individuals and by the teeth of many more, from a number of different sites in South and East Africa. The geological date of the South African sites remains undecided; it may well be late in the Early Pleistocene. At Olduwai the Australopithecines have been dated to the Villafranchian, some 1,750,000 years back (Leakey *et al*, (1961).[37] Technical descriptions of the Australopithecinae have been published in monographs by Broom and Schepers (1946), Broom, Robinson, and Schepers (1950), and by Le Gros Clark (for references see Clark, 1949), Robinson, (1956).[38] Preliminary accounts of the East African forms have been given by Leakey (1959, 1961a).[39] The outstanding features are the coexistence of hominid and ape-like characters in skull and dentition, the general ape-like appearance of the face and head, a cranial capacity probably not much beyond the gorilla range, pelvic and limb bones and skull characters indicative of an erect posture. To fit a creature displaying this combination of hominid and non-hominid characters into existing taxonomic schemes, and thereby to pass judgement on its evolutionary ranking, has led already to sharp controversy. From the beginning Dart himself (1959)[36] and some others such as Gregory (1934) and Broom (1950) regarded the form as 'almost human' and approximated it to the Hominidae. Others have questioned this view (Kern and Strauss, 1949; Ashton and Zuckerman, 1950), and some are even now not yet convinced that other than an ape status is justified, although the presence of hominid features in the dentition and skeletal anatomy of the Australopithecinae is now widely recognized. At the present time the majority not only accept these creatures as hominids but entertain the strong likelihood that some of them were actually the first tool-makers.

There is one large topic on which our evolutionary insight still remains meagre—the emergence of the peculiar attributes of human intelligence, temperament, and social organization. Wide as the morphological gap is between men and apes, we know there are distant ancestral links between them. How far is this apparent also in the working of the brain, and in behaviour? Close students of the great apes seem to share Hebb's view that 'exposure to a group of adult chimpanzees gives one the overwhelming conviction that one is dealing with an essentially human set of attitudes and motivations'. The rudiments of what Hebb calls 'syntactic behaviour' as manifested by man in language and social relations are to be found in the great apes, or at least in the chimpanzee. Anatomical and physiological studies of the brain sufficiently attest to the common neurological organization of man and apes which would make for some degree of behavioural similarity. Another biological resemblance of far-reaching social implication which the apes share with man is the prolonged period of dependence of the infant on the mother and the social group. We know also from the pioneer work of Carpenter and Zuckerman that much of the biological basis of the diverse social life of monkey and ape groups is to be sought in sexual drives and in patterns of reproductive and endocrine physiology. The variety of social organization and of social status which can be established through the operation of these processes has suggested to some a possible genesis for the organization of the most primitive human family groups. A stimulating synthesis of our available knowledge can be found in a recent discussion by Bartholomew and Birdsell (1953).[40]

Man of the Pleistocene

As guides to the geo-chronological background to the history of man and his works in the Pleistocene, Zeuner's recent publication (1946) (1952)[41] is indispensable. Zeuner has done much to bring order into Pleistocene dating and has given detailed reconsideration to the principal sites in all main regions of the world. With the agreement reached in 1949 (King and Oakley, 1949) on the geological designation of the Pliocene-Pleistocene 'boundary' and the incorporation of the Villafranchian period into the first part of the Lower Pleistocene (Oakley, 1962),[42] the geo-chronological time-scale of hominid evolution should in future be used with less ambiguity. Moreover, the application of the fluorine-dating test by Oakley (1949), whereby the relative age of bones from the same geological deposit can be compared, has already proved extremely fruitful. With the help of this test the dating of the Piltdown (Oakley and Hoskins, 1950; Oakley, (1955),[43] Galley Hill (Oakley and Ashley-Montagu, 1949), Swanscombe and Fontéchevade specimens (Oakley, 1949) has been clarified. Recent reconsideration of the geology of the site of Rhodesian man by Oakley and Clark (J. Desmond Clark et al., 1947) and of the Eyasi (Africanthropus) site by Leakey (1946) indicates an Upper Pleistocene date for both these fossils. In the Far East, the dating of the Pithecanthropus specimens (as well as of contemporary implements) has also been established (Howells, 1949; von Koenigswald, 1950). On the other hand the dating of the Kanam and Kanjera fragments remains unresolved (Boswell, 1935), though their attribution to the Pleistocene seems likely (Zeuner, 1950). Carbon-14 dating (Oakley, 1962)[42] has placed many of the fossils of the Late Pleistocene in perspective, and the Potassium-Argon method has proved its worth in supplying dates for the East African hominid finds (Leakey, Evernden, and Curtis, 1961.)[37] In general, it may be fairly said that over the last decade the validity of geo-chronological assessment has been considerably enhanced both through the use of chemical methods and by faunal analysis (Hooijer, 1962).[44]

Though Dubois in 1935 saw fit to renounce his belief in the hominid status of his famous Pithecanthropus discovery and to re-assess it as a gibbon, there has been no acceptance of this *volte-face*. Indeed, the splendid discoveries at about the same time by von Koenigswald (1947) of additional Pithecanthropus specimens in Java, taken together with the close affinities these bear (Zuckerman, 1933; Weidenreich, 1943) to the tool-using, cave-dwelling, fire-making Pithecanthropus sinensis has served firmly to establish the status of these forms as true hominids (Le Gros Clark, 1955).[13]

Weidenreich's (1943)[112] masterly and devoted study of the Chinese fossils stands out as an exemplary achievement in view of the subsequent loss of the original material in the war. Less technical descriptions of these Archanthropinae—as Weidenreich terms the Chinese and Javanese representatives of the earliest phase of human evolution—are to be found in standard text-books of which that by Boule and Vallois (1957)[15] may be singled out. With some assurance we can say today that a palaeolithic subsistence food gathering economy was established and maintained over many thousands of years of the Early and Middle Pleistocene by creatures of a physical type in many ways distinguishable from modern man, carrying ape-like features in the face and skull and possessed of a smaller average brain capacity. Yet these Archanthropinae had undergone the essential human transformations—the achievement of an erect posture and locomotion and a decisive enlargement and modification of the brain and brain case (Weidenreich, 1946).[112] The appearance of an erect posture (and hominid dentition) in advance of full cerebral development seems characteristic of the course of hominid evolution and is a phenomenon foreshadowed in the Australopithecinae. At the present time an undecided problem remains with regard to the exact status to be accorded to the specimens named Meganthropus by von Koenigswald, and which the late Dr Weidenreich (1946)[112] believed to give testimony to a giant phase in human ancestry.

Of recent years (Vallois, 1958;[45] Le Gros Clark, 1955,[13] Howells, 1959)[3] it has come to be accepted that Homo sapiens in an early but recognisable form in Europe reaches back to an antiquity greater than that indicated by the long-known Aurignacian groups of Cro-Magnon and Grimaldi—in fact, to a Riss-Würm (third interglacial) date in the case of the Fontéchevade skulls (discovered by Mlle Henri-Martin in 1947), and in the case of the Swanscombe skull fragments (discovered by A. T. Marston in 1935) and the Steinheim skull to the second interglacial. It seems that these early forms of Homo could well have given rise to both later Sapiens men as well as Neanderthal and Rhodesian man, but the actual course of evolutionary differentiation is still a matter of discussion (Weiner, 1958).[46] The old claim of Galley Hill man to represent a third Homo sapiens of a like antiquity has, however, now been decisively removed (Oakley and Ashley-Montagu, *Bull. British Mus.*, Geology 1, No. 2, 1949).

Of the fossil remains in Europe of men of the Homo sapiens type of the later stages of the Pleistocene, where they are known in some abundance (Boule, 1946; Coon, 1939), there have not been so extensive or detailed studies in this last period as those (for example) of Arthur Keith or Morant before 1935. On the other hand more information has been forthcoming on the presence of Homo sapiens in other continental regions. The Tepexpan skull (de Terra *et al., Viking Pub. in Anthrop.* No. 11, 1949) has raised anew a *prima facie* case for recognition as an Upper Pleistocene man of the New World, whereas the claims for the Minnesota remains have not found support (Hrdlička, *Amer. Journ. Phys. Anth.*, 22, p. 175, 1936). At the moment both these fossils remain uncertainly dated. The upper layers of Choukoutien have yielded evidence of Mongoloid elements of Upper Pleistocene age according to Weidenreich (1939).[112] Of a like antiquity seems to be the 'proto-Australoid' group comprising the Wadjak skulls in Java and the more recently discovered Keilor skull near Melbourne (Wunderly and Adams, *Memoir of the Nat. Museum, Melbourne*, No. 13, 1943; Wood Jones, *Nature*, CLIII, p. 211, 1944). From South Africa ancestral Negroids and Boskopoid precursors to the Bushman-Hottentot complex have been reported (Wells, 1948; Tobias, 1959).[47] It seems likely that the East African finds (Leakey, 1935; Cole, 1954)[48] include Upper Pleistocene individuals not dissimilar from present-day types of that region. In sum, the palaeontological evidence testifies to a widespread regional proliferation in the Upper Pleistocene of men bearing features of the recognized racial groups of the present day.

A large problem, and one which of recent years has in some ways become more complex, concerns the relationship of the Pleistocene representatives of Homo sapiens to varieties of Homo neanderthalensis. The dates to be ascribed to the individuals of these two categories (for example as set forth in Zeuner, 1950, and Oakley, 1962)[42] have assumed a fundamental relevance to the solution of this problem. In the final stages of the Upper Pleistocene in Europe the Homo sapiens forms have apparently no contemporaries of certain Neanderthal affinity. At an earlier period (the later Mousterian) the last Neanderthal representative survivors are present and are anatomically very distinctive. They belong to a group which for morphological reasons are nowadays referred to as the 'classic' or 'conservative' Neanderthal. They display in marked degree the typical Neanderthal features seen in what may be taken as the prototype, the specimen from La Chapelle-aux-Saints

(Boule, 1946). In recent years an important accession to these 'typical' Neanderthal specimens has come from San Feliceo Circeo (Blanc, *Rendiconte Accademia dei Lincei*, Rome, XXIX, 6, 1, 5, p. 205,1939; Sergi, *Man*, XLVIII, p. 91, 1948). At a still earlier time there are individuals who do not conform to the extreme Neanderthal type; they display a variety of resemblances to Homo sapiens. To this category of 'generalized' or 'unspecialized' Neanderthal man belong the Ehringsdorf cranium and that from Steinheim found in 1933 (Weinert, 1936),[53a] and so, very likely, do those from Saccopastore (Sergi, 1948). The Steinheim skull is particularly noteworthy for its strong resemblances to Homo sapiens as well as for certain similarities to Pithecanthropus (Le Gros Clark, 1949). Neanderthaloid specimens bearing Homo sapiens features have long been known in the Krapina collections. The crowning example of the coexistence of Neanderthal and *sapiens* features is provided by the Mount Carmel Levalloisian-Mousterian populations reported on by McCown and Keith (1939). The specimens from the two caves of Skuhl and Tabun are linked in many features but those from the latter are more pronouncedly Neanderthaloid, those from Skuhl more Neanthropic and Cromagnard. In Rhodesian man, too, further studies undertaken by Wells (J. Desmond Clark *et al.*, *J.R.A.I.*, LXXVII, p. 7, 1947) have reaffirmed the coexistence of modern and Neanderthal characteristics. A notable event has been the discovery of a second specimen at Hopefield in the Cape Province (R. H. Singer, 1954).[49]

This brief outline indicates sufficiently the phyletic complexity of the Hominidae; any interpretation must account for the changing morphology of Homo neanderthalensis, of the temporal relations between sapiens and non-sapiens forms, and it must further take into account the very early Heidelberg non-sapiens jaw; but there is now no need (already pointed out in the previous edition of this book) to 'find a place for the far more refractory Piltdown specimen'. The simplification that would accrue without Piltdown man was also indicated in the previous edition as follows: Leaving 'Eoanthropus' out of account, one quite consistent scheme would be the sequence connecting Pithecanthropus to a generalized Neanderthal stock; from this, one radiating line becomes pronouncedly Neanderthal and the other definitely Sapiens. There are difficulties in this as in other views; further discussion of hominid relations can be found in papers by Sergi (1948), Vallois (*Amer. Journ. of Physical Anthrop.*, VII, p. 339, 1949), Le Gros Clark (1955),[13] Howell (1951),[50] and Weiner (1956).[51]

Mention has already been made of the regional proliferation of Homo sapiens in Late Pleistocene times to yield varieties with characteristics of modern racial groups. For a regional distribution of the Pithecanthropine and Neanderthal phase or stage some new evidence can also be adduced. Pithecanthropines outside Java and China may well be represented by the Ternifine specimens in North Africa, by the East African Chellean man (Leakey, 1961),[39] and possibly by Heidelberg man in Europe. Outside Europe, Rhodesian man is the representative of Africa of a non-sapiens stage of Homo, and the Florisbad skull may be regarded as ancestral to Boskopoid and 'Bushmanoid' types (Wells, *Broom Commem. vol.*, R. Soc. S. Africa, 1948). The Eyasi (Africanthropus) (Weinert, 1939),[53b] skull remains seem too fragmentary for firm conclusions to be drawn. In the Java-Australian area there are the skulls from Solo (Oppenoorth, in *Early Man*, ed. MacCurdy, Philadelphia, 1937) resembling both Pithecanthropus and Rhodesian man.

Gates (*Human Ancestry*, London, 1948) argues that the main three or four 'racial 'varieties of today are on palaeontological grounds really species, on the assumption that they represent the end-products of long-separated lines which have developed in parallel through the Archanthropic-Palaeanthropic-Neanthropic sequence. Gates's views go far beyond the palaeontological facts and have not gained critical support from palaeontologists. On the diametrically opposed hypothesis (Dobzhansky, *Amer. Journ. of Phys. Anthr.* II, 1944) a case is made for regarding the whole hominid line as a genetic matrix or common pool out of which modern races have obtained, through selection and other agencies, their somewhat different present-day genetic assemblages. The palaeontological situation as interpreted by some workers in Europe, South Africa, and Australia could fit this suggestion (see for example Weiner, 1958,[46] Napier and Weiner, 1962).[52]

In recent years concepts drawn from general evolutionary biology have been increasingly employed in explanations of the course of human evolution (see Cold Spring Harbor Symposium, 1950,[6] Vol. XV). Such explanations need to account firstly for the transition from a prehominid to a hominid stage, a transformation characterized by at least three special features, the change to an erect posture, the enlargement of the brain and associated remodelling of the brain case, and the prolongation of immaturity; and secondly for the diversification within the species with the formation of subspecific entities such as 'races'. For guidance to the anthropologist faced with these difficult questions, Julian Huxley's *Evolution: the Modern Synthesis* (1942) and Rensch's *Evolution Above the Species Level* (1960)[53] are indispensable contributions. These works emphasize the over-riding role of natural selection acting on the genetic variability provided by mutation and genic recombination as the chief agency of evolutionary change. These agencies suffice as explanations of the multiformity of the pathways which this process takes in the animal kingdom. Huxley's and Rensch's neo-Darwinian views are inimical to orthogenetic explanations of the evolution of human posture and brain form such as those advanced by Weidenreich (1946, 1947).[112] The neo-Darwinian view is expounded also in two works by G. G. Simpson (*Tempo and Mode in Evolution*, 1944, *The Meaning of Evolution*, 1950), both of great value to the anthropologist. Simpson pays particular attention to the phylogenetic changes which may be brought about by mutational changes which alter development and differential growth. This topic is considered also as a general evolutionary phenomenon by De Beer (in *The New Systematics*, ed. J. S. Huxley, 1940) and by Rensch in relation to Bolk's well-known foetalization theory according to which the large brain or the absence of heavy bone ridges, for example, are regarded as foetal characters which by a slowing of development have become part of the adult stage (Rostand, *Rev. Gen. Sci. Pures et Appl.*, 52, p. 211, 1945; Schultz, *Archiv. d. Julius Klaus Stiftung*, XXIV, p. 197, 1949).

Discussion in the recent period of the causes of subspecific differentiations has been rather less speculative. The factors which must be considered are mutation, selection, isolation, mixture, and the size of the breeding unit. Mutation rates for man have been estimated notably by Haldane (1935b, 1947; see also Penrose, 1961)[54] and shown to be similar to mutation rates observed in other organisms. The action of selective advantage conferred by various kinds of genotype (by mutation) in altering the genetic constitution of a population have been treated mathematically by Fisher (1930) and Haldane (1935a); important applications have already been made in explanation of present-day distribution of genes such as those of the Rh series (Haldane, 1942) and the gene responsible for the sickle cell trait (Allison, 1954).[55] Julian Huxley's work (*Evolution, the Modern Synthesis*, 1942) calls attention to the significance of different modes of distribution such as 'clines' as indicative of genetic penetration of one population by another. A particularly good example, given by Mourant (1954),[10] concerns the steady change in frequency of the Rh chromosomes passing from the Negro to the Mediterranean peoples. The presence of sharp discontinuities in distribution, especially of apparently non-adaptive characters finds its explanation in the Sewall Wright phenomenon of random fixation of characters in small isolated groups. The Wright effect has been evoked in order to explain the present-day distribution of certain of the blood groups (Boyd, *Genetics and the Races of Man*, Blackwell, Oxford, 1950), but there is fairly good evidence that selective agencies due to disease may well be concerned (Aird *et al.*, 1954).[56]

Perhaps the most important general consequence of the application of modern evolutionary principles to the anthropological field is the conviction it engenders that differences between human groups are entirely of a subspecific kind and the outcome of factors (mutation, isolation, adaptation, and ecological selection) which seems to be operative in local and geographical race formation in the animal kingdom generally.

THE DIVERSITY OF MODERN MAN

In the period since 1935 the physical characteristics of modern man have continued to be the subject of study by numerous investigators. The work falls naturally into two large categories differing in technique and in material. There are the investigations of 'racial history' and 'racial' differences on skeletal (post-Pleistocene) remains referable to a known archaeological or cultural context; and there are the investigations carried out on living populations.

The Study of Skeletal Remains

A falling off in the systematic metrical description of large regional or 'racial' collections of skulls and other skeletal parts appears to have taken place in the last few years, though reports on bones from particular excavations continue to be issued steadily. The value of such work in a known archaeological provenance may be gleaned, to give a few recent examples, from the reports on the skulls and physical types from the Mohenjo-daro excavations,* those from Sialk (Vallois, 1939), Alisar Hüyük (Krogman, *Oriental Inst. Publ.* XXX, p. 213, 1937) or Lachish (Risdon, *Biometrica*, XXXI, p. 99, 1939). Of the comprehensive 'regional' studies certain are noteworthy as examples of method. Publications by Morant and his colleagues rank especially high here. One may single out the papers of Egyptian and Nubian craniology (Batrawi, *J.R.A.I.*, LXXVI, 1946, *Biometrika*, XXXIV, 1947) which cover the long period from Late Predynastic to Roman times and which present an analysis of the 'racial' history of this important archaeological province. The detailed and painstaking monographs by Schreiner (*Craina Norvegica*, 1946) contain a complete résumé of Norwegian racial elements from prehistoric times and from the Middle Ages to modern

*See Sir John Marshall, page 246

times. In his study of Greek racial history, Angel (*Human Biology*, XVIII, 1946) has attempted an original interpretation of the cultural and social significance of changes in physical type. Kappers (1934) deals comprehensively with the Near East and offers various hypotheses of race movements in this area. A region from which skeletal remains receive consistent attention is the Amerindian; many papers continue to appear in the *American Journal of Physical Anthropology*; an excellent reference source is now available in the annual *Boletin Bibliografico de Antropologia Americana* produced by the Instituto Panamericano de Geografia é Historia, Mexico. An introduction to research in South Africa may be obtained from accounts by Galloway (1948), Dart (1939), Wells (1948), and Tobias (1959).[47] These papers deal with the complexities in the interpretation of the relations between present Negroid inhabitants and Boskopoid and other pre-Bush and pre-Negro types. An important criticism of the Boskop race concept has been offered by R. Singer (1958).[57] Notable for their high standard of biometric analysis are the African Monographs from the Duckworth Laboratory (Mukherjee, Rao and Trevor, 1955;[58] Talbot and Mulhall, 1962).[59] As a guide to knowledge of modern man in Europe from his bony remains, Coon's (1939) book is indispensable. Some information on skeletal finds in the U.S.S.R. of Late and post-Pleistocene age is given by Debetz (1956).[60] An interesting paper on European skeletal remains, specially of the Mediterranean area, is that by Barnicot and Brothwell (1959).[61] Reviews are now available for Australia (McCarthy, *Australian Museum Mag.*, IX, p. 184, 1947), Indo-China (Embree, *Amer. Journ. of Physical Anthr.*, VII, p. 39, 1949), and the East Indies (van Bork-Feltkamp, *Supp. Anthr. Bibliographie van den Indischen Archipel*, Leiden, 1940, *Man*, XLIX, *51*, 1949). Krogman's bibliography (1941) covers the period till 1939. A work of collation (of which many more are required) is the handbook by Cameron on the Neolithic Skeleton in Britain (1934).

It is fair to claim, even from the few publications quoted, that in the exact description of bony remains, especially of the skull, the methods and the most useful measurements (van Bork-Feltkamp, *Man*, L, *15*, 1950) are now reasonably well established. In the achievement of precise and standardized techniques in the field of physical anthropology much is owed to Martin's *Lehrbuch* (Saller, 1957),[62] Hrdlička's *Practical Anthropometry* (T. D. Stewart, 1952),[63] and to the endeavours of the Biometric School as exemplified in various papers by Morant, in the practical handbook of craniometry by Buxton and Morant (1933), and in the well-known work of Tildesley (*J.R.A.I.*, LVIII, p. 351, 1928), who has been responsible in recent years for co-ordinating the endeavours of anthropometrists of different countries towards standardizing techniques. American anthropologists as a body have given critical attention to the improvement of method and to nomenclature, as may be seen, for example, from papers in this recent period, by W. W. Howells (*Amer. Journ. of Phys. Anthr.*, XXII, 1937), Ashley-Montagu (*A.J.P.A.*, XXIII, 1938), and T. D. Stewart (*A. J.P.A.*, XXIII, 1937). From the Biometric School there has come an extension of exact metrical methods to the malar bone (Woo, *Biometrica*, XXIX, 1937), mandible (Morant, *Biometrica*, XXVIII, 1930; Cleaver, *Biometrica*, XXIX, 1937) and long bones (Münter, *Biometrika*, XXVIII, 1936); Comas (*B.S.P.*, Paris, X, 1949) has considered the osteometry of the femur; to these may be added the scapula (Bainbridge and Genoves, 1956),[64] and the pelvic bones (Washburn, 1948;[65] Oetteking, 1950), as skeletal parts for which improved metrical methods are available. A more critical attitude has grown up lately in the interpretation of the markings found on endocranial casts. This matter is discussed in the monographs by Hirschler 1942)[65a] and Connolly (1949).[65b]

Some findings of general significance which have accrued from the examination of skeletal remains deserve comment. The variability of the populations of a given region is known to change somewhat from time to time, but prehistoric men (judged from bony remains) were quite as variable as modern populations, so that no evidence emerges from craniometry or osteometry of the former existence of 'pure' or homogeneous races. It is known, too, that populations do not necessarily remain stable in their average skeletal dimensions. Chronological comparison of series of skulls from particular regions has revealed in various areas in Europe and the Middle East the existence of a trend in skull shape which Weidenreich (1946)[112] terms 'the recent brachycephalization' of man. This has been variously interpreted as due to selective action (Boyd, *Genetics and the Races of Man*, Oxford, 1950)—which, if true, weakens the cephalic index as an index of race—or to an admixture with incoming brachycephals, a view which Weidenreich finds unacceptable. The racial history of Great Britain, however, indicates that changes in skull shape may follow a more complicated course (Giot, *L'Anthropologie*, LIII, p. 240, 1949). An important development was sent on foot by Washburn (1947)[66] in applying experimental morphology to the solution of developmental problems. Washburn showed (in rats) how the form of crests on the skull is dependent on muscle action. Profound modification of strongly developed supra-orbital ridges for example, could therefore come about through functional processes.

Wolffson (1950)[67] has made similar studies on the relation of scapula shape to muscle action. The profound alterations in skull shape which follow a change from a quadripedal to a bipedal posture have been demonstrated experimentally by Lisowski *et al.* (1961).[68] The sex and age identification of bony remains has yielded a certain amount of interesting demographic data for prehistoric communities of various types. It is possible to extract some demographic data even from cremated remains (Gejvall, (1948, 1951);[69] Weiner and Longton, (*Ashmolean Rep. on Excav. at Winchester*, 1951). From the contributions of Vallois (1937, 1960),[70] Senyurek (*A.J.P.A.*, 1947), Angel (*J. Gerontol*, 1947), J. G. D. Clark (*Archaeology and Society*, 1947), Nougier (*Bull. de la Société Prehist. Franc.*, XVI, p. 3, 1949), and Howells (1960),[71] a general finding emerges of the reduced expectation of life in aboriginal and prehistoric communities (Cook, *Human Biology*, XIX, 1947). An explanation of this phenomenon would no doubt require a better knowledge than we possess of the demographic characters of modern primitive communities, and poses a problem as to the interaction of social, biological, and environmental factors in determining the expectation of life. Valuable studies on disease as revealed in skeletal material have been made by Brothwell (1961).[72]

The Study of Living Peoples

In the anthropological description of living peoples there is discernible in this period under review the important difference of approach as between the 'traditional' characterized by the time-honoured criteria of anthropometry and anthroposcopy (as set forth, for example, in Martin's *Lehrbuch*), and that which aims at a strictly genetic analysis. The first relies essentially on morphological differences to establish the existence of 'racial' differences. Much was once hoped from Pearson's 'Coefficient of Racial Likeness' as a statistical device for expressing, by reference to a number of characters considered together, the degree of affinity between different groups. Serious weaknesses in the coefficient have been pointed out both in its theory and its use (Fisher, *J.R.A.I.*, LXVI, 1936; Seltzer, *A.J.P.A.*, XXIII, 1937). Recently, in Mahalanobis's 'Generalized Distance Statistic', a greatly improved method for making such group comparisons has become available and has been applied in an increasing number of studies (Mahalanobis, Majumdar, and Rao, 1949; Trevor, 1947; Talbot and Mulhall, 1962).[59] In the 'traditional' classificatory schemes (expounded in a thorough manner by Hooton (*Up from the Ape*, 1946), a strong *a priori* element attaches to the constellation of criteria whereby the 'racial' allocation is achieved. Such schemes will vary in their results according to the criteria chosen.

The alternative method, the genetic, is now superseding the older method since, by specifying the frequencies of certain genes in a given group, comparisons of racial affinity become entirely objective. Boyd (*Genetics and the Races of Man*, Oxford, 1950) has fully discussed the limitations and weaknesses of the older approach. These are ultimately traceable to the use of phenotypic criteria whose genic constitution is unknown, for with such criteria it is left an open question whether apparently similar characters necessarily denote similar genotypes (and this may well be a difficulty with criteria such as indices of shape); furthermore, the extent to which phenotypic expression may suffer modification through use and disuse and other environmental agencies remains uncertain. Investigation of recent years has established the certainty of such modification affecting many of the usual criteria. It may be shown by comparisons between identical twins (Newman *et al.*, 1937; Newman, 1937; 1940, see page 286). The effect of change of environment in altering, for example, the head shape of the descendants of immigrants has been demonstrated more convincingly recently by Shapiro (1939) and Lasker (1946) than in Boas's pioneer investigation criticized by Morant and Samson (1936). Other evidence is provided by the widely recognized secular alteration in body heights (Mijsberg, 1940; Meredith, 1944; Morant, 1950; Tanner, 1962).[73] The influence of function on form has been the subject of experimental proof by Washburn (1946, 1947).[66] The degree of affinity between groups; using the phenotypic criteria, can at best be expressed only formally. On the other hand the use of characters of known genetic constitution enables the gene frequency to be enumerated so that exact comparisons between groups can be made. On the basis of morphological comparisons studies of race 'mixture' remain essentially descriptive (though they are often very informative, e.g. Trevor, 1953):[74] genetic analysis, on the contrary, makes possible analysis of the rate, extent, and results of hybridization. Application of genetic analysis represents certainly the most important advance since the introduction of exact statistical methods. Discussion of this all-important development can be found in articles by Standskov (1942) and Mourant (1947), and is more extensively dealt with by Stern (1960),[8] Boyd (1950), Glass (1955),[75] and Li (1955).[25]

The fact that genetics has assumed so important a place is largely attributable to the discoveries (Mourant, 1954)[10]—additional to the long-known Landsteiner ABO system—of blood-group antigens of the

MNS system, and more important, of those of the Rh system; and to the elucidation of the gene systems underlying these and other blood groups. The genic constitution of a population may now be specified in terms of a considerable array of genes and of genes in particular combination. A number of other genes which fluctuate in their distribution and are anthropologically of importance can also be detected—such as those controlling sub-groups of the A blood groups, the genes responsible for haemoglobin and haptoglobin variants (see Harrison, 1961),[76] and the gene responsible for the ability or non-ability to taste the substance phenylthiocarbamide. Full technical accounts of the blood-group systems have been published by Wiener (1943)[76a] and Race and Sanger (*Blood Groups in Man*, Oxford, 1950); their anthropological uses are discussed by Mourant (1947), Barnicot (*Science Progress*, CLXIV, p. 702, 1948), Stern (1960),[8] and Boyd (1950).* See aslo Harrison (1961).[76]

There is every reason why 'traditional' anthropometric and anthroposcopic observations (which in the period under review have been undertaken extensively) should retain a place in the technique of physical anthropology. One is, that the genetics of traits, such as eye, hair and skin colour, may in the near future become known. Then again, where genetic analysis is concurrently made, observations (for example) of bodily dimensions may well take on a clearer significance in indicating the operation of environmental factors and of population affinities (Pollitzer, 1958;[77] Sanghvi, 1953).[78] Moreover, the accumulation of exact morphological data and a detailed knowledge of their geographical and climatic distribution remains essential; for in some cases presumptive evidence of the adaptive or ecological significance of a character may be forthcoming (e.g. Schreider, 1950,[79] on the geographic distribution of the body weight/body surface ratio).

Reports on many racial groups of physical characters or blood groups, or both, are noticed in impressive number in the *Year Book of Physical Anthropology* and in the *Boletin Bibliografico de Antropologia Americana*, as well as in the periodical literature. Useful bibliographies are given in the *Anthropologischer Anzeiger* and in *L'Anthropologie*. The intensity of physical anthropological work judged by these activities is at the present time undoubtedly very great and widespread. In Europe, the last war did not by any means always hinder such works as appears from a report by Fagg (*Nature*, CXLVIII, p. 46, 1946). In the period since 1935, field investigations have gradually become more intensively

* The Royal Anthropological Institute has now established a Blood Group Reference Centre (1951).

prosecuted in territories where peoples of relatively simple material culture are still to be found e.g. Pygmies (Gusinde, 1948), Andaman Islanders (Lehmann, 1954),[80] Kalahari Bushmen (Tobias, 1957;[81] Weiner and Zoutendyk, 1959),[82] Australian aborigines (Abbie, 1951, 1961;[83] Gates, 1960,[84] Simmons, *et al.*, 1957)[85] and Caribs (Firschein, 1961).[86] Other studies in remote areas include those in East Africa (Oschinsky, 1954),[87] Sudan (D. F. Roberts *et al.*, 1955),[88] Polynesia (Simmons and Graydon, 1957),[89] Malaya (Polunin and Sneath, 1953),[99] the East Indies (e.g. Keers, 1948; Kleiweg de Zwaan,*Mededeel ingen den afdeeling Volkenkunde van het Kolonial Institut*, 1942), Cyrenaica (Puccioni, *Antropometria delle genti della, Cirenaica*, Florence, 1934), and Indo-China (Embree, *A.J.P.A.*, VII, p. 39, 1949). American workers have maintained a special interest in the Near and Middle East (see, for example, papers by Field and Shanklin in the *American Journal of Physical Anthropology*), and with South American workers are responsible, of course, for many investigations of American Indian tribes (Hrdlička, Steggerda, Stewart, Comas, Seltzer, Woodbury, Goldstein, Salzano, and others), and of Negroes of the New World. The latter have continued to be the subject of Herskovits's illuminating sociophysical interpretation. Continuing that of Hrdlička is the study of 'Old Americans' by Bean (*A.J.P.A.*, XX, p. 171, 1935), Hooton (see page A.J.P.A. 22, 1936), Gould, and others. In the Polynesian area Shapiro's work, and in the Arctic, Laughlin's studies (*Science* 1963, p. 33) are notable.

An active centre for physical anthropology has arisen in India (see Majumdar), where notable work has been done in connexion with the census (Guha, 1935; Mahalanobis *et al.*, 1949), and from where important contributions to anthropological statistical theory have come (Mahalanobis *et al.*, 1949; Rao, 1948). Turkey (Senyürek and his colleagues), South Africa (see, for example, Dart, 1939; Keen, 1947; Tobias, 1959;[47] Cluver *et al.*, 1946), and Australia (notable for field-work by Abbie and Simmons and their co-workers) are also important centres of anthropological study.

In sum, it is true to say that during the last fifteen years in no important region has the physical anthropology been left untouched.

Despite a continuous accession of information it must be admitted that the 'non-genetic' method has produced few solutions to many long-standing problems. Standard queries of racial affinity such as the relation between Oceanic and African Negro, or Oceanic to Congo Pygmy, of Veddah to Australian, of Australian and Ainu to one another and the Caucasoid, continue to receive only tentative answers in terms of the usual 'categorical' systems of classification; and the same may be said of the most general question of all—the nature of the relationship, present and past, between the four or five large 'racial' divisions of today.

It is precisely these questions of racial affinity between larger or smaller groups to which a genetic analysis can provide an objective answer satisfactory both in an evolutionary and a taxonomic sense. Enough has already been done with the blood-group systems and other genetically known characters to enable one to expect this confidently. Even when the ABO system was still the only one available, the information it gave of gene frequencies (Boyd, *Tabulae Biological*, XVII, 1939) provided quite a clear picture of undoubted genetic difference, e.g. between Mongoloid (high group B frequency), American Indians (virtual absence of B, variable in A), and Europeans (low B, high A). For the presence of group B in Europe, Candela's paper (*Human Biology*, XIV, p. 413, 1942) made an impressive case for its introduction along with brachycephaly into Europe through invasions of historic times. Another example of infiltration from a neighbouring high B area is seen in Australia, where B is absent except in the extreme north. The curiously uneven distribution of the A group as in North America may well be explained in terms of random extinction or perpetuation (the Sewall Wright effect). A genetic distinction between Negroes and Papuans is the relatively high incidence in the former of sub-group A^2 (Simmons *et al.*, *Med. J. of Australia*, XXXII, 1945).

The refinements of genetic analysis made possible by the discoveries of new blood groups and sub-groups has already enabled Boyd (1949, 1950), following Wiener (1943),[76a] to formulate a picture of racial differentiation in terms of six main genetic races. The six genetic races are: Early European (represented by modern Basques), European (Caucasian), African (Negroid), Asiatic (Mongoloid), American, and Australian. This classification, which is based essentially on a demonstrable restriction on genetic interchange between the postulated races, embodies also the factor of geographical isolation, a situation which goes far to meet the requirements of an objective definition of race (Stern, 1960).[8]

The origins of these different races, or rather how they came to possess these particular gene frequencies, are discussed by Boyd. He argues, for example, for a common origin for the Australian and European, with subsequent differentiation. That present European peoples represent an admixture with an older (Rh-negative) race represented by the Basques is plausible not only on genetic, but other grounds (Mourant, *J.R.A.I.*, LXXVII, p. 39, 1947). It is already certain that the concept of 'serological' races even in its present tentative form will greatly influence anthropological interpretation.

For anthropology (in a wider sense) it is worth mentioning here the use which can be made of genetics in comparing the genic context of breeding units, or 'isolates', which are usually cohesive social groups in which preferential mating systems or other social barriers to random mating obtain. An interesting example is the detection by Fraser Roberts (1942) of a significant difference in ABO frequency in North Wales between families with Welsh and those with non-Welsh family names. It has been applied to a comparison of Indian endogamous groups (Sanghvi and Khanolkar, 1949), with the finding of large differences between certain of them, not at all apparent physically; and by Darlington (1947) in relation to linguistic distributions.

It is one of the most important developments of present-day anthropology that agencies working at a fairly high selective advantage (or disadvantage) can in fact be shown to be at work. One example is furnished by the selective mortality of Rh-positive offspring born to Rh-negative mothers. A more striking instance is the selective action of disease. Blood group A is significantly more common among cases of stomach cancer than among the general population; blood group O in sufferers from duodenal ulcer. Here the agents responsible for these diseases—and these will vary in different environments—are effective in altering blood group frequencies. The wide fluctuations in observed ABO frequencies do, in fact, suggest that they are the outcome of relatively more rapid selection than is the case with other blood group genes.

Selection can be shown to be effective in maintaining polymorphism in human populations (Allison, 1955).[91] A striking example is one where the heterozygous carriers ('sicklers') of the gene for sickle-cell anaemia are (probably in childhood) less susceptible to malaria than are the homozygotes with normal haemoglobin. The homozygotes carrying two genes for the abnormal haemoglobin die of severe anaemia but the reproductive superiority of the heterozygotes is effective in those malarial regions in maintaining the sickle-cell gene at a high frequency. The balance between the three types of individual maintained at a level in these conditions will be quite different from that of non-malarious regions (Allison, 1954).[55] This mode of balanced environmental selection on gene frequencies is likely to be a widespread phenomenon.

The biology of adaptation and fitness represents one of the most promising fields for anthropological exploration and carries far-reaching implications for preventive and clinical medicine.

The situation today is that comparative observations on living populations will prove of limited value unless blood-grouping and other genetic examination is undertaken; but, as already remarked, it would be entirely a retrograde step to curtail morphological and metrical observations. The need is rather for an intensified use of observations of potential value (such as skin colour and certain anthropometric measurements (Tildesley, *Man*, L, p. 14, 1950), and for their improvement and standardization (Davenport, *A.S.P.A.*, XXIII, p. 91, 1937)); and secondly for the introduction into field work of observations which will yield more data on the individual as such—on his physique (Brozek and Henschel, 1961),[92] growth (Tanner, 1962);[73] fitness, nutritional state, and his functional state generally.

In both these respects the indications are favourable. Standardization of measurements on the living as on the skeleton is well understood as a matter of concern by European workers and in America, as exemplified in the work of Ashley-Montagu, Ciacco, and Stewart. The evaluation of the reliability and precision of methods is more generally in evidence today (Tildesley, *Man*, XLVII, 1947; Meredith, *Child Development*, VII, 1936; Marshall, *Child Development*, VII, 1937; Tanner and Weiner, *A.J.P.A.*, VII, 1949; Howells, (1951).[93] Improved (and agreed) techniques for non-metrical observations are still badly needed, but efforts to remedy deficiencies are being made (e.g. Grieve and Morant, 1946). The exact estimation by Edwards and Duntley (*Amer. J. Anat.*, LXV, 1939) of skin colour spectro-photometrically has led to the general introduction of this method in a simplified and portable form. (Weiner, 1951).[94] Where the facilities become available the use of X-rays will greatly extend the range of comparative observations. An immediate application would be to the assessment of the skeletal maturation (Tanner, 1962)[73] of non-European children which has so far been carried out in only a few instances (e.g. Pillai, *Indian J. of Medical Res.*, XXIII, 1935; Lall and Townsend, *Indian Med. Gaz.*, LXXIV, 1939, Weiner and Thambipillai, (1952).[95] American work has been such that in the standards of skeletal maturation introduced by Todd, and further developed by Greulich and Pyle (*Radiographic Atlas of Skeletal Dev. in Hand and Wrist*, 1950), a satisfactory basis for valid comparative study has been provided. X-ray pelvimetry (Nicholson and Allen, *Lancet*, CCL, p. 192, 1946; Reynolds, *A.J.P.A.*, V, 1947) and the estimation of muscle and bone growth by X-rays (Stuart *et al.*, *Mon Soc. Res. Child Dev.*, V, No. 3, 1940; Tanner, 1962)[73] are two other examples of techniques awaiting a wider application.

We have undoubtedly arrived at a stage where a better insight into the functional and physical state of the individual of different races and communities could be attained. In the last few decades American anthropologists and biologists (following the tradition of Boas and Davenport) have produced a most impressive body of data on the growth and maturation of children. This work, as exemplified by such studies as those of Shuttleworth (*Mon. Soc. Res. Child Dev.*, II, ser. 12, and III, ser. 18, 1937), Bayley (*Child Development*, XIV, 1943), and Meredith (*Univ. Iowa Studies*, XI, No. 3, 1935), is of high accuracy in execution and presentation. Knowledge of the growth characteristics of European children has now advanced to a point (Tanner, 1962)[73] where similar work on non-Europeans might be expected to reveal the influence not only of genetic and racial, but also of climatic and nutritional factors (D. F. Roberts, 1960;[96] Acheson, 1960).[97] As yet, very little direct comparison has been attempted; pioneer studies are those of Steggerda (1941) and of Meredith (1946).

The onset of sexual and reproductive maturity plays a peculiar part in primitive society as a social and cultural determinant. The biology of female reproductive maturity and specially the phenomenon of the pubertal sterility period in the female have been the subject of a thorough exposition by Ashley-Montagu (1946). Mills (*Human Biology*, XXII, 1950) has for long urged that in the humid tropics menstruation (and development generally)—contrary to laymen's views —is in fact retarded, and Ellis (*British Medical J.*, I, p. 85, 1950) has recently confirmed this in the case of Nigerian girls, by comparison with his own and other British data (Wilson and Sutherland, *Brit Med. J.*, July 16, 1949). There is, however, little data on the effect of nutrition and race, as of climate, on the maturation of both sexes. The subject is fully reviewed by Tanner (1962).[73]

Some anthropologists are inclined to lay great stress on the possible relation between physical type (or constitution) and temperament and personality, and this is one reason for the comparisons which have been made on the incidence of Kretchmerian types in different races (Bergman and Amir, *Gen. tijd. N.I.*, LXXVI, 1936, *Ibid.* LXXVII, 1937). There are many other anthropological reasons for comparative studies of physique which so far have been indifferently pursued. The introduction of Sheldon's (*Varieties of Human Physique*, 1940) somatotype system is undoubtedly a positive advance, rather less perhaps for the system itself than for the standardized photographic technique on which it depends. The technique can be adapted for rapid large-scale survey (Tanner and Weiner, *A.J.P.A.*, VII, 1950). Sheldon's somatotype procedure does provide a basis for the assessment of body habitus which has the merit that it can be objectively checked. Whatever genetic, developmental or psychological significance will come to be attributed to the somatotype—and there are indications that it is modifiable by diet (Lasker, *A.J.P.A.*, V, 1947), and bears little or no relation to temperament (Fiske, *L.J. Applied Psychol*, XXVIII, 1944; Hunt, *L.A.J.P.A.*, VII, 1949)—its assessment undoubtedly makes possible an exploratory analysis of physical type. Most data so far relate to Europeans; a survey made of East Africans (Danby, 1956)[98] and of Japanese (Kraus, 1951)[99] indicates the value of somatotyping as an approach to comparisons with the European. This is not the only approach to physique now available. Burt *Psychometrika*, XCI (1947), Thurstone (*A.J.P.A.*, V, No. 1, 1947), and Howells (1951),[93] have shown how factorial analysis may be applied to anthropometric data to specify parameters of components making up the physique.

Of physiological techniques which hold out promise in the anthropological field the assessment of fitness for different types and grades of work deserves consideration. Certain fitness tests (Johnson, Brouha, and Darling, *Rev. Canad. Biol*, I, No. 5, 1942) have been extensively used on Europeans. Cullumbine (*Lancet*, 1949a, *Journ. Appl. Physiol.*, II, b) has used these and many other tests on a large scale in Ceylon, and has found differences in performance according to region and race, much of it ultimately attributable to differences in body dimension and limb girth. It seems clear that by the use of such tests as well as the available methods of nutritional assessment (Sinclair, *Vitamins and Hormones*, VI, 1948), information might be obtained of the influence of social (as well as racial) factors on the individual's well-being in different types of community. The testing of individuals of different racial groups for adaptation to work in hot climates, using more exact physiological procedure than that of Robinson *et al.* (1941), has recently been undertaken for Negroes (Weiner, *Brit. J. Indust. Med.*, VII, 1950a; Ladell, *J. Physiol*, CXII, 1951; Wyndham *et al.*, 1952),[100] and Asiatic groups (Weiner, *Man*, 50, 1950).

Advances in physiology will undoubtedly continue to provide the physical anthropologist with many more techniques for use in the field. In the coming period it is quite likely, for example, that comparisons of endocrine function on an anthropological scale may be possible, in view of the current interest in biochemical methods of hormone assay. One such study is that by Barnicot and Wolffson (1952) which revealed a relatively low output of 17-ketosteroid by West Africans. The significance of this requires further work.

The Question of Race

The situation in the study of man's 'racial' characteristics today is manifestly one of transition. Nevertheless, in recent years physical anthropologists have been able on the available evidence to deal critically and fruitfully with the question which looms so large in these times—the problem of race difference and race discrimination. This contentious issue in both its biological and ethnic aspects has been given the most serious examination by anthropologists such as Huxley and Haddon (*We Europeans*, 1935), Morant (*Ann. Rep. Smithsonian*, 1939), Dahlberg (*Race, Reason, and Rubbish*, 1942), Ashley-Montagu (1945), Washburn (*The Races of C. Europe*, 1945), Boas (*Man's most dangerous Myth, Race and Democratic Society*, 1945), Boyd (1950), and Count (*This is race*, New York, 1950). Views which have occasioned acute controversy are those promulgated by Gates, (*Human Genetics*, 1946, *Human Ancestry* 1948) and Keith (*A new theory of Human Evolution*, 1948). The views both of those who would deny the existence of racial differences in any scientific sense of the term and those who, like Gates, believe mankind to be split into distinct species are generally rejected by geneticists and non-geneticists alike. The great majority have for long agreed that in the traditional classification the three or four major categories rank sub-specifically as 'races'; but this was a conviction derived largely from analogy with animal systematics. A biological definition of race in genetic terms is attainable (Boyd, 1950; Stern, 1960[8]), and the serological races can be justified as such (Boyd, 1950); in the result the genetically defined human races confirm the traditional 'morphological' designations. The sub-divisions of mankind possess just those subspecific characteristics which would result from limited periods of isolation with subsequent admixture. Differentiation between such partially isolated groups could not go so far as to produce absolutely distinct categories. In phenotypic characters there is often a gradation from one race to another and there is overlapping in respect to various characters; genotypically, this situation is reflected in the fact that similar alleles are common to various groups, but differ only in their frequency; there may be a gradient in the gene frequency from the territory of one race to the other (e.g. the B blood group gene in Eurasia). The actual genes concerned in racial differences must be relatively few (Glass, 1943; Strandskov, 1942); while the limited degree of sub-speciation has modified the 'gene complex' in so minor a degree that hybridization entails no genetic incompatibility. A good example of this is furnished by the Bushman-European pedigree described by Tobias (1954).[102] Hence in describing human races, the fact of their essential polymorphism, variability and intergradation requires them to be treated as abstractions which can only be specified statistically. In sum, from morphological and genetic considerations, there seems little reason why the taxonomic relationship between human groups should constitute a topic of disagreement. The biology of race is the subject of an important statement on race (UNESCO, 1952) and of a UNESCO publication. 'The Race Question in Modern Science' (1956). The issue of 'racism' has recently flared up again (Comas, 1961).[103]

Human Distribution and Human Adaptation

In the formation of the more or less distinct races of the single human species natural selection undoubtedly plays its part along with other differentiating forces. The geographical distribution of mankind and its adaptation to a wide variety of habitat might thus, in some degree, rest on racial traits (genotypes) of adaptive value. To stipulate these exactly is impossible in the face of the present deficiency of proven fact, a situation which the work of the last twenty-five years has done something to redress. There is the well-known suggestion of Arthur Thomson of the adaptive significance of the shape of the nose, and this has been given further statistical support by Davies (*J.R.A.I.*, LXII, 1932) and Weiner (1954).[104] Coon, Cairn and Birdsell (*Races, a study of the problem of Race formation in Man*, Illinois, 1950), have recently, and with commendable caution, gathered together the evidence (largely *a priori*) for the adaptive value of a number of traits such as the facial and bodily architecture of the Eskimo in contrast to that of the Nilotic Negro, and the significance of eye shape in relation to snow and desert glare. That body shape and size are related to environmental temperature has been established by the studies of Schreider (1950),[79] D. F. Roberts (1953),[105] and Newman and Munro (1955).[106] The adaptive significance of skin colour (Boyd, 1950) seems reasonably certain, particularly in view of Fleure's (*Geogr. Rev.*, XXXV, 1945) demonstration of the geographical relationship between skin pigmentation and intensity of ultra-violet light. Of interest here, and as an example of a plausible physiological 'proof' of adaptive value are the recent clinical reports of O'Brien (*Brit. J. Dermatol Syph.*, LIX, p. 125, 1947), and experiments of Thomson (*J. Physiol.*, CXII, p. 22, 1951) on the effect of ultra-violet burns in damaging the sweat glands. This implies that heat regulation (by evaporation) could be seriously interfered with in the absence of skin pigment protective against ultra-violet radiation. The adaptive value of pigmentation specially in relation to heat regulation and to protection against ultra-violet light and skin cancer has been critically examined by Barnicot (1959)[27] and Harrison (1961).[107]

But does the geographical distribution of the human species necessarily or to any large extent depend on the possession of adaptive racial genotypes? How far does the human in this respect conform to animal (and plant) species where, in general, according to Mayr (1949) 'each population of a species has been modified by selection to be adapted to the local environment' and 'this adaptation is due to a balance of genetic factors' so that 'the wide distribution' (of particular animals) 'depends on the ability to become reconstituted genetically'?

From the evidence we have, the case of man appears to be rather different. The widespread adaptive ability of man is manifestly a major property of the species as such. It depends on a physiological equipment, evolved by the species, which confers on the individuals of all racial groups the physiological power of adaptation and acclimatization to a wide range of environmental conditions (Dill, 1938; Monge, 1948; Newburgh, 1949; Barnicot, 1959).[27] This proposition of 'human plasticity' (see also Le Gros Clark, 1949; Cuenot, 1942; Gordon Childe, 1941) may be considered from a number of aspects. Firstly, it is reasonably certain that a climatic distribution map would show that communities of the main races are capable of living in extremes of climate and surviving extremes of weather, e.g. the Amerind of the Amazon and Tierra del Fuego, the Australian aborigines inhabiting both desert and high mountains (Goldby et al., 1938; Hammel et al., 1959),[108] the Negro in West Africa as well as in the East African and Basuto Highlands—but the special hardihood which some groups display may certainly indicate special adaptations. The Australian aborigine displays a marked degree of cold tolerance even if tested in the summer months or in hot regions. Hammel et al., (1959)[108] are inclined to see this as an instance of inherited physiological superiority. A priori, for geographical reasons, we should expect that physiologically, the human heat regulating mechanism would exhibit a wide range of adjustment. In the second place, recent work shows that the extent of individual adaptation can be put to the test. After acclimatization, Europeans can work in tropical heat quite as well as Negroes (Weiner, 1950a; Ladell, 1951), and the process of acclimatization to severe heat is similar in these groups (Hellon et al., 1956)[109] and in Asians (Weiner, 1950b). One effect of prolonged residence in hot climates is the lowering in the basal metabolic rate (Ahmad et al., 1938; Wilson, 1945; Duran-Quevedo, 1946; D. F. Roberts, 1952)[110] but the evidence seems to favour this as a response not specific to any particular tropical group, for it occurs in a large proportion of Europeans after some months in the tropics (Mac-Gregor and Loh, *J. Physiol.*, XCIX, 1941; Munro, *J. Physiol*, CX, 1949). Again, it may be argued that these are tests of only a particular response to heat and that successful survival depends on other properties, some of which are innate. On *a priori* grounds certain differences in physique may well confer such advantages, as may skin colour.

Finally, it is important for the anthropologist in attempting to account for the survival and spread of human communities to consider biological adaptability (either 'racial' or 'physiological') in the light of the ecological control achieved by the technology and social organization of the community. As Wulsin (in *Physiology of Heat Regulation and Sci. of Clothing*, ed. Newburgh, 1949) has indicated, the attainment of climatic control (as judged by the physiological adequacy of clothing and the thermal conditions inside dwellings) varies with different communities even under similar conditions. Similarly, the degree of success in attaining optimum nutrition represents a problem of ecological control of simultaneous biological and anthropological interest (Thompson, 1949; Platt, 1946, 1947; Richards, 1939, 1946; Fox, 1953).[26]

Man's dominating position in the animal kingdom is a product of his general adaptability and flexibility of response in relation to which any adaptive racial traits—and very few 'racial' features yet with certainty appear as such—assume a minor significance. Plasticity of response is to an important extent a property of the human physiological make-up, as may be instanced by the wide adjustments of the heat-regulating system or the metabolic ability for utilizing diets of widely differing composition, but as Dobzhansky and Ashley-Montagu (1947), in a stimulating essay, have put the matter, 'the genetically controlled plasticity of mental traits, is, biologically speaking, the most typical and uniquely human characteristic.' And, as they point out, the educability which this makes possible, is a unique human property socially as well as biologically. The neutral mechanisms underlying this are exceedingly complex (Lashley, *Quart. Rev. of Biology*, XXIV, 1949), and involve the integrative properties of complicated nerve nets or lattices of interacting nerve cells; so that the correlation of behaviour with the properties of the nervous system must deal primarily with this complex organization. It is not surprising that in recent years there is less inclination to attach undue significance to differences in external features of brain morphology such as convolutional and fissural pattern of various racial groups. Such comparisons have as a matter of fact been decreasingly pursued in this recent period since the reports on the aboriginal

Australian (Shellshear, 1937), on Chinese (Shellshear, 1937; Chi and Chang, *L.A.J.P.A.*, 28, p. 167, 1941), on Siberian peoples (Bushmankin, 1936), and on Negroes and Whites (Connolly, 1950). The extraordinary variability of fissural pattern within any of the racial groups emerges as the only certain finding; for these studies do not carry conviction that any distinctive difference has been established as Duckworth (1947) pointed out, or Levin earlier (1936). Differences in brain size, it is recognized, must be taken in conjunction with general body size (Bonin, *J. Gen. Physiol.*, XVI, 1937; de Beer, in *The New Systematics*, ed. Huxley, 1940); on this basis some culturally simple peoples possess the largest relative brain volume (Bushmakin, *A.J.P.A.*, XXI, 1936). Differences in intelligence due to racial genetic endowment, if they do exist, have yet to be demonstrated; so far all tests go to prove that environment and not race is the governing factor (Klineberg, 1945, 1956,[111] Jenkins, 1948); nor has it been possible to show so far that racial characteristics play more than a minor part as determinants of personality (Seltzer, *J. Gen. Physiol.*, LXXII, p. 221, 1948).

REFERENCES

1. HARRISON, G. A., WEINER, J. S., TANNER, J. M. and BARNICOT, N. A., *Human Biology*, Clarendon Press, Oxford, 1964.
2. ASHLEY-MONTAGU, M. F., *An Introduction to Physical Anthropology*, 3rd ed., Charles C. Thomas, Springfield, Ill., 1960.
3. HOWELLS, W. W., *Mankind in the Making*, Doubleday: New York, 1959.
4. BARNETT, S. A., *The Human Species* (A Biology of Man), London: Penguin Books, 1957.
5. COMAS, J., *Manual of Physical Anthropology*, Charles C. Thomas, Springfield, Ill., 1960.
6. COLD SPRING HARBOR, *Symposia on Quantitative Biology*, xv (1950), xx (1955), xxiv (1959), Cold Spring Harbor L., New York.
7. EXCERPTA MEDICA: Anatomy, Anthropology, Embryology and Histology. Issued monthly by Excerpta Medica Foundation, Amsterdam.
8. STERN, C. *Principles of Human Genetics*, 2nd ed., Freeman, San Francisco, 1960.
9. GARN, S. M., *Human Races*, Charles C. Thomas, Springfield, Ill., 1961.
10. MOURANT, A. E., *The Distribution of the Human Blood Groups*, Blackwell, Oxford, 1954.
11. WEINER, J. S., *The Piltdown Forgery*, Oxford University Press, 1955.
12. WEINER, J. S., OAKLEY, K. P. and LE GROS CLARK, W. E., 'The Solution of the Piltdown Problem' *Bull. Brit. Mus. (Nat. Hist.)* ii, 1953, p. 141.
13. LE GROS CLARK, W. E., *The Fossil Evidence for Human Evolution*, Univ. Chicago Press, 1955.
14. LE GROS CLARK, W. E., *History of the Primates*, British Museum, London, 1960.
14a. LE GROS CLARK, W. E., *The Antecedents of Man*, Edinburgh University Press, 1960.
15. BOULE, M. and VALLOIS, H. V., *Fossil Men*, Thames & Hudson: London, 1957.

16. CLARK, P. J., 'The heritability of certain anthropometric characters as ascertained from measurements of twins,' *Amer. J. Hum. Gen.*, viii, 1956, p. 49.
17. OSBORNE, R. H. and DE George, F. V., *Genetic Basis of Morphological Variation*, Harvard University Press, 1959.
18. LASKER, G. W., 'Environmental growth factors and selective migration', *Hum. Biol.*, xxiv, 1952, p. 262.
'The question of physical selection of Mexican migrants to the USA', *Hum. Biol.*, xxvi, 1954, p. 52.
19. PENROSE, L. S., 'Distance, size and shape', *Ann. Eug.*, xviii, 1953, p. 105.
20. ASHTON, E. H., HEALY, M. J. R. and LIPTON, L., 'The descriptive uses of discriminant functions in physical anthropology', *Proc. Roy. Soc. B.*, cxlvi, 1957, p. 552.
21. DUNN, L. C., 'Cross currents in the history of human genetics', *Am. J. Hum. Gen.*, xiv, 1962, p. 1.
22. WASHBURN, S. L., 'The new physical anthropology', *N.Y. Acad. Sci.*, xiii, 1951, p. 298.
23. WEINER, J. S., 'Physical anthropology: an appraisal', *Amer. Scientist*, xlv, 1957, p. 79.
24. ROBERTS, D. F. and WEINER, J. S. (editors), *The scope of physical anthropology and its place in academic studies.* (Symposium of the Society for the Study of Human Biology) 1958.
25. LI, C. C., *Population Genetics*, University Chicago Press, 1955.
26. FOX, R. H., *A study of the energy expenditure of Africans engaged in various rural activities*, Ph.D. Thesis, University of London, 1953.
27. BARNICOT, N. A., 'Climatic factors in the evolution of human populations', *Cold Spring Harbor Symposia*, xxiv, 1959, p. 115.
28. NESTURKH, M., *The Origin of Man*, Foreign Languages Publishing House: Moscow, 1959.
29. PRIMATOLOGIA: *A Handbook of Primatology*, ed. by H. Hofer, A. H. Schultz and D. Starck, S. Karger: Basel & New York, 1956.
30. HILL, W. C. O., *Primates: comparative anatomy and taxonomy*, I Strepsorhini, 1953; II Haplorhini, 1955; III Pithecoidea, 1957; IV Cebidae, Part A, 1960, Edinburgh Univ. Press.
31. SIMONS, E. L., 'New fossil primates; a review of the past decade', *Amer. Scientist*, xlviii, 1960, p. 179.
32. SCHULTZ, A. H., 'Postembryonic age changes', *Primatologia*, i, 1956, p. 887.
33. HURZELER, J., 'Oreopithecus bambolii Gervais', *Verh. Naturf. Ges. Basel*, lxix, 1958, p. 1.
'The significance of oreopithecus in the genealogy of man', *Triangle*, v, 1960, p. 164.
34. SCHULTZ, A. H., 'Einige becbachtungen und masse am skelett von oreopithecus', *Z. Morph. Anthrop.*, 1, 1960, p. 136.
35. STRAUS, W. L. K., 'The phylogenetic status of oreopithecus bambolii', *Phila. Anthrop. Soc. Bull.*, xiv, 1961, p. 12.
36. DART, R. A. and CRAIG, D., *Adventures with the Missing Link*, Hamish Hamilton: London, 1959.
37. LEAKEY, L. S. B., EVERNDEN, J. F. and CURTIS, G. H., 'Age of Bed 1, Olduvai Gorge, Tanganyika', *Nature*, cxci, 1961, p. 478.
38. ROBINSON, J. T., The dentition of the Australopithecinal. *Transvaal Museum Memoir* No. 9, 1956.
39. LEAKEY, L. S. B., 'A new fossil skull from Olduvai', *Nature*, clxxxiv, 1959, p. 491.
'New finds at Olduvai Gorge', *Nature*, clxxxix, 1961, p. 649.
40. BARTHOLOMEW, C. A. and BIRDSELL, J. B., 'Ecology and the Protchominids', *Amer. Anth.*, lv, 1953, p. 481.
41. ZEUNER, F. E., *Dating the Past*, London: Methuen, 1946, 3rd ed., 1952.
42. OAKLEY, K. P., 'Dating the emergence of man', *Adv. of Science*, xviii, 1962 p. 415.

317

43. OAKLEY, K. P., 'The composition of the Piltdown hominoid remains: further contributions to the solution of the Piltdown problem', *Bull. Brit. Mus.*, ii, No. 6, 1955, p. 254.
44. HOOIJER, D. A., 'Palaeontology of hominid deposits in Asia', *Adv. of Science*, lxxv, 1962, p. 485.
45. VALLOIS, H. V., 'La Grotte de Fontéchevade: Anthropologie', *Arch. Inst. Paleont. Hum. Mem.*, Part 2, xxix, 1958.
46. WEINER, J. S., 'The pattern of evolutionary development of the Genus Homo', *S. Afr. J. Med. Sci.*, xxiii, 1958, p. 111.
47. TOBIAS, P. V., 'Some developments in South African physical anthropology 1938–1958, In: The Skeletal Remains of Bambandyanaco, Univ. of Witwatersrand Press, 1959, p. 129.
48. COLE, S., *The Prehistory of East Africa*, London: Penguin Books, 1954.
49. SINGER, R., 'The Saldanha Skull from Hopefield, South Africa', *Amer. J. Phys. Anthrop.*, xii, 1954, p. 345.
50. HOWELL, F. CLARK, 'The place of Neanderthal Man in human evolution', *Amer. J. Phys. Anthrop.*, ix, 1951, p. 379.
51. WEINER, J. S., *The evolutionary taxonomy of the Hominidal in the light of the Piltdown investigation.* Selected Papers of the Fifth International Congress of Anthropological and Ethnological Sciences, Philadelphia: Univ. of Pennsylvania Press, 1956, p. 741.
52. NAPIER, J. R. and WEINER, J. S., 'Olduvai Gorge and Human Origins', *Antiquity*, xxxvi, 1962, p. 41.
53. RENSCH, B., *Evolution above the species level*, Methuen: 1960.
53a. Weinert, H., 'Der Urmenschenshädel von Steinheim', *Zeitschrift für Morphologie und Anthropologie*, xxxv, 1936, p. 463.
53b. Weinert, H. 'Africanthropus', *Zeitschrift für Morphologie und Anthropologie*, xxxviii, 1939, p. 18.
54. PENROSE, L. S., *Recent Advances in Human Genetics*, J. & A. Churchill Ltd., London, 1961.
55. ALLISON, A. C., 'Notes on sickle-cell polymorphism', *Ann. Hum. Genet.*, xix, 1954, p. 39.
56. AIRD, I., BENTHALL, H. H., MEHIGAN, J. A. and ROBERTS, J. A. F., 'The blood groups in relation to peptic ulceration and carcinoma of colon, vectum, breast and bronchus', *Brit. Med. J.*, ii, 1954, p. 315.
57. SINGER, R., 'The Boskop "Race" problem', *Man Art.*, ccxxxii, 1958, p. 173.
58. MUKHERJEE, R., RAO, C. R. and TREVOR, J. C., *The Ancient Inhabitants of Jebel Moyà (Sudan)*, Cambridge Univ. Press, 1955.
59. TALBOT, P. A. and MULHALL, H., *The physical anthropology of Southern Nigeria*, Cambridge Univ. Press, 1962.
60. DEBETZ, G. F., *Summary of palaeo-anthropological investigation in the USSR.* Selected papers of the Vth International Congress of Anthropological and Ethnological Sciences, Univ. Pennsylvania Press, 1956, p. 34.
61. BARNICOT, N. A. and BROTHWELL, D. R., 'The evaluation of metrical data in the comparison of ancient and modern bones". In: *Medical Biology and Etruscan Origins*, London: J. & A. Churchill Ltd., 1959.
62. SALLER, K., *Martin-Saller Lehrbuch der Anthropologie*, 3rd ed., Austav Fischer Verlag, Stuttgart, 1957.
63. STEWART, T. D., *Hrdlička's Practical Anthropometry*, 4th ed., Wistar Institute, 1952.
64. BAINBRIDGE, D. and GENOVES, S., 'A study of sex differences in the scapula', *J. Roy. Anth. Institute*, lxxxvi, 1956, p. 109.
65. WASHBURN, S. L., 'Sex differences in the pubic bone', *Am. J. Phys. Anthrop.*, vi, 1948, p. 199.
65a. HIRSCHLER, P., 'Anthropoid and human endocranial casts', N.V. Noord-Hollandische Uitgerers Maatschappij, Amsterdam, 1942.
65b. CONNOLLY, C. J., *External Morphology of the Primate*, Brain, Springfield, Illinois.
66. WASHBURN, S. L., 'The relation of the temporal muscle to the form of the skull', *Anat. Rec.*, xcix, 1947, p. 139.

67. WOLFFSON, D. M., 'Scapula shape and muscle function, with special reference to the Vertebial Barber', *Am. J. Phys. Anthrop.*, viii, 1950, p. 331.
68. LISOWSKI, F. P., VAN DER STEIT, A. and VIS, J. H., 'Upright posture: an experimental investigation', *Acta F.R.N. Univ. Comen.*, v (Anthrop.), 1961, p. 127.
69. GEJVALL, N. G. and SAHLSTROM, K. E., 'Gravfältet pä kyvkbacken i Horns socken Västergötland.' II Antropologisk del Kungl. Vitterhets Historie Antikvitets Akademiens Hand., Del-60, 1948, p. 153.
   Ibid., 'Gravfältet i Mellby by Kallands härad". II Antropologisk del Västergötlands Fornminnesförenings Tidskrift, v, 1951, p. 53.
70. VALLOIS, H. V., 'Vital statistics in prehistoric populations as determined from archaeological data" In: *The Application of Quantitative Methods in Archaeology*, Wenner-Gren Foundation for Anthropological Research, 1960, p. 181.
71. HOWELLS, W. W., 'Estimating population numbers through archaeological and skeletal remains' In: *The Application of Quantitative Methods iu Archaeology*, Wenner-Gren Foundation for Anthropological Research, 1960, p. 158.
72. BROTHWELL, D. R., 'The Palaeopathology of Early British Man', *J. Roy. Anthrop. Institute*, xci, 1961, p. 318.
73. TANNER, J. M., *Growth at Adolescence*, 3rd ed., Blackwell: Oxford, 1962.
74. TREVOR, J. C., *Race Crossing in Man*, Eugenics Lab. Memo, 36. Cambridge Univ. Press, 1953.
75. GLASS, B., 'On the unlikelihood of significant admixture of genes from the North American Indians in the present composition of the Negroes of the United States', *Amer. J. Hum. Gen.*, vii, 1955, p. 368.
76. HARRISON, G. A. (ed.), *Genetical Variation of Human Populations*, Pergamon Press, 1961.
76a. WIENER, A. S., *Blood groups and Transfusion*, Springfield, Ill., 1943.
77. POLLITZER, W. S., 'The Negroes of Charleston; a study of hemoglobin types, serology and morphology', *Am. J. Phys. Anthrop.*, xvi, 1958, p. 241.
78. SANGHVI, L. D., 'Comparison of genetical and morphological methods for a study of biological differences', *Am. J. Phys. Anthrop.*, xi, 1953, p. 385
79. SCHREIDER, E., 'Geographical distribution of the body weight/body surface ratio', *Nature*, clxv, 1959, p. 286.
80. LEHMANN, H., 'Distribution of the sickle-cell gene', *Eugenics Rev.*, xlvi, 1954, p. 3.
81. TOBIAS, P. V., 'Bushmen of the Kalahari', *Man Article* 36, 1957.
82. WEINER, J. S. and ZOUTENDYK, A., 'Blood group investigation on Central Kalahari Bushmen', *Nature*, clxxxiii, 1959, p. 843.
83. ABBIE, A. A., 'The Australian Aborigine', *Oceania*, xxii, 1951, p. 91.
   'Recent field work on the physical anthropology of Australian Aborigines', *Austral. J. Sci.*, xxiii, 1961, p. 210.
84. GATES, R. R., 'Racial elements in the aborigines of Queensland, Australia', *Z. Morph. Anthrop.*, 1, 1960, p. 150.
85. SIMONS, R. T., SEMPLE, N. M., CLELAND, J. B. and CASLEY-SMITH, J. R., 'A blood group genetical survey in Australian aborigines at Haast's Bluff, Central Australia', *Am. J. Phys. Anthrop.*, xv, 1957, p. 547.
86. FIRSCHEIN, I. L., 'Population dynamics of the sickle-cell trait in the Black Caribs of British Honduras, Central America', *Am. J. Hum. Genet.*, xiii, 1961, p. 233.
87. OSCHINSKY, L., *The racial affinities of the Baganda and other Bantu Tribes of British East Africa*, Heffer: Cambridge, 1954.
88. ROBERTS, D. F., IKIN, E. W. and MOURANT, A. E., 'Blood Groups of the Northern Nilotes', *Annals of Hum. Gen.*, xx, 1955, p. 135.
89. SIMMONS, R. T., GRAYDON, J. J. and SEMPLE, N. M., 'A bloodgroup genetical survey in Australian aborigines', *Am. J. Phys. Anthrop.*, xii, 1954, p. 599.

'A bloodgroup genetical survey in Eastern and Central Polynesians', *Am. J. Phys. Anthrop.*, xv, p. 357.

90. POLUNIN, I. and SNEATH, P. H. A., 'Studies on blood groups in South East Asia', *J. Roy. Anthrop. Institute*, lxxxiii, 1953, p. 215.
91. ALLISON, A. C., 'Aspects of polymorphism in man', Cold Spring Harbor Symposia on Quantitative Biology, xxii, 1955, p. 239.
92. BROZEK, J. and HENSCHEL, A., *Techniques for measuring body composition*, Nat. Acad. Sci.-Nat. Res. Council, Washington, D.C., 1961.
93. HOWELLS, W. W., 'Factors of human physique', *Am. J. Phys. Anthrop.*, n.s. ix, 1951, p. 159.
94. WEINER, J. S., 'A spectrophotometer for measurement of skin colour', *Man* Article No. 253, 1951, p. 152.
95. WEINER, J. S. and THAMBIPILLAI, V., 'Skeletal maturation of West African Negroes', *Am. J. Phys. Anthrop.*, x, 1952, p. 407.
96. ROBERTS, D. F., 'Effects of race and climate on human growth as exemplified by studies on African children' In: *Human Growth*, ed. by J. M. Tanner. Pergamon Press, 1960, p. 59.
97. ACHESON, R. M., 'Effects of nutrition and disease on human growth' In: *Human Growth*, ed. by J. M. Tanner. Pergamon Press, 1960, p. 73.
98. DANBY, P. M., 'A study of the physique of some native East Africans', *J. Roy. Anthrop. Institute*, lxxxiii, 1956, p. 194.
99. KRAUS, B. S., 'Male somatotypes among the Japanese of Northern Honshu', *Amer. J. Phys. Anthrop.*, n.s., x, 1951, p. 347.
100. WYNDHAM, C. H., BOUWER, W. V. D. M., DEVINE, M. G. and PATERSON, A.E., 'Physiological responses of African labourers at various saturated air temperatures, wind velocities and rates of energy expenditure', *J. Appl. Physiol.*, v, 1952, p. 290.
101. BARNICOT, N. A. and WOLFFSON, D., 'Daily urinary 17-ketosteroid output of African Negroes', *Lancet*, i, 1952, p. 893.
102. TOBIAS, P. V., 'On a Bushman–European hybrid family', *Man*, cclxxxvii, 1954, p. 179.
103. COMAS, J., '"Scientific" Racism again?' *Current Anthropology*, ii, 1961, p. 303.
104. WEINER, J. S., 'Nose shape and climate', *Amer. J. Phys. Anthrop.*, xii, 1954, p. 1.
105. ROBERTS, D. F., 'Body weight, race and climate', *Am. J. Phys. Anthrop.*, n.s., xi, 1953, p. 533.
106. NEWMAN, R. W. and MUNRO, E. H., 'The relation of climatic and body size in the U.S. males', *Am. J. Phys. Anthrop.*, n.s., xiii, 1955, p. 1.
107. HARRISON, G. A., 'Pigmentation' In: *Genetical Variation in Human Populations*. Pergamon Press, 1961, p. 99.
108. HAMMEL, H. T., ELSNER, MESSURIER, D. H. LE, ANDERSEN, H. T. and MILAN, F. A., 'Thermal and metabolic responses of the Australian aborigine exposed to moderate cold in summer, *J. Appl. Physiol.*, xiv, 1959, p. 605.
109. HELLON, R. F., JONES, R. M., MACPHERSON, R. K. and WEINER, J. S., 'Natural and artificial acclimatization to hot environments', *J. Physiol.*, cxxxii, 1956, p. 559.
110. ROBERTS, D. F., 'Basal metabolism, race and climate', *J. Roy. Anthrop. Institute*, lxxxii, 1952, p. 169.
111. KLINEBERG, O., Race and Psychology In: *The Race Question in Modern Science*, Unesco: Sidgwick & Jackson Ltd., 1956.
112. WEIDENREICH, F., 'On the earliest representatives of modern mankind recovered on the soil of East Asia', *Peking Natural History Bull.*, 1939, p. 3; *The Skull of Sinanthropus Pekinensis*, Chunking: Geological Survey of China, Pehpei, New Series D, No. 10. Whole Series No. 127, 1943; *Apes, Giants, and Man*, Chicago, 1946; 'The trend of human evolution', *Evolution* I, 1947, p. 221.

IV. AMERICANIST STUDIES
by Beatrice Blackwood, B.Sc., M.A., F.S.A.

The Americas offer an especially favourable opportunity of illustrating the point of view taken in other parts of this book, that archaeology and ethnology belong together as the past and the present of the same subject. In some areas, although there has been contact with our own civilization for more than three hundred years, so much of the ancient culture still survives that excavated objects can be recognized by comparison with their modern counterparts, and their meaning and use ascertained by reference to present-day practices. This is not true everywhere, of course, for many tribes have become extinct, and others, though they survive, have changed so much that they view with astonishment the achievements of their forbears when these are shown or explained to them.

A regional arrangement has been adopted for the major part of this review of Americanist studies, because it has seemed to the writer the best framework in which to fit the material available. It has, however, the disadvantage that it tends to obscure the importance of the part played in the development of anthropology in the Americas by the great many-sided scholars of the past such, for example, as Franz Boas, who contributed to our knowledge of every branch of anthropology in most parts of the continent, and who, when he died, was acclaimed 'the world's greatest anthropologist' (Kroeber, *M.A.A.A.*, No. 61, 1943, p. 5). This disadvantage perhaps becomes less cogent in the present, for as the subject grows, its exponents tend of necessity to specialize either in scope or in area. Probably there can never be another Boas, although some of his pupils, notably A. L. Kroeber and R. H. Lowie, also flung their nets widely.

A survey of this nature is like an anthology of poetry, in that whatever is offered, there will always be readers who disagree with the selection. Space is limited, and apologies are hereby tendered to those who think their names should have been mentioned. Murdock's *Ethnographic Bibliography of North America* (third edition 1960), is invaluable for publications up to that date.

Before the regional survey, in which archaeology and ethnology will be considered together, some general methods of approach will be briefly discussed.

An outstanding characteristic of recent years, in America as elsewhere, has been the development of new methods of tackling the problems of chronology. The most important of these, here as elsewhere, is that known as radiocarbon or carbon 14 dating (see p. 256). American archaeologists rely heavily on it, in some cases perhaps too heavily with regard to the degree of accuracy at present attainable. Radio-carbon dates will be quoted on many of the following pages; while they are the best available at the time of writing, the possibility must always be kept in mind that new refinements of technique may cause them to be radically altered. Other methods, such as thermoluminescence, the hydration rate of obsidian, and soil analysis, are being developed. It is reasonable to expect great advances in the accuracy of dates put forward both for sites and for individual specimens in the not-too-far-distant future.

The publication of a new and much enlarged edition of Clark Wissler's *The American Indian* in 1938 (the first edition appeared in 1917) brought renewed discussion as to the validity of his 'culture area' theory (see p. 237). A. L. Kroeber, in 'Cultural and Natural Areas of Native North America' (*U.C.P.A.A.E.*, 38, 1939) justified the method, if further justification were needed, by presenting a revised and more detailed scheme, meeting the more cogent of the objections levelled against Wissler's arrangement. A later comment by Kroeber (*Am. Anth.*, 56, 1954, p. 559) is pertinent: 'It has long been obvious that the weakest thing about culture areas as we deal with them in American ethnology is their boundaries. . . . (If) it is a certain aggregation or mass of culture rather than its limits that is conceptually meaningful, the question is what gives the mass such characterizable unity as it has? There are three main answers: environment, subsistence and what may be called ideology or free creativity.' In practice, the 'culture area' idea has proved its usefulness again and again and has also been fruitfully applied to other continents.

A considerable amount of work has always been and continues to be done on that aspect of our subject called in England culture contact and in America acculturation: the nature of the impact upon each other of two peoples whose ways of life are different. Of recent years, this has broadened its base, and has become a study of the dynamics of culture change. Although investigations are now undertaken of various European and Oriental immigrant groups, an aspect largely neglected until recently, this review will deal only with the situation as it applies to the American Indian. Here a perhaps rather unexpected fact seems to be emerging. At a conference on American Indian affairs organized by the Wenner-Gren Foundation held in 1954, the results of which were published as *The American Indian in Transition* (Provinse, *Am. Anth.*, 56, 1954), 'the conference agreed that despite external pressures and internal change, most of the present identifiable Indian groups residing on reservations (areas long known to them as homelands) will continue indefinitely as distinct social units, preserving their basic values, personality, and Indian way of life, while making continual adjustments, often superficial in nature, to the economic and political demands of the larger society' (p. 389).

The intensive study and analysis of changes resulting from contact received great impetus from the publication by the Social Science Research Council of 'A Memorandum for the Study of Acculturation' by Redfield, Linton, and Herskovits in 1936, followed by a general study by Herskovits, *Acculturation, the Study of Culture Contact*, in 1938. A series of essays, *Acculturation in Seven American Indian Tribes*, edited by Linton (1940), was the first attempt to define various types of contact and to find reasons for the differences between them. A general review of the position as it appeared ten years later took place at the Twenty-ninth International Congress of Americanists, the most important results of which were published as *Acculturation in the Americas* under the editorship of Sol Tax (1952). The Social Science Research Council continued its support, and in 1956 made possible an inter-university summer research seminar attended by six well-known anthropologists, each of whom had been engaged in field research over several years with the Indian group on which he reported. Out of this grew the most important recent publication on the subject. *Perspectives in American Indian Culture Change*, edited by Edward H. Spicer (1961), a significant contribution, which while describing conditions in six contrasting and widely-spaced Indian communities, adds greatly to our knowledge of different types of change and of the principles underlying culture change in general.

The other side of the picture has not been overlooked. In two studies dealing with the impact of the American Indian on American culture, A. Irving Hallowell[1] elaborates upon a sentence quoted from M. L. Williams's edition of Schoolcraft's classic Indian legends:[2] 'The American Indian has left an indelible mark upon the culture of America, upon its customs, its habits, its language and even upon its modes of thought.'

Not dependent on, but often associated with the interest in culture change is the attention paid to psychological techniques in anthropological work, with the result that the boundary between anthropology

[1] *Am. Anth.*, 59, 1957, pp. 201–17 and paper in *The Frontier in Perspective*, ed. by W. D. Wyman and C. B. Kroeber, Madison, Univ. of Wisconsin Press, 1957.

[2] E. Lansing, Michigan State Univ. Press, 1956.

and psychology is becoming more and more blurred. The focus, formerly on 'intelligence', is now largely transferred to 'personality', for the assessment of which a whole battery of 'projective tests' has been evolved. Those most frequently used are the Rorschach (description of a series of ink-blots) and Thematic Apperception (interpretation of a set of simple pictures) tests. Detailed descriptions of these and others will be found in the Andersons' *An Introduction to Projective Techniques* . . . (1951). Arguments for and against the suitability of these tests for use in the anthropological field will be found in the report of a symposium, 'Projective Testing in Anthropology', published in the *American Anthropologist* (LVII) 1955, pp. 245–70). Their value is there stated to be that they are 'an objective check on the anthropological report', and that they 'provide information of a kind not procurable by direct observation'. On the other hand it may be argued that the material is not always suitable for cultures other than that for which it was originally intended; that the administration of the tests puzzles and may confuse or worry the victim, and so invalidate the result; and that the interpretation of the answers by the anthropologist may introduce a subjective element, especially if the anthropologist has not undergone a thorough training in their use.

Developments in the relationship between anthropology and psychology up to 1945 have been reviewed by B. J. Meggers (*Am. Anth.*, 48, 1946). Since then the output has increased enormously. Among later papers involving the use of the Rorschach test may be cited Kaplan's study of responses in four cultures (Zuñi, Navaho, Mormon, and Spanish-American, *P.P.M.*j 42, 1954) and Spindler's work on acculturation among the Menomini (*U.C.P.C.S.*, 5, 1955). Studies of groups are sometimes termed 'modal personality' studies. By 'personality' is meant, in this connexion, the character of the group or of the individual as shown not only by overt actions in response to situations, but also by emotional reactions. The idea of 'modal personality' (not the term) seems to stem from Ruth Benedict's *Patterns of Culture* (see p. 214), although those who have followed her have not always agreed with her. Recent studies along these lines have been published by Wallace on the Tuscarora (*B.A.E. Bull.*, *150*, 1952), Hallowell on the Ojibwa (published under the title *Culture and Experience*, 1955), and comparative studies by Driver and Massey (*Trans. Am. Phil. S.*, 47, 1957) and G. and L. Spindler (1957). A considerable amount of criticism has been directed against the validity of 'modal personality' on the grounds, among other objections, that it involves a dangerous amount of generalization and that the traits used in assessing it may be arbitrarily selected. Taking everything into consideration, the disadvantages in the use of projective tests in anthropological work seem to the present writer to outweigh any advantages they may have, and the objections raised against them appear to be valid.

Possibly connected with the increased interest shown by anthropologists in psychology is the number of investigations into the effects of the use of peyote and other narcotics. Peyote is a small cactus (*Lophophora williamsii*) which grows in the Rio Grande Valley and parts of northern Mexico. It contains alkaloids (including mescaline) which, when the cactus is eaten or a concoction of it drunk, produce certain sensory and psychic phenomena. It was eaten ceremonially in pre-Columbian times and is used in many Indian societies at the present time for both secular and religious purposes. The first full account of it was published by W. La Barre in 1938 (*Y.U.P.A.*, 19); the same writer summed up developments since then with a very full bibliography in 'Twenty Years of Peyote Studies', published in *Current Anthropology* in 1960. Peyote music, a noteworthy feature of the cult, is dealt with by McAllester (*V.F.P.A.*, *13*, 1949) and Merriam and d'Azevedo (*Am. Anth.*, 59, 1957). The peyote cult has spread rapidly during the present century, and has in many areas acquired the status of a religion, with accretions from Christianity. Its popularity is thought by some to be the result of the Indians' frustration and despair at the change in their way of life made necessary by modern conditions.

It is perhaps worth while to put on record some more or less recent developments which help in the collection of information and the collation of results. There has been a notable increase in the number of undertakings in which a comprehensive plan of campaign is worked out for a given region or subject and the aid of several specialists is invoked, to work either separately or in various combinations as occasion requires. These projects are made possible by subventions from universities and various other organizations such as the Rockefeller Foundation, the Carnegie Corporation, and the Wenner-Gren Foundation for Anthropological Research (formerly the Viking Fund). The value to anthropology of the support of these bodies is incalculable. An outstanding example of co-operative research of this kind is the Viru Valley project, in which geologists, and ethnologists took part under the joint sponsorship of eight institutions (see p. 350).

Another method of co-operation which has increased in popularity of late years is the symposium, in which a central theme is discussed by a number of specialists from different angles and different points of view. Papers read and discussed at such symposia have been published in *American Anthropologist, American Antiquity*, and other journals. An exchange of opinion among experts obtained by correspondence is a feature of *Current Anthropology*, the lively periodical edited by Sol Tax, which keeps track of the latest developments in all branches of anthropology in all parts of the world. The increasing amount of co-operation between specialists is part of a larger movement towards breaking down the border lines between disciplines which is discussed in another part of this book.

EARLY MAN

The first discovery of human artefacts which could, from the associated remains, be regarded as of considerable antiquity was made in 1926 at a site near Folsom, New Mexico, where a carefully worked stone projectile point, the human origin of which could not be questioned, was found embedded in the clay matrix surrounding two ribs of a fossil bison thought by geologists to have been extinct for many thousands of years. The block of clay containing the two ribs with the point still in place was removed and sent to the Colorado Museum at Denver (F. H. H. Roberts, *S.M.C.*, 94, 1935). It is on exhibition in the Hall of the Prehistoric People of the Americas at the Colorado Museum (now renamed the Denver Museum of Natural History).[1] This find indicated an antiquity for man in America so much greater than had previously been thought possible, that scientists were sceptical of its authenticity, but later excavations at the Folsom site produced other points of the same type in even closer association with bison bones, providing conclusive evidence that the men who made the points were contemporaries of the animals. This special type of point, with a characteristic longitudinal groove, was given the name Folsom point. Unfortunately, conditions at Folsom were such that there was no means of obtaining even an approximate date. Search in other places led to the discovery in 1936 of the Lindenmeier site in Colorado, where a Folsom point was found firmly embedded in a bison's vertebra. By geological evidence (for which see Bryan and Ray, *S.M.C.*, 99, 1940) the strata in which these remains were found could be dated at not later than 10,000 and possibly as early as 25,000 years ago. This site was the first to provide a definite complex of associated implements, whereas before only isolated points had been found. A detailed account of the Lindenmeier discoveries was published by F. H. H. Roberts in 1935 (*S.M.C.*, 94) and 1936–37 (*S.M.C.*, 95). The Lindenmeier site has recently provided material from which a date of about 8800 B.C. has been obtained (10,780 ± 375 years ago, see Bushnell, *Antiquity*, XXXV, 1961). One site, Lehner in Arizona, has provided a

[1] Letter to the author from the director of the Museum, May 31, 1962.

radiocarbon date earlier than this (rather before 9000 B.C.). Claims have been made for much greater antiquity for finds from other sites, but experts are not agreed on dates for these. It seems clear, however, that nothing may be expected in the New World of an antiquity comparable with that of the Palaeolithic period in Europe. If, as is generally agreed, man entered America from Asia at a time when the two continents were joined by land across what is now the Bering Strait, the possible time of his arrival must have been between 23000 B.C. and 9000–8000 B.C., the last time that this condition obtained as indicated by radiocarbon dating (Hopkins, *Science*, 129, 1950).

Several other types of stone projectile point have been described, clearly akin to though not identical with Folsoms. The name 'fluted points' has therefore been suggested to cover the whole series, but many writers still use the historic term. They are clearly not the work of beginners in the art of flaking stone, since they exhibit a high degree of control over a very difficult medium. Nothing like them has been found in the Old World. It now seems to be established that the men who made them flourished around 9000–7000 B.C. and were wandering hunters living a life not unlike that which we know existed in northern Europe during the early art of the Mesolithic period. As well as stone-pointed weapons, they possessed several varieties of stone tools, including scrapers, gravers, and hammer-stones. Scraps of animal bone have been found, some ornamented with incised designs. There is no evidence of cultivation, and no pottery.

No human remains have yet been found in conjunction with artefacts belonging to the 'Folsom complex'. But some progress has been made in our knowledge of the physical type of early man in the New World. It is now generally accepted as a crucial fact that there were never any anthropoid apes in the New World; investigators therefore no longer seek, as they once did, for remains of pre- or proto-human type, but realize that the earliest comers need not have been, and indeed probably were not, very different in physical type from the present Indians. Recent archaeological work has tended, on the whole, to increase the possibility that at least one of the claimants for antiquity actually belongs to the Late Pleistocene period, i.e. 'Minnesota Man'—actually a girl—(Jenks, *Pleistocene Man in Minnesota*, 1936), while 'Brown's Valley Man' also from Minnesota (Jenks, *M.A.A.A.*, 49, 1937), and a skeleton found near Abilene, Texas (Ray, *Science*, 98, 1943), may be Late Pleistocene or early post-glacial in date. But owing to the circumstances of their excavation, the possibility can never become a certainty. For a discussion of the evidence see F. H. H. Roberts (*An.*

Rep. Smithson. Instn., 1944). An attempt was made by Wilford (*Am. Antiq.*, 21, 1955) to date the 'Minnesota Man' site by the radiocarbon method, using a section of the elk-antler dagger which accompanied the skeleton, but 'its carbon content proved to be almost entirely of inorganic carbonate, attesting to the high degree of mineralization of the specimen, and inadequate for a determination of age' (p. 130). However, as is pointed out by Wormington (*Ancient Man in North America*, 4th ed., 1957, p. 235), such a high degree of mineralization is in itself an indication of antiquity.

The shadow of doubt as to intrusion, and as to the correct interpretation of the geological data, rests also on another discovery of supposed early man in the New World. In 1947 a human skeleton (of 'modern' type) was found in the sediments of the dry bed of Lake Texcoco in the Valley of Mexico. It is interpreted by its finder, Helmut de Terra, as that of a man drowned in the lake between 11,000 and 12,000 years ago. A full account has been published in *Tepexpan Man*, by H. de Terra, J. Romero, and T. D. Stewart (*V.F.P.A.*, No. 11, 1949). For a critical discussion, students should consult the paper by Black in *American Antiquity* (1949) and the review by Krieger in the same journal (1950). Although, for the reasons there given, the antiquity of Tepexpan man will never be absolutely certain, evidence supporting the correctness of de Terra's estimate has been provided by later excavators. In 1952 artefacts of undoubted human workmanship were found in association with mammoth bones (one projectile was lodged between two ribs) at Santa Isabel Iztapan, about a mile and a half south of Tepexpan. This find was seen *in situ* by a number of experts from Mexico and the United States, and there can now be no doubt that men and mammoths were contemporary in the Valley of Mexico. Radiocarbon dates from soil samples obtained at this site range from about 9000 B.C. (11,003 ± 300) to more than 16,000 years ago (Libby, *Radio Carbon Dating*, 1955).

Parts of a human skeleton to which considerable antiquity is generally accorded were found in 1953 near Midland, Texas. In contrast to the circumstances attending the discovery of the bones previously mentioned, 'Midland man' (the name given to the Texas find, though the bones are those of a female) was seen *in situ* by specialists who directed their excavation. Palaeontological and archaeological evidence suggest a date somewhere about 12,500 years ago, but radiocarbon tests have proved unsatisfactory owing to lack of suitable material. Here again, a high degree of mineralization in the bones is an indication of considerable age. Later work confirmed the stratigraphic sequence but again failed to provide satisfactory material for radiocarbon dating (Wendorf and Krieger, *Am. Antiq.*, 25, 1959).

A more detailed history of the discovery of early man in America up to publication dates will be found in the symposium *Early Man*, edited by G. G. MacCurdy (1937), and in two papers by F. H. H. Roberts (*S.M.C.*, 100, 1940, *An. Rep. Smithson Instn.*, 1944). A later summary and discussion of sites, stone industries, and physical types, with bibliography, is contained in H. M. Wormington's useful monograph *Ancient Man in North America* (fourth edition, 1957).

Turning to South America, the work of Tschopik and Cardich in Peru, Menghin and Ibarra Grasso in Bolivia, Mayer-Oakes and Bell in Ecuador, and Bird in Chile and in Patagonia has demonstrated, with the help of radiocarbon dating, that man arrived there much earlier than was formerly supposed. References to this work will be found in an illuminating survey of early man in Central and South America given to the Royal Anthropological Institute by S. K. Lothrop in his Huxley Memorial Lecture for 1960 (published in *J.R.A.I.*, 91, 1961). Shortly before the lecture was due to begin, a cable from Junius Bird announced that an age of 10,700 ± 300 years ago (roughly, between 8000 and 8500 B.C.) had been assigned to Fell's Cave in Patagonia. Although the exact relationship of the South American finds to those farther north remains uncertain, 'there is no longer any question that man, as an early hunter, moved over most of the Americas during or shortly after the Wisconsin advances' (Willey, *Am. Antiq.*, 27, 1961). The bearing of so early an arrival at the southernmost tip of the continent on the date of man's first crossing from Asia has yet to be worked out. Authenticated early human remains are still lacking south of the Valley of Mexico.

There is abundant evidence that the people we have been considering depended for their subsistence mainly if not exclusively on the hunting of big game: mammoth, bison, horse, camel, mastodon, and others, all of species which later became extinct. Up to about ten years ago, there was a break in our knowledge between them and the later prehistory, in some sites represented by a sterile layer. This gap has since been filled, partly by excavation, partly by a revision of ideas about chronology, and a continuous succession has now been worked out for many, if not yet for most, parts of North America, and less completely for South America. It is now clear that contemporary with the big-game hunters, but beginning rather later, there were, over a large part of the United States, and later still in Canada, people whose subsistence depended not on big-game hunting but on gathering wild seeds, berries, roots, or shellfish with hunting (of small animals only) as a minor source of food. This complex has been given the name 'Archaic' (perhaps an unfortunate designation as it was at one time used for a series of much more advanced cultures in Mexico). Jennings and Norbeck (*Am. Antiq.*, 21, 1955) gave to a comparable complex in the Great Basin the name 'Desert Culture', and this term is now applied over a wider area. A number of sites have been dated by the radiocarbon method between 8000 and 5000 B.C. Among the earliest, possibly between 9500 and 9000 B.C., is Danger Cave in Utah, where a continuous succession of cultures has been traced to the early years of the Christian era (Jennings, *M.S.A.A.*, 14, 1957). A study of the Northern Paiute Indians, who still live in the area, produced a number of parallels showing that this simple food-gathering culture survived with but little change almost to the present day (Steward, *U.C.P.A.A.F.*, Vol. 33, 1933). 'Danger Cave' has been singled out from a growing list as an intensive study of a single site. A general account ranging over a wide area will be found in Byers's paper 'An Introduction to Five Papers on the Archaic Stage' (*Am. Antiq.*, 24, 1959); the papers which follow give more detailed regional surveys.

The South-west

It was in this area that the former gap between the earliest hunters and later cultures was first bridged by the work of Martin, Rinaldo, and Antevs (*Fieldiana: Anthropology*, 38, Chicago Nat. Hist. Mus., 1949) in the south-eastern corner of Arizona and adjacent parts of New Mexico where they found evidence of direct succession from the latest stages of the Cochise culture to the Mogollon. Other areas furnished similar sequences, and continuity is now well established. 'These cultures, or this culture, which featured small-game hunting and the gathering and processing of wild plant products, formed the base from which the later sedentary cultures evolved' (Lister, *Am. Antiq.*, 27, 1961). A good summary of what is known about this is to be found in *The American Southwest: a Problem in Cultural Isolation* by J. D. Jennings and others (*M.S.A.A.*, 11, 1956).

The sedentary cultures begin with the Basket-makers, who have been proved to be the founders of the Pueblo cultures, and not a separate development as was earlier thought. To this Basket-maker–Pueblo sequence has been given the name 'Anasazi' (proposed by Kidder in 1936) from a Navaho word meaning 'the ancient ones'. Two Basket-maker and five Pueblo periods (not to be considered as divided by hard and fast lines) are distinguished, of which the greatest was

Pueblo III, about A.D. 1050–1300, which produced the bulk of the impressive buildings at Mesa Verde, Pueblo Bonito, Pecos, and other well-known sites. Pueblo V, beginning about A.D. 1700, continues to the present time. This same culture, modified but by no means extinguished by white influence, still flourishes in at least some of the modern Pueblos.

Besides the Anasazi sequence, two other important early cultures have been defined in the South-west: (1) the Hohokam, in Central and southern Arizona, with five periods from about 300 B.C. (some would put it later) to the present, now represented by the Pima and Papago Indians, who still live in the same area, but have lost far more of their heritage than have the Pueblo Indians; (2) the Mogollon, in southeastern Arizona and south-western New Mexico, which may have arisen out of the early Cochise culture. The Mogollon culture seems to have died out about A.D. 1450. An account of it up to A.D. 1000 has been published by J. B. Wheat (*M.A.A.A.*, 82, 1955).

Kidder's masterly *Introduction to the Study of Southwestern Archaeology* (1924) was the first general scientific study of the area; on it much of the later archaeological work in the South-west has been based. Martin, Quimby, and Collier's *Indians before Columbus* (1947) is especially good on this area, where one of the authors (Martin) has worked. Later syntheses are Wormington's *Prehistoric Indians of the Southwest* (1951) and Gladwyn's *A History of the Ancient Southwest* (1957).

The South-west has for a long time been a favourite hunting-ground for archaeologists. Following the early work of Cushing, Fewkes, and others in the late nineteenth and early twentieth century, came that of E. L. Hewett, whose major contribution to south-western archaeology, besides numerous publications, was the founding in 1909 of the School of American Archaeology, later re-named the School of American Research at Santa Fe, New Mexico, of which he was Director for thirty-seven years. Two important series of excavations were carried on under the leadership of Kidder at Pecos between 1915 and 1929 and Judd in Chaco Canyon during the 1920's. The Pecos material was published between 1930 and 1936 in the series *Papers of the Phillips Academy Southwestern Expedition*. A final volume published in 1958 deals with a number of points previously omitted or hurried over, and continues the story into the historic period, tracing the relations of the Pecos Indians with other Indians and with the Spaniards, until the final abandonment of the pueblo in 1838. The physical anthropology of the Pecos Indians was dealt with by Hooton (1930). The results of the Chaco

Canyon investigation have appeared at long intervals.[1] Some are still unpublished.

The first volume of the Chaco Canyon series is noteworthy as giving the first account of a technique which had a profound effect on south-western archaeology. In *Dating Pueblo Bonito and Other Ruins of the Southwest*, A. E. Douglass explained his method of calculating the date of a building by making use of the variations in the size of the annual growth rings of timber, later to be known as dendrochronology. Dr Douglass, a physicist and astronomer, had begun the investigation early in the present century as a possible means of studying changes in climate. Its possibilities for archaeology were first realized in 1914, when Dr Clark Wissler supplied Douglass with pieces of prehistoric beams from the ruins of Pueblo Bonito. During the next twenty years records were collected, but it was not until 1935 that the results were published. Since then a complete tree-ring record from the beginning of the Christian era to the present time has been built up, and details are published in the *Tree-Ring Bulletin* (Laboratory of Tree-Ring Research, Tucson). Sequences have been worked out for other parts of America, such as that of Giddings for parts of Alaska, where he plotted a series going back for more than a thousand years (*M.M.U.M.P.*, 1952). Attempts have been made to use the method in Europe, but in general the acquisition of suitable material has proved difficult and costly. With the development of radiocarbon dating, dendrochronology has become less important, but it played a very useful part in elucidating south-western archaeology. There are, of course, complications, and certain precautions must be observed. Details of these will be found in *Principles and Methods of Tree-Ring Analysis* by W. S. Glock (*C.I.W.P.*, 486, 1937) and in a note by Deric O'Bryan in *American Antiquity*, Vol. 15, October, 1949. The originator of dendrochronology naturally followed with interest the development of radiocarbon dating. At the time of his death at the age of ninety-four on March 21, 1962, a comparison of the results obtained by the two methods was being carried out by Dr Paul Damon at Tucson (*The Times*, March 22, 1962). The result of this work will be of great interest when it becomes available.

An important advance which has been made of recent years is the extension of the area comprised in the term South-west on all sides to

[1] A. E. Douglass, *Dating Pueblo Bonito and Other Ruins of the Southwest*, Washington, D.C., Nat. Geog. Soc. Pueblo Bonito Series I, 1935.

K. Bryan, 'The Geology of Chaco Canyon, New Mexico, in relation to the life and remains of the prehistoric peoples of Pueblo Bonito.' *S.M.C.* 122, 1954.

N. M. Judd, 'The Material Culture of Pueblo Bonito'. *S.M.C.*, 124, 1954; 'Pueblo del Arroyo, Chaco Canyon, New Mexico'. *S.M.C.*, 138, 1959.

make up the complex now known as the Greater South-west, which includes most of Arizona, New Mexico, Colorado, and Utah, with adjacent parts of states to east and west, together with sections of Sonora and Chihuahua in northern Mexico. A further result of recent research is to highlight the extent to which south-western cultures were influenced by those of Nuclear America (see p. 343 for an explanation of this term). 'It is apparent that initially maize spread from south to north, followed by pottery-making, and then by such elements as certain architectural forms, clay figurines, pottery forms and decorative styles, shell ornaments, copper bells, mosaic discs and so forth. Some of these elements may be associated with religious complexes that reached the Southwest perhaps carried by such peoples as the Toltecs' (Lister, *Am. Antiq.*, 27, 1961).

As with archaeology, so with ethnology; the South-west has attracted the attention of some of the great pioneers. Bandelier's historical studies, the publications of Cushing, Fewkes, Hodge, Hough, and M. C. Stevenson on the Pueblos; of Matthews on the Navaho and of Russell on the Pima, are all classics of the late nineteenth and early twentieth centuries. Bandelier's charming story about Pueblo life, *The Delight Makers* (1890), must have given pleasure to many who would not read his more formal works.

Choice thereafter becomes difficult. Names that spring instantly to mind are those of Kroeber, Goddard, Bunzel, and Parsons. For Kroeber, the South-west was one of many interests. Goddard worked chiefly among the Apache, and Bunzel at Zuñi. Elsie Clews Parsons devoted much of her long working life to the study of south-western ethnology, and there are few pueblos on which she has not contributed something of value. Her last work on the south-west, *Pueblo Indian Religion*, appeared in 1939.[1]

An interesting example of a technique increasingly used by field-workers, the recording of the life-history of a single individual in his own way, is *Sun-Chief: The Autobiography of a Hopi Indian* (edited by L. W. Simmons, 1942). While not strictly an autobiography, *Maria: The Potter of San Ildefonso* by Alice Marriott (1948) gives an intimate account, based on personal conversations, of the most famous modern expert in one of the oldest Pueblo industries.

Marriott's book is about the potter rather than her pots. For a technical account of pottery-making, Guthe's *Pueblo Pottery Making*

---

[1] A posthumous book 'Isleta Paintings' consisting of reproductions with her introduction and comments, edited by E. S. Goldfrank, was published in 1962 as *B.A.E. Bull.*, 181.

(1925) should be consulted. Bunzel's *The Pueblo Potter* deals especially with form and design (*C.U.C.A.*, No. 8, 1929). Bunzel wrote also on the pottery of Zuñi (*A.R.B.A.E.*, 47, 1930) and Chapman on that of Santo Domingo (*Santa Fe*, 1936).

A considerable amount of work has been done on the Navaho. They have been shown on linguistic and other grounds not to belong to the Anasazi tradition, but to be intruders from the north (see Sapir, *Am. Anth.*, 38, 1936). References to early publications may be found in Kluckhohn and Spencer's *A Bibliography of the Navaho Indians* (1940), and later works in Kluckhohn and Leighton, *The Navaho* (1946), a comprehensive and well-documented account of the tribe as it was in the 1940's. An appraisal of Kluckhohn's work, including that on the Navaho, with a bibliography, appeared in the *American Anthropologist*, Vol. 64, 1962. Among numerous other publications on the Navaho may be mentioned Dyk's *A Navaho Autobiography* (*V.F.P.A.*, 8, 1947) and an intensive study of Navaho religion by Gladys Reichard (1950).

The Plains

Unlike the South-west, the Plains have until the last twenty-five years or so attracted little attention from archaeologists, in spite of the fact that Wissler had, as early as 1907, drawn attention to the lateness of the Plains Indian culture as it was in historic times, and to the need for archaeological work before the connecting links between the historic and the prehistoric cultures were destroyed by the plough.

The first systematic study was Strong's paper 'The Plains Culture Area in the Light of Archaeology' (*Am. Anth*, 35, 1933), followed by his 'An Introduction to Nebraska Archaeology' (*S.M.C.*, 93, 1935). By 1940, things had advanced sufficiently for Wedel to formulate a tentative culture-sequence for the Central Plains; the advance since then can be measured by the difference between that paper and the same author's *Prehistoric Man on the Great Plains* (1961). In the earlier publication Wedel points out that 'because the tribes resident there were for many years in contact with white men, the Plains offer an excellent opportunity to tie in the archaeological record at its upper end with written history and ethnography' (Wedel, *S.M.C.*, 100, 1940, p. 296). This 'upper end' has especially occupied the attention of archaeologists and ethnologists in the eastern Plains or Village Indian area, where 'there is incontrovertible proof of long-continued occupation' (Wedel, *Am. Antiq.*, 27, 1961). At the lower end of the archaeological record the tie-up has been with the hunters of mammoth and bison ten or twelve thousand years ago or possibly longer. In the western and north-western Plains this hunting or hunting and gathering economy lasted into historic times, largely, probably, because of geographical and climatic conditions, while in the eastern Plains, with a more favourable environment, we find, perhaps at about the beginning of the Christian era, sedentary or semi-sedentary groups, who understood the cultivation of maize and a few other crops, made pottery and lived in villages of earth-covered pit houses; these groups gradually increased in size. It was not until the seventeenth century that they were partly displaced and partly assimilated (except for some marginal groups) by invaders coming, at first on foot and later with horses, from the north-east, under pressure of other tribes and subsequently of white settlers.

The picturesque elements in the culture of these later tribes of wandering bison-hunters, especially after their acquisition of horses, caught the popular imagination, at first through the work of James Fenimore Cooper and other writers, and later through motion pictures and television, and they became the Red Indians of whom every schoolboy knows. The history of one of these incoming tribes has been traced from the time of its origin until 1878, by G. E. Hyde in *Red Cloud's Folk, a History of the Oglala Sioux Indians* (revised edition 1957).

The literature on the historic Plains Indians is very voluminous, and reference to it must be limited. Among the early writers are D. I. Bushnell, J. O. Dorsey, A. C. Fletcher, and J. Mooney, whose work 'The Ghost Dance Religion' (14th *A.R.B.A.E.*, 1896) is a classic. Clark Wissler contributed many important papers on Plains Indian tribes between 1904 and 1934, and it was he who first enlisted the interest of Robert H. Lowie. These two, with the addition of Kroeber, produced or inspired practically all of the more recent work on the ethnology of the Plains Indians. Lowie identified himself more particularly with the Crow, to whom he returned again and again. He records that when he first visited them their culture 'was spiritually very much alive', and when he returned in 1931 'the rise of a literate generation and the advent of the automobile had not been able to kill it utterly'. This was no longer true in 1950, he told the present writer sadly. A complete bibliography of Lowie's writings, including the posthumously published *Crow Texts*, will be found at the end of his autobiography, *Robert H. Lowie, Ethnologist: A Personal Record*, completed just before he died and published in 1959.

Among other noteworthy publications on the Plains Indians are those of Mandelbaum. Working in 1934–35 among the Plains Cree, he obtained from three old men who had been famous warriors and hunters in their young days, first-hand accounts of warfare and buffalo hunting before the last of the buffalo in their country were killed off about 1880 (*The Plains Cree*, 1940). A monograph by W. D. Wallis on the Canadian Dakota (*A.P.A.M.N.H.*, 1947) fills a gap in our knowledge of those of the Plains tribes who live in Canada, on whom much less work has been done. Outstanding work on the Blackfoot was published by John C. Ewers in 1955 and 1958.[1] The later work is a historical study of the tribe from its first contact with white men until the present time, and the earlier a detailed analysis of the role of the horse in the culture of the central plains, taking a somewhat different line from that of Wissler's paper on the same subject published in 1914. Ewers's *Plains Indian Painting* (1939) is a beautifully illustrated discussion of this interesting form of art.

East and North-East

Sites assignable to the Archaic period have been excavated in many parts of the East and North-east. An account of them will be found in Byers' paper 'The Eastern Archaic' (*Am. Antiq.*, 24, No. 3, 1959). Radiocarbon dates from sites both in the North-east and South-east give results of the order of 7000–6000 B.C. (Byers, *Am. Antiq.*, 24, No. 4, 1959). Lewis and Kneberg (*Am. Antiq.*, 25, No. 2, 1959) trace the Archaic period in Kentucky, Tennessee, Alabama, and Georgia from about 7000 B.C. to the early centuries of the Christian era. All this agrees very well with the radiocarbon dates obtained for the South-west.

Intensive study of the later archaeology was stimulated by Shetrone's *The Mound Builders* (1930) and the historical researches of John R. Swanton (for which the bibliography of Swanton in *Smithsonian Miscellaneous Collections* No. 100, 1940, may be consulted). Attempts to reduce to order a vast mass of material led to a number of different systems of classification being tried out, found wanting, and discarded. One which has survived is known as the Midwestern Taxonomic Method (see McKern, *Am. Antiq.*, 4, 1939). It makes use of five major divisions: focus, aspect, phase, pattern, and base, progressing from localized details to large general classes.

The work of Shetrone and those who followed him took the almost legendary builders of the (sometimes spectacular) earthworks which are a feature of the eastern states out of the realm of fantasy and revealed them as the bearers of a number of different cultures of dates varying between about A.D. 500 and about A.D. 1600. A detailed account of these

---

[1] 'The Horse in Blackfoot Indian Culture', *B.A.E. Bull.*, 159, 1955; *The Blackfoot: Raiders on the Northwestern Plains*', Norman, Okla., Univ. of Oklahoma Press, 1958.

as recognized up to 1947 is given in *Indians before Columbus* (Martin *et al.*). Radiocarbon dating is now pushing the earlier figures back a thousand years or more. The radiocarbon dates so far available are given in an appendix to the magnificent volume *Archaeology of the Eastern United States* (1952) prepared in honour of the retirement of Fay-Cooper Cole, who did so much to promote the study of the area. Edited by J. B. Griffin, the twenty-eight papers it contains give a complete conspectus of eastern archaeology up to the late 1940's; the volume will be a standard work of reference for a long time to come. A general appraisal of the situation about a dozen years later is given in Haag's paper in *American Antiquity*, 1961. An interesting development of recent years is the increase of evidence pointing to connexion with the civilizations of Nuclear America (Caldwell, *M.A.A.A.*, 88, 1958; Willey, *Am. Antiq.*,27, 1961).

The question of the relationship between prehistoric cultures and historically known and still existing Indian tribes has received and is receiving attention, notably in several papers of the symposium 'Man in Northeastern North America' (edited by F. Johnson, *P.P.F.A.*, 3, 1946) and in the contribution by F. Eggan to *Archaeology of the Eastern United States*. Beginning at the other end, work on the past of historically known tribes such as Wintemberg's on the Roebuck prehistoric village site (*N.M.C. Bull.*, 83, 1936) has also demonstrated continuity. In the south, J. R. Swanton's *The Indians of the Southeastern United States* (*B.A.E. Bull.*, 137, 1946) brings the history of the area up to our own times, when those who remain have 'gradually adapted themselves to the civilization about them'.

The Iroquois have been a magnet attracting anthropologists and archaeologists alike for more than a hundred years, from Lewis Morgan's famous *The League of the Iroquois* (1851), on which so many theories have been based (see p. 123), to the 'Symposium on Cherokee and Iroquois Culture', edited by Fenton and Gulick in 1961 (*B.A.E. Bull.*, 180), which deals with both archaeology and ethnology. Among the important publications of the intervening period may be mentioned the papers of J. N. B. Hewitt, who during the fifty years of his service on the staff of the Smithsonian Bureau of American Ethnology made himself the leading authority on the organization and customs of the Iroquois League. His publications range from 1889 to 1926.[1] The tradition has been continued by W. N. Fenton from 1936 onwards. In

[1] Most of Hewitt's work appeared in the various publications of the Smithsonian Institution. See particularly 'Iroquoian Cosmology', Pt. I, *A.R.B.A.E.*, 21, 1900; Pt. II, *ibid.*, 43, 1926.

'Problems Arising from the Historic Northeastern Position of the Iroquois' (*S.M.C.*, 100, 1940), Fenton discusses the part played by this group of tribes in American history during the last 400 years. Cultural persistence among the modern Iroquois is dealt with by Freilich (*Anthropos*, 55, 1958).

The ethnology of the North-east has been well served by Frank G. Speck, notably in *Naskapi, the Savage Hunters of the Labrador Peninsula* (1935) and *Penobscot Man, the Life History of a Forest Tribe in Maine* (1940). R. S. and W. D. Wallis have written on the Micmac (1955) and the Malecite (*N.M.C. Bull.*, 148, 1957). The Indians of the sub-arctic North-east came in for a share of the attention of the Fifth Thule Expedition (see p. 340), resulting in Birket-Smith's volume on Chipewyan ethnology (1945).

West and North-west

Work done on the prehistory of California, the Plateau area and the North-west Coast has appeared in a number of papers scattered through various periodicals. It is well summarized up to 1947 in Part VI of *Indians before Columbus*, to which the reader is referred for the relevant references. Later information on California, some of which is still at the tentative stage, is given by Meighan (*Am. Antiq.*, 24, 1959). 'Recent evidence shows rather clearly that the west coast was occupied as early as any other part of the country, rather than being marginal and only lately settled by migrants from the east or north. There is reason to believe that California was occupied by people who were contemporaneous with the Folsom and perhaps the Clovis cultures of the Southeast and Plains' (p. 289).

A controversial note is sounded by George Carter who maintains that the story of man in California and adjacent regions goes back far beyond the usually accepted period for the presence of man in America. In *Pleistocene Man in San Diego* (1957) he claims that there is in California a Lower Palaeolithic 'core tool culture' going back about 40,000 years but his evidence has not been accepted by all specialists on the area.

Among recent monographs, two must be singled out for mention. A valuable paper by Alice Hunt, 'Archaeology of the Death Valley Salt Pan, California' (*Univ. of Utah Anthrop. Papers*, 47, 1960), gives a record of an area much larger than that indicated by the title, from the end of the Pleistocene down to historic times. The results of excavations carried out by Cressman and others between 1952 and 1956 at The Dalles, Oregon, show that the exploiting of salmon as one of the major sources of food in the North-west began much earlier than had been thought. Their monograph (*Trans. Am. Phil. Soc.* N.S. 50, pt. 10, 1960), combined with Cressman's *Klamath Prehistory* (*ibid.*, 46, pt. 4, 1956), has added a great deal to our knowledge of western North America.

A pioneer in the archaeology of British Columbia was Harlan I. Smith, who published 'Archaeological Investigations on the North Pacific Coast' in 1900 (*Am. Anth.* N.S. 2) though he later devoted most of his attention to ethnology.

Frederica de Laguna, who was herself responsible for collecting much of the field material, published in 1947 a synthesis of what was known at that time of the prehistory of the Indian tribes of the sub-arctic North-west (*M.S.A.A.*, 3). She has also contributed to our knowledge of their present by collaborating with Birket-Smith in a study of the Eyak Indians of Alaska (1938). This work, with that of Osgood on the Kutchin (1936), the Tanaina (1937), and the Ingalik (1940, 1958);[1] and of Honigmann on the somewhat more southerly Kaska (1949, 1954),[1] has added significantly to the data available on an area which was for long one of the least-known parts of North America.

The father of north-western ethnology is undoubtedly Franz Boas. His interest in the Indians of British Columbia began in the early 1880's, and he was still writing about them in the 1940's. His favourite tribe was the Kwakiutl, of whom he made a special study in 1897 as a member of the Jesup North Pacific Expedition. An analysis and appreciation, by H. Codere, of Boas' work on the North-west Coast, with a list of his most important contributions, will be found in a volume celebrating the centenary of his birth, *The Anthropology of Franz Boas*, edited by W. Goldschmidt (*M.A.A.A.*, 89, 1959). Another product of the Jesup North Pacific Expedition was Swanton's monograph on the Haida (*M.A.M.N.H.*, 8, 1909).

For information on the ethnology of California, the standard reference book is Kroeber's 'Handbook of the Indians of California' (*B.A.E. Bull.*, 78, 1925) which is definitive up to its date of publication. Mention must be made of Goddard's intensive work on the life and culture of the Hupa (*U.C.P.A.A.E.*, No. 1, 1903) followed by a volume of Hupa texts (*ibid*, 1904). Among outstanding later publications on the North-west are those of D. Jenness on the Sekani Indians (*B.C.D.M.*, 84, 1937), T. F. McIlwraith on the Bella Coola (1949), and H. G. Barnett on the Coast Salish (1955). Barnett published a valuable study of the nature of the potlatch in 1938 (*Am. Anth.*, 40). Inverarity's

[1] All published in *Y.U.P.A.*

Art of the Northwest Coast Indians (1950) contains excellent illustrations of the characteristic art of this area and also supplies a number of useful references to work on other North-west Coast tribes. An important general study of culture history and culture change is *The Indians of British Columbia* by Hawthorn, Belshaw, and Jamieson (1958). F. de Laguna's monograph 'The Story of a Tlingit Community: A Problem in the Relationship between Archaeological, Ethnological and Historical Methods' (*B.A.E. Bull.*, 172, 1960) demonstrates how fruitful can be the results obtained by the conjunction of these complementary disciplines.

The Arctic

The names of those who have made major contributions to our knowledge of the Arctic are so numerous that only a very short list can be given here. Many have investigated both the past and the present. Again Boas appears as a pioneer. Among those whose work began at the turn of the century or only a little later are Holm, Hrdlička, Jochelson, Steensby, and Thalbitzer, of whom Hrdlička and Thalbitzer were still active in the 1940's. In the next decade came the work of Jenness as a member of the Canadian Arctic Expedition, 1913–18, although his intensive studies of the Copper Eskimo were not published till later.[1] The Fifth Thule Expedition, which set out from Copenhagen in 1921 under the leadership of Knud Rasmussen, resulted in important papers on the geology, meteorology, and botany of the area as well as on archaeology and ethnology. The anthropologist members of the expedition were Knud Rasmussen, Kaj Birket-Smith, and Thirkel Mathiassen. The report of the expedition runs into thirty-four monographs, published in Copenhagen at intervals from 1927 onwards. The latest, probably the last, consists of some posthumous notes by Knud Rasmussen on the Alaskan Eskimo, compiled by H. Osterman, and appeared in 1952.

Although Boas and others were concerning themselves with problems of origin and migrations in the 1880's, the present complications of Arctic archaeology are the product of the last thirty years or so. Most of the earlier field-workers concentrated on providing as comprehensive an ethnographical study as they could on a specific area or group, laying a good foundation on which theories could be built up.

Two diverse theories of the origin of Eskimo culture eventually emerged. Put rather baldly, one is that the Eskimo were first of all an inland people, now represented by the Caribou Eskimo, and later pushed

[1] *Report of the Canadian Arctic Expedition*, Ottawa, vols. 12, 1922; 13, 1924; 15, 1928; 16, 1946.

to the shore where they adapted themselves to life by the sea. The other theory is that they began on the coast and that the Caribou Eskimo represent a degenerate rather than an early form, having moved inland and lost those elements of their culture connected with the sea. The arguments on both sides are stated in papers by Mathiassen and Birket-Smith in the *American Anthropologist* (1930). Yet a third solution of the problem has been suggested by Spencer (*B.A.E. Bull.*, 171, 1959): 'that the inland-maritime dichotomy represents not one system which evolves into another, but rather two specialized kinds of development in the domain of a common culture.' Here the matter rests for the present.

From questions of development it was a short step to problems of ultimate source. As archaeological work proceeded, it began to seem probable that the origin of Eskimo culture as a whole must be sought on the north-eastern coasts of Asia. Good accounts of the position up to publication dates will be found in papers by H. B. Collins (*S.M.C.*, 100, 1940) and F. G. Rainey (*A.P.A.M.N.H.*, 38, pt. 4, 1941). In 1948 Larsen and Rainey, in their report on extensive excavations at Point Hope, Alaska (*A.P.A.M.N.H.*, 42), produced evidence indicating possible connexions much farther to the west than had previously been imagined, perhaps in the western Siberian–eastern Russian area. They pointed out particularly striking parallels between certain animal carvings characteristic of the Ipiutak culture (so-called from the Eskimo name for the Point Hope site) and the 'Scytho-Siberian' animal style of art, together with other similarities which they considered too close to be fortuitous. The bearing of this new evidence on Eskimo problems in general is discussed by Birket-Smith in his paper 'Recent Achievements in Eskimo Research' (*J.R.A.I.*, 77, 1947).

A possible connexion between Eskimo and European art, though at a much earlier time, was first suggested by Sollas in *Ancient Hunters and Their Modern Representatives* (1911); he draws a parallel between the Eskimo and the hunters of the Magdalenian period in palaeolithic western Europe. This is discussed in detail by F. de Laguna in 'A Comparison of Eskimo and Palaeolithic Art' (*Am. J. Arch.*, 36, No. 4; 37, No. 1, 1932–33). Her conclusion is that there are fundamental differences between them, but she suggests that in view of the known changes in Alaskan art from the Old Bering Sea period to modern times, perhaps we should not expect Eskimo and palaeolithic art to have too much in common, even should they have been related in the past, and that archaeological work in Siberia may bring to light new material which will bridge the gap.

A very important discovery which seems to point towards the Old World was made by Giddings at the bottom of a site on Cape Denbigh on the north Bering Sea-coast of Alaska. Here there were stone implements, including burins and microliths, comparable in technique with those of the European Upper Palaeolithic (Giddings, *Am. Antiq.*, 16, 1951). This collection of implements is known as the Denbigh Flint complex. Comparable finds have since been made in north-eastern Canada (MacNeish, quoted by Larsen, *Am. Antiq.*, 27, 1961). Since this complex is unlike anything previously associated with the Eskimo, the question arises of its relationship to the already known Eskimo cultures, or even whether it should be considered as Eskimo at all. A discussion by Giddings of this and other points raised by recent excavations in the Bering Strait region, with comments by Collins and others, will be found in *Current Anthropology* for March, 1960, and a general appraisal of recent work in the whole Arctic area by Helge Larsen in *American Antiquity* for July, 1961.

The archaeology of Siberia, Japan, and other parts of eastern Asia is becoming increasingly known, and might be expected to provide comparable material. But while it is true that there are microlithic industries in a number of regions, they are everywhere associated with pottery or immediately precede it. Taking into account the results of recent Russian and Japanese excavations, Chard (*Antiquity*, XXXII, 1959) has put forward a suggestion that 'the Asiatic evidence at the moment suggests an original movement to America of crude chopping-tool cultures . . . and the indigenous development of all early New World cultures on this simple foundation'. Bushnell and McBurney (*ibid.*, 1959), however, reviewing the same evidence, take a different view: 'We are still inclined to attribute a dominant role to the great events of Upper Palaeolithic spread between the twenty-fifth and twentieth millenia B.C. rather than to possible survivals of primitive indigenous traditions of the Far East.' So the debate continues. It may be that Sollas's long-discredited theory of a connexion between the Eskimo and the Magdalenian hunters will prove not to have been so fantastic after all.

Radiocarbon dating on material from the Arctic is particularly difficult for a number of reasons. Progress is, however, being made with it. A summary of what has been done is given by Rainey and Ralph (*Am. Antiq.*, 24, 1959). After a statement of the limitations of the method as applied to Arctic material, their concluding paragraph (p. 373) runs as follows: 'However, we believe that this radiocarbon study has gone far enough so that we can state with some assurance that men had already occupied the Arctic coast of North America all the way from Alaska to Greenland some time before 2000 B.C. . . . Just when the Eskimos (as defined in specific physical, linguistic and cultural terms) arrived on the scene remains an open question.'

Much has been written on the skill of the Eskimo in coping with Arctic conditions. Perhaps the best single work from this point of view is Weyer's *The Eskimos: Their Environment and Folkways* (1932). A not too highly specialized general survey, touching both past and present, will be found in Birket-Smith's *The Eskimos*, first published in 1936. In a new edition (1960) the author gives his present views on the origin of Eskimo culture. For a vivid picture of Eskimo every-day life by one who shared it, Jenness's *The People of the Twilight* has never been surpassed.

Although concerned with Indians as well as Eskimo, Turner's 'Hair Embroidery in Siberia and North America[1]' is relevant here because 'knowledge of the special suitability of reindeer, caribou and moose hairs as a decorative medium . . . was exploited, with no significant break in continuity, from western Siberia to eastern Canada'. But evidence as to the antiquity of this practice, and of the method of its spread, is so far lacking.

Nuclear America

The relevance of the term 'Nuclear America' as a heading for this section is a sign of the recent trend towards synthesis arising from more detailed knowledge showing connexions between areas once thought to be separate. It was first suggested by Kroeber in 1948 but did not come into general use until some time later.

Nuclear America embraces all the country beginning approximately at the northern margin of the Valley of Mexico, through Central America to the Andean portions of Peru and Bolivia. It thus includes the three major pre-Columbian civilizations of the New World. Two of these had previously been linked under the term Mesoamerica, proposed by A. V. Kidder, who showed for the first time that certain parts of the Maya culture complex could be tied in with certain parts of the prehistory of the Valley of Mexico, providing clear evidence of what had before been only suspected, that the Mexican and the Maya areas can be considered as a cultural entity. For this great advance the work of Kidder at Kaminaljuyu in Guatemala (*C.I.W.P.*, 561, 1946) was mainly responsible.

The inclusion of parts of South America with Mexico in one culture

[1] *Occasional Papers on Technology*, No. 7, 1955, Pitt Rivers Museum, Oxford.

area was first suggested by Spinden[1], who postulated an early farming culture spreading southwards from the Valley of Mexico to Peru and beyond. To this he gave the name 'Archaic', a rather unfortunate term, since it was in no sense a beginning. His hypothesis was challenged, mainly by Vaillant, whose excavations in Mexico produced evidence of a much more complicated situation than that suggested by Spinden. Vaillant's book, *Aztecs of Mexico* (1947), is a masterly synthesis of his own and all other available data, giving the first coherent picture of the sequence of cultures in the Valley of Mexico from the earliest then known up to the Spanish Conquest. Realizing that the cultures described by him represented 'a mid-point between the rude life of hunters and the complex society in developed American Indian civilization', he left the bottom section of his time-and-sequence chart vacant, and called his earliest finds 'Lower Middle Cultures', putting them at about the beginning of the Christian era. Radiocarbon dating has pushed them back by roughly a thousand years[2], and the space he left has been filled. In the filling of it justification has once more been found for the inclusion of South America. A suggestion which aroused considerable controversy at the time of its publication was made by M. N. Porter (*V.F.P.A.*, 19, 1953), arising out of her excavations at Tlatilco in the Valley of Mexico, where she found not only connexions with the people of the Gulf Coast and parts of Guatemala, but also similarities with the Chavin culture of Peru. Subsequent work is described in a survey by Willey (*Am. Antiq.*, 27, 1961). The result has been that we now have, at about the beginning of the first millenium B.C., a chain of mutually related early village agricultural complexes from Central Mexico to South Peru.

The spectacular finds of Matthew Stirling at La Venta, which led to the discovery of the La Venta or Olmec culture, were followed by further investigations at this and other sites. A discussion of these, and an evaluation of the place of the Olmec culture in Mexican prehistory, will be found in 'Excavations at La Venta, Tabasco' by Drucker, Heizer, and Squier (*B.A.E. Bull.*, 170, 1959). While emphasizing its importance, these writers do not endorse the theory put forward by Covarrubias that the Olmec culture was in fact the foundation on which was built the later Mexican and Maya civilizations.

Vaillant's *Aztecs of Mexico* is still the best introduction to the subject. A few other outstanding contributions must, however, be noted.

[1] *Ancient Civilizations of Mexico and Peru*, 1917, 3rd ed. revised, 1928. Am. Mus. Nat. Hist., New York.

[2] e.g. Zacatenco 1359 $\pm$ 250 B.C. *Amer. Anth.*, 57, 1955, p. 796.

The Swedish archaeologist S. Linné, who published his *Archaeological Researches at Teotihuacan* in 1934, followed this in 1942 with *Mexican Highland Cultures*, in which he considered the place of this enormous site in the general picture of Mesoamerican culture history. The identification of Teotihuacan with Tollan, the capital of the Toltecs, has since been given up, because Acosta's excavations at Tula in Hidalgo showed conclusively that it has the better claim (Armillas, *Runa*, 3, 1950). A full discussion of the evidence for Tula being the capital of the Toltecs is given by B. Dutton (*El Pal.*, 62, 1955). It is important because of the close resemblance of sculptures found at Tula to those of Chichén Itzá, with all the implications of contact between the Toltec and the Maya.

A work of outstanding importance to the understanding of Mexican prehistory is Noguera's *La cerámica arqueológica de Cholula* (Mexico 1954), a detailed and magnificently illustrated monograph on the pottery of this interesting site and its relationship to Teotihuacan, a problem which still remains unsolved.

The most important event that has happened for a long time for students of the Aztec is the publication of the Anderson and Dibble edition of the Florentine Codex.[1] This is a mid-sixteenth century account of the Aztec compiled by the Spanish friar Bernadino de Sahagún with the help of Aztec informants. Anderson and Dibble have for the first time given us a translation of the Nahuatl text, which is far richer in detail than Sahagún's Spanish paraphrase. To illustrate his manuscript, Sahagún had illustrations drawn by Indian artists. Pictures and text show that, in spite of some modifications, the Aztec way of life still persisted to a considerable extent at least a generation after the Conquest. The Anderson and Dibble edition—a really great achievement—has been coming out in parts for some time, and some are still to come, but as each book is complete in itself, the order in which they appear does not matter.

One of the best-known studies of modern Mexican Indians is Redfield's *Tepoztlan* (1930). References to other ethnographical work will be found in the bibliography to a paper by Beals, Redfield, and Tax (*Am. Anth.*, 45, 1943).

In southern Mexico an outstanding contribution to knowledge was made by the series of excavations carried on by Alfonso Caso at Monte Alban and at Mitla, in the state of Oaxaca, which have shed much light on the prehistory of the Zapotec and Mixtec Indians who still occupy

---

[1] *General History of the Things of New Spain* (*Florentine Codex*), School of American Research, Santa Fe, New Mexico, 1950—.

that region. The highlight of the excavations was the finding of the unrifled tomb of eight Mixtec officials. The sight of the treasures of gold, silver, crystal, pearls, turquoise mosaics, carved jades, and other examples of unsurpassed craftsmanship, now in the Oaxaca Museum, is an unforgettable experience. The official reports of these excavations were published in Spanish by the Instituto Panamericano de Geografía é Historia. The results obtained have been discussed by Covarrubias in *Mexico South* (1946) and by H. Berlin in *American Antiquity*, Vol. 13, No. 4 (1948). Covarrubias follows his description of 'the Zapotec heritage' with a summary of their history after the conquest, and with a vivid picture of their life at the present time, when 'the Isthmus Zapotecs are among the most progressive and enterprising of the more primitive communities in Mexico'. The interplay of Spanish and Indian elements in a modern Zapotec village is brilliantly analysed by E. C. Parsons in *Mitla, Town of the Souls* (1936).

The father of Mayan archaeology may be said to be John L. Stephens, who made a special journey in search of ruins vaguely reported by others. He took with him an English artist, Frederick Catherwood, whose remarkable sketches illustrating Stephens' book *Incidents of Travel in Central America, Chiapas and Yucatan* (1839) caught the imagination of A. P. Maudslay, who became the pioneer of intensive Mayan studies, working in the field between 1881 and 1894 and publishing his results in five magnificently illustrated volumes (1889–1902). Maudslay not only described the ruins but took paper squeezes of many of the stelae and other sculptures. From these casts were made which, together with some originals, Maudslay presented to the British Museum. His work was continued by W. H. Holmes and later by T. A. Joyce. Joyce had charge of Maudslay's gifts, some of which he illustrated in *Maya and Mexican Art* (1927). Joyce's *Mexican Archaeology* (1914) was the first attempt at a synthesis of the knowledge then available on the subject.

Linking these pioneers with our own time is the life of Sylvanus Griswold Morley, whose first published work on the Maya appeared in 1910, and the last shortly before his death in 1946. In this, *The Ancient Maya*, he painted a vivid and glowing picture of the achievements of the people to whom he had devoted most of his long and full life. A list of his more important writings on the Maya is included in its bibliography. A third edition, drastically revised by G. Brainerd, including some later material, appeared in 1956. But this book is no longer Morley's.

346

Morley made his first contribution to the study of Maya hieroglyphic writing in 1915, but his major works on that subject are *The Inscriptions at Copan* (1920) and *The Inscriptions of Peten* (five volumes, 1937-38).

A long step towards our comprehension of Maya writing, and of the Maya themselves, was taken in J. Eric S. Thompson's *Maya Hieroglyphic Writing* (1950; second edition with some additional matter, 1960). This book, which will undoubtedly become a classic, not only offers interpretations of hitherto untranslatable glyphs, but also, and more important, makes a notable contribution towards a better understanding of the structure of Maya hieroglyphic writing as a whole. It also forges two important links: with the glyphs used by people to the north of the Maya area, and with the books of Chilam Balam, thus 'establishing the continuity of Maya ritualistic practice'. Of special interest is the author's insistence throughout on 'the essentially poetical, even mystical' character of Maya glyphic writings. Many problems remain unsolved—some perhaps are insoluble—but Thompson's work has contributed significantly towards the ultimate objective of such studies, which, as he puts it (p. 295), 'is not the literal word-for-word decipherment of the glyphs, but a fuller comprehension of the mentality, the poetic concepts, and the philosophical outlook of the Maya'. Other methods of explaining the glyphs have been advanced by various scholars, notably by Y. V. Knorosov, who interprets the individual signs on a syllabic basis. Thompson discusses this and other problems connected with the interpretation of the glyphs in *American Antiquity*, Vol. 24, 1959.

Bound up with the interpretation of the glyphs is the vexed question of the relation of Maya chronology to our own. Largely owing to the work of Thompson, the dating known as the Goodman-Martinez-Thompson correlation has been widely adopted, putting all dates 256 years later than the system elaborated by Spinden (1924) from suggestions originally made by Morley (who, however, uses the other correlation in his later writings). This question is discussed in detail by Kidder and Thompson in 'The Correlation of Maya and Christian Chronology' (*C.I.W.P.*, 501, 1938), where the method of arriving at these different correlations is explained. With the introduction of radiocarbon dating, this question has again come to the fore. At first it seemed that the dates worked out by this method, using wood from beams of temples dated by inscriptions, supported the Spinden dating, but the results of later work, using a greater number of specimens and new refinements of technique, have turned out to be strongly in favour of the Goodman-Martinez-Thompson correlation (see Satterthwaite and Ralph, *Am. Antiq.*, 26, 1960).

Detailed descriptions of the Maya sites, such as Chichén Itzá, Copan, Kaminaljuyu, Palenque, Piedras Negras, Quirigua, Tikal, Uaxactun, and Yaxchilan, to mention only a few of the best known, have been published in monograph form by the Carnegie Institution of Washington and the Peabody Museum of Archaeology and Ethnology of Harvard University. These are for the specialist. For those who are interested in knowing something about the Maya without wanting to specialize, there can be no better introduction than Thompson's *The Rise and Fall of Maya Civilization* (1956), where references for further reading, including the site reports, may be found.

A recently discovered Maya site calls for special mention. The extraordinary mural paintings in the temple at Bonampak, Chiapas, throw fresh light on Maya life and activities, as well as being remarkable works of art. They are beautifully reproduced in colour from copies by Antonio Tejada in the monograph by Ruppert, Thompson, and Proskouriakoff (*C.I.W.P.*, 602, 1955).

Tatiana Proskouriakoff, who was responsible for that portion of the book on Bonampak dealing with the artistic aspects of the paintings, has also made Maya studies more vivid by her brilliant sketches bringing to life the great sites as they must have looked in their prime. These, based on all the information available from excavations and descriptions, were published as *An Album of Maya Architecture* (*C.I.W.P.*, 558, 1946). We are also indebted to her for *A Study of Classic Maya Sculpture* (*C.I.W.P.*, 593, 1950).

It is impossible within the scope of this review to do justice to all the important work that has been done by the many eminent scholars who have been attracted by the Maya. But any record, however brief, must include the name of A. M. Tozzer, field-worker and, perhaps even more important, inspirer of others to a more than ordinary degree. In his posthumously published work on Chichén Itzá (*M.P.M.*, 10, 1957) he deals in detail with the modern discoveries confirming the connexion between the Maya and the Mexican Toltec which he had adumbrated nearly thirty years earlier. Among many useful services to Maya scholars he translated and edited Bishop Landa's *Relación de las cosas de Yucatán* (1941). This sixteenth-century work by a Spanish friar gives information on Maya history, customs, and religion, which Tozzer explains and amplifies in his extensive notes, adding greatly to the usefulness of the publication. He had lived among the descendants of the people about whom Landa wrote, the Lacandon Maya, where he found striking parallels. In his introduction to the *Relación* he says: 'Working from the sixteenth century both back into the past and forward to the present, a fairly consecutive picture of the history of Yucatan is given, starting perhaps in the twelfth or thirteenth century . . . to the present Maya of Yucatan.'

Thanks to the work of other scholars, students of Maya history have at their disposal records compiled by the Maya themselves. Chief of these are the books of Chilam Balam, one of which was translated by R. L. Roys (*C.I.W.P.*, 438, 1933); *Popul Vuh: the Sacred Book of the Ancient Quiché Maya*, translated into Spanish by A. Recinos (1947) and into English by D. Goetz and S. G. Morley (1950); and *The Annals of the Cakchiquels*, translated by A. Recinos and D. Goetz (1953).

Besides Tozzer's paper on the Lacandon Maya previously referred to, many other works on the modern Maya have appeared. Studies showing both changes produced by contact and survivals from ancient times include Redfield and Villa, *Chan Kom, a Maya Village* (*C.I.W.P.*, 448, 1934); Redfield, *A Village That Chose Progress, Chan Kom Revisited* (1950) and *The Folk-Culture of Yucatán* (1941); and Steggerda, *Maya Indians of Yucatan* (*C.I.W.P.*, 531, 1941). The last-named study gives a detailed description of methods of cultivation, which appear to have changed very little. Links with the past are mainly in this and other aspects of material culture, for the higher learning was in the hands of the priests and the ruling classes and did not long survive the Spanish Conquest. That the Maya can cope with modern conditions is shown by the remarkable story of successful adaptation told by M. Nash in 'Machine-age Maya', (*M.A.A.A.*, 87, 1958) of a farming community which absorbed a textile mill into its structure without appreciable injury. A detailed account of the economic activities of a small community is given by Sol Tax in *Penny Capitalism: A Guatemalan Indian Economy* (1953).

A *Handbook of Middle American Indians* is in course of compilation under the general editorship of Dr Robert Wauchope, Director of the Middle American Research Institute, Tulane University, New Orleans. The plan is for eleven volumes, to be issued separately as completed, dealing with the geography, archaeology, ethnology, social anthropology, physical anthropology, linguistics and ethnohistory of the Indians of Mexico and Central America. Each volume is being edited by a specialist in these fields. (Personal communication from Dr Wauchope).

The labours of all who seek information on South American archaeology and ethnology have been greatly lightened by the appearance of the *Handbook of South American Indians* (Bulletin 143 of the Bureau of American Ethnology) under the general editorship of Julian Steward. Abandoning the encyclopaedic form and alphabetical order of the *Handbook of North American Indians* (Bulletin 30) it consists of a series of articles, with extensive bibliographies, each by an expert on his area, grouped under the headings Marginal Tribes (1946), Andean Civilizations (1946), Tropical Forest Tribes (1948), Circum-Caribbean Tribes (1948), Comparative Ethnology (1949). The sixth volume, published in 1950, deals comparatively with physical anthropology, linguistics, and cultural geography. The seventh (1959) provides a general index to the whole series. In the second volume, dealing with the area with which this section is concerned, Rowe's work on the Inca is especially noteworthy. The remainder of the section will be concerned with work published after the appearance of this volume.

Since Max Uhle published his discussion of the distribution of styles of pottery, sculpture, and textiles throughout the Peruvian area in 1903, much attention has been paid to 'horizon styles' and latterly to their synthesis into the 'Peruvian co-tradition' as defined by Wendell Bennett at a conference held in 1947. The results of this conference were published in a valuable series of papers under the title 'A Reappraisal of Peruvian Archaeology' (*M.S.A.A.*, 4, 1948). This volume gives a good idea of the situation at that time. Sufficient progress had then been made in correlating the various Andean cultures, coastal and highland, north, central and south, to make possible a fairly coherent picture, with the relative chronology reasonably well established. Though the time sequence has been elaborated in places, it has not been substantially altered. A chart setting out the generally accepted sequence of culture periods in Peru will be found in J. Alden Mason's useful book *The Ancient Civilizations of Peru* (1957). This shows that although the relative chronology is fairly satisfactory, that is not the case with the absolute chronology. Mason's chart gives two columns, one showing dates computed by the usual archaeological methods, the other using the few radiocarbon dates then available. Although other dates have since been worked out, much more work needs to be done before a satisfactory absolute chronology for the Andean region will emerge. A summary of the position as of 1961 is given by Bushnell in *Antiquity* (Vol. XXXV, 1961).

The appearance of Collier's *Cultural Chronology and Change as Reflected in the Ceramics of the Virú Valley, Peru* (1955) marked the completion of an important piece of work known as the Virú Valley project which had for its aim 'to make an intensive, co-operative study of human adaptation and culture growth in a single coastal valley over the total span of human occupancy' (Preface). Other volumes in the series were contributed by Ford and Willey (*A.P.A.M.N.H.*, 43, 1949), Wendell C. Bennett (*Y.U.P.A.*, 43, 1950), Strong and Evans (*C.S.A.E.*, 4, 1952); and Willey (*B.A.E. Bull.*, 155, 1953). Taken together, the volumes of this series are a valuable contribution to knowledge.

The publications mentioned so far have all been regional in scope. A few works dealing with special industries must be added.

Nuclear America has long been famous for the excellence and variety of its textiles, perhaps unsurpassed anywhere in the world both for beauty and for intricacy of weave. Their chief exponent has been Lila O'Neale, who continued until her death the work she began in 1930 in association with Kroeber. Her last book, *Textiles of Pre-Columbian Chihuahua*, was published posthumously in 1948 (*C.I.W.P.*, 574). Junius Bird has continued the tradition with his *Paracas Fabrics and Nazca Needlework* (1954).

In many places the art of weaving has continued without a break from the earliest known periods until the present, and fine textiles are still being produced with the same techniques and on the same type of loom as was used in pre-Columbian times. O'Neale's *Textiles of Highland Guatemala* (*C.I.W.P.*, 56, 1945) deals with some of this modern work. Her 'opposite number' in England, L. E. Start, published 'The McDougall Collection of Indian Textiles from Guatemala and Mexico' in the Pitt Rivers Museum series of *Occasional Papers on Technology* in 1948. As the title of the series indicates, it is written from a different angle and complements O'Neale's work without competing with it.

Turning to pottery, no list, however short, could omit Kroeber's series of papers (*U.C.P.A.A.E.*, 1924–27) on the collection brought back by Max Uhle from a number of Andean sites. For Central America, Lothrop's monographs on the pottery of Nicaragua and Costa Rica (*Contr. Mus. Am. Ind.*, 8, 1926) and of Coclé (*M.P.M.*, 7, No. 1, 1937) are the chief sources of information. In 1935 Osgood formulated a classification for Chiriqui pottery based on the earlier work of Holmes and MacCurdy (*Am. Anth.*, 37). Two general surveys may be mentioned, especially as they contain illustrations not generally available. In *Ancient American Pottery* (1955)—which also includes some pieces from the South-west—Bushnell and Digby draw upon the collections of the British Museum and the Cambridge University Museum of Archaeology and Ethnology. Bushnell in his book on Peru (1956) was fortunate in being able to illustrate some of the treasures in the private collection of

Señor Rafael Larco Hoyle. Although many modern tribes still make pottery, the tradition of fine craftsmanship does not seem to have survived as it did in weaving.

Problems of Origin of the Higher Civilizations of the New World

The question whether the higher civilizations of the New World were indigenous or whether they stemmed from, or at least were influenced by, the civilizations of the Old World (and if so, when and how much) has for a long time been one of the most hotly debated subjects in American archaeology, and there are champions of both sides prepared to defend their views with vehemence. The discovery of early simple cultures throughout the Americas, described in the section on early man, has destroyed the argument that because no early stages were known, the higher civilizations of America cannot have been indigenous but must have been imported from somewhere ready-made, a contention pushed to its uttermost limits in Gladwyn's preposterous, provocative, and amusing book *Men out of Asia* (1947), out-diffusing the diffusionists and deliberately designed to give orthodox anthropologists a heart attack.

An important part of this problem turns on the origin of agriculture —more correctly described as horticulture, since the plough was unknown in the New World until it was introduced by Europeans. A combination of plant genetics and radiocarbon dating is helping to solve this problem. It is now clear that not one but several centres of domestication are involved. The investigations of MacNeish and others have made it known that the first food plants to be cultivated were a species of squash (*Cucurbita pepo*) and one, or possibly two, species of bean (*Phaesolus* spp.), which may possibly go back as far as 7000–5500 B.C. and certainly as far as 4000–2300 B.C. (Crane and Griffin, *Science*, 127, p. 1105, 1958). These were found in caves at Ocampo, Tamaulipas, Mexico (Whitaker, Cutler, and MacNeish, *Am. Antiq.*, 22, 1957). Maize (*Zea mays*), once thought to be the first plant to be cultivated in the New World, has now been shown to be later than squash and beans, but it was certainly being grown in north-east Mexico by 2500 B.C. and perhaps earlier farther south. Radiocarbon dates suggesting a much earlier beginning have been worked out but need further checking. Maize, 'while not yet tracked down to its ultimate beginnings, probably was cultivated first in southern Mesoamerica; but either it spread early to Peru or the idea of cultivating wild corn spread there, for well back in the archaeological past the majority of races of Peruvian maize differ from those of Mexico or Central America, (Mangelsdorf, quoted by

Willey, *Am. Antiq.*, 27, 1961). The situation as at present known is summed up by Willey (p. 47) as follows:

The picture of the rise of Nuclear American farming which emerges ... is that of a pattern slowly forming through time. Experimentation with plants and an improvement of them, together with their diffusion and cross-diffusion within the Nuclear American zone, appears to have lasted from 7000 to 1500 B.C. in Mesoamerica and from at least 2000 to 1000 B.C. in Peru. This era of experimentation and dissemination—or stage of 'incipient agriculture'—was terminated by the attainment of the threshold of village agriculture. It may be that then, explosively, the new fully-formed subsistence pattern spread from some one center within Nuclear America; or perhaps there were several such centers responsible for the propagation of an 'established' agricultural way of life. This we do not know, and it remains a major next step in our learning about the origins of agriculture in native America.

It would seem from this that there is no need to look outside the New World for the origin of this very important concomitant of higher civilization. But for a statement of the opposite point of view see G. F. Carter's 'Plants across the Pacific' (in *M.S.A.A.*, 9, 1953).

A scholar who holds strong views on the question of Asiatic influence on the higher civilizations of America is Heine-Geldern, who presents arguments in favour of the diffusion of the knowledge of metal-working across the Pacific to Peru (*Paideuma*, 5, 1954) and stresses resemblances between Indian and Chinese art and architecture and that of certain sites in Mexico and Peru (1959; and with Ekholm, 1951).[1] Ekholm discusses a number of possible parallels in the symposium on *Transpacific Contacts* (ed. M. W. Smith, *M.S.A.A.*, 9, 1953). These and other ideas must be taken into consideration, but it may well be argued that many of the resemblances, some of them slight, may have quite other explanations.

That there was some contact across the Pacific at some time is, of course, practically certain on botanical evidence, but after careful consideration of all the available evidence, it seems likely that the majority of Americanists would agree that the case for the indigenous origin and development of the higher civilizations of Nuclear America still stands.

It will be noted that Maya civilization is unique in the world in that it arose and flourished in a lowland region of tropical forest. This question is discussed in two interesting papers, 'Cultural Ecology of Nuclear Mesoamerica' by William T. Sanders and 'An Agricultural Study of the Southern Maya Lowlands' by Ursula M. Cowgill (both in *Am.*

---

[1] Papers in *Actas del XXXIII Congreso Internacional de Americanistas*, Vol. I, San José, 1959. With G. F. Ekholm in *Selected Papers of the Twenty-ninth International Congress of Americanists, 1949*, Chicago, 1951.

Anth., 64, 1962). These authors give references to other works on the subject.

Lowland South America and the Caribbean

What was known on the archaeology of the tropical lowlands up to 1949 is summarized by Bennett in *Andean Culture History*. He there predicted that 'lowland archaeology will eventually be correlated with the Andean sequence'. The investigations of G. and A. Reichel-Dolmatoff in Colombia, Cruxent and Rouse in Venezuela, Meggers and Evans in Ecuador, and Lathrap in eastern Peru all point in that direction. The question is discussed by Irving Rouse in *American Antiquity*, 1961 (pp. 56–62), where bibliographical references to all this work will be found.

The most important event in the history of Caribbean anthropological research was the launching in 1933 of the Yale Peabody Museum Caribbean Anthropological Program, which has since sponsored by far the major part of the work done in the area. It was due to the initiative and enthusiasm of Cornelius Osgood, who has contributed important papers, and to whom a volume marking the twenty-fifth anniversary of the program is dedicated (edited by S. Mintz, *Y.U.P.A.*, 57–64, 1960). One of its principal supporters and contributors is Irving Rouse, who was the first to formulate a chronology for the area (*Y.U.P.A.*, 21, 1939) and who has been responsible for a large number of the publications listed in the anniversary volume. His paper 'Archaeology in Lowland South America and the Caribbean' (*Am. Antiq.* 27, 1961) provides a survey of the state of our knowledge up to 1960. The islands seem to have been peopled from South America, chiefly from Venezuela, and their role as a route into the south-eastern area of North America seems to have been negligible.

The present-day Indians are particularly well served by the Handbook of South American Indians (J. H. Steward, B.A.E. Bull 143 1946–59), to which the reader is referred. A less highly specialized, well-illustrated account, ranging in space over the whole of South America and in time from the earliest prehistory to the present day, largely based on the material in the 'Handbook', is presented by Steward and Faron under the title *Native Peoples of South America* (1959). Since then, a number of anthropologists have worked in the field. Among these may be mentioned A. Leeds with the Yaruro, Becher with the Suràra and the Pakidai, N. Fock and J. Yde with the Waiwai, O. Zerries and H. Schuster with the Waica-Guaharibo-Shirianá, A. J. Butt with the Akawaio and neighbouring tribes, and D. Maybury-Lewis with the Shavante and the

Serente. All these have so far published only scattered papers, but their full reports, when they appear, should add very considerably to our knowledge of these Indians. Intensive work has been carried out in Venezuela on the Warrau, which has resulted in the publication of *Los Guarao del Delta Amacuro* in 1956 and of *A Warrau Dictionary* in 1957 by Basilio Ma de Barral.

STUDIES OF SPECIAL SUBJECTS

There remains to be considered work which has been done on subjects rather than on areas, and so has been omitted from the foregoing sections.

Linguistics

Following the lead given by J. W. Powell (see p. 92), it is not surprising that the study of languages has always claimed a large share of the interest of Americanists. A glance through the titles of the volumes published by the Bureau of American Ethnology is clear evidence of this. As so often, a leading part was played by Boas, who edited and contributed to the *Handbook of Indian Languages* (Part 1, 1911; Part 2, 1922), which he described as 'an attempt to prepare a revised edition of Major J. W. Powell's "Introduction to the Study of Indian Languages" . . .' From the 1880's onwards, hardly a year passed without some contribution on language coming from his pen (see *Bibliography* by H. A. Andrews and others, *M.A.A.A.*, 61, 1943). Most of those who have worked in this field since have been his pupils, either directly or at one remove. Their names are too numerous to mention, but the shortest list must include those of Kroeber and Sapir.

Most of Kroeber's linguistic work, chiefly but not exclusively on the Indians of California, was published in the University of California *Publications in American Archaeology and Ethnology*. Some of it was done in collaboration with R. B. Dixon. An appraisal of his contribution by D. H. Hyme appeared in the periodical *Language* (1961). Sapir's main interests were in linguistic change and in tracing hitherto unrecognized relationships between languages so that the number of distinct linguistic stocks might be reduced. His work on Southern Paiute, the first intensive study of a Shoshonean language, proved conclusively the validity of linking it with Nahuatl in the Uto-Aztecan stock[1] that on the Athabascans led to the formulation of the Na-Dene group and to the recognition of the true position of Navaho (*Am. Anth.*, 38,

[1] *Journal Soc. des Americanistes de Paris*, X, 1913, XI, 1915; *Proc. Amer. Acad. of Arts and Sciences*, 65, 1930.

1936). His work ranged far beyond the bounds of linguistics (see p. 237), but his *Nootka Texts*, published posthumously in 1939 by the Linguistic Society of America, showed that his early interest had persisted. He also collected songs from the Nootka in the course of his work on the Northwest coast in 1910 and 1913–14. These were published, with some later additions, by Helen H. Roberts and Morris Swadesh in 1955 (*Trans. Am. Phil. Soc.*, 45). His influence remains potent in the work of his students; witness the important papers published in a memorial volume, *Language, Culture and Personality* (edited by L. Spier, A. I. Hallowell and S. S. Newman, 1941), and in *Linguistic Structures of Native America* by H. Hoijer and others (*V.F.P.A.*, 6, 1946).

Sapir was also the begetter of one of the latest developments in the study of languages, the technique variously known as glottochronology and lexicostatistics. This is based on his generalization that 'the greater the degree of linguistic differentiation within a stock, the greater is the period of time that must be assumed for the development of such differentiation'. Morris Swadesh and others, developing this idea, worked out a comparative technique based on the assumption of a constant rate of change in basic vocabulary. It is explained by R. B. Lees in *Language* (1953). Arguments for and against it will be found in *Current Anthropology* for January, 1960, and April, 1962, with extensive references on the subject. Like so many other tests, it seems to work on material similar to that on which it has been standardized, but, like them, its usefulness and reliability on quite different material are not yet established.

How much still remains to be done in the field of American Indian linguistics was brought out in the papers given at a symposium held in 1951 and published in the University of California *Publications in Linguistics*, No. 10, 1954. Rowe, in his paper on problems of linguistic classification in South America, summed up the situation as regards that continent by saying, 'We know less about more languages in South America than about any other continental area.'

So far as the present writer has been able to ascertain, no valid relationship has yet been established between any American Indian language and any linguistic stock in the Old World.

Art

In accordance with a trend not confined to America, there has been an upsurge of interest in aboriginal art. Impetus was given to it by the excellent Indian section of the Golden Gate International Exposition held in San Francisco in 1939, for which F. H. Douglas and René d'Harnoncourt were largely responsible. Their book *Indian Art of the United States* (1941), together with Vaillant's *Indian Arts in North America* (1939), spread this interest widely. Their example has been followed at intervals by H. U. Doering's *The Art of Ancient Peru* (1952), Groth-Kimball and Feuchtwanger's *The Art of Ancient Mexico* (1954), and Wendell C. Bennett's *Ancient Arts of the Andes* (1954), all consisting mainly of excellent illustrations with a minimum of comment.

An interesting special study with considerable ethnological significance is the work of F. G. Speck on designs in birch-bark[1]

The two sumptuous volumes by Pál Kelemen, *Medieval American Art* (1943), provide a treasury of illustrations, with comments, of the finest examples of pre-Columbian architecture, sculpture, pottery, weaving, metal-work, the carving of precious and semi-precious stones, and paintings, both mural and manuscript, ranging from the South-west to the Andes. Anthropological interpretation is not attempted; the work is, to quote from a review by Vaillant, 'a straight appraisal of Indian art in terms of western culture'. A new edition, in one volume, appeared in 1957, with the addition of a number of important discoveries made since 1943.

Miguel Covarrubias, who combined in himself the skill and knowledge of the practising artist with those of the ethnologist, contributed two books on Mesoamerican art: *The Eagle, the Jaguar and the Serpent* (1954) and *Indian Art of Mexico and Central America* (1957). In the former volume he offers a survey of North American Indian art forms, and sets out his theories on the debt of American Indian art to Asia.

Museums have now begun to treat Indian art as art as well as ethnology. For this we have to thank in great measure the acumen of Robert Woods Bliss, connoisseur and collector, who began in 1912 to buy, as opportunity offered, objects which appealed to him from Mexico, Central America, and Peru. In 1947 he offered the collection, by then of large size, on loan to the National Gallery of Art, Washington, where it was placed on exhibition as 'an interesting experiment'—and where it still remains on exhibition, but no longer as an experiment. In 1957 a catalogue with articles by specialists was published which, aided by the progress made of late years in the technicalities of colour printing, must be the most magnificent volume of its kind ever issued: *Pre-Columbian Art: The Robert Woods Bliss Collection* (Lothrop, Fosberg, and Mahler, 1957).

[1] 'Montagnais Art in Birchbark, a circumpolar trait,' *Indian Notes and Monographs*, 11, No. 2. Mus. of the Am. Indian, Heye Foundation, New York; 'Art Processes of the River Desert Algonquin', *B.A.E. Anthrop. Papers*, 17, *Bull.*, 128, 1941.

The name of Samuel Kirkland Lothrop is also associated with a very stimulating volume of essays entitled *Pre-Columbian Art and Archaeology* (1961), in which a number of eminent specialists discuss points of interest arising out of their own researches ranging from Mexico to Patagonia.

A short but significant summary of the art of South American Indians, past and present, by A. L. Kroeber appears in the fifth volume of the *Handbook of South American Indians*.

In recent years, consequent upon the influx of non-Indian artists into the South-west, the Indians have themselves taken to painting pictures, a departure from their own tradition which looks upon painting as essentially a medium for decoration. They have evolved a distinctive style, a hybrid between the traditional art styles and modern sophisticated art, but a hybrid sufficiently well bred to attain a distinction of its own. It has been described by C. L. Tanner.[1] Modern Mexican art, in the hands of masters such as Miguel Covarrubias, Diego Rivera, and others, is beyond the scope of this review.

In this connexion may be mentioned the renewal of interest in the study of petroglyphs, which are found in many areas, both incised and painted. A general survey will be found in Steward's 'Petroglyphs of the United States' (*A. R. Smiths Inst.*, 1937). Other studies include that by Gebhard and Cahn in Wyoming (1950) and by Agnes C. Sims in New Mexico (*San Cristobal Petroglyphs*, 1950). For South America there is a summary with bibliography by Irving Rouse in Vol. V of the *Handbook*.

Music

All students of American Indian music must acknowledge their great debt to Frances Densmore, who has done more than anyone else to advance our knowledge of the subject. Her first published work was on Chippewa music in 1910; the latest known to the present writer is 'Music of Acoma, Isleta, Cochiti and Zuñi' (*B.A.E. Bull.*, 165, 1957). A list of the many volumes published between these dates will be found in its bibliography. She always considers music in its setting, so that each volume is in effect an ethnographic study of the people dealt with. Apart from these numerous special studies she has published a general work, *American Indians and Their Music* (1926).

Another scholar to contribute to our knowledge of Indian music is George Herzog, who read a paper on 'Musical Styles in North America' at the Twenty-third International Congress of Americanists in 1928.

[1] *Southwest Indian Painting*, Tucson, 1957; 'The Influence of the White Man on Southwest Indian Art', *Ethnohistory*, 7, Bloomington, Ind., 1960.

He followed this with 'The Yuman Musical Style' (*J. Am. Folklore*, 41, 1928), 'A Comparison of Pueblo and Pima Musical Style' (*ibid.*, 49, 1936), 'Special Song Types in North American Indian Music' (*Z.f.v.M.*, 3, 1935), 'Plains Ghost Dance and Great Basin Music' (*Am. Anth.*, 37, 1935), and 'Salish Music' (in *Indians of the Urban Northwest*, ed. by M. W. Smith, 1949).

The special music associated with the peyote cult has already been mentioned (p. 325). David McAllester has also published a study of social and esthetic values as seen in Navaho music (*P.P.M.*, 41, 1954).

There is now available a large corpus of recorded and annotated music from a number of tribes throughout the Americas. The foundations for a synthetic and analytical study were laid by Helen H. Roberts, whose initial training was that of a musician, in her 'Melodic Composition and Scale Foundation in Primitive Music' (*Am. Anth.*, 34, 1932), 'Form in Primitive Music' (1933), and 'Musical Areas in Aboriginal North America' (*Y.U.P.A.*, 12, 1936). It is a major loss to anthropology that circumstances have prevented her from doing further work along these lines.

For a study of culture changes in music we go back once more to Frances Densmore, whose paper 'Traces of Foreign Influence in the Music of the American Indians' (*Am. Anth.*, 46, 1944) is the first of its kind known to the present writer. A later paper on the same subject by Willard Rhodes, *Acculturation in North American Indian Music*, is one of the series of papers on acculturation edited by Sol Tax.[1]

Metal-working

In pre-Columbian times true metallurgy occurs only in Nuclear America, but in many other areas metal, generally copper, was accessible in a natural state which could be worked cold, i.e. treated as if it were stone. This technique gradually spread over the eastern half of North America, but did not reach Mexico. A good account of it is given by Rickard (*J.R.A.I.*, lxiv, 1934). Copper was worked in the Great Lakes region at least 3,500 years ago by radiocarbon dating; this appears to be 'the only case in the entire world where the use of metal preceded the use of pottery' (Lothrop in *Pre-Columbian Art*, p. 63). Some Indian and some Eskimo groups also made use of natural iron (Rickard, *J.R.A.I.*, lxxi, 1941).

The first metal of which we have evidence in Nuclear America is gold, and the earliest technique, so far as is known, was the hammering

---

[1] *Acculturation in the Americas.* Selected papers of the Twenty-ninth International Congress of Americanists. Chicago University Press, 1952.

of gold into thin sheets which were then cut into various shapes and embossed, or joined by a process entailing the use of heat. Ornaments made in this way were found by Tello (*Am. Anth.*, 9, 1943) associated with the Chavin horizon, dated during the last few centuries B.C. Other metals worked in pre-Columbian times were silver, copper, tin, lead, and, surprisingly, platinum (Bergsøe, 1937[1]) with several alloys including bronze, perhaps first made in the region of Lake Titicaca about A.D. 1000, and a gold-copper alloy known as tumbaga which was invented in Colombia and spread from there. Iron was unknown.

There appear to have been two centres of development, one in Colombia, extending northwards through Panama into Costa Rica (Root, in *Pre-Columbian Art and Archaeology*, 1961) and one in southern Peru. The variety of highly skilled techniques known to the ancient Peruvians and Colombians (they differ slightly in the two regions) is amazing. An account of them, with a good bibliography, by W. C. Root, can be found in the article 'Metallurgy' in Vol. V of the *Handbook of South American Indians*. The same author's paper 'The Metallurgy of the Southern Coast of Peru' (*Am. Antiq.*, 15, 1949) gives a number of metallurgical analyses.

There seems to be general agreement that metal-working was not an independent development in Mexico but came from the southern centres, but there are differences of opinion about the route by which it travelled. Willey (*Am. Anth.*, 57, 1955, p. 584) endorses the theory put forward by Rivet in 1946 that it was the result of direct sea trade with Peru or Ecuador; Lothrop, in his monograph on the metal objects dredged from the *cenote* of sacrifice at Chichén Itzá (*M.P.M.*, 10, No. 2, 1952), which he takes as an opportunity for a survey of metal-working throughout Mesoamerica, gives evidence for thinking that a route via Panama is more likely. In any case, there is no evidence that metal was worked in Mexico before the end of the ninth century A.D., although trade objects are not uncommon earlier. Easby, in a paper contributed to *Pre-Columbian Art and Archaeology*, has the final word: 'When and where metal-working began in the New World, how it developed and the extent to which metals were extracted from ores must still be viewed as an open question. There is plenty of debate but very little of what, as a lawyer, I could call evidence.'

In parts of the Andean area and in Mexico, the practice of metal-working has continued, like that of weaving, without a break until the present day. Silver and copper ornaments are now the principal prod-

---

[1] 'The Metallurgy and Technology of Gold and Platinum among the Pre-Columbian Indians.' *Ingeniervidenskabelige Skrifter*, 44, Copenhagen, 1937.

ucts, and are sold commercially. Anderson's *The Art of the Silversmith in Mexico, 1519–1936* (published in 1941) may be consulted on this subject.

The art was never part of the ancient culture of the South-west. It is now flourishing there, but as a new development learnt from the white man, probably not earlier than the beginning of the nineteenth century when the Navaho and Pueblo Indians learnt from the Mexicans how to make the silver ornaments which are now so characteristic of both groups. The history, present position, and possible future of this art are discussed in *The Navajo and Pueblo Silversmiths* by John Adair (1946).

As a corollary to this review of metal-working there may be mentioned a very useful summary of what is known of the mining and use of gems and ornamental stones by American Indians, written by S. H. Ball (*B.A.E. Bull.*, 128, 1941), which includes an extensive and interesting bibliography.

CONCLUSION

The criticism has been levelled at Americanist studies that they tend to be carried on in water-tight compartments, and that workers in one part of the field take too little account of what those in other parts are doing, and do not seek for points of contact. It will have become apparent from the preceding pages that this criticism is now less valid, and that overall pictures of larger areas are becoming possible. At the same time, the treatment of Americanist studies in a separate section of this book, and its mainly regional arrangement, still seem best to fit the present state of our knowledge. It may be, as suggested in 1946 by J. M. Cooper at the close of his brilliant contribution to the symposium *Man in Northeastern North America*,[1] that in the future 'the study of any single culture in North America must reckon also with South America, and that Pan-America viewed as a cultural unit must reckon both with Asia and with world culture as a whole'. That time is not yet, but the work of the last sixteen years has brought it appreciably nearer.

V. GENERAL ETHNOLOGY AND SOCIAL ANTHROPOLOGY

So far, we have been describing the development of studies of cultures, past and present, and of their elements, and also of races and individuals now, and in the past, implying that ethnology and prehistory are a part of the same subject, the one dealing with peoples and their cultures now, and the other with origins of peoples and of cultures,

[1] Edited by F. Johnson, *P.P.F.A.*, Vol. 3, 1946.

and their development in early times. It is possible, by using both the records of ethnology and of prehistory, to show many examples of the origin, development, diffusion, and geographical variation of the elements of culture, especially of material culture, and sometimes it is even possible with the help of objects to discover the broad facts of social organization, religion, law, economics, and the like. We are on safe ground in dealing with many of the artefacts of material culture. For example, we can proceed experimentally with subjects like metallurgy and music or stone implements, and discover exactly what we want to know as far as the evidence available will allow us. We can then make comparative and analytic studies in a scientific manner, and not worry ourselves about the social setting of these artefacts, when it is irrelevant. But when we come to other elements of culture, such as social, religious, legal, or economic customs, whether partly expressed in the use of objects or not, we are not on the same safe ground, whether we gather our evidence archaeologically or ethnologically, that is from an ancient or a modern people. Even when we have historical records, there is a difference in the two classes of elements. A musical instrument or a copper axe can be studied outside its social context, and what happens in one area can be compared with that of another. But the capital difficulty in dealing with social, religious, legal, or economic customs is that they must be considered in their whole context, since often it appears that two customs or more which may seem identical when abstracted from their context appear to have quite different origins and purposes when studied as a part of their whole cultural setting. This business of studying *social customs* in a comparative and analytic way has always been a main difficulty in ethnology, as opposed to ethnography, which confines itself to the study of individual cultures and peoples.

It is, of course, social anthropology which devotes itself to a study of social organization, religion, law, economics, and the like, usually, though not always, among the simpler and smaller and more self-contained societies which can be directly observed as wholes, and which are so different from our own that it is comparatively easy to study them objectively. These studies are first made ethnographically of the whole society before the social anthropologist can deal with any feature of it intensively, such as the legal system. In this way, to my mind, the social anthropologist differs from the sociologist, who usually studies particular problems in civilized societies, often with a formidable array of statistics. Thus, in *African Political Systems*, edited by M. Fortes and E. E. Evans-Pritchard, the reader can observe the societies described by the various social anthropologists as wholes, and the part of the political system in them, and abstract principles which may be compared, while a sociological work on any problem such as the incidence of crime, strikes, or divorce does not give a whole view of the society or societies from which the evidence is collected. Moreover, the work of the sociologist is often undertaken with a view to social planning, while that of the social anthropologist is generally not concerned with such matters.

There are many different views about the best methods to use in investigating societies, all sincerely held by eminent social anthropologists, and divergences have become especially marked. The most notable differences of approach are broadly those between the Old and the New World. Four very valuable recent studies of the problems and methods involved are R. H. Lowie's *The History of Ethnological Theory* (1937), A. L. Kroeber's *Anthropology* (1949), E. E. Evans-Pritchard's *Social Anthropology* (1951), and a chapter by Meyer Fortes entitled 'Social Anthropology' in *The Development of Scientific Thought in the Twentieth Century* (1951), edited by A. E. Heath.

The work of American social anthropologists was summarized up to 1946 in a paper by Betty J. Meggers in the *American Anthropologist* (Vol. 48, No. 2, 1946, pp. 176-214), on 'Recent Trends in American Ethnology,' already quoted (p. 324) by Beatrice Blackwood. In a long bibliography, the author gave all of the outstanding work of recent years in America. 178 titles are devoted to psychological studies of societies or individuals, 49 to acculturation or culture contact, 22 to community studies, and 111 to distribution of culture-elements, culture areas, religion, law, social organization, and other such subjects, as well as to studies of the sociology of war and peace. These tendencies, in varying degrees, appear to continue.

It is quite natural that a great number of works should be devoted to psychological studies. From about 1930, the idea became current in America that to explain culture, you must have psychological studies of men, who are the creators of culture.

From 1936, when R. Redfield, R. Linton, and M. J. Herskovits published 'A Memorandum for the study of Acculturation' in the *American Anthropologist* (Vol. 38, pp. 149-52), a considerable number of books and papers have appeared on the subject of the contact of cultures, which is understandable in a country where thoughtful men live so close to so great a number of races and peoples. These works are generally descriptions of a society in its present stage of adjustment, with an attempt to separate the items introduced from those that are indigenous. Some writers state that the ultimate aim is to make generalizations about culture change, and also admit that such generalizations are not easy to achieve.

An interesting development of the last few years has been the study of European or American communities by the same methods that would be used in the investigation of the Trobriands or the Galla. Some of these studies, like those of C. M. Arensberg on *The Irish Countryman*, published in London in 1937, and Julian Pitt Rivers on *The People of the Sierra*, London, 1954, are good ethnological field-work; others are more sociological and statistical. Most, though not all of them, are self-contained, and it is not always possible to abstract material from one which can be compared with another so as to arrive at generalizations.

The idea of the culture area, so ably presented for the first time by the late Clark Wissler, and further developed by A. L. Kroeber in 'Cultural and Natural Areas of Native North America' (Berkeley, California, 1939), and *Configurations of Culture Growth* (1944), has proved especially useful in a country where the archaeological and ethnological run into each other in some areas, and is especially valuable for the classification of a vast amount of material which would otherwise be chaotic and incoherent. One has the feeling, however, that there is a difficulty in some of the culture-element distributions which are so often done in America. One can extract cooking pots and fishing tackle more easily than a religious or social custom, and be on safer ground in coming to general conclusions.

Betty Meggers ultimately decided that 'psychology has already claimed man, and sociology has cast its lot for society', and that 'if anthropology is to become an independent and self-consistent science, it must concede these fields and devote itself to the one as yet relatively untended—culture'.

It has been noted that the article was entitled 'Recent Trends in American Ethnology', and it is clear that the greater number of works cited are on subjects generally treated by social anthropology. Again, there is a very large number of psychological studies, both of individuals and of groups, their aim being to interpret culture. There is an insistence on culture and culture-elements, and finally there is a desire to abstract elements which can be compared with other elements, so as to arrive at generalizations.

All of these methods have in view the explanation of culture or cultures, and it has been said that 'there are twelve gates to Jerusalem, and all lead to the temple'. Before making any comment on any of these gates or roads, it may be as well to put down the very different development of social anthropology in the Old World.

During the time that has elapsed since the first edition of this book, the influence of Émile Durkheim[1] and of his pupils has greatly increased in England and in the Dominions, mainly through the earlier work of Malinowski and the later work of Radcliffe-Brown. As Evans-Pritchard said in his B.B.C. lectures on social anthropology:[2] 'All of us now teaching the subject in England and in the Dominions are directly or indirectly, for the most part directly, their pupils.' I am greatly indebted to him for allowing me to see these valuable lectures while they were still in typescript, and consider their publication to be a most important contribution to the history, theory, and aims of the subject.

It may be as well to summarize Durkheim's general principles very generally, as my earlier account in this book may not make clear his influence on present workers. Durkheim maintained that social facts cannot be explained in terms of individual psychology, because such facts exist outside and apart from those individual minds. Evans-Pritchard chooses a language as an example, which exists before an individual is born into the society which speaks it, and will exist after he is dead, the individual merely learning to speak it as his ancestors did and descendants will. The language is a social fact which can only be understood in relation to other facts of the same order, that is, as part of a social system, and in terms of its functions in maintaining the system.

Social facts such as language, customs, morals, legal and political institutions form a more or less stable structure which lasts in essentials for many generations, the individual from birth to death passing through the structure which is in being when he arrives and goes on after he has gone, for the system is not psychic but social, with a collective consciousness different in kind from individual consciousness. In the main, the structure of social facts is compulsory, and the individual who does not conform has to meet disapproval or penalties. By 'collective consciousness' Durkheim does not mean 'collective mind'. His 'collective representations' refer to the common body of values, beliefs, and customs which individuals accept and transmit. In connexion with Durkheim's analyses of social activities, we must also remember Lucien Lévy-Bruhl's analyses of the ideas associated with these activities in such books as *Les fonctions mentales dans les sociétés inférieures* (1910), and *La mentalité primitive* (1912).

---

[1] *De la division du travail social: Étude sur l'organisation des sociétés supérieures*, 1893; *Les régles de la méthode sociologique*, 1895; *Les formes élémentaires de la vie réligieuse*, 1912; *Le système totémique en Australie*, 1912. See also his work in *L'Année Sociologique* from 1898, and articles by Hulbert and Mauss.

[2] Published as follows: E. E. Evans-Pritchard, *Social Anthropology*, Cohen and West, London, 1951.

The work of Durkheim had a profound effect on the field work of Bronislaw Malinowksi, the first anthropologist, so far as I know, to live as a native among natives for months on end, taking part in work and play and conversing with them in their own language, so that he was able to analyse their social structure and the ideas associated with it.[1]

While the functional method was implicit in Malinowski's field work and teaching, it became explicit in the teaching of A. R. Radcliffe-Brown from about 1935,[2] at any rate in England. Basing the concept of function as applied to human societies on an analogy between social life and organic life, he defined the function of a social institution as the contribution which it as a partial activity makes to the total activity of which it is part. Social institutions are thus considered as functioning with a social structure made up of individuals 'connected by a definite set of social relations into an integrated whole', and the social life of a community is the functioning of its structure. In another place, speaking of social integration, he states that 'the function of culture as a whole is to unite individual human beings into more or less stable social structures, i.e., stable systems of groups determining and relating the regulations of those individuals to one another, and providing such external adaptation to the physical environment, and such internal adaptation between the component individuals or groups, as to make possible an ordered social life.' That assumption (he says) 'I believe to be a sort of primary postulate of any objective and scientific study of culture or of human society.'[3]

As the social anthropologist who follows Durkheim, Malinowski, and Radcliffe-Brown studies social structures, and the social institutions which are part of them, it follows that such workers must study these structures as wholes in the field and in the language of the people being studied, and observe the place of the institutions within the structures. Failing this, they must depend on the work of others who have used their method. For it would appear that they are dealing with societies rather than with cultures, and the relations between members of a society and between social groups, rather than with the body of customs which represents the culture of a society. We have already noted the difficulty of the ethnologists in comparing customs whose similarity may well be deceptive (p. 362), since the same function in any two given societies

[1] See 'The Natives of Mailu,' *Trans. Royal Soc. S. Australia*, Vol. XXXIX, 1915, and *Argonauts of the Western Pacific*, London, 1922.

[2] 'On the Concept of Function in Social Science,' *American Anthropologist*, 1935, pp. 394-97.

[3] 'The Present Position of Anthropological Studies,' Presidential Address, *British Association for the Advancement of Science*, Section H, 1931, p. 13.

may be represented by two quite different customs, or two tribes or peoples may have two quite different cultures, and have basically the same social structures.

It is evident then, that the social anthropologist of this school must go farther than describing the culture of a society, and make abstractions from it in the light of the problems which he wishes to investigate. Speaking of the work of the social anthropologist, Evans-Pritchard says:[1]

If these are problems of social structure, he pays chief attention to the social relationships of the persons concerned in the whole procedure rather than the details of its cultural expression. This methodological distinction is most evident when comparative studies are undertaken, for to attempt both kinds of interpretation at the same time is almost certain to lead to confusion. In comparative studies what one compares are not things in themselves, but certain particular characteristics of them.

He takes as an example an interpretation of ancestor worship which is consistent with family or kinship structure, and explains: 'If one wishes to make a sociological comparison of ancestor cults in a number of different societies, what one compares are sets of structural relations between persons. One necessarily starts, therefore, by abstracting these relations in each society from their particular modes of cultural expression. Otherwise one will not be able to make the comparison.'

Radcliffe-Brown would consider the collection of the evidence in the field, the abstractions from it, and the comparison of the abstractions as a scientific process, while Evans-Pritchard has argued that such work is a historical procedure. In his Marett Lecture for 1950 on 'Social Anthropology: Past and Present' (*Man*, 1950, No. **198**), he contends that when the social anthropologist has lived among a people, speaking their language, thinking in their concepts, and feeling in their values, and translated all this into terms of his own culture, he has done what the historian does, the difference being that he has made a direct study of social life while the historian has made an indirect study through documents and other surviving evidence. Moreover, when the social anthropologist goes a step farther, and tried by analysis 'to disclose the latent underlying form of a society or culture,' he is 'studying the same things in the same way and . . . reaching out for the same kind of understanding of them' as Fustel de Coulanges, Vinogradoff, or Maitland. Finally, when the social anthropologist compares the social structures his analysis has revealed in a number of societies, he is still working as a philosophical historian. 'In some historical writers comparison and

[1] *Social Anthropology*, London. 1951.

367

classification are quite explicit; always they are implicit, for history cannot be written except against a standard of some kind, by comparison with the culture of a different time or people, if only with the writer's own.'

The former attitude displays the difficulty of basing the concept of function as applied to human societies on an analogy between social and organic life, with the assumption that social systems are natural systems which can be reduced to sociological laws, and that the history of these systems has no scientific relevance. It appears to me to be dangerous to argue from analogies, that is, to say that something resembles something else and that we can therefore postulate of the something what we can postulate of the something else. Strictly, I suppose, an analogy is a resemblance of form or function between things essentially different, and I find it difficult to believe that because there may be some resemblances of form or function between society and an organism that we can therefore pursue the same methods of study for both, and arrive at the same sort of conclusions. The fact, too, that no laws of sociology comparable with laws of the natural sciences have been discovered, leads some functionalists to seek a new orientation. Again, now that social anthropologists are beginning to study societies belonging to historical cultures, they recognize that 'the past is contained in the present as the present is in the future',[1] and a good example of such a study is Evans-Pritchard's own social history, *The Sanusi of Cyrenaica* (Oxford, 1949).

If we leave out the analogy altogether, forgetting the organism and concentrating on society, we have a reasonable working hypothesis of a social structure connected by a definite set of social relations into an integrated whole. It would appear that the abstraction of sets of social relations out of masses of concrete customs, and then the comparison of such abstractions from various societies, was a scientific process, and that historians who use such methods were working in a scientific manner. As one who has worked both in natural science and the humanities, I have seen that scientific methods have been used in the study of the humanities, and believe that, in the study of mankind, we must often be crossing the boundaries, and not confine ourselves rigidly within a particular method.

For this reason, I have considerable sympathy with all the methods of social anthropology. The particular interest of the investigator may require a psychological approach, or he may wish to examine the impact of one culture on another, or examine the interaction of various social activities in a community, or discover the function of particular in-

[1] E. E. Evans-Pritchard, *Social Anthropology*, 1951.

stitutions in a community. All such interpretations result in valuable ethnological books or papers and, from whatever view they are written, they throw light on some aspect of the many that one must consider in the study of humanity, and are one more piece of evidence that helps to show that people do not live in their own peculiar way in order to annoy us, but because they have very good reason to do so. All add to our sympathetic interest in and knowledge of each other.

The business of discovering general laws on a big scale need not worry us unduly. Already social anthropology has a considerable body of theory. Apart from overt similarities between primitive societies all over the world, these societies can to some considerable extent be classified by such structural analysis as we have mentioned into a limited number of types, so that it is possible to prepare a student to investigate societies in any part of the world.

We have already mentioned ethnological studies and ethnographical studies relating to human biology and to material culture, and it remains to mention some which deal mainly with social, religious, economic, political, and such-like subjects.

Apart from Evans-Pritchard's *Social Anthropology*, already discussed, other notable recent works on social anthropology are his *Nuer Religion*, 1956; *Les structures élémentaires de la parenté*, 1949, by Claude Lévi-Strauss; Rodney Needham's *Structure and Sentiment*, 1962; Lloyd A. Fallers on *Bantu Bureaucracy*, 1956; J. Middleton's *Lugbara Religion*, 1960; Godfrey Lienhardt's *Divinity and Experience*, 1961; E. R. Leach's *Political Systems of Highland Burma*, 1954; Audrey Richards (editor), *East African Chiefs*, 1960; Louis Dumont's *Une sous-caste de l'Inde de Sud*, 1957; John Middleton (editor), *Tribes without Rulers*, 1958; and Max Gluckman's *The Judicial Process among the Barotse of Southern Rhodesia*, 1955.

There has been a general interest among social anthropologists and ethnologists in economics. That old stand-by, Daryll Forde's *Habitat, Economy, and Society*, goes into edition after edition as the first book generally recommended to those who begin the study of anthropology. His 'Land and Labour in a Cross River Village,' *Geographical Journal*, 1937, and with R. Scott, *The Native Economies of Nigeria*, 1946, can be recommended. Others are: A. I. Richards, *Land, Labour, and Diet in Northern Rhodesia*, International Institute of African Languages and Cultures (now the International African Institute), 1939; R. W. Firth, *Primitive Polynesian Economy*, 1939, and *Malay Fishermen: Their Peasant Economy*, 1946; Rosemary Firth, 'Housekeeping among the Malay Peasants,' London School of Economics Monographs on Social

Anthropology, No. 7, 1943; M. J. Herskovits, *The Economic Life of Primitive Peoples*, including an extensive bibliography, 1940; W. Watson, *Tribal Cohesion in a Money Economy* (Mambwe of Northern Rhodesia), 1958; F. G. Bailey, *Caste and the Economic Frontier*, 1957; J. C. van Leur, *Indonesian Trade and Society*, 1955; D. F. Thomson, *Economic Structure and the Ceremonial Exchange Cycle in Arnhem Land*, 1949; and *Viehzucht und Hirtenleben in Ostmittel Europa*, edited by L. Foldes with M. Belenyesy and B. Gunda for the Hungarian Academy of Sciences, 1961.

For works on African ethnology and ethnography, the reader should above all consult the ethnographic surveys of the International African Institute, London and Paris, since 1950, edited by C. Daryll Forde, as well as the lists of publications issued by the Institute from Fetter Lane in London. There are also the journals *Africa*, London, 1928–, and *African Affairs*, formerly the *Journal of the Royal African Society;* and before that the *Journal of the African Society*, 1901–. A few books may be mentioned: E. E. Evans-Pritchard, *Witchcraft, Oracles, and Magic among the Azande*, 1937, and *The Nuer*, 1940; Meyer Fortes, *Marriage Law among the Tallensi*, 1937; *The Dynamics of Clanship among the Tallensi* (International Institute of African Languages and Cultures, later International African Institute), 1945, and *The Web of Kinship among the Tallensi*, 1949; John Beattie, *Bunyoro: An African Kingdom*, 1960; Colin Turnbull, *The Forest People* (Pygmies), 1961; and numerous publications by I. Schapera, including *The Bantu-speaking Tribes of South Africa* (1937), *Select Bibliography of South African Native Life and Problems* (1941), *A Handbook of Tswana Law and Custom* (1938), *Native Land Tenure in the Bechuanaland Protectorate* (1943), *Tribal Legislation among the Tswana of the Bechuanaland Protectorate*, (1943), and *Migrant Labour and Tribal Life in the Bechuanaland Protectorate* (1947).

Two valuable periodicals for the ethnologist are *Man in India*, 1921; and the *Journal of the Malayan Branch of the Royal Asiatic Society*, 1923–. A few of the fairly recent books on Asiatic peoples are: A. Aiyappan and L. K. Bula Ratnam, *Society in India*, 1956; Frederick Barth, *Political Leadership among Swat Pathans*, 1959; Ursula Graham Bower, *Naga Path*, 1950; G. Coedès, *Les États Hindouises d'Indochine et d'Indonesie*, 1948; Judith Djamour, *Malay Kinship and Marriage in Singapore*, 1959; E. H. Dobby, *South-east Asia*, 1950; E. S. Drower, *The Mandaeans of Iraq and Iran*, Oxford, 1937, and *Water into Wine*, 1956; Thomas Fitzsimmonds, *Cambodia*, 1957; Maurice Freedman, *Chinese Family and Marriage in Singapore*, 1957, and *Lineage Organiza-*

tion in South-eastern China, 1958; Hsiao-Tung Fei, *Peasant Life in China*, London, 1939; I. H. N. Evans, *Negritos of Malaya*, 1937; J. M. Gullick, *Indigenous Political Systems of Western Malaya*, 1958; D. G. E. Hall, *A History of South-east Asia*, 1955; A. M. Hocart, *Caste*, 1950; Verrier Elwin, *The Baiga* (1939) and *The Agaria* (1942); Basile Nikitine, *Les Kurdes*, 1956; Fosco Maraini, *Meeting with Japan*, 1959; G. B. Sansom, *Japan, a Short Cultural History*, 1952; M. E. Spiro, *Kibbutz*, 1956; and M. N. Srinivas, *Religion and Society among the Coorgs of South India*, 1952. Joseph Needham's great work on *Science and Civilization in China* has been mentioned on page 255.

Students will find *Oceania*, Melbourne, 1930–, and *The Journal of the Polynesian Society*, New Zealand, 1892–, invaluable for the islands of the Pacific. We may recommend such books as A. P. Elkin, *The Australian Aborigines*, 1938; R. W. Firth, *We, the Tikopia*, 1936; Felix Speiser, 'Versuch einer Siedlungsgeschichte der Südsee' in *Denkschriften der Schweizerische Naturforschenden Gesellschaft*, 1946; K. O. L. Burridge, *Mambu, a Melanesian Millennium*, 1960; B. A. L. Cranstone, *Melanesia, a Short Ethnography*, 1961; I. H. N. Evans, *The Religion of the Tempasuk Dusuns of North Borneo*, 1953; R. W. Firth, *Social Change in Tikopia* (1959), and *History and Traditions of Tikopia* (1961); J. D. Freeman, *Iban Agriculture*, 1955; W. R. Geddes, *The Land Dyaks of Sarawak*, 1954; Clifford Geertz, *The Religion of Java* (1960) and *The Javanese Family* (1961); Jean Guiart, *Espiritu Santo*, 1958; L. Langewis, *Lamak and Malat in Bali and a Sunda Loom*, 1956; R. L. Mellema, *Wayang Puppets*, 1954; A. Métraux, *Easter Island*, 1957; Douglas L. Oliver, *A Solomon Island Society*, 1955; C. P. Mountford, *Brown Men and Red Sand*, 1948; L. H. Palmier, *Social Status and Power in Java*, 1960; Andrew Sharp, *Ancient Voyages in the Pacific*, 1956; Alexander Spoehr, *Majuro, a Village in the Marshall Islands*, 1949; W. E. H. Stanner, *The South Seas in Transition*, 1953; W. F. Wertheim (ed.), *Bali*, 1960; and J. E. de Young, *Village Life in Modern Thailand*, 1955.

I have already mentioned the *Biennial Review of Anthropology* (p. 262). In this and in *The American Anthropologist*, 1890–, one can find summaries and bibliographies of the work done in various countries. *The Index to Current Periodicals* of the Royal Anthropological Institute, London, will be invaluable in keeping up to date.

We noted earlier that ethnology was the comparative and analytic study of races or peoples by any or all of the methods of anthropology, and in another place (p. 363) that Betty Meggers' paper which was largely on the work of Social Anthropologists was called 'Recent Trends in American Ethnology'. It is clear enough by whatever method one works, whether in human biology, material culture, past and present, or in social subjects, one generally ends with a book which can be called ethnography, if purely descriptive, or ethnology, if comparative and analytic. It has been possible for a long time to use the facts afforded by physical anthropology and material culture (what we have called prehistory and technology) in a comparative and analytic manner. The social anthropologists who classify societies on the basis of their social structures rather than of their cultures, and define their subject matter as social relations rather than culture, claim to have found a scientific manner of studying their part of the complex which is ethnology, and to have established a discipline independent of it, in the same way that physical anthropology, prehistory, and technology have independent disciplines and yet contribute to ethnology.

VI. POSTSCRIPT

In the first edition of this book I prophesied a future, and we had a war instead. My general view of human biology being linked through psychology with cultural anthropology on the grand scale has not proved to be workable so far, and something else has happened; indeed, many other things have happened. The most cheerful event has been the increase of interest in the whole complex of studies, largely due, I think, to the many young people who have served in many parts of the world and want to know more about what they saw. All universities have more pupils than before the war, and more opportunities are available, or students make more opportunities, to undergo the long training for, and the hard discipline of, field work. At Oxford, to give one example, a year at least is spent in the diploma course, followed by one or two years of research into the available material for the area to which the student wishes to go. Then, if funds can be made available, he is expected to spend a period among the people he is to study, then return and work up his material under academic supervision, before going again for a further period to the people he is studying. The discipline has become harder, then, and more intensive.[1]

Readers who compare the part of this book which was written in 1935 with that written in later editions will call me inconsistent, and I admit at once that the two parts of the book are written from quite different points of view. After a quarter-century of teaching and administration, I have found that in working with my colleagues, the general divisions which I have used in later editions are the categories

[1] See Evans-Pritchard, *Social Anthrolopogy*, 1951.

into which our several abilities seem best to fall, and the ones which work best in passing on the subject to our students.

In the first edition, I spent the greater part of my space in describing the developments of the disciplines of anthropology, which I still believe is a science of methods, and devoted little time to ethnology, the comparative and analytic study of races and peoples by all or any of the methods of anthropology.

In this second part, I have taken the view that the aim of all of the anthropological disciplines is ethnology, now and in the past, and that the ultimate aim of all of them, physical anthropology, prehistory, technology, and social anthropology, is to add to our knowledge of ethnology, which helps us to understand peoples as they are and as they have been.

ABBREVIATIONS

Abhandl. der Königl. Bayerischen Akad. Wissen. Abhandlungen der Königlichen Bayerischen Akademie der Wissenschaften (later *Abhandlungen der Bayerischen Akademie der Wissenschaften*), Munich.

Acta F.R.N. Univ. Comen. Acta Facultatis rerum naturalium Universitatis comenianae, Bratislava.

A.J.P.A. American Journal of Physical Anthropology, Philadelphia.

Am. Anth. American Anthropologist, Lancaster, Pa.

Am. Antiq. American Antiquity, Menasha, Wis.

Am. J. Anat. American Journal of Anatomy, Baltimore.

Am. J. Arch. American Journal of Archaeology, New York.

Am. J. Pharm. American Journal of Pharmacy, Philadelphia.

Am. J. Physiol. American Journal of Physiology, Boston.

Anat. Anzeiger. Anatomischer Anzeiger, Jena.

A.P.A.M.N.H. Anthropological Papers, American Museum of Natural History, New York.

A.R. Anthropological Review of the Anthropological Society of London.

Arch. Inst. Paléont humaine. Archives de l'Institut de paléontologie humaine, Paris.

Arch. Zool. Expér. Archives de zoologie expérimentale et générale, Paris.

A. R. Smiths. Inst. Annual Report of the Smithsonian Institution, Washington, D.C.

Atti d. Soc. Ital. di Sci. Nat. Atti della Società Italiana di Scienze Naturali, Milan.

B.A.E. Bureau of American Ethnology, Smithsonian Institution, Washington, D.C.

B.C.D.M. Bulletin, Canada Department of Mines, National Museum of Canada, Ottawa.

Brit. Sch. Arch. British School of Archaeology.

B.S.A. British School of Athens.

B.S.A. de Paris, Lyon, etc. Bulletin de la Société d'Anthropologie de Paris, Lyon, etc.

Bull. Geol. Inst. Upsala. Bulletin of the Geological Institute, University of Upsala.

Bull. Soc. d'Anthr., Paris. *Bulletin de la Société d'Anthropologie*, Paris.

Bull. Soc. Geol. de France. Bulletin de la Société geologique de France, Paris.

C.D.G.A. Correspondenzblatt der deutschen Gesellschaft für Anthropologie, Ethnologie und Urgeschichte (Supplement to *Archiv für Anthropologie*, Brunswick).

C.I.A. Congrès International d'Anthropologie et d'Archéologie préhistorique.

374

C.I.S.A.E. *Congrès International des Sciences Anthropologiques et Ethnologiques.*

C.I.W.P. *Carnegie Institution of Washington Publications*, Washington, D.C.

C.P. de Fr. *Congrès Préhistorique de France*, Périgueux.

Contr. Mus. Am. Ind. *Contributions from the Museum of the American Indian*, Heye Foundation, New York.

C.S.A.E. *Columbia Studies in Archaeology and Ethnology*, New York.

C.U.C.A. *Columbia University Contributions to Anthropology*, New York.

Denkschr. Ak. Wien *Denkschriften, Akademie der Wissenschaften*, Vienna.

Denkschr. der Kais. Akademie der Wiss, Wien. *Denkschriften der Kaiserlichen Akademie der Wissenschaften*, Vienna.

El Pal. *El Palacio*, Museum of New Mexico, Santa Fe.

Eph. Αρχκιολογικὴ ἐφηίιερῖς, Athens.

E.R.E. Hastings *Encyclopaedia of Religion and Ethics.*

Gen. Tijdsch. N.I. *Geneeskundig Tijdschrift voor Nederlandsch Indië*, Batavia.

Hastings *E.R.E.* See *E.R.E.*

Imago. *Imago. Zeitschrift für Anwendung der Psychoanalyse.* Leipzig and Vienna.

Intern. Z. f. ärztl. Psychoanal. *International Zeitschrift für (ärztliche) Psychoanalyse.* Leipzig and Vienna.

J. Abn. Psych. *Journal of Abnormal (and Social) Psychology*, Boston.

J.A.I. *Journal of the Anthropological Institute* of Great Britain and Ireland.

J. Anat. and Physiol. *Journal of Anatomy and Physiology*, London.

J.A.S. *Journal of the Anthropological Society* of London.

J. Biol. Chem. *Journal of Biological Chemistry*, Baltimore.

J.E.S. *Journal of the Ethnological Society* of London.

J. Exper. Med. *Journal of Experimental Medicine*, New York.

J. Exp. Zool. *Journal of Experimental Zoology*, Philadelphia.

J. Gerontol. *Journal of Gerontology*, Springfield, Ill.

J.H.S. *Journal of Hellenic Studies*, London.

J. Lab. and Clin. Med. *Journal of Laboratory and Clinical Medicine*, St Louis, Missouri.

J.N.E.S. *Journal of Near Eastern Studies*, Chicago.

J. Physiol. *Journal of Physiology*, London and Cambridge.

J.R.A.I. *Journal of the Royal Anthropological Institute* of Great Britain and Ireland, London.

Konin. Akd. v. Wetensch. *Koninklijke Akademie van Wetenschappen*, Amsterdam.

K.S. Ges. Wiss. *Königliche Sächsische Gesellschaft der Wissenschaften.*

M.A.A.A. *Memoirs of the American Anthropological Association*, Lancaster, Pa.

M.A.G.W. *Mitteilungen der anthropologischen Gesellschaft in Wien.*

M.A.M.N.H. *Memoirs of the American Museum of Natural History*, New York.

M.A.S.L. Memoirs of the Anthropological Society of London.

Matériaux. Matériaux pour l'histoire de l'homme (included in *L'Anthropologie*, Paris, 1890–)

Mém. Soc. d'Anthr., Paris. Mémoires de la Société d'Anthropologie, Paris.

M.M.U.M.P. Museum Monographs, University Museum, Philadelphia.

Mon. Soc. Res. Child Dev. Monographs of the Society for Research in Child Development, Washington, D.C.

M.P.M. Memoirs of the Peabody Museum, Harvard University, Cambridge, Mass.

M.S.A.A. Memoirs of the Society for American Archaeology, Menasha, Wis. and Salt Lake City, Utah. (Published as supplements to *American Antiquity*.)

N.M.C. Bull. Bulletin of the National Museum of Canada, Ottawa.

O.E.C.T., Oxford Edition of Cuneiform Texts.

Paideuma. Paideuma. Mitteilungen für Kulturkunde. Frankfurt.

Pal. Sin. Palaeontologia Sinica. Peking.

Peking Nat. Hist. Bull. Peking Natural History Bulletin.

Phil. Trans. Philosophical Transactions of the Royal Society, London.

P.P.F.A. Papers of the Robert S. Peabody Foundation for Archaeology, Andover, Mass.

P.P.M. Papers of the Peabody Museum of American Archaeology and Ethnology, Harvard University, Cambridge, Mass.

P.R.I.G.B. Proceedings of the Royal Institution of Great Britain.

Proc. Amer. Phil. Soc. Proceedings of the American Philosophical Society, Philadelphia.

Proc. Nat. Aca. Sci. Proceedings of the National Academy of Sciences, Washington, D.C.

Proc. Prehist. Soc. Proceedings of the Prehistoric Society (Cambridge 1935–. Before that was added 'of East Anglia', London 1908–35.)

Q.J.G.S.L. or *Quart. Journ. Geol. Quarterly Journal of the Geological Society* of London.

R.A.Q. Répertoire de l'art quaternaire (Reinach).

R.B.A. Report of the British Association for the Advancement of Science.

R.E.A. or *Rév. de l'École d'A. Révue mensuelle de l'École d'Anthropologie* de Paris.

Runa. Runa: Archivo para las ciencias del hombre, Buenos Aires.

S.M.C. Smithsonian Miscellaneous Collections, Washington, D.C.

Trans. Am. Phil. Soc. Transactions of the American Philosophical Society, Philadelphia.

Trans. Royal Soc. S. Australia. Transactions of the Royal Society of South Australia, Adelaide.

U.C.P.A.A.E. University of California Publications in American Archaeology and Ethnology, Berkeley.

U.C.P.C.S. University of California Publications in Cultural Sociology, Berkeley.

Verh. Ges. Phys. Anthrop. Verhandlungen der Gesellschaft für physische Anthropologie, Stuttgart.

Verh. Naturf. Ver. in Brünn. Verhandlungen des Naturforschenden Vereins in Brünn.

V.F.P.A. Viking Fund Publications in Anthropology, New York.

Wien Klin. Woch. Wiener Klinische Wochenschrift, Vienna.

Y.U.P.A. Yale University Publications in Anthropology, New Haven, Conn.

Z.E. Zeitschrift für Ethnologie, Berlin.

Zentbl. f. Parasit. u. Infekt. Zentralblatt für Bakteriologie, Parasiten kunde und Infektions-Krankheiten, Jena.

Z. f. Immun. exp. Therapie. Zeitschrift für Immunitäts-forschung und experimentelle Therapie, Jena.

Z.P. Zeitschrift für Psychologie, Leipzig.

Z.f.v.M. Zeitschrift für vergleichende Musikwissenschaft, Berlin.

INDEX